798

D1161336

Transgressing the Bounds

Recent titles in

RELIGION IN AMERICA SERIES
Harry S. Stout, General Editor

Transgressing the Bounds

Subversive Enterprises among the Puritan Elite in Massachusetts, 1630–1692

Louise A. Breen

OXFORD
UNIVERSITY PRESS
2001

OXFORD
UNIVERSITY PRESS

Oxford   New York
Athens   Auckland   Bangkok   Bogotá   Bombay   Buenos Aires
Calcutta   Cape Town   Dar es Salaam   Delhi   Florence   Hong Kong
Istanbul   Karachi   Kuala Lumpur   Madras   Madrid   Melbourne
Mexico City   Nairobi   Paris   Shanghai   Singapore   Taipei   Tokyo   Toronto

and associated companies in
Berlin   Ibadan

Copyright © 2001 by Louise A. Breen

Published by Oxford University Press, Inc.,
198 Madison Avenue, New York, New York 10016

Oxford is a registered trademark of Oxford University Press

All rights reserved. No part of this publication may be reproduced,
stored in a retrieval system, or transmitted, in any form or by any means,
electronic, mechanical, photocopying, recording, or otherwise,
without the prior permission of Oxford University Press.

Library of Congress Cataloging-in-Publication Data

Breen, Louise.
Transgressing the bounds : subversive enterprises among the Puritan elite in
Massachusetts, 1630–1692 / Louise Breen.
p.   cm. — (Religion in America series)
Includes bibliographical references and index.
ISBN 0-19-513800-7
1. Puritans—Massachusetts—History—17th century. 2. Puritans—Massachusetts—
Social conditions—17th century. 3. Elite (Social sciences)—Massachusetts—History
—17th century. 4. Civil-military relations—Massachusetts—History—17th century.
5. Ancient and Honorable Artillery Company of Massachusetts—History—17th century.
6. Antinomianism—History—17th century. 7. Massachusetts—History—
Colonial period, ca. 1600–1775. 8. Massachusetts—Social conditions—17th century.
9. Massachusetts—Church history—17th century.   I. Title.
II. Religion in America series (Oxford University Press)
F67 .B82 2000
974.4'02'08825—dc21   00-026310

9 8 7 6 5 4 3 2 1

Printed in the United States of America
on acid-free paper

Acknowledgments

This is a wonderful opportunity to thank the fine individuals and institutions that have helped me along the way. First and foremost, I have been blessed with wonderful teachers. Karen O. Kupperman, my major professor during my graduate career at the University of Connecticut, and a mentor to me in the years thereafter, has shared her enviable knowledge of early American history, and, through her own pursuit of excellence, has been a source of constant inspiration. From the dissertation stage forward, she has read and commented upon successive drafts of this manuscript, offering encouragement and criticism at all the critical junctures. Harry S. Stout, whom I encountered initially as the tremendously enthusiastic instructor of my first university-level U.S. History survey class, showed me that history was an interpretive enterprise, and offered what, at the time, I took to be a preposterous suggestion: that I pursue an advanced degree in the subject. Later on, after I acted on his advice and enrolled in his seminar on New England history, he instilled in me an abiding interest in the Puritans. Harry S. Stout showed me what was possible; his words of encouragement at such an early stage made a tremendous impression, and led me ultimately to a career in history. I do not have words sufficient to express my thanks for the time and effort these two generous scholars have expended on my behalf.

During the research and writing of the dissertation out of which this book grew, I received short-term research fellowships from the Masachusetts Historical Society and the John Carter Brown Library, as well as a year-long dissertation fellowship from the Harry Frank Guggenheim Foundation. After joining the history department at Kansas State University, I was granted a Faculty Fellowship from the Pew Program in Religion and American History at Yale University, which afforded me the tremendous gift of a free year in which to rethink portions of my work, and to revise the manuscript into its present form. During my time at the University of Connecticut, I benefited greatly from the instruction and advice of Richard D. Brown and Shirley A. Roe, and from the friendship of James F. Cooper Jr., Kenneth P. Minkeman, Cynthia, J. Van Zandt, Walter W. Woodward, and Philip Zwick. I would also like to thank the anonymous readers who commented on my manuscript when it was being considered for publication.

On a personal level, I must acknowledge my very supportive family. My parents, Dorothy E. Breen and Robert L. Breen, provided encouragement both moral and material as I pursued graduate study. My husband, Saeed M. Khan, sustains me in innumerable ways, and has manifested his affection by somehow learning to live with the Puritans. Finally, I owe my colleagues in the History Department at Kansas State University a debt of gratitude for providing a stimulating and good-natured atmosphere in which to teach, write, and reflect.

I have incorporated into this book materials previously published in Louise A. Breen, "Religious Radicalism in the Puritan Officer Corps: Antinomianism, the Artillery Company, and Cultural Integration in Seventeenth-Century Boston," *New England Quarterly*, 68 (March 1995), 3–43; and "Praying with the Enemy: Daniel Gookin, King Philip's War and the Dangers of Intercultural Mediatorship," in *Empire and Others: British Encounters with Indigenous Peoples, 1600–1850*, ed. Martin Daunton and Rich Halpern (Philadelphia: University of Pennsylvania Press, 1999), 101–22. I thank the pulishers for allowing me to use portions of these essays in this book. Quotations and citations from manuscript collections owned by the Massachuetts Historical Society and the Massachusetts Archives at Columbia Point appear here by permission of those institutions.

L.A.B.
Manhattan, Kansas

Contents

Transgressing the Bounds

Introduction

I n February 1638, John Winthrop confided to his journal that he and
other magistrates harbored strong misgivings about a petition that had
recently come before the Massachusetts General Court. The petition,
subscribed by some of Boston's most prominent citizens, requested permission to establish a private military company modeled upon the fashionable
"artillery gardens" of London and other English cities. But the Court, said
Winthrop, recognizing "how dangerous it might be to erect a standing
authority of military men, which might easily, in time, overthrow the civil
power, thought fit to stop it betimes." For reasons that Winthrop did not
explain, these doubts were overcome within a few months' time. The Court
not only granted permission to organize what would subsequently be known
as the Ancient and Honorable Artillery Company of Boston but also extended broad privileges to the fledgling organization, providing a one-
thousand-acre tract of land for the Company's support, allowing it to as-
semble in any Massachusetts locality, conferring upon it the right to elect
its own officers, and instructing towns to schedule military trainings and
town meetings so as not to conflict with its musters. The Artillery Company
emerged rapidly as a key institution in Puritan Massachusetts, functioning
not only as an elite social club but as a prime recruiting ground for military
leadership over virtually all the colony's trainbands, militias, and expeditionary forces.[1]

Winthrop's account of a muted controversy over the commissioning
of the Artillery Company concealed as much as it revealed about his true

apprehensions. The Massachusetts governor couched his arguments in vague, general terms with which few Puritans could disagree, carefully linking his own reservations about the Company's potential threat to the civil government with the longstanding and well-documented antipathy Puritans in England held for the exactions, including forced loans and troop billetings, that had accompanied Charles I's attempts to create a "perfect militia."[2] But while it was certainly true that Bay Colony Puritans were eager to place military affairs firmly under the control of godly, local civil authorities, it is difficult, both from the perspective of the role of artillery gardens in England and from the dynamics of the local situation, to understand how Winthrop could seriously have reached a conclusion so harsh as to warrant a comparison between the proposed Artillery Company and the "Pretorian band among the Romans, and the Templars in Europe."[3]

Far from being dominated by forces hostile to Puritan interests, the English officers' clubs on which the Artillery Company was patterned were populated both by the "new merchants" who played important roles in Britain's colonial enterprise and by Puritan "grandees" like Lord Brooke, who saw military leadership as an important talent for civil magistrates to cultivate.[4] In Massachusetts the four men who pressed for a charter—Robert Keayne, Robert Sedgwick, Nathaniel Duncan, and William Spencer—were substantial Puritans who held important civil and military positions at the town and colony levels. An officers' company, moreover, would seem to constitute a sensible precaution at a time when colonists felt themselves to occupy a vulnerable niche in their New World setting and when there existed no counterpart to the modern joint chiefs of staff. As events unfolded, the Artillery Company did indeed provide a forum where several times per year men interested in military pursuits, many of whom were the duly elected officers of the colony's trainbands and militias, had the opportunity to meet, interact, and drill. Still, Winthrop's uneasiness about private officers' companies persisted. As late as 1645, long after a "covenanted" citizen soldiery had been firmly established in Massachusetts, Winthrop recorded with dismay that the General Court had approved a request to create local officers' companies—"thought by diverse of the court to be very unfit, and not so safe in times of peace"—in the counties of Essex, Middlesex, and Norfolk.[5]

WINTHROP'S MISGIVINGS CONCERNING the Artillery Company had less to do with the balance between civil and military power (although this was certainly a factor) than with his recognition that the Company reified a temperamental split at the center of the colony's ruling elite; the organization attracted a heterogeneous yet prominent membership whose diversity contrasted with the social and religious ideals propounded by the majority of magistrates and settlers. The Artillery Company burst upon the stage of Massachusetts just as the "antinomian" controversy was winding down. In March 1638, only one month after Winthrop mentioned the Artillery Company petition in his journal, the famous religious dissident

Anne Hutchinson began her exile in Aquidneck, Rhode Island.[6] It must have given pause to the colony's "orthodox" leaders to learn that ten of the twenty-four individuals listed on the Company's first roster had aligned themselves in some way with the antinomian menace.[7] And subsequent events proved that the Artillery Company would remain a magnet for ideas and people at variance with New England orthodoxy.[8] Given the prestige of the organization, a surprising number of Artillery Company members continued during the first decades of colonization to stand out either as advocates of a broader toleration or as actual subscribers to heterodox opinion. Although these men were charged in their official roles with protecting the social and religious boundaries of Massachusetts, they could at times be seen willfully to transgress them.

Men affiliated with the Company, many of whom held positions of trust in the colony at large, spearheaded efforts to gain more flexibility in the relationship between church and state and to reverse the colony's preoccupation with uniformity and parochial isolationism. Such leading lights in the Company, and the colony, as John Leverett, Robert Sedgwick, Edward Gibbons, Edward Hutchinson, Nehemiah Bourne, Thomas Clark, and William Tyng could be found at various times and in various combinations petitioning for toleration of Anabaptists; requesting an amelioration of the stringent laws against Quakers; resisting establishment of the Cambridge Platform as a legislated form of orthodoxy; and evincing support for the petition of Robert Child (a member) to make civil rights conditional on property ownership rather than "visible" sainthood.[9]

The elite men who congregated in the Artillery Company cannot be said to have shared an identical religious outlook. But the Artillery Company as an institution, even though it contained many men whose orthodoxy could never be doubted, embodied a heterogeneous ideal that clashed with the coordinated system of civil, social, and religious convenants known to historians as the New England Way. The inclusion of Pequot War hero and incorrigible antinomian John Underhill on the first roster at a time when the captain's future in the colony was in serious doubt testified to this greater openness. So too did the fact that in later decades prominent men who either could not or would not become church members and consequently had no political rights—individuals like Robert Child, Thomas Lechford, Robert Saltonstall, Samuel Maverick, and John Nelson—could look to the Artillery Company as the only semiofficial locus of authority and honor open to them.[10] Henry Dunster, who was forced out of the presidency of Harvard in 1654 because of his Anabaptist views, was also a member of the Company. Although Dunster had no observable interest in things military, he could associate in that organization with men who questioned the exclusivity of the New England Way, such as sea captain John Milam; indeed, in 1655, Milam bore to Dunster a letter inviting him to minister to an Anabaptist congregation in Ireland, Milam being entrusted to "contrive your passadge and advise you as to the state of the country and the Christians amongst us."[11] While John Winthrop was ready to close off debate on the proper shape of Massachusetts society almost as soon as he delivered his famous *Arbella* sermon on Christian charity, other prominent Bay Colony residents were just beginning to enter the discussion.

The diversity found in the Artillery Company, hence within the colony's elite (especially its trading community) belies the myth perpetuated by John Winthrop of a single-minded, monolithic Puritan enterprise in New England; it also calls into question the historiographic conceit that the ranks of dissenters from the New England Way were filled primarily with persons marginalized by class or gender. The disproportionate support for heterodox opinion among merchants and military men came because orthodoxy, as defined in the Bay, did not adequately fulfill the needs of cosmopolitan-minded individuals habitually called to play roles on a stage wider than Massachusetts. As merchants, and as military officers, Artillery Company members, many of whom possessed strong transatlantic ties, were positioned to recognize both the value of alternative points of view within the large spectrum of Puritan belief and the importance of achieving greater flexibility in the New England Way.[12] These sorts of individuals were uncomfortable with the parochialism, enforced religious uniformity, and communalism that the New England Way imposed. In this context, "antinomianism" was attractive because it provided a theological discourse capable of underwriting a society more cosmopolitan, more individualistic, and more heterogeneous than orthodox Puritanism would allow.

While the New England Way upheld social goals and religious ideals with which the "middling" colonists of the Bay felt comfortable—economic "competency" and an accessible form of Puritanism where external appearances and spiritual reality were understood normally to coincide—defenders of "antinomianism," and later of religious toleration, tended to be interested in more grandiose (and therefore more dangerous) economic and military plans, and they favored a form of Puritanism in which external appearances and reality were understood almost always to conflict.[13] The antinomian controversy, understood in these broad terms, should be seen not as the end of significant disagreement about the New England Way but as the opening salvo in a series of debates concerning communal definition, theological boundaries, and socioeconomic goals that remained hotly contested down to the end of the century and beyond.

The great conflict of the 1630s left as its enduring legacy two coded languages that not only expressed the dichotomies residing at the center of the Bay Colony, but also structured people's understanding of their choices. The orthodox victory over antinomianism was tantamount to a triumph of provincialism over internationalism; and it was no mere coincidence that it was achieved at precisely the same moment when, as Karen O. Kupperman has shown recently, disaffected colonial leaders were distancing themselves from the worldwide interests (especially alternative colonizing ventures) and religious expansiveness of English Puritan "grandees."[14] The New England Way—which allowed only church members to have a political voice, which achieved spiritual homogeneity by assigning less importance to the private experiential dimension of faith than outwardly observable and communally agreed-upon manifestations of its presence, and which punished all overt dissenters—provided a means of uniting the local community while establishing a degree of "independency" from well-intentioned but meddling outsiders. The category of orthodoxy, renegotiated by each succeeding generation, was by no means static. Still, orthodoxy always retained as its main priority the preservation of New England's regional integrity and its status as a place where ordinary people could achieve some form of political and economic "independency."[15]

Orthodox ideology justified New England's aloofness from imperial schemes, whether designed by Puritan grandees, the Cromwellian commonwealth, or the restored Stuart monarchy. And in the second half of the century, as the colony's leaders adopted a new orthodoxy that favored the genealogical "seed" of New England in church admissions, the isolationist strain integral to Puritan orthodoxy blossomed into a more virulently tribal definition of community.[16] This reinvigorated tribalism eventuated, during the King Philip's War era, in the popularly motivated exclusion of Indians, whether Christian or "pagan," from any claim to colonial citizenship. In their rejection of "praying" Indians, New Englanders broke with a missionary impulse that was near and dear to the hearts of internationalist English Puritans and post-Restoration latitudinarian Anglicans alike. The break signaled the maturation of a trend that had lasted for nearly a century of believing that the transatlantic world and the Indian frontier harbored dangers similarly capable of reducing English colonists to a slavelike, "dependent" status. In his memoirs the migrant Roger Clap remembered having dreamed that the Massachusetts polity would "knit together" the hearts of all who "feared God," whether "rich or poor," "English or Indian," "Portugal or Negro." But such a multiethnic dream was not to become reality in Massachusetts.[17]

To be sure, antinomianism as a discrete theological challenge to New England orthodoxy did not long outlast the exile of Anne Hutchinson; but the principled objection to a circumscribed, isolationist New England Way did. Those who chafed against the boundaries of religious and social orthodoxy, although they may not have been antinomian in a theological sense, continued to speak in the language of protest forged during that crisis. Demands for greater religious toleration, for a more traditionally English means of distributing political and civil rights, and for a more meaningful engagement in transatlantic imperial affairs came from a variety of dissenting traditions. But, as I will show, all these demands were, at some level, consistent with what had erroneously been defined as the "antinomian" impulse that took hold of the Massachusetts trading community in the 1630s. Men who had been identified as antinomians, like Captain Edward Hutchinson, the son of Anne and William, later lent support to others seeking a wider toleration. And in 1637, Henry Vane, the secular leader of the antinomian party, saw no inconsistency in conspiring against

John Winthrop with Samuel Maverick, a curmudgeonly Anglican who lived on Noddle's Island. Winthrop related how the two men plotted to embarrass him socially:

> The differences grew so much here, as tended fast to a separation; so as Mr. Vane, being, among others, invited by the governor [Win-throp] to accompany the Lord Ley [a distinguished visitor to the colony and a friend of Vane] at dinner, not only refused to come (alleging by letter than his conscience withheld him), but also, at the same hour, he went over to Nottle's Island to dine with Mr. Maverick, and carried the Lord Ley with him.

Maverick, who later remigrated to England and appeared again in 1664 as one of the hated royal commissioners sent by the restored monarchy to investigate New England, regarded the orthodox Winthrop, not the anti-nomian Vane, as the deviant fanatic. In a pamphlet designed to expose the Bay Colony's failure to accord citizens their due English liberties, Maverick, who also signed the Child petition in 1646, cited the injustices done during the antinomian controversy: "Witness also the Banishing so many to leave their habitations there, and seek places abroad elswhere, meerly for differing in Judgment from them as the Hutchinsons and severall families with them."[18] Maverick and Vane (a regicide) clearly did not see eye to eye on religious issues: but in the context of the antinomian controversy, they found more common ground with one another than with Winthrop.

John Winthrop's orthodox party emerged victorious in 1638 not because it represented oligarchic rule but rather because the framers of the New England Way successfully associated their brand of orthodoxy with the freedoms that most "middling" colonists sought to attain when they emigrated to the new world—widespread access to freehold land tenure and economic "independency," rough egalitarianism among house-holding patriarchs, and a greater concern for the local "tribe" of saints than the international community of faith. If any one tradition in early New England was protodemocratic, in the sense of being responsive to the needs of ordinary people, that tradition was orthodoxy and not antinomianism. When Thomas Lechford, who had once "hung upon" the preaching of Hugh Peter in London, became disillusioned with Massachusetts, it was to a large degree because he felt stifled by the egalitarian ideal permeating both church and civil affairs. There were certain intrinsic "mysteries" to good rulership that the humble colonists of the Bay would never possess: "Are there not some great mysteries of State and government? Is it possible, convenient, or necessary, for all men to attain to the knowledge of those mysteries, or to have the like measure of knowledge, faith, mercifulnesse, wisdome, courage, magnanimity, patience?" If not, cautioned Lechford, it were "Better" to "yeeld to many pressures in a Monarchie, then for subjects to destroy, and spoile one another."[19] The specific theological issues broached during the antinomian controversy may gradually have faded from view in the years after 1638; but rank-and-file colonists of Massachusetts, with the encouragement of certain magistrates and ministers, continued to view an evolving orthodoxy as a protective covering that could shield the colony from the transatlantic world and the frontier, both of which were thought to be rife with danger and diversity.

SCHOLARS OF SEVENTEENTH-CENTURY Massachusetts, regardless of whether they focus on social or intellectual history, have tended to follow the lead of Perry Miller in finding consensus rather than conflict in the Puritan colony's early history.[20] Scores of town studies, incorporating Miller's theme of religious "declension," have traced how communities that originally enjoyed great cohesion in their first decade of settlement, gradually became more individualistic, more worldly, and somehow less "Puritan" as they responded to a series of changes—including the expansion of the capitalist market, the resumption of royalist rule in England, and the land shortages affecting second-generation sons—that intruded ever more insistently on their "closed," "utopian" world during the second half of the seventeenth century.[21] Central to most of these studies is the assumption that the elite men of the first generation were essentially in agreement on the basic principles around which their society would be organized and that they were prepared, when necessary, to impose that vision on others.[22] Even historian Stephen Innes, who has recently mounted a far-reaching Weberian challenge to the assumption that communally oriented New Englanders were diffident toward capitalist growth, has simply replaced one consensus view of Massachusetts exceptionalism with another.[23] Yet Winthrop's misgivings about the formation of the Artillery Company, inscribed within the larger controversy over antinomianism—together with his immediate assumption that his high-ranking peers needed to be reminded that their organization would be "subordinate to all authority"—reflects a degree of distrust and disagreement among the colony's leading men rarely acknowledged in the literature.

This book argues that the people of Puritan Massachusetts were deeply and consistently divided, no less in 1638 than in 1692, over where the colony's social and religious boundaries should be drawn and how their society should relate to the wider transatlantic world. Focusing on the lives of elite men (not marginalized outsiders) who endeavored to stretch the intellectual and social bounds of orthodoxy, I will demonstrate that the dangers posed by the outside world and various sorts of "others" were perceived in very similar terms over the course of the seventeenth century. The tendency to form opposing factions, insisting on the one hand on isolation from that world and on the other on involvement in its growing diversity, also remained relatively constant, having been fixed during the antinomian controversy. The old declension model suggested that Massachusetts fell away from its original purity as alien outside forces impinged ever more heavily on its residents; this study argues that dueling versions of the good life, pitting localism against cosmopolitanism and homogeneity versus heterogeneity, competed with one another persistently throughout the entire century and beyond.[24] In pursuing the idea that there existed two different, while not completely distinct, versions of the Puritan good life, I will extend the lines of reasoning set forth in recent works by Janice Knight and Karen O. Kupperman, both of whom have shown that the Puritan world view was volatile and highly contested and have argued that in Puritan New England the dominant orthodoxy was created by individuals less well known, and less prominent, on the world stage.[25]

CHAPTER I ANALYZES the antinomian and orthodox discourses of the late 1630s with an eye toward explaining why each appealed to distinct social constituencies and how each could be used to construct very different social worlds. In explaining why antinomianism had broad appeal in the trading community, I break with the venerable historiographic tradition that links orthodoxy with capitalist growth. According to that tradition, Puritans acquired the abstemiousness and diligence necessary for the accumulation of wealth because, in their spiritual lives, they were taught to "prepare" themselves for salvation, even though "works" had no power to alter the predestined outcome of their salvific lives. Rather than linking orthodox "preparationism" with economic growth in this Weberian fashion, I will argue that the mystical strains of antinomianism were, ironically, more in tune with market values than a rationalistic, work-a-day orthodoxy. Orthodoxy functioned in Massachusetts to affirm the local colonial identity, to privilege the public sphere over the private, and to draw people together, toward communalistic goals, in a shared geographic space. Antinomianism and the market were not identical; but both, in contrast to orthodoxy, were gendered feminine; both operated similarly to blur communal identities; both emphasized private needs (whether spiritual or economic) over those of the community; and both abstracted individuals from their discrete localities.[26]

In addition to challenging the wisdom of applying Weberian principles to Puritan Massachusetts, in chapter 1 I also depart from the notion that antinomianism stood for marginalized, perfectionist fanaticism. The people and opinions comprehended under the antinomian rubric were incredibly diverse, including, to name a few, William Aspinwall, a future Fifth Monarchist, Thomas Lechford, a future returnee to episcopacy, Thomas Savage, a future champion of the "halfway" covenant, and Edward Hutchinson, a future defender of toleration (and enemy of the "halfway" covenant). These oppositional figures, and their sympathizers, cannot be said to have shared a single, cohesive alternative theological vision for the colony; rather, they struggled to alter the placement of the religious, social, and cultural boundaries preferred by the majority of colonists and the dominant faction of magistrates. Antinomianism was far more than a discrete set of heretical opinions; it was an open-ended critique of the New England Way.

In chapters 2 and 3 I use the lives of key elite individuals to illustrate how the market, intercultural contact (both hostile and cooperative), and religious heterodoxy or tolerationism inhabited a shared intellectual universe that was inimical, though not wholly so, to the religious and social goals of orthodoxy. In chapter 2, which focuses on the ordeal of John Underhill, I argue that the exiled captain turned to antinomianism because it approximated more closely than orthodoxy the honor culture to which he aspired. Underhill, who depended for his livelihood on the salary he received from the Massachusetts Bay Company, could not pursue the "independency" that defined manhood in Massachusetts. His sense of his own masculinity, therefore, came to depend on his martial feats and his role in the worldwide struggle for a broadly defined Puritanism—a perspective that was shaped in part by his experiences as a soldier in the Netherlands. In the wake of his 1641 exile, Underhill hoped that he might return to respectability (and power) in Massachusetts, if only his heroic qualities might come to be appreciated in the hostilities that he believed would break out between New England and New Netherland in the early 1650s. When Massachusetts proved reluctant to allow the Anglo-Dutch War then raging in Europe to extend into the colonies, Underhill began to depict himself as a transatlantic actor whose life's ambitions had been thwarted and destroyed by a group of sanctimonious provincials who put their own well-being above that of the commonwealth.

Underhill was rash, even capricious, in his actions and pronouncements. But he was not the only man of note in the Bay Colony whose questioning of the New England Way was contextualized by transatlantic experiences and commitments. Chapter 3 shows how the broad transatlantic interests of men like John Leverett, Edward Gibbons, Robert Sedgwick, Edward Hutchinson, and John Humphrey, to name a few, provided a framework for dissent from the New England Way. All of these men were prominent merchants who held high military rank; all participated in extracolonial affairs that could both support and compromise the goal of creating a Bible commonwealth in the "wilderness"; and all, to various extents and through various means, expressed frustration with the spirit of religious persecution that had taken hold of Massachusetts.

During the middle decades of the seventeenth century, these men, in addition to questioning the wisdom of the New England Way, involved themselves in schemes with which orthodox magistrates were ill at ease—participation in the Protector's Western Design, intervention in the struggle between two rival leaders in New France, involvement in various episodes of privateering, and entanglement in schemes to overthrow the governor of New Netherland (which required the cooperation of the exiled Underhill). These exploits were suspect because they were intended not solely to promote the security of the Bay Colony but rather to enhance individual fortunes and reputations for valor, as well as to advance the goals of empire. An isolationist orthodoxy discouraged these sorts of exploits, while, conversely, a broader attachment to the Protestant interest in the world infused them with cosmic meaning. The "middling" colonists of the Bay Colony, who saw their new world habitation as a refuge and as a place where they could establish a "competency" for their families, did not approve of such dangerous, destabilizing activities. Robert Child complained that even those who had fought valiantly for the Puritan (Independent) cause in England, expending "bloud and estate in the Parliaments Service," were sometimes unwelcome in the Bay.[27] The orthodoxy framed and enforced during the first few decades of settlement shaped, but also reflected, the popular sense that grand exploits and broad toleration were elitist constructions that might threaten the needs of the vast majority of ordinary folk.

In chapter 4, which is organized around (but not limited to) the experience of Daniel Gookin, I explore how the isolationist orthodoxy of the early seventeenth century hardened into a racialized tribalism during the King Philip's War era of the 1670s. At that time the common people of the Bay Colony turned against Gookin and other leading men, including John Leverett and Thomas Savage, who argued that Christian Indians should be treated as "citizens" and trusted to fight on the Bay Colony side during the war, which was an all-out struggle that pitted most of the region's Algonquian peoples against the English. Unlike other figures introduced in this study, Gookin was adamantly opposed to religious toleration. But the new orthodoxy of the 1660s and 1670s, framed in response to the Restoration of the Stuart monarchy, had taken a racialist turn, emphasizing that certain genealogical "seeds" were more disposed to godliness than others. In this context, Gookin's ideas about trusting Indians represented the worst possible deviation from orthodoxy, as it was popularly understood.

Ordinary New Englanders had never been enthusiastic about the imperialist plans coordinated by English Puritan leaders, least of all the missionary enterprise. But with the outbreak of what amounted to a race war, the Anglican takeover of the London-based missionary society with which Gookin was affiliated and the advent of a new orthodoxy that magnified a preexisting isolationism, Indian-hating seemed almost patriotic. Royal officials, who were believed to be plotting against the colonists' liberties, had counseled the accommodation of both friendly Indians and religious dissenters. And Daniel Gookin, despite his pronounced opposition to the extension of royal authority into the Bay, was perceived as someone who allowed dangerous transatlantic and frontier influences to infiltrate the colony. Gookin's commitment to the integration of Indian peoples into colonial life had been shaped, I will argue, not by his understanding of the New England Way but by his family's experiences as colonizers of Ireland; indeed, Gookin was denounced at one point as an "Irish dog . . . never loyal to his country."[28]

Daniel Gookin and John Leverett, this study will show, disagreed on a wide range of issues, most notably religious toleration. But the two men had more in common than either would have cared to admit. Because of their involvement in the transatlantic world, both challenged the isolationism and homogeneity enshrined at the heart of the New England Way. And once the Puritan cause was lost in England, neither was able to disengage from the mandates of a wider world. While both worked assiduously against political accommodation with the Crown, each, one suspects, would have adapted well (had they lived long enough) to the economic, social, and cultural implications of the impending anglicization. Men who had learned during the commonwealth period to think in international, multiethnic terms could not easily shrink their vision to the contours of a province.

Chapter 4 demonstrates how, during the King Philip's War era, colonists manifested fear not only of Indians but of military leaders whose vested interest in the frontier, whether in trade or missionary work, was thought to have blinded them to the dangers of Indians who only pretended to be converts or allies so that they could later betray the English. Chapter 5, which revolves around the witchcraft accusation made against John Alden in 1692, shows how these same suspicions, combined with an ongoing fear of religious diversity, persisted into the 1680s and 1690s. Alden was vulnerable to witchcraft charges because he traded heavily on the eastern frontier with both Frenchmen and Indians; because he occasionally associated himself in business with Boston-based Anglican merchants, such as John Nelson, who specialized in the Nova Scotia (or Acadia) trade; and because, while ostensibly an orthodox member of Third Church Boston, he had married into a heretical family. William Phillips, Alden's father-in-law, was a wine merchant, high-ranking militia officer, and broker of Maine lands who had moved to Saco in the 1660s and collaborated briefly with an attempted royalist takeover of the region, probably so as to allow his wife—Bridget Hutchinson Sanford Phillips, the daughter of Anne Hutchinson—a measure of freedom to practice her Quaker religion. Alden—who had befriended Anglicans and Quakers alike, who had betrayed his own son in an aborted captive exchange just weeks before being cried down as a witch, and who was accused both of miscegenation and trading arms to the colony's French and Indian enemies in King William's War—symbolized the vices thought to accompany religious heterodoxy, imperial control, and a biracial frontier.

The deposed Governor Edmund Andros, foisted on Massachusetts two years after its charter was revoked in 1684, had chided New Englanders for their abominable treatment both of Indians and of Englishmen who dissented from their particular religious way. While Andros's rule was swept away in the Massachusetts variant of England's Glorious Revolution, the new monarchs, William and Mary, in granting a charter, required Bay colonists to abide by the Toleration Act of 1689—an eventuality that made it impossible to continue persecuting Quakers. The image of Alden the "witch" encapsulated popular fears of how the freedoms achieved under the New England Way, and its cultural distinctiveness, might degenerate into thralldom under the crush of imperial mandates and trade. These fears and resentments differed in intensity, but not in kind, from those expressed earlier toward the internationalist pretensions of the Cromwellian Protectorate.

The perspective I offer in this book avoids the historiographic pitfall of assuming that early New England's religious idealism rendered it qualitatively different from other regions of British colonial North America.[29] The New England Way helped migrants to achieve the liberties and privileges widely sought by colonists in other regions of the Anglo-American world. By limiting political rights to male church members, the Bay Colony managed to ensure that most magistrates and deputies would share the particular communal interests of the colonists, thereby establishing a measure of local "independence" from transatlantic operators, including even prominent English Puritans, who sought to make the colony serve broader interests than its own. In addition to a de facto regional "independence" from forces that might thwart the will of their "middling" way, Puritan Massachusetts also made freehold land tenure widely accessible and protected individual families from falling into a dreaded "dependent" status.

The attainment of personal "independency"—the single most important guarantor of liberty as well as a comfortable living standard in early America—was, as Jack Greene has shown, a goal shared by Englishmen living in all colonial regions. New Englanders behaved no differently in securing and defending this all-important right from settlers elsewhere. When at midcentury the second generation's access to productive land on the Massachusetts frontier was blocked by the presence of Indians, English traders, and missionaries, the common people turned to a racial consensus similar to that adopted by Virginians during Bacon's Rebellion. In both colonies ordinary Englishmen, demanding that all Indians be treated indiscriminately as enemies, challenged and condemned as elitist those English officials and colonial elites (like Gookin) who favored the idea of cooperating, making alliances, and sharing resources with friendly or Christian Indians.

All over colonial British North America, the various "middle grounds" of trade and proselytization established during the initial stages of intercultural contact eventually crumbled as land-hungry settlers pushed onto the frontier, widening their own conceptualization of liberty at the expense of the native peoples whom they displaced from the land. Massachusetts was no exception to this general pattern.[30] The logic of the New England Way did nothing to halt its progress. Reflecting the will of the people, the evolving orthodoxy of the mid to late seventeenth century moved in an increasingly tribalistic direction. Clergymen like Increase Mather, who condemned the Indian-hating talk and behavior he observed in the 1670s, nonetheless preached up the sins of frontier trading houses and insisted that godliness usually flowed "through the loyns of godly parents." This clerical message simultaneously called into doubt the wholesomeness of intercultural trade and placed a biological imperative on conversion, making it increasingly difficult—even if this was not Mather's intention—to incorporate the Indian "other" into any productive or admirable role within the colony.

In the 1680s, the New England Way merged with a Whiggish defense of liberty and property rights, as colonial leaders endeavored to justify to

English authorities, in resonant secular terms, their overthrow of the Stuart-appointed Edmund Andros. But unlike their peers in the home island, New England pamphleteers injected into their polemics a racial dimension that continued to be an important part of the imperial conversation, ultimately emerging as a distinctive American voice. The anti-Andros tracts written in defense of the colony's Glorious Revolution show that the royal governor's history of making alliances with Indians had counted very much against him, giving rise to the rumor that he had plotted against the Bay Colony with "friends" among the Indians and French. Partisans of Andros, meanwhile—as well as religious dissidents, like the Quaker Thomas Maule of Salem—continued to excoriate Massachusetts for treating the Indians unfairly and provoking war. During the 1670s, Massachusetts elites, many of whom, like Gookin, had profited from their contacts on the frontier, hung back from criticizing frontier trading activities. But, given the need to win popular support, and with Andros challenging their own claims to land, the mercantile elite of the 1680s helped to forge a language that pitted colonial liberties against imperial schemes involving Indian alliances.

THE RELIGIOUS SQUABBLES of Puritan New England have often seemed remote from the secular debates that engaged the new nation in the revolutionary and early national periods. But the issues raised during the antinomian controversy concerning whether Massachusetts should be localist or cosmopolitan in its orientation, homogeneous or heterogeneous in its culture, remained endemic for generations; these questions, indeed, became the stuff of American politics.

The New England Way, in the final analysis, provided a fitting bridge to what has been called the republican synthesis of the eighteenth century; both traditions extended extraordinary privileges to "independent" patriarchal householders; both asserted the rights of the periphery over those of the center; both regarded cultural diversity with suspicion; and both mistrusted mercantile guile, conflating it with feminine wiles.[31] Still, the countervailing demand, first voiced by antinomian dissenters, for a more individualistic, more cosmopolitan, and more heterogeneously-constructed society, persisted. This ethos continued to resonate at many levels for a long and diverse series of dissenters from a multivalent orthodoxy. Much later, it worked its way into the "liberalism" associated with New England trading interests (and self-interest) in the early national period. By the beginning of the nineteenth century, critics from other regions could charge that anti-"republican" forces connected with commerce and manufacturing had taken possession of a New England, which had itself become a cultural "center" bent upon imposing its own "imperial" will—including the social integration of Indians and blacks—on the rest of the nation.[32]

1

The Antinomian Moment

A Contest of Cultures in
Puritan Massachusetts

In November 1637, at the height of the Bay Colony's antinomian controversy, magistrate Israel Stoughton proved an unlikely ally of Anne Hutchinson. During the civil trial that culminated in the banishment of the accused woman, the Dorchester captain adamantly supported the antinomian party's demand that the Court require hostile witnesses, including ministers, to swear oaths as to the truth of their most damaging accusation against the "American Jezebel": that Hutchinson had dishonored her figurative parents, the colony's leaders, by charging openly that most Bay Colony ministers "did preach a covenant of works [rather than grace] . . . and that they were not able ministers of the new testament, and that they had not the seal of the spirit."[1] Interestingly, Stoughton persisted in requesting oaths even after the majority of magistrates had concluded that Hutchinson's hard words—most notably her bold warning that the Court should "take heed what they did to her" for fear of incurring the wrath of God—confirmed that "she walked by such a rule [immediate revelation] as cannot stand with the peace of any state."[2]

Like her infamous brother-in-law John Wheelwright, exiled for having preached a fast-day sermon that countenanced civil "combustions" and created disruptive "divisions" between the people of "grace" and those of "works," Hutchinson had long been considered a seditious woman. But this suspicion could not be proved until there came from "her owne mouth" a scandalous tirade in which Hutchinson admitted that the same "immedi-

ate" voice that taught her how to "distinguish between the voice of my
beloved and the voice of Moses [gracious and works-righteous preaching]"
had also foretold her suffering in Massachusetts at the hands of those inferior to her in grace and her ultimate vindication (by "miracle") once the
Lord ordained the destruction of her enemies: "if you go on in this course
[of persecution] you begin," Hutchinson intoned at the climactic moment
of her civil trial, "you will bring a curse upon you and your posterity and
the mouth of the Lord hath spoken it."[3] These words sealed Hutchinson's
fate, for they mirrored almost exactly certain phrases, already judged seditious, that had appeared in a petition protesting Wheelwright's banishment: "wee beseech you consider the danger of medling against the Proph-
ets of God," the petitioners had written, "for what yee do unto them, the
Lord Jesus takes as done unto himselfe."[4] After months of uncertainty and
backbiting, Hutchinson, whose gender had precluded her from signing the
antinomian petition, could finally be found guilty of "countenancing and
incouraging such as have sowed seditions amongst us."[5]

Hutchinson's use of the prophetic voice to threaten the colony, Winthrop asserted, demonstrated once and for all that her "bottomlesse revelations" were at the "root of all the [seditious] mischief," the "tumults and
troubles," that had preceded the trial. The potential damage attributed to
Hutchinson's—or anyone else's—prophetic voice could never be contained solely within the church, he argued, but must spread to the commonwealth, for the ability to determine unerringly which ministers should
be heeded and which ignored implied also the ability to determine which
magistrates should be obeyed and which treated with "contempt"; "if they
[direct revelations] be allowed in one thing, [they] must be admitted a rule
in all things; for they being above reason and Scripture, they are not subject
to controll." Under these conditions, Winthrop wondered, how long might
it be before the people began to act upon groundless conceits concerning
who were the friends of Jesus and who his enemies; how long before they
would endeavor to "take up arms against their prince and to cut the throats
one of another"?[6]

Stoughton, a moderate Puritan from Dorsetshire, was no antinomian.[7]
In fact, at the fateful moment when Hutchinson pronounced her famous
"curse" on New England, a startled Stoughton exclaimed "Behold I turn
away from you."[8] Such a reaction is not at all surprising, for the orthodox
party interpreted Hutchinson's boast that "she must be delivered by miracle
and all we must be ruined" as evidence of a longstanding plot, concealed
under the "faire pretence of the Covenant of free Grace," to "fetch a revelation that shall reach the Magistrates and the whole Court, and the
succeeding generations."[9] Yet even after recoiling in apparent horror from
Hutchinson's fighting words, Stoughton quickly recovered his composure
and once again joined the antinomian party in a renewed call for oaths:

> The censure which the court is about to pass in my conscience is as
> much as she deserves, but because she desires witnesses and there is

none in way of witness therefore I shall desire that no offence be taken if I do not formally condemn her because she hath not been formally convicted as others are by witnesses upon oath.[10]

Stoughton ultimately voted for banishment with the majority, accepting the prevailing view that Hutchinson's "words" and the "frame of her spirit" were "pernicious." Still, Stoughton was the only magistrate, except for those who actually went into exile, to insist on oaths so late in the trial.[11] Indeed, when Thomas Weld and John Eliot were finally sworn in, Winthrop observed trenchantly that it was in "regard Mr. Stoughton is not satisfied."[12]

How are we to account for Stoughton's having aligned himself so closely with Hutchinson that at one point he perceived himself as having turned "away" from her? John Winthrop, in his *Short Story of the Rise, Reign, and Ruine of the Antinomians, Familists and Libertines*, was intent on proving to an English audience that the dissenters had been prosecuted not for their beliefs, or "matter of conscience," but rather because they had offered "speciall contempt . . . to the Court . . . which the Church could not judge of." Wheelwright, in particular, by recommending that believers contend for the true faith and by making clear distinctions between those who relied on grace and those who remained enthralled to works, "stirred up" certain colonists to "joyn in the disturbance of that peace, which hee was bound by solemn Oath to preserve." Yet Winthrop's tract, polemical as it was, shows that there was considerable disagreement concerning both the broad definition of "sedition" employed by the orthodox party and the appropriateness of allowing the government to "proceed in cases of conscience without referring them first to the Church."[13] Israel Stoughton, who had himself suffered through an earlier conviction on charges of sedition, was bound to be wary of the orthodox party's loose definition of that crime in the cases of Wheelwright and Hutchinson. And, like many other Bay Colony Puritans, he may have been disturbed by the hardening rigidity of the New England Way, especially since his own church of Dorchester had, at the outset of the antinomian troubles, been denied the "approbation" of a visiting committee of ministers and magistrates.

Stoughton's use of the antinomian controversy to register his discomfort with certain aspects of an all-encompassing New England Way was by no means unique. William Jennison, a General Court deputy from Watertown, Pequot War captain, and merchant, refused point-blank to vote "one way or the other" on Hutchinson's banishment, offering to share his thinking on the subject only "if the court require it."[14] Edward Gibbons, a General Court deputy from Charlestown, merchant, and lieutenant of the antinomian captain John Underhill, made a short-lived attempt to prevent the admonition of Hutchinson at her subsequent trial before the church, recommending that, though Hutchinson was a "lost woman," the congregation might "wayte a little longer to see if God will not help her to see the rest [of her errors] and to acknowledge them" so as to avoid "this Censure."[15] Robert Saltonstall, a wealthy Bay Colony resident unable to attain freeman status because of his disagreement with the emerging New England Way, lent money to accused antinomian Stephen Greensmith so that the latter could post bond for the enormous fine he had been assessed after proclaiming that "all the ministers except A, B, C [Cotton Wheelwright and, interestingly, Hooker] did teach a covenant of works."[16] In a shadowy incident related to the antinomian controversy, Thomas Hawkins, a merchant, shipwright, and General Court deputy from Dorchester (and later Boston), was compelled to acknowledge his "indiscretion in roughly addressing a member of the court while in session."[17] And Anthony Stoddard, a young merchant commencing his public life in the position of constable, was fined and enjoined to confess at church and in court the wrongfulness of his solicitude toward Francis Hutchinson, the twenty-one-year-old son of William and Anne, who was arrested in 1641 upon arrival from Barbados. Although Stoddard took custody of Hutchinson as directed, he used the opportunity to admonish the governor: "Sir, I came to observe what you did, that if you should proceed with a brother otherwise than you ought, I might deal with you in a church way."[18]

THE ORTHODOX ASSERTION of supremacy in 1638 was an unmistakable act of communal self-definition by which its expounders sought, consciously or not, to create a protonationalistic, self-regulating, provincially oriented, "godly" society based on humanistic values and dominated by ordinary "middling" people. Once the franchise was made contingent on church membership, the "visible" saint necessarily became the spiritual reflection of the good citizen, and diversity in the means of reaching or evidencing salvation had to be curtailed. Proponents of orthodoxy such as John Winthrop, Thomas Shepard, and Peter Bulkeley emphasized the connection between the worlds of nature and of spirit in such a way as to forge community by standardizing the ways the spirit could be understood to interact with the saints. While antinomians thought that an individual's reliance on objective, external standards—either for attaining church membership or for gaining a personal sense of assurance—would prevent him or her from experiencing the transports of a spiritual world that operated in a manner contradictory to mere human reason and logic, upholders of orthodoxy insisted that a person's outward behavior should be considered the most reliable indicator of his or her spiritual estate.[19]

Antinomian doctrine, in contrast, because it emphasized how observed reality diverged from spiritual reality, posed a direct threat to the close relationship between civil and religious authority emerging in the late 1630s. Although this form of dissent has often been associated with perfectionist fanaticism, it was feared, in reality, because of its ability to underwrite a more heterodox godly society, attuned to the transatlantic community rather than the geographically circumscribed locality and composed of saints who came to God by their own idiosyncratic routes.[20]

The emphasis in antinomianism on the inviolable interiority of the soul, and the worth of individual private judgment, seemed almost calculated to appeal to would-be leaders, ambitious merchants, and fractious military officers who expected their singular opinions to be heard with respect, who harbored doubts about the close relationship evolving between church and state, who resented what they sometimes experienced as the tyranny of consensual politics, who craved a secret internal space free of public scrutiny, and who could tolerate more (albeit limited) diversity in religious "opinions" than the newly established orthodox majority.[21] Israel Stoughton was such a man; and his experience opens a window on how the social, as opposed to the narrowly theological, meanings of orthodoxy and antinomianism were negotiated in a new world setting. Israel Stoughton might not have been a likely candidate to stand up in defense of a heretic, but he himself had been made to feel vulnerable in the face of orthodoxy; and Hutchinson's determination not only to protect her private self from public judgment but to assert her opinions resonated strongly with him.

Historians of the antinomian controversy have often followed orthodox chroniclers in obscuring one of the key social realities of the period: that the antinomian movement attracted prominent men of affairs who were not necessarily antinomian in a theological sense but who gave varying degrees of support to the dissenters out of frustration with (but not total alienation from) the type of community emerging as the social counterpart of orthodoxy. This occurred because the antinomianism that was "polemically constructed" in the 1630s was capable of legitimizing self-assertive behavior normally condemned in a communally oriented orthodoxy; its intellectual contours approximated the shape and feel of the "boundless" transatlantic market; and its central tenet of sundering spiritual from temporal things promised to admit some degree of toleration, or religious diversity, into the Bay.[22]

STOUGHTON'S SOLICITUDE IN 1637 for Hutchinson's right to a trial in which all testimony was properly sworn and his concern that her private exchanges with clergymen not be made grist for the public mill must be traced to his harrowing experience, two years earlier, as a political dissident—an opponent of magisterial supremacy.

In 1635, Stoughton, a General Court deputy, had argued that the magistrates' assumption of discretionary powers—the so-called negative voice—was a violation of freemen's rights as spelled out in the Bay Colony charter. Demanding actually to see this document, Stoughton had contended that it was the freemen or their representatives, the deputies—not the magistrates—who possessed the power to make laws; and he had written a tract elucidating his views on the proper exercise of government under the Massachusetts Bay charter.[23] The tract, as he later explained in a letter to his brother, John Stoughton, was considered seditious because it was thought to have "denied the assistants to be magistrates and made them but ministers of justice." For this transgression, the Court not only disqualified Stoughton from holding office for a period of three years but also required him to request personally the destruction of the offending manuscript as a didactic symbol of "how little I esteemed ought of mine."[24] Although a petition from the town of Dorchester asking that Stoughton's eligibility for office be restored was summarily denied, Stoughton's fortunes began steadily to rise when, during the governorship of Henry Vane, the ban on officeholding was mysteriously lifted, perhaps in an effort to forestall his migration to Connecticut.[25] Once he regained full civil liberties, Stoughton quickly emerged as Dorchester's leading citizen and was voted into the magistrate's chair, his ascent aided by the removal to Windsor of the prominent Roger Ludlow, a leading man of Dorchester who had clashed with the rulers of the Bay.[26]

Stoughton's history does not in any way suggest that he was a fellow religious traveler with the antinomians; indeed, as a migrant from Dorsetshire, gathered into the church of John Warham and John Maverick prior to emigration from England, Stoughton was not likely to have been a "high" Calvinist.[27] Furthermore, he advanced to the magistracy in the same election that displaced the antinomian governor Vane and returned Winthrop to the position of chief magistrate; he was granted land near the Neponset River on the same day that Wheelwright, steadfast in his opposition, was banished; and he was deemed trustworthy enough to be designated Wheelwright's keeper should the latter fail to depart the jurisdiction in the allotted time.[28] In view of these facts, some historians, ignoring Stoughton's behavior at the Hutchinson trial, have described him as wholly within the orthodox camp.[29] Still, it is easy to see how the Wheelwright sedition trial, opening up old wounds barely healed, may have inspired an understandably diffident Stoughton to go on record later in demanding, at the Hutchinson trial, that the Court adhere closely to what he regarded as the proper course of "justice."

The proceedings surrounding Wheelwright were highly contested. The antinomian party insisted that a charge of sedition could not be seriously entertained unless the accused person "bee culpable of some seditious fact, or his doctrine must bee seditious, or must breed sedition in the hearts of his hearers." None of these conditions, they said, obtained in the Wheelwright case because the preacher's doctrines had been "no other but the very expressions of the Holy Ghost himselfe" and because no seditious acts had been committed: "wee have not drawn the sword . . . neither have wee rescued our innocent Brother."[30]

Stiff punishments were meted out to those signers of the antinomian petition who stubbornly refused to acknowledge their mistake. But Winthrop's highly biased writings show that misgivings about Wheelwright's banishment were nonetheless widespread. The dominant faction, for example, found it necessary to write an "apology" explaining their thinking on the issue because some "Members of the Court (both of the Magistrates and Deputies) did dissent from the major part, in the judgement of the cause of Mr. Wheelwright, and divers others have since censured the proceedings against him as unjust, or (at best) over hasty."[31] At the same time, eager to preserve the appearance if not the reality of consensus, the Court had also turned down a request that information about the difference of opinion be placed in the official records: "such of the Magistrates and Deputies, as had not concurred with the major part in the vote, (some of them) moved that the dissent might be recorded (but it was denied)."[32]

During the period when Wheelwright was being questioned before the Court, partisans tried to block questions concerning the clergyman's unspoken intentions, or state of mind, at the time when he described "works-righteous" people as "enemies" of the saints of God and compared them with "Antichrists," "enemies," "Philistims," "Herod," "Pilate," and the "persecuting Jews."[33] The Court held that because Wheelwright knew that most Bay Colonists operated under what he (falsely) described as a "covenant of works," he must have intended to "traduce" the reputations of men of rank, both ministers and magistrates, and hold them up to public ridicule and contempt, grounds for sedition in English practice because of the threat to authority.[34] Magistrates accordingly asked Wheelwright "whether before his [fast-day] Sermon he did not know, that most of the Ministers in this jurisdiction did teach that doctrine which he in his Sermon called a Covenant of works"—a question that went to the heart of this issue. Some in the Court, however, accused the interrogators of using tactics similar to those employed by the hated Court of High Commission, which silenced Puritan ministers in England; and Wheelwright, for his part, refused to answer, seeming to concur with the view that the "Court went about to ensnare him and to make him to accuse himselfe."[35] Although Wheelwright protested that he had not condemned specific persons of any rank, the Court had a ready answer: "he who designes a man by such circumstances, as doe note him out to common intendments, doth as much as if he named the party," just as "when Paul spake of those of the circumcision, it was as certaine whom he meant as if he named the Jewes."[36]

Beyond the question of whether Wheelwright had set out deliberately to insult the colony's ruling men, Winthrop, speaking for the orthodox party, cited classical sources and Scripture alike to prove that the sedition-monger was no more and no less than one who "sets mens minds at difference and begets strife."[37] Wheelwright had made "sides" when he preached the "covenant of grace" in a manner that was at variance with the understanding of most of the colony's leaders. It had been his duty to consult with his peers, to convince them of the righteousness of his opinions, and, failing that, to desist rather than to "publish" them abroad to the people. Setting aside questions concerning Wheelwright's doctrines as matters for "conscience" and not courts, Winthrop condemned this misguided elder for failing to exercise due discretion or, in effect, to censor himself. An educated man should have known better than to preach words that he knew to be "divisive": "his reading and experience might have told him how dangerous it is to heat peoples affections against their opposites." If a magistrate "may not appoint a messenger of God, what hee should teach," he "may limit him what hee may not teach," for "every truth is not seasonable at all times."[38]

Stoughton's act of "sedition" had been far tamer than Wheelwright's. Having backed down and suffered the full indignities the Court had to offer, Stoughton may well have believed that the unrepentant Wheelwright had gone too far. Indeed, Wheelwright was so full of pride that he refused even to read the Court's explanation (the "apology") for charging him with sedition. "An Angel would have given milder language to the Devill himselfe," Winthrop complained, than Wheelwright offered to his disputants. Wheelwright, moreover, had had eight months, between the conviction for sedition in March 1637 and the final sentence of banishment in November, to contemplate an apology; and during this time great "paines had beene [vainly] taken" to procure a change of heart and wean him of his "erroneous opinions."[39]

Still, there is no doubt that Stoughton had highly resented the draconian censure of his own views, which he most likely knew were contrary to consensus but as an elite man like Wheelwright, thought he had the right to discuss. It is thus noteworthy that in the Hutchinson trial, although he was obviously disturbed by Hutchinson's venomous revelations, Stoughton insisted that there be sworn testimony pointing toward specific incidents in which she had "traduced" the ministers, not just vague allegations concerning her presumed intentions.

Winthrop described in melodramatic detail the long- and short-term consequences of the antinomian-inspired divisions. To those willing to concede that the disturbances had harmed only the colony's "unity" and not its "utility"—and therefore could not be considered sedition—Winthrop pointed out that some antinomian hotheads had refused to serve in the Pequot War and had snubbed chaplain John Wilson, not even turning up to bid him farewell when he went off to join the troops, "for when brethren shall looke one at another as enemies and persecutors . . . how shall they joyne together in any publike service?" Winthrop also dilated on the long-term consequences that might flow from "inflamed passions" and a partisan spirit by bringing to mind the religious wars on the Continent and the Anabaptist-inspired massacre at Munster, under John of Leyden, a century earlier: the "warres in Germany," he warned, began "first" with "contentions" bred "by disputations and Sermons[,] and when the minds of the people were once set on fire by reproachfull termes of incendiary spirits, they soone set to blowes, and had alwayes a tragicall and bloudy issue."[40] Stoughton was no less concerned about the social order than Winthrop. But having endured Winthrop's fulmination that his own authorship of a small pamphlet on the charter made him a "troubler of Israel," a "worm," and an "underminer of the state," the Dorchester magistrate, who well appreciated the damage that could be wrought when the governor "too much forgot and overshot" himself, was inclined to regard Winthrop's agitated predictions with a grain of salt.[41]

Moving ahead to the Hutchinson trial itself, Stoughton's actions are thrown into bolder relief, for his correspondence suggests reasons why the former political dissident might have perceived in the Hutchinson case certain disturbing parallels to the sequence of events leading to his own temporary downfall. During his time of troubles, Stoughton complained that fellow colonists had encouraged him to articulate his ideas and then twisted his words around so as to make him more culpable, and more singular in his failure to be humble, than, in his own mind, he really was:

> The patent makes their [the magistrates'] power ministerial according to the greater vote of the general courts and not magisterial according to their own discretion. These were my very expressions, whereby I intended and meant that their power—call it ministerial or magisterial or magistratical (which you will)—was not so great that they could do ought or hinder ought simply according to their own wills, but they must eye and respect general courts, which by patent consist of the whole company of freemen. And this is in very deed the magistrates' own judgment and the judgment of every man in the land that hath expressed himself, and yet for this my expression they would have me to affirm they were no magistrates, and these my words should be a proof of it.[42]

Stoughton was particularly incensed that his enemies had played upon his religious scruples in order to get him to "confess" his differences with the magistrates; he reported having been approached by several church brothers who encouraged him to commit his political views to paper, and "pressed my conscience that I sinned if I refused. . . . Now no sooner had Mr. Warum [the Dorchester pastor] the thing but he (without my privity) carries it to the ministers, presents it at their meeting, which for aught I ever heard was well approved by every man of them"—at least until the accusations began to fly.[43]

Just as Stoughton suggested that his coreligionists deliberately encouraged him to make certain injudicious statements, so too did Hutchinson complain that she had been ensnared by those who presented themselves as being most earnest to save her soul. As Mary Beth Norton has recently shown, the controversy over oathtaking in the Hutchinson trial had arisen when the defendant demanded that her accusers affirm before God their recollection of the exact words they alleged she had used in defaming them and the precise times and places where these words had been spoken.[44] Understanding that the ministers might not remember the verbatim utterances, or the actual sequence, of Hutchinson's remarks (now almost a year old), and believing that such issues were but trifling "circumstances and adjuncts to the cause," Simon Bradstreet had tried to dissuade the accused from placing her detractors in jeopardy for bearing false witness: "admit they should mistake you in your speeches you would make them to sin if you urge them to swear."[45] But Hutchinson remained obdurate. While conceding that she had described some of the colony's ministers as preaching the covenant of grace "more clearly" than others, she categorically denied having said that the orthodox ministers preached a "covenant of works" or that they were not "sealed." Hutchinson allowed that in private conference with the ministers or other saints she might have used sterner expressions. But these conversations, particularly her examination at the house of her favorite minister, John Cotton, were not, in her opinion, intended for public consumption: "It is one thing for me to come before a public magistracy and there to speak what they would have me to speak and another when a man comes to me in a way of friendship privately there is difference in that."[46] Hutchinson argued further that the orthodox preachers' motives were suspect because they had "come [to court] in their own cause," to protect their professional reputations and not the colony's; thus their testimony should not be accepted without an oath.[47]

Stoughton's claim that his private differences with the magistrates had been purposely elicited, publicly presented, and then systematically deformed had much in common with the defense Hutchinson tried to mount at her civil trial. And just as Stoughton believed that his own earlier humiliation had come at the hands of people jealous to augment their own powers, so too did Hutchinson denounce her accusers for serving unfairly as "witnesses of their own cause." This charge threatened to trivialize the proceedings by framing Hutchinson's offense as a slander against private individuals rather than a serious breach of authority carrying momentous consequences for the colony as a whole. Sensing the danger in this line of defense, Winthrop responded that "It is not their cause [the minister's] but the cause of the whole country and they were unwilling that it should come forth, but that it was the glory and honour of God."[48] Still, Hutchinson's insight was compelling. The antinomian captain John Underhill, for example, in pleading on behalf of Stephen Greensmith, another individual who had questioned the orthodox ministers' ability to preach grace, raised precisely this issue in a reproachful letter to Winthrop: "Yow knowe itt (Greensmith's insult) is nott an offence against Christ, butt the callings of me[n] and I hope for peace sake God will moove your hearte to preferre the peace of his Church before the rightt of your owne cause."[49]

If Stoughton had his differences with believers the likes of Hutchinson and Underhill, many of their criticisms of the Bay leadership rang true in his ears. Stoughton believed that the Court permitted his accusers to read aloud parts of his book in such a fashion that it would appear to be saying what his accusers wanted it to say rather than what he had been trying to express; and he had watched in frustration as the Court accepted hostile testimony from witnesses who were allowed to "affirm" their accounts of what he had said in conversation on various occasions simply "upon their credit" and without oath.[50] Like other dissenters, Stoughton was discomfited by the forced homogeneity of the impending New England Way and its emphasis on the good of the community over the dignity and private judgment of the individual.

It would be a mistake to view Stoughton's obstreperous behavior at the Hutchinson trial solely as an attempt to gain some small retribution for the political injuries he had suffered. Stoughton's disinclination to censure Anne Hutchinson even though he disagreed with her religious views suggests that he was comfortable allowing a number of different, even slightly contradictory, opinions to float freely beneath the surface of majority opinion—a position he may have arrived at after experiencing personally just how confining religious orthodoxy could be.

In April 1636, just as the colony's ministers had begun to explore their differences, Stoughton's church, organized anew under Richard Mather after many of the original inhabitants removed to Windsor, had been denied "the approbation of the other churches and of the magistrates." This "publique approbacion" of new congregations was mandated by an ordinance, passed in the March session of the General Court, that denied the privileges of freemanship to the members of any church gathered without the approval of the magistrates and "the greater parte of the said churches." By Winthrop's account, Dorchester's "confession of faith" was deemed sound, but the members themselves were unable properly to "manifest the work of God's grace in themselves," having "builded their comfort of salvation upon unsound grounds, viz., some upon dreams and ravishes of spirit by fits; others upon the reformation of their lives; others upon duties and performances, etc." If the proposed Dorchester church contained persons of both the antinomian and the "Arminian" persuasion, both Israel Stoughton and Nathaniel Duncan, a fellow member of the Artillery Company and church pillar—not to mention Mather—must have been willing to tolerate this diversity. But Thomas Shepard, demonstrating the same concern for uniformity and discipline that would inform his stance during the full-blown antinomian controversy, counseled Mather on the dangers of "false hearts" and the need to be "very wary and very sharp in looking to the hearts and spirits of those you sign yourself unto."[51] The key roles that Winthrop and Shepard played in the rejection of Dorchester church could only have added to Stoughton's reservations about a regime that had once silenced his political criticisms.

Stoughton could not ingenuously claim to have been discreet in his criticism of Bay Colony government; yet he genuinely resented how his private opinions had been wrested from him and forced out into the open by an orthodoxy intent on exposing and punishing all dissent, whether political or religious. Stoughton did not, in all situations, want to submit his private self to public scrutiny, and he viewed as inappropriate efforts to force Anne Hutchinson to do the same. When, after considerable discussion regarding the merits of oaths, John Eliot and Thomas Shepard asked "to see light why we should take an oath," Stoughton, echoing a remark that Hutchinson had earlier made to him, responded curtly, "Why it is an end of all strife and I think you ought to swear and put an end to the matter."[52] Having encountered unforeseen, and, to his mind, unwarranted constraints in his New World setting, Stoughton was driven, by force of circumstance, to adopt, very gingerly, what looks much like an inchoate, anachronistic due process mode of viewing judicial affairs.[53] Yet his was a world where champions of such views were seen not as populist defenders of civil liberties, and certainly not as good Puritans, but rather as courtier-like manipulators who purposely bent the truth for the advantage of known malefactors.[54] Winthrop's contention that the Court should ignore legal niceties and simply "believe so many godly elders in a cause wherein we [already] know the mind of the party [Hutchinson] without their [the elders'] testimony," while typical of the early modern world, is jarring to modern sensibilities.[55] But to the "middling" colonists of Puritan Massachusetts, Winthrop's views, like the religious orthodoxy in which they were embedded, had the compelling ring of plain common sense, while Stoughton's interest in legal niceties seemed elitist and ungodly.

IN 1633 THE future Presbyterian pamphleteer William Prynne reacted to the disorder that abounded in Stuart England by publishing a weighty tome, Histrio-Mastix, that condemned theatricality in all its forms. Confused and frightened by the "crisis of representation" that radiated out from the market and insinuated itself into every aspect of life in early-seventeenth-century England, Prynne longed for the clarity, honesty, and simplicity that he attributed to a God devoid of mystery, a God "who is truth itselfe, in whom there is no variablenesse, no shadow of change and no feigning." Events in England held out little hope that Prynne could escape into a halcyon world where all creatures possessed "a uniforme distinct and proper being . . . the bounds of which may not be exceeded" and where people followed closely the godly injunction always to be "such in shew, as they are in truth."[56] The orthodox saints of Puritan New England, however, suffering from the same angst, attempted to create such conditions in their corner of the New World. And there they too came into conflict with a sensibility that denied and scoffed at the desire for a close correspondence between terrestrial/external/public realities and spiritual/internal/private ones. They labeled this sensibility antinomianism, and it elicited the same fear—whether manifested in the secular realm (as sedition) or in the religious (as licentiousness)—that theatricality did for Prynne.

Historians have hotly debated the extent to which "real" antinomian views could be found in the preaching of John Wheelwright and John Cotton, the two Boston clerics most closely associated with the party of dissenters.[57] In England the term "antinomian" referred to the Eatonite circle of mystical preachers—John Eaton, Robert Towne, John Traske, Tobias Crispe, and Roger Brierley—who denied that God saw the stains of sin upon his elect, cried down the "law," and emphasized the doctrine of unmerited free grace to such an exaggerated extent that they left themselves open to charges of libertinism.[58] Neither Cotton nor Wheelwright were as extreme as these radical spirits or, for that matter, Hutchinson, who had carried their ideas to the utmost extremes. Yet even if the orthodox party falsely invoked the scandalous epithet "antinomian" to discredit their opposition, the fact remains that real differences existed in religious sensibility in Puritan Massachusetts. These differences, capable of supporting divergent social visions, and viewed as particularly dangerous at the outset of a godly experiment, placed Cotton and Wheelwright in opposition to most of the other Bay Colony ministers, especially Thomas Shepard of Cambridge and Peter Bulkeley of Concord.

Because Wheelwright so adamantly rejected consensus, refusing to consult with "flesh and bloud," he was the only clergyman actually punished during the crisis. But Cotton shared with Wheelwright the root belief that human and divine things were ineluctably opposed, that the "eie of faith" saw things differently from the "eie of reason," and that sanctified behavior could not be used as evidence that one had been saved. In the clerical conferences preceding the antinomian trials Cotton regarded with a jaundiced eye those colleagues and believers who seemed presumptuously and erroneously to assume that the spirit would conform to human law and logic: "God is not wont to witness upon the sight of our gracious dispositions," warned Cotton, "but upon the sight of our great ungodliness, that so the glory of Grace, and the vertue and value of Christs righteousness may be the more magnified."[59] In a setting where "sanctification" played a major role in determining who would be admitted to "visible" sainthood and where church membership in turn conferred upon men the privilege of the franchise, any deviation from the essential truth that the spiritual and temporal worlds were commensurable had to be regarded as bordering on the seditious. The hallmark of orthodoxy for Thomas Shepard was the belief that it was God's "common wonted dispensation" to order "all parts of his work both of faith and holiness" in "Symmetry and proportion."[60] And because Cotton, even in the wake of Anne Hutchinson's expulsion, "doth stiffly hold the revelation of our good estate still, without any sight of word or work," Shepard concluded that his rival remained a dangerous hidden antinomian.[61]

The orthodox party during New England's antinomian crisis insisted that those who were banished, disarmed, or disfranchised in 1637 had been guilty of sedition, not heresy. But in a polity where church membership was made a precondition for full citizenship, Winthrop's claim that only the "application" of Wheelwright's doctrines and not the religious ideas themselves had been condemned was strained. Wheelwright could easily be proceeded against because he allegedly "taught" that the "former Governour [Vane] and some of the Magistrates then were friends of Christ and Free-grace [not works-righteousness], but the present [Winthrop et. al.] were enemies."[62] Yet Winthrop saw too that the tendency to view contemptuously those who were "exceeding holy and strict in their way," even when engaged in by the peace-loving John Cotton, would injure efforts to construct a cohesive godly community based on "visible" churches and the "law of love."

If Winthrop hung back from explicitly denouncing false doctrine—an office befitting a minister but not a magistrate—he nonetheless expressed freely his disregard for the way that Wheelwright attributed belief in a "covenant of works" to those who based their "assurance" of salvation not on their "justification," or the silent whisperings of the spirit to the sin-sick soul, but rather on their "sanctification," the active belief, godly behavior, and "mourning" for sin that were thought to flow from "justification" but could easily be "counterfeited" by hypocrites. Not only might the discrediting of sanctification open the door to "sin without fear," but the censorious spirit exemplified in Wheelwright's preaching might sap the Christian "charity" vital to fellow-feeling and trust, attributes sorely needed in an infant plantation. With these considerations in mind, Winthrop was willing to say that Wheelwright, in pronouncing as "enemies" those who were only "visibly" godly, was theologically wrong, guilty not only of an unbending will and contemptuous "manner" but also of spreading fallacious "matter" adverse to the "truth of the Gospel":

> wee may safely deny that those speeches were truths, which the Court censured for contempt and sedition, for a brother may fall so farre into disobedience to the Gospel, as there may bee cause to separate from him, and to put him to shame . . . all hee spake was not true, and by this is the offence more aggravated, for if it were seditious only in the manner, it must needs bee much worse, when the matter it selfe also was untrue.[63]

Wheelwright's greatest failing in Winthrop's eyes was that he evinced hostility, not "tendernesse of heart," toward those whom he described as works-righteous. Winthrop was by no means willing to concede that the majority of Bay inhabitants were mired in a "covenant of works." But he argued that if a preacher *were* to encounter such individuals, he should nurture them up to a correct way of thinking and "use all gentlenesse, instructing them with meeknesse." Instead, Wheelwright had treated all who differed with him as incipient persecutors, even though they had "denied themselves for the love of Christ as farre as he hath done, and will be ready (by Gods grace) to doe and suffer for the sake of Christ, and the honour of Free-grace as much as himselfe." If Wheelwright had exercised due "charity," he would have treated fellow New Englanders as "true Christians," not "Turks or Papists." Colonists who "professe their faith in Christ only, etc. and are in Church fellowship, and walk inoffensively, submitting to all the Lords Ordinances in Church and Common wealth," did not deserve to be "branded Reprobates, and arch-enemies of Christ." It was indeed criminal for "such [good people, especially the prominent among them] to be publikely defamed, and held forth as enemies to the Lord Jesus and persecutors like Herod and Pilate, and the uncircumcised heathen."[64]

John Cotton, unlike Wheelwright, was universally regarded as mild of manner. Yet in exchanges with orthodox ministers even he was accused of being insufficiently charitable, for his views were thought to deprive professed Christians of the peace of mind that might come from right living and striving after faith. Cotton denounced all mere outward sanctification as "counterfeit treasure" and argued that anyone who based their assurance on such appearances alone—rather than the direct witness of Christ—was a "hypocrite" who deserved to be "blamed of going aside to a Covenant of Works . . . unless it be a fault to call a sin by its proper name."[65] Those who would use works to corroborate their justification manifested not their holiness but their lack of faith, placing their trust "not on him that justifieth the ungodly (which is the faith of the Gospel) . . . but on him which justifieth the Godly: which is such a faith as Adam might have, and so belongeth to the Covenant of Works."[66] Orthodox elders were appalled that Cotton allowed "signs delivered by the Holy Ghost in Scripture [sanctification]" to "be of use only to them that are assured already, and so have least need, and of no use to them that want assurance and so have most need of them."[67] But Cotton was certain that a true saint was one whose "very iniquity shall not make him afraid; there is such a state in Christianity, and not all men know it."[68] Thomas Shepard depicted the authoritative Christian community, headed by the minister, as providing a more stable source of assurance than the individual's own fickle intuition:

> Do not think there is no compunction or sense of sin wrought in the soul, because you cannot so clearly discern and feel it, nor the time of the working and first beginning of it. I have known many that have come with complaints they were never humbled . . . nor yet could tell the time when it was so, yet there hath been and many times they have seen it by the help of other spectacles, and blest God for it.[69]

Cotton, in contrast, cautioned people to rely on themselves, and not on the judgment of others, to gain hope for the positive outcome of their spiritual journeys. The good Christian should listen respectfully to what others had to say, but in the end could rely for assurance only upon private communication with the spirit:

> another Christian of better discerning, may justly . . . apply [seemingly sanctified acts] to him as good Evidences of his justified estate. But neverthelesse he will still seeke and wait for further and clearer Fellowship with Christ, till the Spirit of God himselfe do witnesse to him, the gracious thoughts of God towards him in a free Promise of Grace, before he can plead his owne good workes . . . for good Evidences of his Justification.[70]

Historians have focused—and rightly so—on the belief of Cotton's interlocutors that his way of faith was too "free and easie" for those who would take advantage of it and sin without fear. But it is important to recognize that at the same time, they also worried that it was too harsh and dispiriting for the average colonist.

Whatever else the antinomian controversy was "about," it certainly had much to do with social engineering. Winthrop had claimed that, even if Wheelwright's doctrines were correct, he had promulgated them in the wrong "season," the infancy of a new society being a time to build the sinews of community, not isolate people from one another. Given this social perspective, Cotton's ideas were just as dangerous as Wheelwright's, for, if taken to extremes, they might put off too many of the right sort of people—those humble, modest souls who hung back from the promises— while encouraging proud, "ambitious," unruly spirits, like Hutchinson, who preferred their own intuitions over the admonitions of the clergy and the brethren. Even Cotton was said to have blanched at the rhetorical question Hutchinson used to explain how she knew that her "revelations" were from God: "how did Abraham know that it was the voyce of God, when he commanded him to sacrifice his sonne?"[71]

Cotton and Wheelwright emphasized subjectivity, intuition, and emotionalism in ways that were socially as well as intellectually out of joint with an evolving New England Way that required applicants for church membership to focus on their sense of "compunction" for sin and outward signs of reformation, not the joy of "assurance" emphasized by Cotton and Wheelwright.[72] The dominant view of salvation, as expressed by Shepard and Bulkeley, held that God chose the elect out of eternity, provided them with the "habit" of grace as a free gift, but did not effectually save them until they actively received faith and consciously believed. After the righteousness of Christ was imputed to them in justification, the saints, both out of gratitude and because God had ordained that a "good tree" must produce "good fruit," began to feel compunction for their sins and to live "sanctified," outwardly moral, lives. While a saint's justification bore no external signs but was evident to the saint who received it, sanctification provided the means by which the godly could be discovered to the community.[73]

The antinomian controversy thus pitted two very different conceptualizations of truth against one another. For orthodox lights, like Shepard, sin and the law operated as a kind of reality check: "The Law is that Glass that sheweth a Man his own Face, and what he himself is. Now if this Glass be taken away, and not set before a deformed Heart, how can a Man but think himself fair? . . . the Mind sets up and bows down to a False Image of Grace."[74] But to Cotton and Wheelwright, the mirror image seemed like a dangerous delusion that might puff up the sanctified-looking hypocrite— who "may for a long time find all his own ends attained in seeking the glory of God"—at the expense of real, albeit errant, saints, "so a poor Christian is discouraged, and an hypocrite is emboldned, seeing himself more sanctified in the outward view than the other."[75] In order to protect the integrity of authentic spiritual experience from the allure of terrestrial appearance, Cotton affirmed how the "assurance of a [Christian] mans good

Estate, may be maintained to him, when the frame of his Spirit [and Course] is grown much degenerate."[76] God, Cotton thought, sometimes incapacitated his people's ability to perform "works" so that they would "lay up all our joy in christ," rather than "our owne songs in the Night [sanctified acts]."[77]

Here it is instructive to return to William Prynne, whose denunciations of the stage exactly mirrored orthodox attacks on antinomianism. Shepard castigated the antinomians for construing the terrestrial and spiritual worlds as so divergent that in the latter the guilt and misery of sin might be ignored. Prynne similarly attacked the theater for having created a privileged space, the stage, where people were not held responsible for their deeds. The invented world of the stage featured actors whose guilt was only apparent and not real, just as the antinomian scheme featured human beings whose sins were of evanescent importance so long as they were saved. In *Histrio-Mastix*, Prynne put forth an understanding of sin so concrete as to suggest that every sinful act depicted in "jest" by a "feined" character on the stage would be punished just as though it had been committed in "real" life by a true malefactor: "no sinne can ever subsist without its proper subject . . . and then this vaine Evasion [that the play was not real] will not helpe" the sinners/actors to escape punishment.[78]

Like orthodox New Englanders, Prynne apprehended sin as a discrete act attributable to a particular "subject." And, as with the New Englanders, this understanding of sin made possible Prynne's sense of worldly order: a sin, though performed only in "jest," was still a sin and needed a "subject" to whose account it could be tallied. If things were not so, "then every man . . . would dayly violate them [Gods commandments] by way of sport, and merriment, not in earnest, and yet they should bee no sinners, because they sinne in jest: and so all Gods Lawes should be evacuated, Religion undermined, and sinne made a jest."[79]

John Cotton and John Wheelwright certainly did not treat sin as a "jest." But Shepard, who said that his opponents "make light of the matter, and say even the best of men sins seven times a day," denounced what he identified as the antinomian message in precisely the same cadences that Prynne used to anathematize the notion that an actor could sin "by way of proxie, or representation onely," and still remain blameless.[80] Speaking to an audience of Harvard students in the aftermath of the antinomian controversy, Shepard depicted the evils of that heresy in the following terms.

> It is therefore a most accursed doctrine of some Libertines, who imagining that (through the bloudshed and righteousness of Christ in their free justification) God sees no sin in his justified people, that therefore themselves are to see no sin, because now they are justified and washed with Christs bloud; and therefore lest they should be found out to be grosse liars, they mince the matter, they confesse that they may see sin by the eie of sense and reason, but (faith being crosse to

reason) they are therefore to see the quite contrary, and so to see no sin in themselves by the eie of faith; from whence it follows, that Christ shed his bloud to destroy all sight and sense of sin to the eie of faith, though not to the eie of reason, and thus as by the eie of faith they should see no sin; so (it will follow) that by the same bloud they are bound to see no law, no not so much as their rule, which . . . in revealing mans dutie declares his sin.[81]

Shepard and other orthodox divines in New England, all of whom emphasized God's great gift in structuring most (but not all) spiritual things to coincide with human perceptions, would have applauded Prynne's argument that appearances normally coincided with reality, such that "if the substance be evill, the shadow of it cannot be good."[82] Such coincidences were indispensable to the survival of morality, religion, and truth in the world; and, more important, they were vital to the construction of a godly local community and "visible" churches. John Cotton, however, like Wheelwright, defined faith as the ability to look beyond earthly chimeras and challenged the notion that it was possible, or even desirable, for people to be "such in shew, as they are in truth." According to Cotton, saints and hypocrites, like actors, were capable of performing equally convincing sanctified acts: "I have seen hypocrites (to outward view) well rooted, and more comfortable than I myself."[83] The ranks of the regenerate and reprobate were rigidly distinct, Cotton held, because the former's possession of true faith allowed them to be "melted into flesh," while the latter were only "melted as iron, which will return again to . . . hardness." Still, despite these very real and fundamental differences, it was impossible for mere human beings to separate spiritual wheat from chaff, for "to distinguish in men between that Sanctification which floweth from the Law, and that which is of the Gospel, is a matter so narrow, that the Angels in Heaven have much ado to discern who differ; a work fitter for Angels . . . then for Ministers of the Gospel, though indeed there be great difference of the one from the other."[84] Although Cotton emerged from the antinomian controversy as a major defender of the New England Way, his belief that well-behaved hypocrites and saints were virtually indistinguishable from one another was potentially devastating to the very concept of "visible" churches.

If outward appearances were as deceiving as the antinomians suggested, then the godly community could be little more than a pleasant fiction with no basis in reality. If true reality inhered in the unbridled interiority of each individual—in the intuition, or emotions, rather than the rational faculties—then it would be impossible for people to agree on or even to know a single truth. No wonder John Winthrop said of the antinomian heresy that it "overthrows" all. Winthrop found it heartening that in the wake of the controversy Anne Hutchinson experienced a "monstrous" birth: some thirty misshapen masses issued forth from the hertic's body, corresponding roughly to the number of erroneous opinions she had spread and physically embodying the social disorganization her ideas implied. The "erronists," however, had a disturbing rejoinder to Winthrop's comfortable conclusion that this—like Hutchinson's compulsion to "deliver" an account of her damnable revelations to the Court—signified how the physical world was constructed to reflect, or "out," God's truth: "This [deceptive evidence of Hutchinson's guilt] is for you, yee legalists, that your eyes might be further blinded, by God's hand upon us, in your legall wayes, and stumble and fall, and in the end breake your necks into Hell, if yee embrace not the truth."[85] Here the spiritual world was depicted not simply as counterintuitive, but as a realm deliberately designed to delude stubborn legalists.

ORTHODOXY WAS PERCEIVED as confining or liberating depending on one's social circumstances. Some historians have viewed orthodoxy as oligarchic or dictatorial because it discredited the individual's ability to apprehend experientially his or her own estate, emphatically shifting control of the whole conversion experience (and the church admissions process) from individual saint to Christian community. But it must be remembered that the New England Way was voted in; it was not imposed. In 1637 rank-and-file colonists overwhelmingly voted Winthrop, hence orthodoxy, back into office. Orthodox ministers and magistrates popularized their message by presenting themselves as the protectors of the Bay Colony's ordinary inhabitants, whom they frequently referred to as "honest husbandmen," from an anticommunal, inegalitarian, mystical antinomianism. The antinomian emphasis on exceptional people or atypical dispensations—as opposed to the way things worked under normal circumstances—did not, in the long run, appeal to the rank and file. In contrast, the balance that orthodox preachers struck between grace and works, Christ and Adam, word and world, upheld a widely acceptable vision of an interdependent community capable of providing good Christian fellowship.[86]

Why would this be the case? The orthodox premise that the seen and unseen worlds were commensurable accorded well with the common sense of ordinary settlers. Puritans knew that mere mortals were incapable of making the invisible and visible worlds coincide perfectly. Yet they wanted to believe that in most cases, and especially in their churches, these two worlds did reflect one another fairly accurately. David D. Hall has shown that this desire was fully consonant with a popular culture, that, far from understanding sin in a metaphorical sense (like the antinomians), was inclined to believe that iniquity left a palpable "stain" upon the land: "sin will out: it cannot hide forever."[87]

The insistence that all saints must approach the work of salvation and receive communal approbation in roughly the same manner, moreover, upheld a kind of egalitarianism, the concept of "salvation-work" providing standards against which all could be evaluated and none excused. The minister and magistrate would, of course, rule; but because of the widespread availability of land and the franchise, this rule would not be perceived as onerous. The antinomian propensity to focus upon the extraordinary rather than the ordinary, possibilities rather than probabilities, went against the grain of orthodox attempts to provide a stable, community-affirming version of the conversion experience that would bring people together rather than drive them apart.

Modern readers have been positively struck by the individuating tendencies found in Cotton's preaching during his antinomian phase; on his distaste for endless "mourning" over sin; and on the singularly positive valuation he placed upon the ecstatic (and erotic) marital union between the saintly bride and the bridegroom Christ, all of these elements seeming somehow more humane, and more inviting, than orthodoxy.[88] Yet in the context of early New England this unrestrained and exaggerated focus on direct union, marital or otherwise, with a spiritual universe operating in a manner that normally contradicted observed reality, seemed to strip the "real" world, and human society, of religious meaning. The orthodox magnification of the human element in the drama of salvation, on the other hand, made religion more accessible to ordinary people.[89]

These contrary understandings of how the material world related to the spiritual, while abstract, clearly reflected different conceptions of the ideal society and its inhabitants. The ideas expounded by orthodox stalwarts Bulkeley and Shepard dominated Massachusetts preaching because they underwrote the values approved of by "middling" residents—communalism, egalitarianism, and parochialism—at a time when the saints were in need of a distinct New World identity that could keep them safe from all challengers.

Far from associating objective means of evidencing faith with hidebound conservatism, defenders aligned orthodoxy with comfort, charity, and communal interdependence. The collective pursuit of an intensely personal spiritual experience that nonetheless followed a prescribed course susceptible to external validation did much to create or enhance the horizontal bonds among the saints. If this experience were construed as unduly mysterious or idiosyncratic, or if outward appearances were believed frequently to mask rather than to reveal the true self, as John Cotton and John Wheelwright would have it, then the bonds of trust that held people together would be severed, and the linkage between the secular and spiritual worlds would be lost. Bulkeley, who had felt particularly forlorn when Cotton and Wheelwright refused to attend his ordination, described how the apparent disparities between the covenants of work and grace would melt away if only people could see how sweetly they complemented one another: his plea to "let us not then dash them one against another" has an unmistakable social as well as theological resonance.[90] Orthodox saints used the peculiarities of the Massachusetts way both to define their nascent community and to exclude others through a series of binary oppositions separating pure from impure and good from evil in the most emphatic manner possible. The utter privatism that antinomian doctrine afforded people in their spiritual lives, combined with the caution that things are rarely what they seem, inspired early modern fears of imposture and dissimulation.

SO WHERE DID Israel Stoughton fit in all of this? Stoughton clearly did not approve of Anne Hutchinson's malicious "carriage." Nor was he bred up to appreciate the high Calvinist position. Yet Stoughton could identify with the antinomian commitment to respect individual opinions and intuition. When John Wheelwright encouraged saints to fight for what they knew to be the correct way of evidencing faith, and when he warned of how souls would be deformed when forced to affirm a salvific script that did not match their owners' inner experiences, Stoughton could apply the lesson to his own life and think back on how his political conscience had been forced to bow down to consensus in the most humiliating possible way. If Stoughton was not a heretic, he did come to understand that orthodoxy was uncomfortably uncompromising in the new world, for New Englanders were using religion to forge the bonds needed to create a cohesive, godly society. The New England Way, moreover, carefully balancing word and spirit, works and grace, seemed bent upon achieving stasis and homogeneity. But Stoughton, as a merchant, was oriented toward change and exchange; and he was not the only New England merchant who learned to speak in antinomian accents when beleaguered by criticism.

The merchant Robert Keayne, founder of the Artillery Company, steered clear of antinomianism; at the close of the controversy, he was one of the few military men blameless enough to be charged with the task of collecting weapons from disarmed antinomians. But Keayne did not stay out of trouble for long. In 1639, he was fined by the Court and admonished by the church for "selling his wares at excessive rates"; in 1642 he was accused of wrongfully seizing and slaughtering a pig belonging to a needy widow; and in 1652, several episodes of public drunkeness forced him to resign his judgeship on the Suffolk County bench. In his last will and testament, a long document of more than fifty-thousand words, Keayne expressed his resentment toward a community that judged and humiliated him without having the ability to understand his true nature; here Keayne evinced an antinomian-like style of reasoning, emphasizing the mysteries of sin and salvation rather than their commensurability with appearances and the natural world.[91]

According to Keayne, the people who sat in judgment of him had no idea of his subjective state, nor of the larger goals—such as generous bequests to the town—that he intended his mercantile success to afford. Keayne admitted that the preservation of civil order, even the well-being of individual souls, demanded some degree of conformity to an externally mandated code of behavior and belief: "the ways of holiness . . . may not be neglected by me without great sin, but are ordained of God for me to walk in them carefully, in love to him, in obedience to his commandments, as well as for many good ends." Yet in expanding on how all my righteousness, sanctification, close walking with God, if it were or had been a thousand times more exact than ever yet I attained to, is all polluted and corrupt and falls short of commending me to God in point of justification, or helping forward my redemption or salvation.

Keayne reproved colonists for setting too much store by outward appearances—a criticism similar to that leveled by Anne Hutchinson. Only God was capable of accurately linking a sinner's actions with his intentions and determining whether sin had been committed: "I answer that time past, present and to come are all one with God. He takes notice of the purpose, and intents of the heart. If it be real he is pleased to accept of the will for the deed and of good actions intended to be done when there is just cause to hinder or prolong them."[92] The latter part of this statement was perfectly orthodox and indeed represented a position that English antinomians abhorred: to propound that the human "will" was capable of performing acts of obedience that would satisfy the requirements for salvation, just as "deeds" had fulfilled these requirements under the covenant of works, was tantamount to placing "conditions" on the free and unconditional covenant of grace.[93] Effortlessly spliced together with the truism that God accepts the "will for the deed," however, was Keayne's statement that "time past present and to come are all one with God." This recognizably antinomian formulation emphasized the eternal constancy of God's election—prior to active belief and even life itself—over the lived, chronological experience of human sin and gradual steps toward salvation.[94]

While Keayne's views, modeled closely on Cotton's preaching, were not exactly unorthodox, he used them deliberately to subvert orthodox assessments of his behavior, much as Anne Hutchinson did when she denied that her verbal "expressions" were equal to conveying accurately her real feelings.[95] In defiance of the whole thrust of seventeenth-century orthodoxy, Keayne was denying that one's true identity, one's whole self, could or should be known by the community. Indeed the secret identity was the spiritual, and therefore the truer, self—the self that knew God.[96]

Both Keayne, with his bristling animosity against those who professed to judge him without understanding his true nature, and Stoughton, with his use of a covering legal fiction at Anne Hutchinson's civil trial, were more comfortable than others with the full complexity of the human character. To some extent, this willingness came easily to individuals of their social status: active merchants and denizens of the transatlantic community. If a multilayered construction of reality seemed devious and dangerously decentered to the average Bay Colony resident, merchants and military men were accustomed to complicated transatlantic dealings in a setting where the extrinsic and intrinsic value of commodities, and of truth claims, remained constantly in a state of flux. Success for these individuals depended on a series of shifting, temporary alliances transacted across cultural (or in the case of the civil wars, where Stoughton met his end, sectarian) lines, or within a market that was increasingly abstracted from the

bounded geographical space so important to orthodoxy, and that was dominated, as Andrew Delbanco has suggested, by fluid capital, a commodity
"whose manipulation for purposes of its own procreation was already linked
with sordid sexual metaphor."[97] The ideas denounced as antinomian in the
late 1630s were those that had the propensity to fragment the local community by deemphasizing the importance of outward forms and appearances
and rendering people strangers to one another.

MORE NUMEROUS IN the antinomian party than people who experienced unbridgeable differences with the emergent orthodoxy were people
who felt religiously and socially connected to the Bay Colony (and wanted
to remain that way) but were dissatisfied with its perceived narrowness.
These people wanted to live in a Scripture-based society; but they recognized too how the establishment of what amounted to a uniform state
church might injure both the true faith and liberty. The crisis of the 1630s
was so severe, according to Winthrop, that orthodox elders facilitated the
magistrates' job of punishing dissenters by agreeing that the churches
should forego their right "publikely" to question magistrates for "any speech
in the court, without the license of the court" and by conceding to the
government the right to "proceed" against "all such heresies or errors . . .
as are manifest and dangerous to the state . . . without tarrying for the
church."[98] But, as I have shown, the chilling specter of John Wheelwright
being told that his sermon stood as the chief "witness" of his sedition
garnered protest. And Anthony Stoddard, in questioning why the General
Court must begin persecuting Francis Hutchinson before he had been dealt
with in a "church way," implied that the two authorities were not, or should
not be, so closely connected as the New England Way stipulated. Hutchinson's crime of having "reviled the church of Boston (being then a member of it) calling her a strumpet," had, after all, been directed at the church
and not the civil government.[99]

Even more pointedly, at Anne Hutchinson's church trial, Thomas
Savage, her son-in-law, who had already apologized to the Court for having
affixed his signature to the "seditious" pro-Wheelwright antinomian petition, was bold enough to suggest that the New England Way, with its
compulsion to prescribe the religious lives of its adherents, had deviated
from the "primitive" Christian practices that Massachusetts Puritans sought
to emulate, and reestablish, in the new world.[100] Referring to 1 Corinthians
15, Savage pointed out that the apostle Paul had detected and denounced
mortalist thinking—precisely the same heresy that Hutchinson was called
to account for during her church trial—in the church of Corinth. But Paul,
unlike the leaders of the Bay Colony, refrained from casting out those who
defended mortalist views.[101] The church fathers and apostles, concluded
Savage, established no precedent for persecution on the basis of doctrinal
error or disagreement, but only for manifest sinfulness:

> Nayther doe I see any Rule why the church should proceed to Ad-
> monition: seeinge that in the most Churches thear hath bine some

Errors or Mistakes held. Yea and in this very Church of Corinth there was many unsound opinions . . . yet wee doe not read that the Church did admonish them for it. Indeed in poynt of fact as in the Case of Incest the church proceeded to Excommunication because it was groce and abominable but not for opinion.[102]

When Hutchinson was excommunicated in March 1638, it was not for holding false opinions but for lying about how long she had held them, for "prevaricating" her culpability in broaching them, and for failing to evince the downcast demeanor that would alone connote true contrition.[103] Still, Savage failed to react to Hutchinson's theological explorations with what pastor John Wilson thought was the appropriate degree of fear and loathing. While Savage blithely cited a scriptural passage that emphasized apostolic forebearance in the face of diverse, even dangerously heretical ideas, Wilson had a very different view of the early church:

> It was usiall in the former Times whan any Blasphemie or Idolatrie was held forth thay did use to rent thear Garments and tare thear hare of thear heads in signe of Lothinge . . . should one mans scruple or doubte hinder all the rest of the Congregation which are satisfied to crye out, that the Lord is God.[104]

Savage's expostulation against persecution for "opinion" came in the phase of the trial that culminated with Hutchinson being admonished for entertaining and spreading dangerous doctrinal errors—a phase in which Savage and his brother-in-law Edward Hutchinson twice attempted to thwart calls for formal censure. Anne Hutchinson, the two men argued, held her "errors" not "peremtorilye" but in a questioning, experimental manner, seeking "information" and "Light" from the colony's best spiritual guides. She had exemplified a willingness to admit theological "mistakes" and might, in due course, be "convinced" of all her errors, thereby obviating the need for admonition. Edward Gibbons made a similar plea. While making sure that his hearers understood he regarded "our sister as a lost woman" and that he never would "open my mouth in the least kinde to hinder the churches proceedinge," he nonetheless expressed clearly the opinion that admonition might not be necessary if Hutchinson were given more time to consider and be convinced that she was wrong:

> but I would humbly propose this to the churches Consideration seeing Admonition is one of the greatest Censures that the Church can pronounce agaynst any offender and one of the last next to Excommunication and to be used agaynst Impenitent Offendors, but seinge God hath turned her hart about allready to see her Error or Mistake as she calls it in some of the poynts. Whether the Church had not better wayte a little longer to see if God will not help her to see the rest and to acknowledge them, than the Church may have no occasion to come to this Censure.[105]

The ministers, including a now-chastened Cotton, were horrified by these men's determination to support Hutchinson in her obstinate course. It was ungodly, they thought, for Hutchinson to persist in some of her most dangerous delusions, particularly her doubts about whether Christ "united with our fleshly bodies" and whether corporeal bodies were to be resurrected on the day of judgment, when virtually every knowledgeable person present in the church agreed that she was wrong and that such heresies would give way to libertinism. Most took offense too at how, even when Hutchinson did concede points, she attempted to minimize her own guilt by mincing words, referring to "so groce and so dayngerous an opinion [the soul's mortality] as a mere "mistake" and not an "error": "I doe acknowledge my Expression to be Ironious," Hutchinson had said, "but my Judgment was not Ironious, for I held befor as you did but could not express it soe."[106] If Hutchinson had not been so puffed up with pride, Thomas Shepard concluded, she would have recognized that her admission of two doctrinal mistakes was enough to throw all into doubt, to render preposterous all former boasts of "revelations . . . as trew as the Scriptures" and to make superfluous any further "paynes" to convince her that she was wrong: "I hope she will . . . suspect herselfe and to know it is not Gods Spirit but her owne Spirit that hath guided her hitherto, a spirit of Delusion and Error."[107]

When the admonition finally came, Savage and Edward Hutchinson were included within its scope because they had encouraged hubris where penitence was due. Cotton attributed the failing to misplaced "naturall affection" and family pride: "you must cast downe her Name and Credit though it be the chiefest Crowne that ayther yourselves or your mother hath at the Feete of Jesus Christ and let that be trampled upon soe his Crowne may be exalted." By having "intercepted the Course" of church justice, Cotton went on, the "sonnes" had done more harm than good for their mother, "hardninge her Hart," "nourishinge her in her unsound Opinions," and keeping her from "seeinge . . . Evells in her selfe." In this they had proved "Vipers to Eate through the very Bowells" of their parent, not "lovinge and naturall Children."[108] Interestingly, Gibbons, who was not related to the Hutchinsons, was excluded from the admonition. And Cotton's tactic of focusing on the issue of family loyalty obscured the more substantive question that Hutchinson, Savage, and Gibbons had raised: Why must the individual always submit to the will of the group?

If Hutchinson's defenders focused on the church's obligation to satisfy the needs of one errant member, the Massachusetts ministers believed that the airing of "grave" theological errors, while possibly edifying to Hutchinson, should be concluded as soon as possible because such discussion might pollute the minds of spectators (especially women). It was "dayngerous," John Eliot thought, to "dispute this Question soe longe in this Congregation."[109] Hutchinson's persistence in debating certain points indicated to the divines a rebellious spirit, not an inquisitive mind; and such a spirit needed to be sharply rebuked, not foolishly indulged, both for her own good and as an example to others. Savage, Hutchinson, and Gibbons, on the other hand, thought that Hutchinson would be persuaded better by learned disputation—the marshaling of "Arguments . . . waytie enough to convince your Mother," as John Davenport derisively put it—than reprimand.[110] Once consensus was reached, the clergymen believed, the individual who scrupled it must either capitulate quickly or face public humiliation. Indeed, Davenport thought of formal rebuke as a means of persuasion, suggesting that Hutchinson's backers might not "oppose" censure if only they understood that this "ordinance of God" was designed to function as a "spetiall and powerfull meanes to convince the partie offendinge as well as Arguments and reasons given."[111]

The framers of orthodoxy, paying heed to the remarks made by men like Savage, Stoddard, and Hutchinson, worried that the diverse positions forced together under the antinomian umbrella would destroy the unity desperately needed in a new plantation dedicated to right religion. The proliferation of antinomian ideas, it was feared, might embolden people to chart their own ecclesiastical destinies and to throw off societal responsibilities. Just as Hutchinson and her followers had flocked to hear Cotton and spurned Wilson, so too might an antinomian victory sanction the practice of shopping, as it were, for the best teacher and fellowship.[112] The antinomian Synod, an official gathering of ministers summoned to enumerate and condemn the recently broached errors, found the dissenters guilty of viewing church membership as a matter of private fulfillment rather than a badge of corporate responsibility and acceptance, so that:

> if a man thinke he may edifie better in another congregation then in his owne, that is ground enough to depart ordinarily, from word, seales, fastings, feastings, and all administrations in his own church, notwithstanding the offence of the Church, often manifested to him for so doing.[113]

Other complaints of the synod reflected the extent to which antinomian principles were believed to nourish individual spiritual needs, or the needs of small groups who felt some emotional affinity for one another, at the expense of the larger community.[114]

As far as the composition of the churches was concerned, an antinomian perspective could accommodate two very different possibilities: membership standards so arcane and exclusive that the churches could never become a significant social building block; or membership standards so inclusive that they would make meaningless any claim that New England was specially blessed with godliness. Following the emphasis found in John Winthrop's writings, historians have focused on the specter of exclusionary fanaticism.[115] But the antinomian synod was sensitive too to the threat of overinclusiveness that followed logically from the idea—found, as I have shown, in Cotton's theological writings—that hypocrites and saints were virtually indistinguishable. Six of the 82 errors specifically identified at the antinomian synod related to the proposition that "Christs worke of grace [the sanctification visible to human eyes] can no more distinguish betweene a Hypocrite and a Saint then the raine that fals from Heaven betweene the just and the unjust."[116]

The seemingly contradictory tendencies found within the antinomian party can be glimpsed through the future spiritual trajectories of Hutchinson and Savage, both of whom soon returned to the Bay Colony after residing for a brief period in Rhode Island. Savage, by the 1660s, became a partisan for the controversial "halfway" covenant, hoping, perhaps, that its more comprehensive policy on church membership would encourage believers to focus on the broad truths they held in common rather than their differences.[117] Edward Hutchinson, in contrast, became a sworn enemy of the "halfway" covenant and a great advocate of a wider toleration. Although he preferred to limit his own congregation to an exclusive membership of saints—turning his back when Wilson inducted "halfway" members whose only claim to sanctity was their descent from a covenanted parent—Hutchinson was not adverse to the existence of other manifestations of "light" and forms of church government within the colony. Savage and Hutchinson both wanted to live in a godly commonwealth, but they did not agree with first-generation New England orthodoxy, or with each other, on how the individual saint should relate to the churches, the civil government, and the society as a whole. This indeterminacy was the most troublesome aspect of antinomianism. To a society that demanded stark dichotomies, antinomian adjuncts preferred misty shades of gray.

To return to the decade of the 1630s, the negotiations of First Church with the Hutchinsonian diaspora in Rhode Island gave immediate substance to the fears regarding the antinomian threat to a sense of communal solidarity. In 1639, the Boston church, operating under the assumption that the exiles remained in fellowship until they were formally dismissed to another congregation, sent three messengers to ascertain how religious matters stood with the brethren and to determine whether any among them might be reclaimed for right religion. Hutchinson, after all, was the only one formally tried and excommunicated; and even she might have been spared the final casting out had she attended her admonition with "fear and Tremblinge" rather than interrupting Cotton to interject the "lie" that "I did not hould any of thease Things" [the theological errors] "before my Imprisonment."[118]

At least two of the messengers, William Hibbens and Edward Gibbons, were chosen with care, so as not to offend the exiles. Gibbons had favored sparing Hutchinson embarrassment at her church trial. Hibbens, hailing from the Hutchinsons' own native Lincolnshire, was a prominent merchant like many of the "erronists." The third messenger, John Oliver, was more problematic. Although he had signed the antinomian petition, he had quickly abjured it and admitted his error once the orthodox tide began to rise; he had also turned against Hutchinson at her church trial, going so far as to suggest that Savage and young Edward Hutchinson be censured along with Anne Hutchinson so that the congregation's decision to admonish might be unanimous—a gesture calculated to communicate his newfound appreciation for communal unity.[119]

In any event, these messengers, whose report was transcribed by Robert Keayne, brought little encouragement that Rhode Island congregations would accede to the demand that they reject the fellowship of all who lay under censure, admonition, or excommunication in Boston until such time as the condemned persons gave satisfaction and gained due dismission from First Church. As events unfolded, the Rhode Islanders remained firm in this position. Dissenters like Edward Hutchinson, William Aspinwall, and Thomas Savage, wishing to return to the Bay, made their peace with the church as individuals; but no relationship was ever established between the church fellowships of Aquidneck or Portsmouth and those of the Bay.[120]

Although the representatives from Boston were received politely enough in Rhode Island, their report revealed, much to the dismay of John Wilson and a now-chastened Cotton, that residents of the communities-in-exile considered themselves free agents as far as religious organization was concerned. In Portsmouth, where the Hutchinsons now resided, residents scrupled to meet as a group to hear the messengers from Boston for fear this would imply some sort of collective submission to First Church:

> But for a meetinge thay did not know what power one church hath over an other church and thay denyed our Comission and refused to let our Letter be read. And they Conseave one church hath not power over the members of another Church, and doe not thinke thay are tide to us by our covenant and soe were we fayne to take all thear Answers by goinge to thear severall Houses.[121]

In the course of these household visits, "Mr. [William] Hutchinson tould us he was more nearly tied to his wife than to the church, he thought her to be a dear saint and servant of god."[122]

This terse statement held profound meaning, for the corrosive appeal of placing private pleasure over public duty in matrimony, a basic social building block, seemed to have influenced the exiles' conceptualization of the church covenant itself, which was in turn closely identified with the marital bond. The chastened Cotton of 1639 certainly interpreted events in this light when he reflected on the status of the exiles: "They were in Covenant with us as a wife to the Husband . . . but like a Harlot she welbe gone for all her Covenant."[123] As far as First Church could discern in 1639, the exiles had chosen to associate with one another in such a manner as to please themselves as individuals but not to fulfill their obligations to the community; such unions, like the proverbial love match, were prone to impermanence and instability. The antinomian diaspora in Rhode Island was destined to fracture both over doctrinal issues and over the question of how church and state should relate to one another; for many years, there was no settled opinion on this issue.[124] It was precisely this lack of a fixed, agreed-on relationship between the sacred and the secular that most terrified the Massachusetts orthodoxy. Winthrop reflected that the antinomians living in Rhode Island "live to this day . . . in great strife and contention in the civill estate and otherwise, hatching and multiplying new Opinions, and cannot agree, but are miserably divided into sundry sects and factions."[125]

Fears of the earthly chaos attendant on antinomianism would also have been increased by concrete knowledge of at least one of the English antinomians, Roger Brierley. In his autobiographical journal, Thomas Shepard admitted to a youthful flirtation with the views of Brierley, pastor of Grindleton in Yorkshire and the only English antinomian pastor whose name was invoked during the crisis of the 1630s. Brierley's influence was known and feared in New England. According to John Winthrop, a law placing constraints upon immigration in the wake of the antinomian controversy was deliberately aimed at the Grindletonians: "it was very probable, that they expected many of their opinion to come out of England from Mr. Brierly his church."[126] Shepard, for his part, explained how he had learned of Grindletonian "perfectionism" at a particularly sensitive juncture in his own spiritual quest, a time when he had been entertaining "atheistic" doubts, wondering "whether there were a God . . . whether Christ was the Messiah, whether the Scriptures were God's word or no" and whether it might be social conditioning rather than undeniable religious truths that caused people to adopt their respective faiths. In this vein he wondered "whether if I had been educated up among the Papists I should not have been as verily persuaded that Popery is the truth or Turkism is the truth." At this point he "at last . . . heard of Grindleton, and . . . did question whether that glorious estate of perfection"—one that threw off all discipline and admitted that genuine faith could be expressed through numerous ecclesiastical forms and different doctrines—"might not be the truth."[127]

Although it is uncertain whether Shepard read Brierley's tracts, he most certainly understood how this brand of antinomianism could undermine the perceived importance of uniform belief and practice. Knowledge of Grindletonian ideas could only have heightened Shepard's worries about the threat to the outward religious forms so central to the New England identity. Brierley in his sermons envisioned a broad community of inclusiveness that built on the commonalities of all spiritual people instead of accentuating their differences; ecclesiastical organization, for Brierley, was a "mere garment," which, like "works," had little to do with true spirituality: "And thus, all Religion almost is but the fruit of mans witt and brain, and not of a troubled heart, but for an end of mans self."[128] Brierley recommended an open-ended approach to outward faith that respected differences among those truly godly rather than forcing all to conform to a prescribed set of beliefs and behaviors. He saw as lost those who insisted on more precise definitions of faith, and who "cut themselves off from Christ and the church, by their singular opinions: and fell into Sects, and would needs joyn Circumcision and fleshly Righteousness with Christ: and so become confident in the flesh."[129] People who did not conform to the "same opinion" and who were not "familiars" could nonetheless live peacefully, for true spirituality is "Opposed against the Pharisees busie pride, and judging others . . . It sets man at work with himself and none else," so that the true Christian should be "against that Religion, thats nothing but busie quarrelling for victorie in this or that opinion. . . . These that are busie with others, not themselves . . . starts quarrels, and suits for trifles."[130]

Shepard no doubt saw shades of Grindletonianism in the willingness of prominent laymen to tolerate a modest variety of religious opinions, so long as they did not injure an essential underlying faith. And he perceived Grindletonian-like ambiguity in the preaching of Cotton and Wheelwright. These two were no Grindletonians. But recent scholarship has shown that Cotton tended to be more flexible in his understanding of church order than most orthodox preachers, especially Shepard. And both Cotton and Wheelwright spoke of stripping away fleshly forms, which were really only tributes to human pride, so as to reveal underlying spiritual realities. Even the all-important concrete sense of sin, which Shepard credited with placing him on the correct path, was belittled by his Bay Colony rivals.[131] The "law killeth," bellowed John Wheelwright in his fast-day sermon: "therefore ought no works of sanctification to be urged upon the servants of God, so as if they had the power to do them, it will kill the soull of a man, and it oppresseth the poore soules of the saynts of God."[132] Cotton, though not so extreme as this, had gone so far as to argue that even the Word was a mere form unless it was quickened by spiritual energy above and beyond it.[133] On the basis of his knowledge of the content of Grindletonian opinion and its attractiveness to so vigilant a Puritan as himself, Shepard feared that it might be but a short step to the conclusion that the worldly church—and with it the godly community—was only a meaningless husk.

In Massachusetts, leaders insisted that faith be embodied in the fleshly form of the "visible" church or the "sanctified" saint, not "allegorized" out of the world, for only in this way could they provide the social glue necessary to hold together a society that, Michael Zuckerman has argued, was naturally "fissive" due to its "revolutionary" attempt to organize itself along ideological lines rather than the discarded traditional culture of "merrie olde England."[134] By figuring religious bonds as indissoluble familial or marital ties, however, the orthodox party successfully reimbued with spiritual meaning those traditional practices—commitment to place, and to family—that rank-and-file colonists already had the propensity to hold dear. In a polity where political enfranchisement, local identity, and communal unity were all bound up with church membership, authorities needed to make sure that the various congregational churches had some binding relationship with one another and that, internally, they were more than ephemeral agglomerations of like-minded people. Antinomianism appeared to exalt private whims over public needs; its rejection of the symmetry between the spiritual and the earthly threatened to pull asunder religious from temporal authority, thereby destroying the whole notion of a geographically bounded godly society.

IT WOULD TAKE a great stretch of the imagination to see the people suspected or accused of antinomianism as sharing identical religious precepts. Included among them were, for example, William Aspinwall, the author of the antinomian petition protesting Wheelwright's banishment, who returned to England in the 1650s and became a ringleader in the Fifth Monarchist disturbances, agitating for the immediate reign of Christ on earth; Robert Harding, a merchant and ensign under John Underhill who turned to Anabaptist beliefs several years after the rapprochement he made with Bay Colony authorities concerning his antinomianism; Hugh Gunnison, the innkeeper and vintner who recanted his antinomianism only to succumb to Quakerism (like Underhill) by the 1650s, when a relocation to Maine placed him beyond the direct control of Bay Colony magistrates. All of these individuals, of course, were congregated on the left side of the Puritan spectrum; but it must be remembered that even Thomas Lechford, a lawyer and nonfreeman who eventually returned to episcopacy, was at one point considered to be an antinomian. Although Lechford disagreed with the antinomians Samuel Collins and Francis Hutchinson, describing their ideas as "dangerous" and "grievously mistaken," he nonetheless wrote sympathetic letters to both men during the time of their imprisonment, offering advice and encouraging words on how they might escape punishment: "so I yet pray for your . . . expediting out of this evil net wherein you are taken."

Lechford's disagreement with the congregational polity—and his firm resolve to "speake according to my light, and dare do no otherwise"—excluded him from church fellowship and made it impossible for him to advance to any place of "preferment." Yet Lechford believed that his religious speculations on proper church government should be respectfully indulged, not only because they were the result of "mature . . . deliberation" undertaken "long before I resolved to betake myself into these parts of the world," but because he was a man of high rank who, though reduced to penury in New England, had received and "forsook" tempting offers from the "Prince of Transylvania and Lord of Lower Hungary" as well as the "Lords of Providence." Lechford reported to a correspondent in England the sense of betrayal he felt in 1638 after requesting Thomas Dudley's opinion of a tract he had written on millennial prophecy; although Lechford had approached Dudley as a "private friend," wondering about his book's prospects for publication, the magistrate had, without permission, circulated the manuscript among other officials, including Winthrop, so that the "next news I had" was that it was regarded as smacking of "heresy" and "fitter to be burned" than printed. It was probably this episode, along with the permanent sense of alienation he felt as a person outside the church, deprived of a voice in government counsels, that prompted Lechford to question "By what Rule . . . are the faults of men to bee so publiquely handled before all the world as to undo them . . . what power have any ordinarie men . . . at all . . . either in admission or excommunication?" When Lechford gravitated back into the episcopal fold, it was because he believed that this afforded more, not less, intellectual latitude; in Massachusetts, the colonists consumed their own, ignoring the talents of important men, for the sake of theological principles that Lechford regarded as petty.[135]

Just as the "evil net" snagged the episcopal-leaning Lechford along with individuals we would more clearly label "spiritist," so too did its most energetic cavilers suggest that antinomianism was consistent with a whole panoply of seemingly incompatible errors. Antinomian ideas were equated with "Monkish imaginations, the goodly cob-webs of the brain-imagerie of those idolatrous and superstitious . . . Monks and friars." Accused of aspiring to be the "very power and familiars of God" upon whom the "blind and simple world" must "admire" and "gaze," they were associated with practitioners of magic, peering, like "adepts," into a secret realm that belonged only to God.[136] Partaking of mysticism, antinomianism was thought to hold within itself a host of distinct, sometimes contradictory impulses not yet bounded by the decisive finality of articulated language, physical embodiment, or church government.[137] Most interesting, perhaps, is the manner in which antinomianism, despite its firm injunction concerning the passivity of humans in the process of salvation, was held to encourage its apparent opposite, Arminianism.

High Calvinists like Cotton might have ignored the dangers of antinomianism, with its heavy emphasis on free grace, because they saw the Arminian threat as the more deadly.[138] But Massachusetts critics charged that in their haste to escape "works-righteousness," antinomian sympathizers had arrived at a position equally assailable for elevating humans to unseemly heights:

> Some that love to be wise above that which is written and not according to sobriety, despise this way [orthodoxy] as fit for novices, but not for such as are perfect as they are. They have their assurance by revelation seeing the very book of life unsealed and opened unto them, so that they may see and read their owne names written in it; it is too low a work for them to descend into themselves, and to examine how it is with them within, whether they be in the faith or no.[139]

Massachusetts antinomians rendered as the central reality of the conversion experience the secret knowledge gained directly from the spirit and the ecstatic subjective experience of the "indwelling" Christ. Although this was intended to counter the conceit that any sort of efficacy might attach to physical forms or human effort—even the act of believing—Shepard and Bulkeley regarded it as making one's assurance subject not to God's constant will but to mercurial human willfulness. Shepard, it will be recalled, warned Anne Hutchinson that she should recognize that "it is not Gods Spirit but her owne Spirit that hath guided her hitherto, a spirit of Delusion and Error."[140] Regardless of what the original intentions might have been of the preachers with antinomian leanings, Shepard seemed to be saying, their doctrine threatened to make individual believers the arbiters of their own spiritual destinies.[141] A single-minded focus on the second Adam, coupled with encouragement to stop "mourning" for sin and to melt into the embrace of a loving Christ, had eventuated in pride, the most maligned of all antinomian vices.[142]

The capacity of antinomianism to blur important theological boundaries went hand in hand with its capacity to soften the distinctions between the Puritan "self" and other. Thomas Shepard warned that antinomian skepticism regarding the diagnostic powers of sin might slip into an Arminian universalism that held that Christ had died for all, not just the elect:

> And verily, if the love of God belong to sinners as sinners, then all sinners shall certainly be saved . . . so that by this principle, as sin hath abounded actually to condemn all, so grace hath abounded actually to save all, which is most pernicious; nor do I know what should make men embrace this principle unless that they either secretly think that the strait gate and narrow way to life is now so wide and broad, that all men shall in Gospel times enter in thereat, which is prodigious, or else they must imagine some Arminian universal redemption and reconciliation, and so put all men in a salvable and reconciled estate (such as it is) before faith, and then the evidence and ground of their assurance must be built on this false . . . foundation viz. Jesus Christ had died to reconcile (and so hath reconciled) all sinners.[143]

Those discomfited by the idea that people were "empty vessels" prior to their union with Christ suspected that "it will follow, that if the spirit of God may unite it selfe to the soule before faith doeth any thing in the union, then by the same Reason it may unite it selfe to the soule, without such a Faith, and so may be united to an unbeliever, to a Reprobate, etc."[144] While the charge that antinomianism might lead directly toward universalism was excessive, the underlying fear that antinomianism would deny the inspired community in Massachusetts the ability to determine who properly belonged and who should be excluded was not.[145] If Cotton thought it unmeet "that hypocrites should wallow themselves in the fellowship of the saints, and alwaies bless themselves in their carnal condition," his doctrines, as I have shown, provided no way for mortals, with their limited vision, to separate them, since "an hypocrite may for a long time find all his own ends attained in seeking the glory of God."[146]

AS THE SOCIAL orthodoxy of the New England Way hardened, antinomianism took on an expanded meaning and was used as a medium for expressing the frustrations of those who, for a variety of reasons, felt constricted. This helps us to understand why such diverse laymen as Stoughton, Hutchinson, Stoddard, Savage, and Keayne variously sympathized with, embraced, or appropriated antinomian themes for their own particular purposes. Since the antinomian heresy drew so much support from the mercantile community (the Hutchinsons comprised the mercantile family par excellence), it is also important to explore this connection.[147] Orthodoxy demanded that the saints be transparent to one another.[148] Merchants, however, were likely to understand the importance of complex truths and secret selves. And while orthodoxy was oriented toward the local polity, the transatlantic market connoted the breaking free from local bounds and the fixed value of commodities and coin.[149] All this taught merchants to view with equanimity, or at least not to be alarmed by, a religious sensibility that encouraged people to look past outside appearances and to situate themselves in a spiritual world that evinced little respect for manmade boundaries.

The intellectual chasm separating concerns about the market from concerns about heresy may seem wide and deep. But a number of seventeenth-century English economic theorists were beginning to conceive of the market—whether they approved of it or not—as a mystical force no longer comprehensible to ordinary rational human beings but only to mercantile adepts. These authors condemned economic regulation with the same passion and in almost the same terms with which antinomians denounced "legalism." Dissenters against New England orthodoxy and champions of the market alike favored the transatlantic world over the local community; and both introduced relativist moral standards denounced, in various contexts, as amoral. Just as antinomians believed in the irresistibility and boundlessness of the spirit, so too did these economic thinkers posit the existence of a mysterious, unsystematized, and cosmopolitan mercantile ethos that resisted the worldly control of local authorities while effortlessly attracting the allegiance of traders everywhere.

The work of Gerard Malynes, an English mint master who chronicled and commented (often unfavorably) on these ideas, was sufficiently well known in New England that the General Court advised a committee charged in the late 1650s with improving the colony's economic position to read his Lex Mercatoria.[150] Unfortunately, we have no explicit evidence of any controversy provoked by the ideas expressed in Lex Mercatoria, which addressed the question of whether government officials should oversee their nations' economies and showed how merchants viewed themselves as near-omniscient figures whose superior knowledge of the sophisticated symbols of the market (currency and bills of exchange) allowed them effectively to usurp the authority of civil servants in economic matters. Still, New England merchants who read the tract must have found its message liberating.

On more than one occasion, the General Court had punished merchants, such as Robert Keayne, for unfair dealing.[151] But Malynes's tract depicted how merchants, who regarded themselves as operating at a level far above the law as conceived by ordinary folk, scorned these types of prosecutions:

> questions are made, whether a Merchant may trafficke with Turkes, Heathens, Barbarians, and Infidels, and perform promises with them? whether a Merchant may sell his commodities as deare as he can, without respect of persons? whether he may use lies (as being officious) in the selling of commodities? whether he may be crafty without deceit? whether learning be requisite to a merchant?

While Malynes made no attempt to answer these question himself, he showed how prior attempts to impose moral standards had failed, "All which determinations can give but little satisfaction to instruct Merchants."[152] In much the same way that antinomians chafed under an outmoded orthodox morality they associated with the "covenant of works," men of trade were shown to resist the meddlesome props and gratuitous instructions accompanying traditional ideas of morality. What seemed immoral or sinful from the outside might ultimately be beneficial. A myopic view of morality, or a human-derived set of laws, it might be gathered, served merely as crutches for those unwilling to face the indeterminacy, or the boundlessness, of raw providence, of spirituality, or of the market.

The most irreverent treatments of authority in the work of free-market theorists can be found in their discussions of exchange rates. While Malynes, as a state-employed assayer, did not approve of how merchants could subvert communal goals, his tract portrayed merchants as capable figures in the art of exchange and valuation, while civil authorities were often ineffectual.[153] Malynes believed that gold and other precious metals were generated by alchemical principles, the understanding of which "God hath revealed to a few humble and charitable men." Once the metals came into existence and were minted into coin, he said, they underwent two valuations: one at the hands of state officials, and the other at the hands of merchants. The statesmen's method came off as static and dead, like human law, while the merchants' method, which "is predominant and over ruleth the former," was flexible, alive, and contingency based. In the same mysterious way that the sun and moon transformed earthly elements into bullion, giving them new life, so too did mercantile valuations elevate the bullion to a new plane, acting as the "Spirit which giveth life unto Coines."

Just as the ability of local authorities to discern the real, as opposed to the apparent, value of money was being questioned in the seventeenth century, so had the antinomians in Massachusetts questioned the ability of their orthodox peers to judge the real value of souls on the basis of sanctification, which signified the mere appearance of "holy walking" and not its substance. The vagaries of the market could no more be manipulated without risk by individual profit-seekers than the mysteries of salvation could be collapsed into a series of discrete steps learnable and performable by strivers after grace. Both endeavors required faith in something intangible and contrary to human reason. In a revealing passage of the *Lex Mercatoria*, Malynes demonstrated that merchants believed that just as the spirit influenced and uplifted the soul and body, so too did "exchange," the economic analog of spirit, energize both money and commodities.

> For as monies do infuse life to commodities . . . so Exchange for monies by Bills of Exchanges (being seated everywhere) corroborateth the Vitall Spirit of Trafficke directing and controlling (by just proportions) the prices and values of commodities and money, as shall be declared . . . To make application of this comparison betweene the Soule and Spirit, we shall find by the following discourse, that even as the Spirit of man is predominant over the Soule and Body in all the actions thereof, which by the bloud are quickned and preserved, even so is the Exchange for monies by Bills of Exchanges, over ruling the course of commodities and monies in all places where the action of money is felt or seene, directing the same (by some due proportions) accordingly.[154]

The admiration among merchants for the intangible concept of uncontrolled, indeed uncontrollable, "exchange," resembled, in temperament if not in substance, the antinomian appreciation for the inscrutable and all-powerful "actings" of the spirit. Like New England dissenters, merchants consciously defined themselves as participants in a divine mystery that could be contained neither within the bounds of law nor the dictates of human reason.

Contrary to the Weberian views resurrected recently by historian Stephen Innes, successful interaction with the market involved far more than promoting a sense of "worldly asceticism" and institutionalizing the "work ethic" as a major societal virtue.[155] The orthodox party in Puritan New England positively encouraged the kind of individualism and hard work necessary to build productive family farms and trading networks. But they were uncomfortable with the manner in which the transatlantic market was detaching itself from bounded space, stable systems of monetary and commodity valuation, and face-to-face transactions.[156] As Jean-Christophe Agnew has recently shown, the market sensibility required people to enter into a new, often counterintuitive type of reality that was strangely disembodied and artificial and that, to the uninitiated, seemed, like the theater, to be alien, false, and treacherous.[157] The market sensibility, understood in this way, paralleled antinomianism on many different levels. This is not to say that all Massachusetts merchants (much less English economic theorists) were antinomian, or vice versa. Rather it is to explain why merchants were especially sensitive (and resistant) to the sorts of boundaries that New England orthodoxy imposed. In the 1630s, antinomianism encompassed, indeed prefigured, the tolerationist urges that, in subsequent decades, lodged themselves disproportionately in the mercantile community.

Historians who associate New England orthodoxy with the growth of market capitalism in Massachusetts have emphasized, time and again, the crucial intersection between religious "preparationism" and the secular work ethic.[158] The merchants of Puritan New England, however, many of whom chafed against orthodox bounds, realized that hard work could go only so far in developing transatlantic markets. The remonstrant Robert Child, for example, who ridiculed Massachusetts for its treatment of the antinomian party, believed that the cultivation of sophisticated, even luxurious, tastes among consumers went hand in hand with productivity. Laying out in a letter to Samuel Hartlib the ills England encountered during the dark days of "Papistry," Child explained how, at that time, "all in this Island were either Souldiers or Scollars":

> And in those times Gentlemen thought it an honour to be carelesse, and to have houses, furniture, diet, exercises, apparell, etc. yea all things at home and abroad, souldier-like: Musick, Pictures, Perfumes, Saunces (unless good stomacks [fortifying]) were counted, perhaps unjustly, too effeminate. In Queen Elizabeth's dayes Ingenuities, Curiosities and Good Husbandry began to take place, and then salt marshes began to be fenced from the seas.[159]

Although Child believed that "a severe law should be enacted against those who run up and down and will not worke," he nonetheless held that, for a fortunate few, the enjoyment of the things of this world—as well as the deliberate creation of artificial wants—would not only beget more work, but also growth, diversification, and change.[160] Child's attempt to realign luxury, or a hunger for "ingenuities" and "curiosities," with masculinity, is especially striking, for a plain, Spartan way of life long continued, under the "Real Whig" tradition that informed the revolutionary generation, to be associated with manly "virtue."[161] Child could not have been ignorant of the fact that the heresies he defended had, like luxury, been gendered feminine in Puritan Massachusetts.

The antinomian party's views on the spiritual economy were strikingly similar to Child's perspective on the material one. Just as Child put a positive spin on the sensual, effeminate pleasures of consumption, so too did antinomians believe that the saints should be free to bask in the spiritual bliss of their justification, arguing that such bursts of otherworldly ecstasy would spur believers on to greater exertion, not render them passive. At both the spiritual and material levels, dissenters from a variety of perspectives feared that the orthodox way, with its emphasis on "work" alone, would retard growth. John Cotton, of course, is known for his strong condemnation of usury and other sharp economic practices; but his mercantile audience was capable of taking different cues from Cotton's emphasis on how believers should consume and enjoy, without guilt or remorse, their grand spiritual inheritance.[162] Indeed, during the period in which he leaned toward antinomianism, Cotton feared that orthodoxy would produce spiritual drones so mired in the repetitive tasks of "mourning" for sin that they would never metamorphose into "new men." These views coalesced strangely with Child's quite different concerns about the cheerless, work-centered orthodox economy; while the work ethic alone might help generations of New Englanders achieve modest "competencies" in their family farms and small trading ventures, Child implied, it would never blossom fully into a diverse and dynamic capitalist economy. The orthodox work ethic, whether manifested in its religious or secular form, was believed, by critics as different as Cotton and Child, to generate stasis rather than change. Ordinary New Englanders preferred this state of affairs because it offered good prospects not just to the chosen few, who would be permitted to wallow in spiritual or earthly riches, but also to "honest husbandmen" and dutiful, would-be saints.

Most New Englanders, in other words, were content with orthodoxy because they were satisfied with modest gains in their economic and spiritual lives, so long as such small gains were widely accessible and relatively evenly distributed. In this context, it was no wonder that Child, doubting "whether the Lord hath blest many in these parts with such eminent political gifts, so as to continue better lawes and customes than the wisest of our nation have . . . composed," implied a causal connection between the Bay Colony's idiosyncratic religious ways, its "arbitrary" government, and God's "not blessing us in any of our endeavors, so as to give us any great hopes of staple commodities."[163]

AS A RELIGIOSITY that privileged the claims of the heart, or inner self, over the claims of the local community, that demanded a converted ministry, and that was linked with the growth of market capitalism, antinomianism can, in some ways, be said to prefigure certain key elements found in eighteenth-century evangelicalism. Historians have clearly shown how evangelical religion and the expanding market economy, locked in a symbiotic embrace, tended in the eighteenth century to break down traditional patterns of association and affiliation.[164] The eighteenth-century awakenings cut a wide swath in the population, to some extent because market dealings, especially consumption, had become far more widely diffused than in the early seventeenth century.[165] Early-seventeenth-century antinomianism, on the other hand, remained relatively isolated in the upper reaches of Bay Colony society, in part because more limited contact with the transatlantic market militated against the temperament required for antinomianism, and in part because the orthodox majority understood implicitly the dangers that market and heterodoxy together posed to a reliable sense of shared identity. The "middling" classes of the eighteenth and nineteenth centuries adopted a variety of religions of the heart that simultaneously reflected, influenced, and helped them make sense of their material and social circumstances. But the "middling" colonists of Massachusetts Bay in the seventeenth century related more easily to the orthodox concerns of communalism, family order, and a worldly discipline that alone could impart a comforting sense of stability. Not only did antinomianism fail to address in a meaningful way the concerns of the majority of people in seventeenth-century Massachusetts, it scared them.

Merchants and their families, however, lived economic lives that became increasingly abstracted from local communities. They grew more at home with the "artificial" world of the market, more confident that "artificial" ligaments of emotion, or interest, could tie people together just as surely as prescription, and more comfortable with a variety of arrangements, sometimes comprising alterations in conventional gender roles, that appeared unnatural and elitist to the majority of colonists.[166] From the vantage point of the early seventeenth century, of course, these changes were a long way off. But in the language of the antinomian controversy, which pitted "honest husbandmen" against subtle, crafty deceivers who would defy nature, and who would impose a religious sensibility that ran contrary to human sense and reason, we can detect their inchoate beginnings.

ANTINOMIANISM WAS FEARED because it threatened to make unworkable and unattainable the homogeneous, traditional society that was so deeply desired in early seventeenth-century New England.[167] Its lay adherents did not necessarily agree on what the relationship between religion and the civil state should be or on how society should be structured. But antinomian doctrine, which appealed broadly in the upper reaches of Bay Colony society, resonated among people who resented the inflexibility of orthodox doctrine, who felt equally at home in a transatlantic and a provincial environment, and who were comfortable with the fluidity of identity found in the world of the Renaissance and of the market.

Orthodox Puritanism, on the other hand, reflected the dreams of the majority of "middling" colonists in Massachusetts, both in the religious and social spheres. The interpersonal bonds that orthodoxy facilitated were especially important in a New World environment. Despite the fact that not all residents of the Bay Colony were able to attain church membership, orthodoxy helped Massachusetts residents to construct the "imagined community" that historian Benedict Anderson has theorized lies at the root of nationalism.[168] The conversion experience, in which people imagined themselves and others passing through a familiar series of "stadia" on the journey toward salvation, functioned in seventeenth-century Massachusetts in a manner similar to the way, centuries later, novels featuring familiar landscapes and activities helped to inspire fellow feeling among readers otherwise unknown to one another in the countries of eighteenth- and nineteenth-century Europe. As Bay colonists "imagined" the horizontal ties that linked them together through a collective yet highly personal conversion experience, so too did they conceive of their communal space as geographically bounded and finite; orthodoxy aimed at a localistic homogeneity that reinforced parochial (and patriarchal) bonds, often at the expense of the transatlantic Puritan community. This met the needs of many, but not all, Bay Colony residents.

The fluidity associated with antinomianism, so shunned by the first generation in Massachusetts, would ultimately assert itself as the colony modernized. Mystical antinomianism was a once and future religious sensibility, simultaneously pointing back toward the universalism of the medieval church and forward toward the cosmopolitanism of the growing market. The antinomian controversy, largely a form of elite intransigence rather than popular protest, was the first incident in which frustration with the relatively closed New England Way was expressed on such a wide scale; but it would not be the last. Indeed, while explicit charges of antinomianism may have faded into the past, the two positions outlined by orthodox and antinomian proponents, with their different social visions, framed debates that would continue to be fought, under different distinguishing labels, for many generations.

2

"I Ame As Jephthah"

Honor, Heresy, and the Massachusetts Ordeal of John Underhill

I n 1653 the antinomian exile John Underhill, having lived among the Dutch in New Netherland for over ten years, wrote a letter to the commissioners of the United Colonies proclaiming his willingness to aid Massachusetts should the colony engage itself in hostilities against New Netherland: "I ame as Jephthah forced to lay my life in my hands to save English blood from destruction."[1] At the time that he made this dramatic pledge to aid a people that had wronged him, Underhill was in fact engaged in a series of risk-laden schemes designed to nudge the English colonies into war with New Netherland.[2] In correspondence with New Haven and Connecticut authorities, Underhill had confirmed fears that the Dutch, in league with the Narragansett Indians, were conspiring against the English colonies; and when civil war veteran and Massachusetts captain John Leverett arrived in New Netherland at the head of a United Colonies delegation charged to investigate the existence of the alleged plot, Underhill grasped at the hope that his deliverance from exile might be near. The disgraced captain's brazen identification of his own position with that of the Old Testament outcast-hero Jephthah reflected both his optimism and his unmitigated boldness, for it revealed to Puritan leaders, who would most certainly grasp the biblical allusion, precisely what he hoped to gain from such a conflict: an opportunity to win back his esteemed place in the halls of Bay Colony power.[3]

Underhill was drawn to Jephthah because he saw parallels between his own situation and that of the Old Testament hero: Jephthah, an exile like

Underhill, labored through military exertions to win back what he believed was his rightful place in his homeland, the biblical Gilead. Because his birth had been illegitimate, Jephthah's brothers, upon their father's death, had denied him his inheritance and cast him out of his home; Jephthah then settled in the peripheral "land of Tob," where he sharpened his military skills by associating with a group of raiders and "vain men." But Jephthah's fortunes were altered when Gilead was endangered by war with the Ammonites, and his former detractors among the elders were forced to seek Jephthah out and beg him to return to Gilead and be their captain. Jephthah was at first reluctant: "Did ye not hate me," he asked, "and expel me out of my father's house? and why are ye come unto me now when ye are in distress?" Only when the elders promised that Jephthah would be their "head" if he won the victory did he agree to return. Jephthah's subsequent vanquishing of the Ammonites did indeed restore him to his rightful place as a judge of Israel—at least for a time.[4]

The trials that Jephthah and Underhill faced in their lives must have seemed uncannily alike, at least in the mind of the one-time Massachusetts captain. While Jephthah's exile was occasioned by the illegitimacy of his birth, Underhill's forced removal from Massachusetts stemmed from his adoption of heretical religious principles stigmatized as the base progeny of a wicked woman.[5] While Jephthah carved out a social place for himself among the "vain men" living on the margins of his homeland, so too did Underhill establish himself as an Indian fighter in New Netherland, a region peripheral to the colony in whose affairs he still longed to play a prominent role. Finally, in the summer of 1653, Underhill believed that an event analogous to Jephthah's meeting with the elders of Gilead had occurred in his own life when the Leverett commission arrived to investigate whether the Dutch had been encouraging the English colonists' Narragansett enemies to make war on them.

But here the similarities in the life courses of the two figures end. The Ammonite threat in the biblical account was real, and the tribes of Israel were eager to go to war; but the dominant governing faction in Massachusetts (as opposed to those in Connecticut and New Haven) was decidedly reluctant to allow the Anglo–Dutch War, then raging in Europe, to spread to the new world. Leverett, while an important man in Massachusetts, represented a prowar faction, composed primarily of merchants, whose views were by no means consonant with majority opinion.[6] Soon after Leverett made contact with Underhill, the Massachusetts General Court, wary of Leverett's growing popularity, instructed the militia committees in the various towns that they should guard against any unauthorized mobilization of troops, reminding them of their power and obligation to "suppresse all raising of souldiers, but such as shallbe by authoritie of this government."[7] In the end, Underhill could only dream of attaining in Massachusetts the kind of influence that Jephthah wielded over Gilead.

Blinded by ambition and his eagerness to abet a conflict that would afford him the opportunity to prove his worth to the Bay, Underhill did not see the vulnerability of his position; not only did he gather testimony for the United Colonies emissaries but also, after their departure, he openly denounced the Dutch governor and fiscal and raised the Commonwealth flag in Hempstead—an action that resulted in Underhill's arrest and subsequent flight from the jurisdiction.[8] While Jephthah was a shrewd bargainer who understood that Gilead's mortal danger would force the elders to grant him concessions, Underhill rashly set aside all evidence that ran contrary to his hopes. Consistent with his lifelong pattern, all his grandiose plans came to nothing. Not only did Underhill place himself in jeopardy in New Netherland, where he was imprisoned for a time, but he allowed himself to appear as a desperate troublemaker, not a returning hero: "Youer agents departed; Newes came to mee to bee gone, our danger is great."[9] If skill in war brought Jephthah back into the ruling councils of Gilead, Underhill's vehicle to restored greatness turned out to be a mere chimera, as the war scare dissipated quickly once Anglo-Dutch hostilities ground to a halt in Europe.

THE DESIRE FOR honor and distinction that Underhill manifested in the foregoing incident was a constant theme throughout his life and helps to account, I will argue here, for his attraction to unorthodox religious ideas. Historians have readily accepted the view, promoted by John Winthrop himself, that orthodoxy was masculine while antinomianism held a uniquely feminine appeal.[10] The case of John Underhill, however, challenges this line of reasoning in important ways. To be sure, the newly established orthodoxy stigmitized antinomianism as a feminine heresy. The great myth-maker John Winthrop, hoping to neutralize antinomianism once and for all and to depict Hutchinson as stirring up controversy where none really existed, denounced the heresy as a "masterpiece of woman's wit," subsequently using the defeat of the antinomian party to reinforce the designation of certain undesirable character traits—secrecy, dissimulation, excessive pride—as feminine. It does not necessarily follow from this, however, that the powerful men who joined the Hutchinsonian party, or took steps to defend heretical or seditious expressions, necessarily viewed matters in this same light—least of all John Underhill.

Anne Hutchinson, throughout the controversy, was depicted as a figure of great strength and mental dexterity, capable of creating bitter divisions among people who were normally amicable and well-disposed toward one another. The preaching of the ordinarily "gentle" John Wheelwright became, as Winthrop told the story, inflamed under her tutelage:

> thence took Mr. Wheelwright courage to inveigh in his [fast-day] sermon against men in a Covenant of works (as hee placed them) and to proclaim them all enemies to Christ . . . whereas before hee was wont to teach in a plaine and gentle stile, and though he would sometimes glaunce upon these opinions, yet it was modestly and reservedly, not in such a peremptory and censorious manner.[11]

It is highly unlikely that Wheelwright's character changed so dramatically under Hutchinson's influence. Still, Winthrop went on to suggest that Hutchinson's talent for malevolent manipulation also made her worthy of comparison with the Old Testament Athaliah, a queen of Judah who killed off all rival claimants to the throne in an effort to consolidate power in her own hands: "see the impudent boldnesse of a proud dame, that Athaliah-like makes havocke of all that stand in the way of her ambitious spirit."[12] Underhill may well have been drawn to Hutchinson's party because she was viewed not as an ideal bride of Christ, but rather as sharing the characteristics of headstrong biblical heroes, like Jephthah and Joab, whom he admired.

That a crucial step in the discrediting of dangerous ideas necessarily involved their feminization tells us much about the way gender was socially constructed and how it was used to bolster the desired social hierarchy in early-seventeenth-century Massachusetts. Historians Marilyn Westerkamp and Ben Barker-Benfield have argued recently that Puritan men were discomfited by the bridal analogies that so often appeared in antinomian discourse. Fearing the implication that women might be construed as more naturally fulfilling the role of bride, these historians have suggested, male leaders delegitimized belief in the unencumbered matrimonial relationship with Christ that was at the center of antinomian thought and insisted instead that education and works, accouterments more attainable by men than women, were crucial for salvation and the exercise of religious leadership. The Underhill case adds a layer of complexity to these analyses. On the one hand, Underhill's dependent status as a salaried Bay Colony employee, unable to pursue his "independency" in the same manner as other householders, may have caused him to share some of the same frustrations as his female antinomian counterparts; but at the same time, a man like Underhill, keenly conscious of how his every action reflected his rank, would never have become an antinomian if he thought that it would call his masculinity into question.[13]

Underhill, whose apostasy was triggered by a perceived demotion in rank, used antinomianism to elide the pain (and shame) of his dependent status.[14] Antinomianism allowed Underhill both to escape the earthly bonds of local authority and to deprecate New England communalism. For Underhill, the emphasis on "preparation" and outward appearances meant that the colonists, desiring some degree of predictability in their spiritual lives, had grown "soft"; it was the ability to contend with the boundlessness and uncertainties of the spirit world and to stand apart from the commonalty that was, in his contrasting view, manly. Just as biblical heroes, like Jephthah, could win battles only when the "spirit of the Lord came upon" them, often in sudden and disconcerting ways, so too must Underhill follow the will of the spirit as his only master. The tremendous empowerment Underhill felt when guided by the spirit was disturbingly obvious to those who condemned him for having signed the pro-Wheelwright antinomian petition:

Being further demanded, how they came so many of them, to bee so suddenly agreed in so weighty and doubtfull a case, hee answered, that many of them being present when Mr. Wheelwright was convict of sedition, they were sore grieved at it, and suddenly rushing out of the court, a strange motion came into all their mindes, so as they said (in a manner all together) Come let us petition; and for his part, from that time to this, his conscience which then led him to it, will not suffer him to retract it.[15]

Antinomianism, for Underhill, represented a release from the "domestic" cares and responsibilities of a polity that demanded consensus and obedience, implying a rough egalitarianism. Underhill not only integrated antinomian thought with his own arrogant conceptualization of male honor but also used it to bolster his opinion that individuals specially linked with the spirit should be accorded privileges and liberties not granted to ordinary citizens—a point of view that grated harshly against the proto-"democratic" principles embraced in the Bay Colony, and that allowed Underhill to place himself above those who tried to diminish him.[16] The antinomian challenge, as mounted by Underhill (and others like him), can be read as evidence that it was not just the gender hierarchy but also the definition of good leadership and the proper distribution of power among men that was being contested during the upheavals of the 1630s.[17] The proper bounds of masculinity, no less than femininity, could be considered contested ground.

Although Underhill, a hero of the Pequot War, was steadily ascending in Bay Colony society at the time of the antinomian controversy, he was not entirely happy with his lot.[18] As I have shown, rank-and-file colonists appreciated the religious and social structure of the Bay Colony because the unprecedented opportunity it provided to gain title to land, to establish a "competency," and to exercise control over the churches compared favorably to the conditions they had faced in England. But for Underhill, Bay Colony aspirations seemed narrow, ordinary, and decidedly unheroic. The ruling faction in Massachusetts conceived of the polity as an extended family and required leading men, as good symbolic fathers or brothers, to cooperate with one another, and to submit to majority opinion, in the building of consensus.[19] Underhill, in contrast, schooled in the art of war, was more interested in playing the role of potent commander than good father; while he craved public adulation, he was not interested in performing tedious public services that required him to compromise his principles or curb his opinions. He insisted on expressing his views forcefully in a political context where contrarians were not tolerated.[20] He remained fixed in this role because he feared that by pursuing the truncated honors available in Massachusetts, he would be participating in his own diminishment. Underhill's desire to gather benefits and praise from the community while treating it as little more than a source of preferments would certainly have been perceived as feminine—or at least not fully masculine—by many of his fellow colonists; but to Underhill this seemed the logical stance for protecting his honor.[21]

Underhill's choice of Jephthah as a role model of sorts reflects his belief that the benefits of the spirit must be pursued in isolating circumstances rather than in the bosom of a loving communal family. The Jephthah story showed not only how one might rescue oneself from obscurity through valiant (and violent) acts but also that one's connection to the world of spirit must sometimes come at the price of one's local or earthly family. Jephthah, while under the influence of the spirit, had made a vow to Yahweh that, in the event of a victory over the Ammonites, he would sacrifice the first creature to come out of his house to greet him upon his return from battle. Tragically, it turned out to be his only daughter, and he was forced to honor his vow. Jephthah pursued his direct relationship with the spirit—and the glorious victory that would flow from this relationship— without considering the possible dangers that such rashness might pose to his family. Yet, while Jephthah's vow might be condemned as self-serving and ill-considered, it was also beyond his immediate control, since the "spirit of the Lord [was] upon him" at the time he uttered it.[22] We cannot know whether Underhill reflected upon this aspect of the story while identifying with the protagonist Jephthah or whether he was wholly engrossed in the idea of an outcast coming back into favor and receiving power from those who had spurned him. It is clear, however, that Jephthah's needless sacrifice of his daughter did not diminish him as a hero in Underhill's eyes. This may be because Underhill tended to regard the "spirit," already "upon" Jephthah at the time of his vow, as a doer of both great and terrible things—things that might even seem evil in the limited sight afforded humans. As I will show in this chapter, Underhill had an exaggerated appreciation for the contingency and danger of the spiritual world; and he entertained a near contempt for the familial bonds that Winthrop valued so highly.

The Jephthah story mirrored Bay Colony antinomianism by emphasizing the asymmetry between the spiritual and temporal worlds and the distinction between human and divine morality. Underhill had no wish to sacrifice his own children; but he was willing to break with what he saw as the artificial morality, the forced consensus, and the false sense of security, of the New England "family." Underhill wished to remain a part of New England, though he wanted to be respected not as a brother or father but as a great leader, who, like Jephthah, could transcend the earthly plane to which "visible" saints were, by definition, confined. Such special abilities, Underhill thought, should bring him special rewards. Just as Jephthah was a figure who "opened his mouth" rashly to man and God, so too did Underhill (who also admired Joab) claim that as a man directly infused with the power of God, he should have the right to "speak roughly" to doubtful social superiors like John Winthrop.

Historians have had a tendency to dismiss Underhill, a convicted adulterer, as a libertine searching for a religion that would allow him an outlet for both his overbearing pride and his libido; Laurence Hauptman has gone so far as to assert that Underhill suffered from an "antisocial personality disorder."[23] By joining with the antinomian party, however, Underhill hoped to change the social priorities of Massachusetts, not make himself odious. Underhill firmly believed that once Massachusetts overcame the limitations of a provincial backwater, men with his talents would finally be appreciated. Until late in life, Underhill remained enough of a Puritan to continue plotting ways to return to the colony in a blaze of glory.

As an antinomian, Underhill aligned himself with those whom he understood to be the better sort of colonists (such as the well-born Henry Vane), and he adopted a religious idiom that had the potential to alter the priorities of a system that not only denied him his social objectives but increasingly tended to define as illegitimate and sinful—or even worse, frivolous—his motivating desire for honor, recognition, and position.[24] The orthodox reaction to John Underhill, conversely, epitomizes how easily the fear of antinomianism could merge with uneasiness regarding men who pursued greatness in unsanctioned ways. Still, the Bay Colony could not have succeeded without the contributions of such men; and, in this chapter I will examine not only how John Underhill came to be a pariah in the Bay Colony community but also how certain of his ideas and character traits grudgingly came to be accepted.

UNDERHILL'S CRAVING FOR honor, distinction, and adventure was rooted, to some degree, in family history.[25] The Massachusetts captain's forebears, who had served for generations as retainers of Queen Elizabeth and her favorite, the earl of Leicester, had come tantalizingly close to the "table of the great." Hugh Underhill, John's great-grandfather, served at Elizabeth's estate in Greenwich as Keeper of the Wardrobe and Keeper of the Queen's Garden. John's grandfather, Thomas Underhill, was similarly situated at Kenilworth, Leicester's Warwickshire estate, and in 1585 he accompanied the earl to the Netherlands, where Leicester directed Protestant efforts against the Spanish.[26] Following Leicester's untimely death in 1589, Thomas Underhill, and after him his son, John Underhill, Sr., the father of the New England migrant, remained at Kenilworth as part of the retinue of Robert Dudley, Leicester's heir and "base-born" son.[27] The young John Underhill, growing up in the shadow of Kenilworth, was so struck by the dashing Elizabethans with whom his family was connected that late in life, when he settled at Oyster Bay, Long Island, Underhill called his estate Killingworth, a name that in seventeenth-century Warwickshire was used interchangably with Kenilworth.

The imprint of the great Elizabethans on Underhill's life went far deeper than estate-naming, for the trajectory of his life, punctuated by betrayal, adultery, scandal, and adventure, bore a remarkable likeness to that of his father's master, Robert Dudley, Leicester's illegitimate son, and, for a time, heir to Kenilworth. Dudley, who may have been married at one point to a relative of the explorer Thomas Cavendish, cultivated a knowledge of maritime affairs, and harbored a deep and abiding interest in voyages for adventure, conquest, and profit. In 1594 Dudley, with John Underhill, Sr., most likely in his entourage, embarked upon a voyage to the West Indies in which he claimed Trinidad for England, attempted to take Spanish prize ships, and tried to find gold along the Orinoco River, anticipating and perhaps trying to compete with Sir Walter Raleigh, who arrived several months later.[28] Soon after returning from this voyage, Dudley served in the Cadiz expedition against Spain. But in 1603, the brash young man ran into difficulties (much like Jephthah) when both his legitimacy and his rightful claim to Leicester's titles and property came under dispute. Unable to bring matters to a successful conclusion, a frustrated Dudley obtained permission in 1605 to travel abroad for three years; instead he abandoned his wife and fled to Florence with his lover, Elizabeth Southwell, conveniently disguised as a page. Dudley and Southwell subsequently converted to Catholicism, entered a bigamous marriage, and enjoyed the patronage of grand duke Ferdinand I, who found Dudley's knowledge of seafaring useful in his endeavor to gain control of the Mediterranean.[29] In the meantime the Underhills, who were supposed to have traveled abroad in Dudley's retinue, ended up in the Netherlands, where father and son found employment as soldiers.

While serving with Protestant forces defending the Netherlands from Spain, John Underhill encountered Lion Gardiner and Hugh Peter and was somehow recruited as a paid military expert for New England. During his first few years in Massachusetts, Underhill performed well: he helped to capture the miscreant Christopher Gardiner; escorted the governor on visits to settlements outside of Boston; traveled to England to solicit donations of arms for the colony; and raised a surprise alarm to demonstrate the lack of military preparedness among the generality of colonists, who responded to the feigned emergency "like men amazed" with no idea "how to behave themselves, so as the officers could not draw them into order."[30] Yet, while his election to the General Court in 1634 would seem to suggest that the captain had earned communal approbation and was successfully adapting to his new world home, all was not well. Underhill was becoming increasingly disenchanted with an emerging New England Way, which seemed almost calculated to thwart his ambitions. Just as Robert Dudley turned, when thwarted, and amid a sexual scandal, to a polity and a religion that Englishmen held in much disdain, so too did Underhill, who would soon be exposed as an adulterer, give over his loyalties to a party and a set of beliefs that orthodox Massachusetts leaders had begun to demonize. Like Dudley, too, Underhill, once disgraced, would engage in a long campaign to regain his lost esteem in the polity that rejected him.

Underhill's disenchantment with Massachusetts reached a crisis point in 1636, when the Massachusetts militia system was reorganized in such a way as to give regimental commands to civil leaders, while the real experts, in Underhill's view, were relegated to subordinate, "hireling" positions such as "muster master." Underhill could not understand, as he explained to

John Winthrop early in 1637, how Bay Colony leaders could "chose" him "to the place of a muster master" instead of promoting him, as he had expected, to a county level regimental command. He wrote accusingly of how this decision "had almost broughtt me to noething, when yow all pretended my advancement."[31] Demanding to know "upon what just grownde yow should be soe fearful to advance me," Underhill was fully aware that his aspirations wore a threatening aspect to the magistrates, who seemed determined to put him down:

> Butt [m]ake itt your owne case; would itt nott trouble your spiritt to sp[end] all your dayes aboute a callinge, and having noething else to liv[e] upon, and yett booth to be slighted, and such as never served onely [adv?]ansed? Nay, would itt nott be a greater tryall to have [?]ge castt in a mans dish to his dishonour? I pray yo[u] [c]ons[ider] of itt, and judge charitablye of my expressions.[32]

By middecade, Underhill was certain that Massachusetts was evolving in a direction that was overwhelmingly disadvantageous to his own interests; rather than allowing gallant, well-trained, worldly men such as himself a path to honor through military accompishment, the colony chose to set up a citizen soldiery that was carefully subordinated to civil rulers whom Underhill did not respect. Not only did the system invest inhabitants with a say in choosing their own officers but it also established conditions in which inferior men might actually be entrusted to convey commissions to militia officers.[33] In a petition submitted to the General Court just prior to the antinomian controversy, Underhill pointed out that the practice of allowing military officers to attain their positions through election, in roughly the same manner as their counterparts in civil government, had the effect of engendering a contempt for military authority that "never was hearde of in any schoole of warre; nor in no Kingedome under heaven."[34] Citing an incident in Salem in which a lowly constable was allowed to confer a lieutenancy upon Nathaniel Turner, who served on the 1636 expedition against the Indians of Block Island, Underhill intimated that, intentionally or not, the General Court was stripping officers of their honor and, presumably, their efficacy:[35]

> The Company standinge togither, as they were ordered, the Constable comes up to the Company, takeinge the authoritie of the majestrate upon him, delivers the partisan to Mr. Turner, and tells him that he is chosen Lieutennant to this Company, and so bids god give him joye.

But "Mr Turner," explained Underhill approvingly,

> understandinge himselfe better then he that broughte it, would not accepte of the place, without order of the Courte. . . . If officers should be of no better esteeme then for constables to place them, and mar-

tiall discipline to proceede disorderly, I would rather lay downe my commande then to shame so noble a Prince, from whome we came.[36]

Massachusetts, Underhill concluded with disappointment, was not at all like the biblical principalities about which he had read, or even the Netherlands, where renowned warriors were permitted to speak roughly to their kings.[37]

Underhill's attraction in 1636–37 to the nascent antinomian movement had polical and social, as well as religious, dimensions. As a General Court deputy and political observer in the early 1630s, Underhill must have been aware that other men besides himself were dissatisfied with the seeming lack of respect they received in the Bay Colony. At the same time he must have taken heart that Henry Vane, the political leader of the antinomian movement and a member of the English gentry, had been attempting, ever since his arrival, to counteract the influence of the political philosophy that had so much to do with Underhill's misery and the dissatisfaction of others like him.

IN THE YEARS leading up to the antinomian controversy, John Winthrop, the Bay Colony's foremost political theorist, presided frequently as governor over a polity that he likened to a large extended family. The family analogy conveyed perfectly Winthrop's desire to establish a society that was simultaneously hierarchical and communal, for, while Winthrop agreed wholeheartedly with the prevailing notion that the well-ordered society must be organized in a rigidly orderly manner, he also believed that the truly godly society must moderate the implicit harshness of such a system by applying to all ranks the "law of love."[38] Officeholders, in Winthrop's view, were deserving of all due respect, but they were to rule in a manner befitting the good patriarch, attentive always to the communal good rather than their own private desire for esteem and the perquisites of rank. This style of governance placed a high premium on consensus and self-denial, even for those who possessed the God-given talent to govern; as David Leverenz has argued, Puritans,

> eager to resist the tyrannous ego in any form, male or female, in the court, the church, the family, or the heart . . . tend[ed] toward a language of clear egalitarian obligations and heavenly dependence, maximizing duties and minimizing powers, securing identity as roles within a communal organism rather than inflating a hierarchy of persons.[39]

While these principles appealed to the majority of "middling" colonists, they were irksome to men who saw themselves as leaders and wished to assert themselves in ways that ran contrary to consensus. Antinomianism, a theological language that gave priority to private intuition over public appearance, proved enticing to certain men of substance who resented the constraints Massachusetts imposed on the independent will.

The high-born Henry Vane, who steadfastly supported the antinomian party during his governorship (1636–37) and departed as soon as the Winthrop faction regained political control, was precisely the sort of individual who felt unduly limited by the New England Way, especially, it would seem, because social, intellectual, and political priorities were so conditioned by the values of ordinary colonists. It is revealing that almost as soon as he arrived in the colony, Vane, in an attempt to discredit the Bay Colony's foremost political architect, tried to rekindle an old political rivalry between Winthrop and magistrate Thomas Dudley in which Dudley had complained of Winthrop's tendency to rule in a fashion that was, for lack of a better word, too populist.

Back in 1632, Dudley, a frequent occupant of the governor's chair, a veteran of the Continental wars, and a man who "must needs discharge his conscience in speaking freely," accused Winthrop of arrogating too much governmental power to himself, most notably through laxity in levying fines and administering other punishments meted out by the court so as to "make himself popular, that he might gain absolute power, and bring all the assistants under his subjection." Winthrop, in turn, had charged that Dudley failed to behave in the self-sacrificing, charitable manner appropriate for the godly magistrate of a chosen community: while the majority of residents were suffering from economic hardship during the colony's first few years, the insensitive Dudley had insisted on decorating his house with wainscotting; if indulging his vanity in this way were not bad enough, he also had sold to "some poor men, members of the same congregation . . . seven bushels and an half of corn to receive ten for it after harvest; which the governor and some others held to be oppressing usury." In the Winthrop–Dudley clash, Winthrop had consistently advanced the position that the key quality of a magistrate was to rule with kindness, like a father, and to set an example by sacrificing his own well-being for the public good. Winthrop argued adamantly that if he had indeed assumed too much power or been too lenient it had not been done "to oppress or wrong any man" but rather, he implied, to protect the public from potentially uncaring rulers. In 1636, he reiterated the latter point more explicitly, asserting that it was his "judgment that in the infancy of a plantation, justice should be administered with more lenity than in a settled state, because people were then more apt to transgress, partly out of ignorance of new laws and orders, partly through oppression of business and other straits." Besides, Winthrop pointed out, it was he who had, at times, "for want of a public stock . . . disbursed all common charges out of his own estate; whereas the deputy [Dudley] would never lay out one penny" of his own money.[40]

Much of what Winthrop said and did could, as Dudley charged, be considered self-serving, especially since his enhancement of gubernatorial power could be construed as violating the charter so as to become more popular. Historians have had a tendency to interpret any individual or group who challenged Winthrop's authority as champions of a more protodemocratic polity. Indeed, the charge that Winthrop clung tenaciously to "discretionary" powers is irrefutable.[41] Still, as far as the Winthrop–Dudley controversy is concerned, it is clear that Dudley was less interested in establishing an equitable distribution of power than in ensuring that he himself would be allowed to exercise certain prerogatives and to achieve the level of dignity he believed naturally belonged to men of his standing and wealth. Dudley, as an individual whose opinion carried weight, thought that he should be able to voice his ideas freely, and take profit where profit was due, without being subjected to lectures about his failure to contribute to the public good; if "the governor thought otherwise of it, it was his weakness."[42]

It is of great significance that in 1636 Vane, perceiving Dudley as a potential ally, had begun a campaign against John Winthrop, agitating for a meeting of magistrates and ministers to rehash the old grievances between the two men. As a member of the General Court, Underhill would have observed these machinations and, having already identified Winthrop as a source of his difficultuies, would have appreciated Vane's efforts to engineer Winthrop's downfall. Vane (and Underhill) well knew that Winthrop's faction was the one that believed in "carrying matters with more lenity" while Dudley's favored "more severity . . . both in criminal offences and in martial affairs."[43] Indeed, when Dudley resigned from office in a huff in 1632, he gave as one of his reasons that "he must needs discharge his conscience in speaking freely; and he saw that bred disturbance."[44] Although Dudley, perhaps comfortable in his position by the time of Vane's intervention, resisted the new governor's overtures, it was clear that this leading antinomian was trying to mobilize an undercurrent of elite dissatisfaction. Such dissatisfaction can be glimpsed in Israel Stoughton's explanation for Winthrop's failure to be elected governor in 1635:

> Mr. Wenthrop had very many hands against him for being either governor (which some attempted) or assistant . . . He hath lost much of the applause that he hath had (for indeed he was highly magnified), and I heard some say they put in blanks not simply because they would not have him a magistrate but because they would admonish him thereby to look a little more circumspectly to himself. He is indeed a man of men, but he is but a man, and some say they have idolized him and do now confess their error.[45]

Much more eloquently than Underhill, Vane delineated the "great disparitye" between a family and a commonwealth. In justifying the General Court's 1637 decision to ban further immigration of those deemed ideologically suspect, Winthrop had argued that just as a "family," or "little common wealth . . . is not bound to entertaine all comers, no not every good man . . . no more is a common wealth."[46] Vane countered in writing that the Bay Colony was not simply a people "consenting to cohabit together under one government for their mutual safetye and well fare," but was subordinate to a king, all of whose subjects had the right to plant so long as they neither denied the land "which they inhabit to be an enlargement of his majesties dominions" nor became "such dissolute and prophane persons as rather doe harden the Indians than be a meanes of their conversion."[47]

Vane, a future regicide, was no friend to Stuart monarchy; but he wished to deny in the most emphatic terms possible the Bay Colony notion that those who differed with the newly defined orthodoxy must be regarded as "strangers" not fit to inhabit the colony: "This law doth crosse many lawes of Christ, Christ would have us render unto Caesar . . . But this law will not give unto the kings majestie his right of planting some of his subjects amongst us, except they please" the orthodox magistrates. While the "maister" of a family had the right to bequeath land and houses at his own discretion, the majority faction of a commonwealth did not. For Vane, the ultimate authority over both church and state was God, whose preference—ever since the gentiles were brought into the covenant—was toward greater inclusivity rather than narrow exclusivity. Just as the Old Testament Jews had no warrant to reject the centurion Cornelius when he saw an angel and converted, Vane argued, so was the orthodox party wrong to question new stirrings of the spirit:

> it is not now left to the discretion of the church whether they would admitte them thereunto or not . . . when Christ opens a door to any there is none may take libertye to shut them out. In one word, there is no libertye to be taken neither in church nor commonwealth, but that which Christ gives and is according unto him.[48]

Ironically, the loose sense of community obtaining among the "king's Christian subjects" appeared closer to Vane's idea of godliness than the constrained family analogy forced upon the Bay Colony in the late 1630s.

In any event, Underhill surely took into consideration Vane's anti-Winthrop stance when it came time for him to choose sides in the impending religious dispute; and he ignored Dudley's commitment to orthodoxy if not his confrontational demeanor. The localistic orientation of the Bay Colony, the overwhelming concentration on the collective public sphere, the tendency to collapse church and state into one another, all proved vexing in one way or another to men who longed for a type of recognition that Bay Colonists were likely to regard as prideful or selfish.

The Watertown deputy and Pequot War officer William Jennison left few clues as to why he abstained from voting in favor of Hutchinson's banishment. But previous and subsequent difficulties Jennison had with the orthodox government suggest that he was concerned that gentleman's private views, and their persons, were being denied due respect. In the aftermath of the antinomian controversy Jennison, summoned before the Court, managed to convince authorities that he was free from the taint of antinomianism; but suspicions about his ultimate loyalty lingered.[49] Back in 1634, Jennison had been fined for "upbraydeing the Court with injustice, uttering theis words: I pray God deliver mee from this Court, professing hee had wayted from Court to Court, and could not have justice done him" in some unspecified action.[50] Jennison's previous residence in the Caribbean, an area "infected with familism," could not have helped his reputation. And by the mid-1640s, with the outbreak of civil war in England, the Watertown captain was again called before the Court, this time to answer for his expression of doubts about whether Englishmen should take up arms against their king.[51] No one, of course, was as vexed by these sorts of questionings as John Underhill.

IF THE ANTINOMIAN controversy pitted the values of certain elite (or aspiring elite) Puritans against those of "honest husbandmen," it made eminent good intellectual and social sense for Underhill to cast his lot with the dissenters. The "lenient" Winthrop faction, listing as it did toward the interests of the majority of "middling" colonists, could not be expected to create the kind of society capable of properly appreciating or rewarding the exertions of a gentleman like John Underhill. But the political maneuvering of Henry Vane, together with the preaching of John Wheelwright, comported well with Underhill's coveted sense of honor and his ideas about the proper way to live one's life. Antinomian ideas, as well as political expediency, attracted Underhill to the party of dissenters. And in March 1637, just one month before his departure for the Pequot War, a disaffected Underhill registered his disapproval of the banishment of John Wheelwright by signing William Aspinwall's antinomian petition.[52]

The condemned fast-day sermon given by Wheelwright, deemed seditious because it might incite antinomians to lay violent hands on their orthodox opponents, appealed to Underhill because it seemed to validate the idea that a Christian life need not always be lived in consensual social harmony and because of its antiauthoritarian overtones. Wheelwright depicted the suffering Christ as an itinerant, persecuted, and contentious figure, with whom men like Underhill, particularly those who had felt the wrath—or at least the disapproval—of authority, could easily identify. Christ, reviled throughout his life as the object and instigator of controversy, argued Wheelwright, was neither meek nor peace-loving when God's word was at stake. The Savior did not hesitate to use "vehement" speech "when he cometh to those that did oppose the wayes of grace." Nor did he scruple to avoid "combustions in church and commonwealth." Indeed, concluded Wheelwright, endemic strife must be embraced as a means of grace, and tranquility avoided, for "did not christ come to send fire upon the earth . . . never feare combustions and burnings . . . it is impossible to hold out the truth of God with externall peace and quietnes."[53]

The suggestion that constant travel, never-ending affliction and incessant controversy characterized Christ's mission on earth fired the imaginations of all who fancied themselves risk-takers, adventurers, and men of action. During a brief trip to England following his banishment from Massachusetts, Underhill published an account of the Pequot War that revealed much about his own state of mind, particularly in its extended meditation on the fate of two young women who had been held hostage by the Pequots. Although the women's plight might have indicated to some that they were providentially disfavored, Underhill wrote, it actually brought them closer to spiritual things, for God identified and tested his "tender ones" through tribulation. Drawn to the image of captivity, Underhill dilated on the advantages that might flow from such a seemingly powerless position: the Lord "is pleased to exercise his people with trouble and affliction that he might appear to them in mercy, and reveal more clearly his free grace unto their souls . . . the greater the afflictions and troubles of God's people be, the more eminent is his grace in the souls of his servants." Underhill, it would seem, considered himself to have been like a captive in a world of orthodoxy. Just as Wheelwright argued that "it is impossible to hold out the truth of God with externall peace and quietnes," so did Underhill insist that the "greater the captivities be of his servants, the contentions amongst his churches, the clearer God's presence is amongst his, to pick and cull them out of the fire, and to manifest himself to their souls."

Underhill found Christ only in dangerous or isolating circumstances. The Boston-centered orthodoxy of John Winthrop and Thomas Shepard paled in comparison with the raw religiosity this not-so-gentle Puritan experienced in frontier violence and religious controversy.

> Better a prison, sometimes and a Christ, than liberty without him. Better in a fiery furnace with the presence of Christ, than in a kingly palace without him. Better in the lion's den in the midst of all the roaring lions and with Christ, than in a downy bed with wife and children without Christ.

The controlled, communal church ordinances provided in non-separating congregationalism were powerless to move a disdainful Underhill, who deplored them as slothful. "Ease is come into the world, and men would have Christ and ease."[54] Antinomian ideas, in contrast, made lives full of movement and conflict appear Christlike and cast people who lived such lives as special emissaries of God.

If an antinomian outlook was capable of elevating adventurous undertakings and fractious behavior to a spiritual level, so too were antinomian, as opposed to orthodox, ideas conformable with seventeenth-century notions of honor and combat. Honor, as the concept had evolved in England since medieval times, was highly individualistic and tended toward antiauthoritarianism, involving the relentless promotion of self in all social or military situations betraying even a hint of competition.[55] But military authors mirrored antinomian conceits in more than their validation of prideful behavior, for they insisted, with Francis Bacon, that divine energy flowed directly to chosen commanders, who, through acts of war, made their "suits of appeales to the Tribunall of Gods justice, when there are no superiours on earth to determine the cause."[56] Just as members of the antinomian party emphasized that "works" of "preparation" would never suffice to capture the spirit, so too did proponents of honor culture hold that this attribute was a divine gift that could neither be earned nor limited to one geographical area; honor was "eternall . . . Generall and dispiersed, not confin'd or bounded within limits, it flyes over all the corners of the Earth, and covers the face thereof as with a Curtaine."[57] Like the antinomian saints, honorable people need not manifest tangible results as proof of their honor: "All fortuens outcasts but Honours darlings."[58] Honor, moreover, was associated with the ability to communicate with or receive visions from God. Francis Markham, a well-known writer of military tracts, emphasized how military success sprang in part from God's direct communication with chosen officers and leaders and from God's providential infusion of courage or talent into his hosts: Moses, for example, was a great leader because God "vouchsafed to speak with him face to face, to direct him in all his designes."[59]

In 1637, when an irate John Underhill confronted John Winthrop, reminding the chief magistrate that in other times and places dissatisfied military officers had been known to "turne publique rebells against their state and kingdome," he was merging antinomian principles with what he must have known of honor. Underhill, as I have shown, was seething with anger over his perceived demotion and subordination to unworthy civil authorities like Winthrop. The wronged captain found solace in Wheelwright's declaration that the "Lord hath given true beleevers power over the Nations . . . they shall break them in peeces as shivered with a rod of yron." He echoed these words to Winthrop, explaining why fractious behavior was uniquely appropriate in seventeenth-century Boston, where soldiers took their orders from the "indwelling spirit." "We may easilie disscerne," wrote Underhill, "thatt where the sworde of God's worde comes sharpened, itt separats a man from himselfe . . . when I meete with the spiritt of Christ, I dare to be the boulder."[60] Underhill's belief that valuable soldiers should be allowed to speak boldly to civil leaders had precedents in the Bible and in Wheelwright's preaching; but such ideas also appeared in military writings of the colonists' generation.[61] Gervase Markham held that "Honour hath also the priviledge of person, for it is held ignoble in any man to doe injury to a noble Captine, and howsoever they may be commanded, yet they may not be tormented." Francis Markham instructed similarly on the respect that civil authorities must show to great military leaders:

> Hence it comes, that the greatest Princes stile all men of Warre their Fellow-Souldiers: and the meanest among them (in the way of Vassalage) disdaine to serve the greatest persons, well may they serve under them, but cannot be truly said to serve them.[62]

Military writers included one other crucial element in their canon, which, again, bore unintended similarities to antinomian thought; they discussed war as an extraordinary circumstance in which the rules of conventional morality did not apply and in which honor absolved the apparent sins of those chosen ones whose blemished lives would ultimately contribute to a greater good. As discussed in chapter 1, Puritan orthodoxy, as it was being constructed in Massachusetts, was disinclined to dwell on those extraordinary circumstances in which moral "weaknesses" should be overlooked, seeking instead to "reduce" all matters of faith and behavior to a "single rule" measurable by external signifiers. But those who wrote about the "art" of war emphasized how wartime affliction catapulted humankind into a lawless, disruptive world-turned-upside-down, which afforded God his "only opportunity to shew himself that it may appear to be himself who worketh all our workes in us, and for us, and this is that which will teach us to give all the honour, prayse and glory to himselfe, who is the Author and Fountaine of all good."[63] In this vein, Markham asserted that in just wars

> Slaughter (a thing most odious to God and Nature) in this case Heaven doth not onely permit it, but commaund it; and men-killers in this Service shall bee crowned ... with Lawrell. ... These doubtlesse (how great soever the streame of Blood be which they spill) shall shine with Martyrs at the last day; yea, though accompanied with weaknesses of more then a tollerable proportion, yet is the cause so good.[64]

Warriors, according to most military tracts, were not bound to live by the same code as other Christians; their accomplishments were so important that they could find eternal glory regardless of their otherwise intolerable "weaknesses."

We cannot know for certain whether Underhill actually read authors like Markham. But according to historian Mervyn James, the prerogatives of honor were becoming increasingly important to the very class to which Underhill aspired; Puritan gentlemen of the 1620s and 1630s, he argues, were attempting to use the chivalric code to justify a revival of the "oppositionist role of the peerage."[65] While such an outlook may have permitted Puritans in England more effectively to oppose the royal government, most Massachusetts authorities assumed that in New England such exertions were no longer necessary, since the colony was under the rule of godly magistrates. New Englanders, during the antinomian controversy, stressed the importance of ordinary, not extraordinary, efforts to accomplish godly ends; to swim against the social tide in Massachusetts was to flout the divine will, not fulfill it.

John Underhill, spending his youth at Kenilworth and undoubtedly listening to his father's tales of service in the continental wars, would have been fully steeped in the culture of honor. As an adult, serving in the Netherlands in the life guard of Prince Frederick Henry and participating in the successful defense of Bergom-op-Zoom, Underhill would have learned, along with the New England migrant Hugh Peter, that honor could be merged with the most extreme of Puritan doctrines. Peter, in fact, wrote an account of how Dutch and English forces turned the Spanish off from an invasion of Bergen Op Zoom, describing the providential grounding of the Spanish ships and the subsequent mist that prevented them from finding their way as a time "allotted us from heaven."[66] It was no wonder, then, that Underhill, perceiving that the "honest husbandmen" of New England were more interested in "works" and "preparations" than divine interventions and extraordinary circumstances, should turn toward John Wheelwright's antinomianism.

Wheelwright contended that the God-inspired individual in society— like the heroic commander in Puritan and non-Puritan English military discourse alike—could, indeed must, strive for and act on a higher truth than that perceived by the common person. At the same time, Wheelwright and other antinomians insisted that outward appearances revealed little about internal spiritual realities and incorporated into their world view an antiauthoritarianism, an individualism, and a disregard for conventional notions of morality that bore a deep resemblance to the isolating nature of honor. In his 1653 letter to the United Colonies, Underhill clearly wanted to convey how his antinomianism might prove to be a boon rather than a danger to the colony. Understanding full well that he had been condemned for aligning himself with a heresy that was "against law," Underhill reminded his correspondents how useful such an attribute could be in war. "It is true often times," he wrote, "Nessesitie hath noe law."[67]

From the perspective of Massachusetts magistrates, honor culture and antinomianism shared the same dangers. John Underhill, as I have shown, used his own blend of antinomianism and honor to ridicule the domestic ties—the "downy bed with wife and children"—that stood at the center of Bay Colony communalism and hierarchy and that, in Underhill's view, made the colony "soft." Both antinomianism and honor, moreover, could corrode the elective, voluntaristic framework of the colony's mutually supportive covenants. Massachusetts leaders assumed that the outwardly godly man could be trusted and thus should be raised to public service through legal mechanisms. But both honor culture and antinomianism held leaders to more elusive standards. In 1637, when John Winthrop was returned to the governor's seat and the Hutchinson faction stood rebuffed, the antinomian sergeants, including Edward Hutchinson, the brother of William Hutchinson, refused to provide the new chief magistrate with an honor guard, explaining that they had escorted Henry Vane while he occupied the office "voluntarily in respect of his person not his place." An indignant Winthrop retorted "the place drowns the person, be he honorable or base."[68] If "orthodox" magistrates held that colonists should revere those in authority because of their "office" or "place," not their popularity or "persons," then antinomians were accused of emphasizing the importance of the "person" over that of the community, going so far as to consider certain chosen individuals to be above the law.

IN NOVEMBER, 1637, when Underhill's unflagging support for Wheelwright was punished with disfranchisement and suspension from all official positions, Underhill refused to believe that his reputation was irreparably lost and for five years struggled to make a rapprochement with Bay Colony authorities so as to regain his social place.[69] During that time the "hero" of the Pequot War, alternating between bouts of remorse and fits of defiance, remained conflicted in his own mind about how far he should go to prove his worthiness. It would be tempting to conclude that the outrageous behavior Underhill manifested during this period meant that he was not a "real" Puritan. Yet, in remaining obsessed throughout his life with the idea of returning to a place of rank in the Bay Colony, Underhill demonstrated that he continued to think of himself as a part of the Puritan community, albeit a member of a party that was temporarily out of favor.

In the immediate wake of the disfranchisement, Underhill, still puffed up by his recent military victory, set forth to England to publish a book on the Pequot War and to investigate alternative options for his own employment. He negotiated in March 1638 for a military position in Providence Island, perhaps having received an entree to the "lords and gentlemen" through the offices of Henry Vane.[70] Choosing not to accept a forthcoming and generous offer from the Providence Island Company, however, he instead returned to Massachusetts. In September 1638, hoping that tempers had cooled sufficiently to overlook his earlier indiscretions, Underhill tested the waters by tendering to the General Court both a retraction of his heretical views and a request for a tract of land that had been promised him in the past. In the petition to the General Court in which he requested his land, Underhill, referring to his absence in England as an instance where his services had been lent temporarily to another power, spoke as though there had never been any rupture between himself and the orthodox party:

> my selfe alledgeing itt to be the custome off Nations thatt if a Commander be lentt to another State, by that state to whome he is a servantt; booth his place and meanes is nott detayned from him, soe longe as he dooth nott refuse the call of his owne state, to which he is a servantt, in case they shall call him home.[71]

Instead of welcoming him home with open arms and allowing him to save face, however, the General Court assailed the errant captain with a barrage of complaints about past behavior and newly revealed evidence of sinful disloyalty. From a fellow passenger on Underhill's return voyage, magistrates learned that the captain had entertained some of his shipmates by making disparaging remarks about the colony, holding forth that "we were zealous here, as the Scribes and Pharisees were, and as Paul was before his conversion." When Underhill tried to deny that he had made such statements, "they were proved to his face by a sober, godly woman" whom he had temporarily "drawn to his opinions." And this was not all: Underhill had told the woman, whom he had apparently also tried to seduce, that he received his assurance of salvation while "taking a pipe of tobacco" and that since then he never "doubted of his good estate, neither should he, though he should fall into sin."[72]

Up to this point Underhill's truculent behavior suggests that he was confident of being again accepted into the Massachusetts fold. Not only had he been well received by Puritan "grandees" in England but he had reason to believe that there were people in Massachusetts sympathetic to his plight; after all, the prominent men of the colony had, despite (or perhaps because of) his uncertain status, included him on the first roster of the prestigious Artillery Company.[73] It was most likely this sense of having what he thought of as powerful allies in the colony, and in England, that emboldened Underhill, who was absent during the period of Anne Hutchinson's church trial, to take actions that seem more calculated to grate on orthodox sensibilities than mollify them.

Underhill was certainly aware of John Winthrop's desire to stem any impending "opinionist" tide. Yet in his history of the Pequot War, the captain pointedly urged those who feared persecution in Massachusetts not to abandon their plans to migrate just because they had heard about troubles in the churches, for it was the responsibility of every Christian to enter the fray and fight for their beliefs. Underhill argued that there must always be conflict, even in the most "pure" of churches, and he insisted that to emulate Christ one must be prepared to champion the cause against those who lacked religious insight. The "cross" that Christ bore, and the source of his "suffering," was having been compelled to live in a world where the "word of his Father could not take place in the hearts of those to whom it was sent. . . . And that is the cross, too, that Christians must expect, and that in the purest churches." Underhill insulted the orthodox majority by implying that those who experienced persecution in Massachusetts were more Christlike than their oppressors, and he defied the will of the magistrates by deliberately attempting to incite an oppositionist stance:

> You that intend to go to New England, fear not a little trouble. More men would go to sea, if they were sure to meet with no storms. But he is the most courageous soldier, that sees the battle pitched, the drums beat an alarm, and trumpets sound a charge, and yet is not afraid to join in the battle. Show not yourselves cowards, but proceed on in your intentions, and abuse not the lenity of our noble prince, and the sweet liberty he hath from time to time given to pass and repass according to our desired wills. Wherefore do ye stop? Are you afraid? May not the Lord do this to prove your hearts, to see whether

you durst follow him in afflictions or not? What is become of faith? I will not fear that man can do unto me, saith David, no, nor what troubles can do, but will trust in the Lord, who is my God.[74]

Having singled out for address those who had reason to fear that they might suffer for their faith in Massachusetts, Underhill could easily be accused of trying to attract disagreeable spirits to the colony.

The contents of *Newes From America* signaled, in a variety of ways, that the exultant military hero was unrepentant. His stirring war stories were calculated to illustrate how the antinomian inclination to follow divine inspiration rather than human law was an appropriate response to the extreme conditions that characterized a new world. The captive girls, for example, with whom Underhill identified, triumphed over physically stronger foes because, as one of them explained after coming safely home, they had learned a crucial lesson: "I will not fear what man can do unto me, knowing God to be above man, and man can do nothing without God's permission." These words were striking in their similarity to Anne Hutchinson's pronouncement at her civil trial that the Court could not harm her so long as she was inspired by God, and Underhill, as though he feared that detractors might accuse him of fabricating the quotation, assured readers that he had been in command of the Saybrook fort when the rescued girl was questioned and that these were indeed the "words that fell from her mouth . . . she spake these things . . . in my hearing."

In his history of the Pequot War, too, Underhill recounted with palpable relish how he himself had experienced a gratifying reversal by upstaging Samuel Stone, the chaplain whose appointment had, in Winthrop's opinion, offended the antinomian party so grievously that some had refused to serve in the war. As Underhill told the tale, a Connecticut militia company headed by John Mason had encountered "threescore Mohiggeners" seeking to join the English and take revenge on the Pequots for having driven them "out of their lawful possessions." The officers who had "chief oversight of the company," however, feared that the "Indians in time of greatest trial might revolt, and turn their backs against those they professed to be their friends, and join with the Pequeats." Much "perplexed" over these untried allies, the English directed the Mohegans to proceed on foot to the Saybrook fort, while they themselves went by water aboard a "great massy vessel, which was slow in coming, and very long detained by cross winds." Present at the fort when the Indians arrived, and witnessing the way they eagerly "fell out" and slew a party of Pequots, Underhill excitedly "rowed up to meet the rest of the forces" to tell them the news. While he "lay under the [oncoming] vessel" in his small boat, Underhill overheard "one Master Stone" praying "solemnly before God, in the midst of the soldiers," begging the lord to "vouchsafe so much favor to thy poor distresed servants, as to manifest one pledge of thy love, that may confirm us of the fidelity of these Indians towards us." A proud Underhill knew exactly what to do. "Immediately myself stepping up," he told Stone "that

God had answered his desire, and that I had brought him this news, that those Indians had brought in five Pequeats heads, one prisoner, and wounded one mortally; which did much encourage the hearts of all, and replenished them exceedingly."

Rising up and revealing his news with almost preternatural accuracy, Underhill savored how his vigorous immediacy eclipsed the ministers' plodding prayer. No reader could mistake how Underhill wanted this event to be perceived: not only had Underhill been, quite literally, the answer to Stone's prayers, but God had allowed Underhill, Moses-like, to transform the news of the day into a divine revelation: the Lord had inspired Stone to ask for a sign concerning the Indians' intentions—"it pleased God to put into the heart of Master Stone this passage in prayer"—and then sent him "a messenger to tell him his prayer was granted." Underhill's place in the limelight that day had therefore been engineered by his creator.[75]

The book *Newes From America* offended in one final way by overtly encouraging settlement of the newly conquered lands of eastern Connecticut, especially the region around New Haven, in a manner that was highly insensitive to Winthrop's well-known insecurities regarding geographical dispersal. Indeed, Underhill went so far as to promise on his book's title page that the work would provide "a discovery of . . . places, that as yet have very few or no Inhabitants which would yeeld special accommodation to such as will Plant there." While not unmindful of the need for careful expansion, the governor had a tendency to regard out-migration as a form of criticism.[76] In December 1638, no less a personage than Thomas Hooker subtly accused Winthrop of trying to sabotage migration into Connecticut by spreading rumors about unfavorable conditions there.[77] And Israel Stoughton, who was in charge of the mopping-up operations in the wake of the Pequot War, chose his words carefully when recommending settlement of Pequot and New Haven: "we will prefer your minds [Winthrop's and the council, on where new settlements should be started] before ours," Stoughton wrote in a letter to Winthrop, but " 'tis clear some must reside here or hereabouts . . . I am confidant we have not the like in English possession as yet, and probable 'tis the Dutch will seaze it if the English do not . . . it is too good for any but friends."[78]

Whatever Underhill's optimistic expectations about his reception in the Bay may have been, he found few defenders in September 1638. Blindsided by the mountain of evidence that had piled up against him, he was ill prepared to respond in a way that would reverse the unexpected tide of ill will. According to Winthrop, Underhill "would not confess nor deny [the testimony of the woman from the ship] but took exceptions at the court for crediting one witness against him." Worse yet, the captain's failed attempt to conceal, and then to obfuscate, his misdeeds seemed to confirm the orthodox belief that antinomianism led inexorably to libertinism and dissimulation. The lies Underhill told about what transpired on the ship inexorably gave rise to doubts about the sincerity of his recantation of support for the antinomian petition. The magistrates now pressed him on whether, contrary to a written statement in which he claimed to have abjured the antinomians and expressed remorse for "his sin in condemning the court," he were still "of the same opinion he had been in about the [Wheelwright] petition or remonstrance." Loath to grovel before the magistrates, Underhill "answered, yes, and that his retraction was only of the manner, not of the matter." In his written recantation, which was now read aloud, however, Underhill had "professeth how the Lord had brought him to see his sin in condemning the court, and passing the bounds of modesty and submission, which is required in private persons, etc., and in what trouble of spirit he had been for it, etc." This cinched the orthodox case, and one day later the errant captain was summarily banished "for abusing the court with a show of retractation, and intending no such thing."[79]

In an effort to restore his dignity and to leave the Bay in a posture of defiance rather than submission, Underhill "made a speech" in church on the following sabbath, "showing that, as the Lord was pleased to convert Paul" at a time when he was persecuting Christians, "so he might manifest himself to him [Underhill] as he was taking the moderate use of the creature called tobacco. He professed withal, that he knew not wherein he had deserved the sentence of the court, and that he was sure that Christ was his."[80] This was a deft move and reflected Underhill's awareness of the theological debates that comprised the antinomian controversy, for in interchanges with his orthodox colleagues Cotton himself had used a similar argument, employing the biblical example of the publican to show how a seemingly profane man could gain election. But now Cotton, recognizing how easily his doctrinal stance could be abused by untutored and unscrupulous minds, clarified his former position without quite denying its veracity: "although God doth often lay a man under a spirit of bondage, when he is walking in sin, as Paul was, yet he never sends such a spirit of comfort but in an ordinance"; therefore, Underhill would do "well to examine the revelation and joy which he had."[81]

Cotton's rebuff, while devastating, did not render Underhill's humiliation complete, for allegations now surfaced regarding his "incontinency with a neighbor's wife." Again it appeared that Underhill had used his deviant religious views to tempt (this time successfully) a woman into sin. When Underhill refused to respond to private questionings about the accusation, he "was publicly questioned, and put under admonition." Suspicions of unsavory goings-on had been aroused when Underhill was observed to call frequently at the house of a woman described as "young, and beautiful, and withal of a jovial spirit and behavior." The captain "was divers times found there alone with her, the door being locked on the inside." Although he admitted that this might have "an appearance of evil in it," Underhill had an excuse: "the woman was in great trouble of mind, and sore temptations, and that he resorted to her to comfort her; and that when the door was found locked upon them, they were in private prayer together."[82]

In the two-year period following this debacle, Underhill removed to the New Hampshire settlement of Dover, where, for a time, he managed to establish himself and the future Anabaptist clergyman Hanserd Knollys, another refugee from the Bay, as the community's temporal and spiritual leaders.[83] Hoping that he had found his niche in New Hampshire, where he persuaded the inhabitants to enter into a "combination," Underhill at first ignored the recurrent pleas from First Church Boston that he submit himself to answer for his crimes, which included adulterous behavior, sedition, "corrupt" opinions, reproach against the church, "revyling the governor and others of the magistrates—threatening revenge and destruction to the Country . . . writing slanderous lies to the state of England," and, worst of all, "feigning a retractation both of his seditious practice and also of his corrupt opinions, and after denying it again."[84] Winthrop dismissed as mere posturing the captain's understandable fear that the license obtained by the church for him to travel to Boston might be insufficient to protect him from seizure; and he regarded as specious and impertinent Underhill's claim that "he had no rule to come and answer to any offence, except his banishment were released."[85] Meanwhile, the governor endeavored to use whatever influence he had to impugn Underhill's character in letters sent to men of stature in New Hampshire, such as Thomas Wiggin, the agent for the group of English investors (including Lord Say and Sele and Lord Brooke) that had purchased a two-thirds interest in Dover in 1633, and Edward Hilton, an influential figure who with his brother William had come to "Pascataquack" to direct the Laconia Company's fishing enterprise.[86]

But Underhill for a time remained undaunted and resolute. At one point in the winter of 1638, Winthrop explained darkly, Underhill and George Burdet, a discredited clergyman from the Bay who briefly served simultaneously as magistrate and minister at Dover, managed to intercept one of Winthrop's letters to Hilton.[87] The two outcasts, Knollys and Underhill, retaliated by writing "presently into England against [Massachusetts], discovering what they knew of our combination to resist any authority, that should come out of England against us." At this time, Underhill's treachery was doubly revealed, for not only did he appear ready to collude with hostile forces in England but also he continued deliberately to misrepresent himself, having given diametrically opposed accounts of his intentions in letters written to John Winthrop and John Cotton. The letter to Cotton, which was probably the more honest, was "full of high and threatening words against us," while Winthrop's letter was written "in very fair terms, entreating an obliterating of all that was past, and a bearing with human infirmities, etc., disavowing all purpose of revenge." To make matters worse, Winthrop knew that Underhill had sent still another letter in early 1639 to "a young gentleman (who sojourned in the house of our governor), wherein he revile[d] the governor with reproachful terms and imprecations of vengeance upon us all." Even more disturbingly, Underhill had styled himself "an instrument ordained of God for our ruin."[88]

While it is uncertain how successful Winthrop's letters were in compromising Underhill's position at Dover, the captain ultimately found the volatile mixture of Puritans and profane fishermen, as well as hostile interventions mounted by the episcopal governor of Portsmouth, too difficult to manage without some kind of external support. At some point in the summer of 1639 a new plan took shape in Underhill's mind; he might possibly regain his lost esteem in the Bay by convincing the people of Dover to submit to Massachusetts rule. In July of that year, having "returned to a better mind," he "wrote divers letters to the governor and deputy . . . bewailing his offenses, and craving pardon"; and in October, he wrote to John Winthrop and Thomas Dudley to assure them that, despite being "dayli abused by malischous tongse," he was not, as the letter of one John Baker claimed, constantly "dronck and like to be cild [killed]" in a series of senseless brawls at Dover. It was true enough, Underhill admitted, that he had drawn his sword on Thomas Warnerton [Wannerton], a steward of the episcopal settlement of Strawberry Bank. But he had done so only because that "insolent and dasterdli sperrite" was "resolutli bent to rout out all gud among us, and advanc there superstischous waye," endeavoring "by boystrous words . . . to fritten men to accomplish his end." Underhill tried to affect a penitent tone; but his letter was shot through with resentment at how he had been misunderstood and apparently forsaken by his countrymen in Massachusetts. He complained that Bay Colony magistrates had responded with "silence" to several of his recent attempts at communication; and he reminded them that "Jesos Christ did wayt; and God his Father did dig and telfe bout the barren fig-tre before he would cast it of[f]." In addition to suggesting that Bay Colony leaders lacked Christian forebearance, Underhill also gestured disapprovingly at their tendency to credit appearances over hidden (and more significant) realities; although Underhill did become involved in altercations at Dover—such as on "ister [Easter?] day" when "on[e] Pickeren their [Strawberry Bank's] Chorch Warden caim up to us with intent to mak som of ourse dronc"—his ultimate aim was to defend the Massachusetts interest by combatting episcopal "intrushon[s]" in the eastern settlements. More important, Underhill confided that he and Knollys were working toward the submission of Dover to Massachusetts rule, a business that required secrecy: "we are prifat in our prosedingse tell [until] a conkluchon, and so desier you [to keep this information in confidence]: for we ar threttend. . . . We shall not rest untel this work be finnist, and youer selfes [in] pouer here." Knowing that the antinomians had been condemned for their failure to be plain and truthful, Underhill had begun his letter by promising to "youse [use] chrischan playnnes. I know you love it." But he concluded cannily on a different note, suggesting that such plainness must sometimes give way to a more judicious secrecy.[89]

In concert with Underhill, Hanserd Knollys also decided to confess his sins and beg forgiveness from the Bay. Knollys, according to Winthrop, had formerly written letters to English correspondents in which "he had most falsely slandered [the Bay Colony] as that it was worse than the high commission . . . and that here was nothing but oppression . . . and not so much as a face of religion."[90] Knowing that one of Knollys's letters had been intercepted and opened in Boston, Underhill wrote to Winthrop in January 1639–40 requesting a copy of the writing so that the court in Dover could "more thorrily dele" with Knollys, who, Underhill announced, was "injenious to confes his falt, and gif du satisfacechen not only to us [the people of Dover], from whence he wrot it, but to youer whole state, which we shall dilligenli furder him in, and shall be willing to my power to dow the like, to the glori of God, and my farther humelyachon."[91] The two men then endeavored to procure safe conducts from Massachusetts and proceeded, at different times, to humble themselves before the existing powers in Massachusetts.

Knollys, who preceded Underhill in making the trek to Boston in early 1640, was well received, having "made a very free and full confession of his offence, with much aggravation against himself, so as the assembly were well satisfied."[92] But Underhill's performance, which Winthrop described in the same journal entry, was unsatisfactory. Underhill confessed to adultery with one woman and an attempt to do the same with another; he admitted the "injury he had done to our state"; and he conceded that all the actions taken against him so far had been just. Still, "all his confessions were mixed with such excuses and extenuations, as did not give satisfaction of the truth of his repentance so as it seemed to be done rather out of policy . . . than in sincerity." Therefore the church excommunicated him.[93] Underhill appeared suitably dejected for the several days he remained in Boston before his return to Dover. But when he arrived in Piscataqua he resumed his old ways, failing to show "proof of a broken heart" and, more dangerously, working to "ingratiate himself," despite all his assertions to the contrary, "with the state of England, and with some gentlemen at the river's mouth, who were very zealous that way, and had lately set up common prayer." To gain credence with these enemies of Massachusetts, Underhill "sent thirteen men armed to Exeter to fetch one Gabriel Fish, who was detained in the officer's hands for speaking against the king."

Underhill's erratic behavior stemmed from what he must have perceived as the successive narrowing of all his options. Not only had his efforts at reconciliation been rejected in the Bay, but the people of Dover, or at least a significant faction of them, were in the process of rethinking Underhill's place in their settlement. As soon as he returned, they requested that he stay away from their court until they had had an opportunity to discuss whether he should continue there. But

> hearing that they were consulting to remove him from his government, he could not refrain, but came and took his place in the court; and though he had offered to lay down his place, yet, when he saw they went about it, he grew passionate, and expostulated with them,

and would not stay to receive his dismission, nor would be seen to accept it, when it was sent after him.

Winthrop attributed the precipitous downturn in Underhill's popularity in Dover to his having been engaged in a dangerous double game with the residents: he spoke out against the attempts of Massachusetts to absorb Dover in an effort to pacify a contingent of episcopal-minded settlers while at the same time he plotted secretly to bring the Piscataqua region under Bay Colony control, presumably so as to ensure his own glorious return to Boston. In the process he blackened the reputations of "the people, especially . . . some among them" by portraying them to correspondents in Boston as the source of hostility against the Bay, when in fact it was he who had incited them in that direction. Underhill's feat in helping to procure the submission of Dover could appear grandiose only so long as its people were thought to be hostile to the idea; but the truth of the matter was that a signficant portion had steadily favored unification with the Bay. Unfortunately for Underhill, the settlers learned of his duplicity before he could accomplish his ends: "they produced against him a letter from our governor, written to one of their commissioners in answer to a letter of his, wherein he had discovered the captain's proceeding in that matter."[94]

With his position in Dover fully eroded, Underhill slunk back to Boston for a second time to make peace, but to no avail. Some of the magistrates thought Underhill should be imprisoned immediately for violating the terms of his exile; his safe conduct, they argued, even though it had not yet expired, was good for only one trip. While calmer minds prevailed on this issue, Underhill returned to Dover within the week without accomplishing his goal, for the church refused even to allow him to speak.[95] Writing to Winthrop from the home of Edward Gibbons, Underhill appeared chastened, conceding that he was "justli deprived of liberti to visset you" and admitting that his "sinnfull lif and backsliding prodigalliti . . . hafe made the blod and deth of Christ of non efeckt." Yet even while admitting the enormity of his sins, Underhill did not expect, and could not fathom, the deep resentment that confronted him; he did "not thorroli understand mense displesure" and was "trobeld that chuch [such] hard reportes should gooe out agaynst me . . . I came simpli to satisfi the chorch, not thincking to haf herd cuch [such] hard reportes agaynst me, thogh som smale ingling [inkling] I had before." In the final analysis, however, Underhill conceptualized the "rumers and fliing reportes gon out agaynst me" not as a true reflection of popular opinion but as the product of demonic delusions, "becase it is Sathan's time, now or nefer, to wage ware agaynst my soule, and prefent [prevent] my reconsilement with His [God's] pepel by his falce alarmse: which sound ale the contri ofer [over]." Underhill thus continued to present himself as a central link in New England's armor, and he advised Winthrop, for the good of the colony, not to allow Satan to distort his opinion: "Sir, be plese to here mee, in the matters of Exceter and Dover, and let not mallics and fare words take place in the bosem of the wise."[96]

Despite his elevated sense of his own importance, Underhill was by this time in truly desperate straits, for he faced a new potential usurper, Thomas Larkham, who had arrived at Dover in 1640 and was making inroads on his authority. Larkham, a Church of England minister spurned from the Bay, gained popularity by accepting into his church all who would put themselves forward, no matter how openly sinful, so long as they promised to reform. The clergyman's immediate aim was to take Knollys's place as religious leader; but, according to Winthrop, he aspired eventually to "rule all, even the magistrates (such as they were)." Open conflict, punctuated on both sides by excommunications, arrests, fines, and even violence, would soon break out between the Larkham faction and Underhill/Knollys supporters. Unable to hold his own, especially when Larkham appealed for help from the governor of Portsmouth, who probably favored the resumption of royal control, Underhill was forced to petition Massachusetts for aid. The delegation eventually sent by the Bay, headed by Hugh Peter, was able to pacify the two sides and seemed at first inclined to recommend continued church governance under Knollys. But then it was revealed that Knollys was "an unclean person" who had "solicited the chastity of two maids, his servants, and to have used filthy dalliance with them." This further compromised Underhill; and even though the desperate captain had already humilated himself before First Church, he could not save his position.[97]

In September 1640, some months prior to the violent altercation with Larkham, the proud captain, with few options remaining, had obtained yet another safe conduct allowing him a final opportunity to mortify himself before the church. Facing what looked to be his last chance, Underhill swallowed his pride and gave the "orthodox" magistrates the spectacle they had long awaited:

> He came at the time of the court of assistants, and upon the lecture day, after sermon, the pastor called him forth and declared the occasion, and then gave him leave to speak . . . He came in his worst clothes (being accustomed to take great pride in his bravery and neatness) without a band, in a foul linen cap pulled close to his eyes; and standing upon a form, he did, with many deep sighs and abundance of tears, lay open his wicked course, his adultery, his hypocrisy, his persecution of God's people here, and especially his pride (as the root of all, which caused God to give him over to his other sinful courses) and contempt of the magistrates. He justified God and the church and the court in all that had been inflicted on him. He declared what power Satan had of him since the casting out of the church; how his presumptuous laying hold of mercy and pardon, before God gave it, did then fail him when the terrors of God came upon him, so as he

could have no rest, nor could see any issue but utter despair, which had put him divers times upon resolutions of destroying himself, had not the Lord in mercy prevented him, even when his sword was ready to have done the execution. Many fearful temptations he met with beside, and in all these his heart shut up in hardness and impenitency as the bondslave of Satan, till the Lord, after a long time and great afflictions, had broken his heart, and brought him to humble himself before him night and day with prayers and tears till his strength was wasted; and indeed he appeared as a man worn out with sorrow, and yet he could find no peace, therefore he was now come to seek it in this ordinance of God.[98]

While some historians have tended to interpret Underhill's attraction to antinomianism as a convenient justification for his sinful ways, it is obvious from his confession that Underhill understood a great deal about how New England leaders conceptualized the difference between antinomianism and orthodoxy. [99] In *Newes From America,* it will be recalled, Underhill had linked true spirituality with social alienation and had scoffed at communally oriented religiosity as slothful and confining: "Ease is come into the world, and men would have Christ and ease."[100] Now he reversed this position and explained how his alienation from society had made him all the more vulnerable to sin. It was not enough that he had come privately to "humble himself" before God "night and day"; now he could get "no peace" outside of a communal "ordinance of God." Following the path marked out by Thomas Shepard, moreover, Underhill admitted that his former sense of assurance had been "presumptuous," deriving from a moment's enthusiasm rather than long striving and the careful corroboration of external evidence (and judgment). It had disappeared, as Shepard's writings predicted, like an ephemeral mood, when the "terrors" returned to stalk him. Garbling, perhaps intentionally, his otherwise well-spoken confession with intermittent "blubbering," Underhill knew that his confession would be best received if it was didactic in tone; thus he "gave good exhortations to take heed of such vanities and beginnings of evil as had occasioned his fall."[101]

All this self-deprecation aside, Underhill could not resist one subtle element of bravado; in speaking of his liaison with the cooper's wife, for which he had been admonished prior to departing the Bay, Underhill gave his listeners to understand that his partner in adultery had "withstood" his advances for "six months against all his solicitations (which he thought no woman could have resisted) before he could overcome her chastity, but being once overcome, she was wholly at his will."[102] Gesturing almost playfully at the role of the gallant knight protecting the soiled reputation of an injured woman, Underhill, in the depths of his greatest humiliation, found a way to recoup some small part of his trammeled honor and to mock his accusers. At least his sexual prowess remained intact; and he found a way to brag about it in a social context where he was virtually unassailable, especially since he was careful subsequently to fall on his knees and plead forgiveness for his sin directly from the husband of his illicit lover.[103]

Underhill's dramatic act of humiliation was successful insofar as it secured his readmission to church fellowship; but the Court, while willing to lift his banishment and pardon him for all except his adultery, refused to "restore him to freedom."[104] Winthrop did credit Underhill in a back-handed way for what he had accomplished in Dover: the captain, he wrote, had faced "eager prosecution . . . because he had procured a good part of the inhabitants [of Dover] to offer themselves again to the government of the Massachusetts."[105] But Underhill gained nothing by his suffering. The final submission of the settlement to Bay Colony rule came through the agency of a group of negotiators headed by Hugh Peter and John Humphrey.[106] By May 1642, Underhill, deprived of his reputation and, presumably, his civil liberties, could find no employment in the Bay Colony and resolved to depart, beginning an odyssey that would lead him finally to New Netherland.[107]

Winthrop, in reflecting on these events, tried to comfort himself with the idea that the Lord would always provide external signs to call attention to those who might threaten the godly community. Just as the governor responded with relief to the way Anne Hutchinson's "monstrous" birth gave physical embodiment to her misshapen ideas, so did he marvel at how God "gave up these two [Underhill and Knollys], and some others who had held with Mrs. Hutchinson, in crying down all evidence from sanctification, etc., to fall into these unclean courses, whereby themselves and their erroneous opinions were laid open to the world."[108] That these critics of the concept of sanctification should be revealed as scoundrels by the outward evidence of their corruption was sweet justice indeed.

On the other hand, Underhill's performance of the role of contrite sinner could also be interpreted as a disturbing reminder of how artfully a sinner's true essence could be concealed. The majority of magistrates, who refused to restore Underhill's civil rights, did not believe that he had really changed; some even appeared to have forgotten that he was reconciled to the church and state, for in 1641, when Underhill came to Boston, he was called to appear before the General Court despite the fact that no outstanding charges remained against him.[109] Anne Hutchinson's efforts at prevarication and equivocation at her civil trial had culminated in her apparent inability to resist proclaiming visions that could be interpreted as seditious threats against the colony; the Lord, it would seem, had structured things so that the truth would "out."[110] But John Underhill's confession, while incredibly affecting even to so hostile an observer as John Winthrop, suggested that duplicity, although it did not succeed in this case, could be extremely powerful.

Even more disturbing in regard to Underhill was the realization, noted by John Winthrop, that the captain's behavior in Dover, which hinged to some extent upon his apostasy, ultimately proved advantageous to the Bay

Colony. Winthrop realized that just as antinomianism played an important role in making Underhill an effective Indian fighter, his guile, a trait linked with apostasy, contributed to the Bay's successful annexation of Dover. No matter how vexing the captain's presence had been, he had accomplished much that was useful. Underhill did not hesitate to play this card in 1653, when he hoped to be swept back into power as a result of hostilities between New Netherland and New England.

JOHN UNDERHILL WAS the perfect vehicle for linking theological antinomianism with pride, honor, and dissimulation and for proving that this particular form of heresy would cause its proponents to sin without fear. The confession before First Church Boston, in which Underhill costumed himself and spoke in a way that denoted his new-found posture of humiliation, was, as David D. Hall has pointed out, a "ritualistic" act that symbolically reversed the sins he had committed.[111] But it was not so easy to represent, or to reverse, the duplicity—a character flaw more than a discrete set of sins—around which suspicions of Underhill centered. The pattern of accusations that arose in relation to Underhill focused on his having lived a double life of deceit and treachery that could have endangered the colony and that was revealed only through seemingly random reports of his private conversations and the contents of intercepted letters. While outwardly manifesting his dedication to the colony, most dramatically through military service on its behalf, Underhill harbored secret doubts, even contempt, for its leadership and its interpretation of "right" religion. Worse, there were times at Dover when he appeared ready to treat with forces that would have preferred a New England ruled by a "general governor" sent from England rather than one sworn to carry out the will of a godly covenanted community.

John Underhill inverted the communal norms prized by orthodox Puritans. In many ways he was more of a danger than Anne Hutchinson herself. At the same time, his exertions had helped to further the temporal aims of Massachusetts. The colony's wrangling with Underhill had revealed an unsettling truth: the orthodox breach with those Puritans who were interested in a more flexible religiosity and a more cosmopolitan focus had been neither eradicated, nor even fully articulated, by the antinomian controversy. The community, after much acrimonious debate, had finally agreed that Anne Hutchinson was beyond the pale; but she had not been observed to focus her religious views in such a way as to contribute to the martial, mercantile, or maritime goals that leaders viewed as significant. For John Underhill, as well as other male antinomians who did focus their religiosity in this way, the break could never be quite so absolute.

Hugh Peter, for example, one of Anne Hutchinson's most avid persecutors, was far more lenient when it came to Underhill and Knollys. Not only did both of these dissidents travel through Salem and receive advice and reassurance from Peter when attempting to effect their reconciliations with the Bay Colony, but Peter obligingly provided letters attesting to

Knollys's good character and requesting Winthrop's "wonted carefull ten-
dernes." As already shown, Peter seemed comfortable with the idea of
Underhill and Knollys retaining their authority in Dover—at least until
Knollys's adulterous behavior was discovered.[112] Although Peter wholeheartedly aligned himself with the orthodox side during the controversy
over Hutchinson, he did not share the orthodox desire for a homogeneous
community attuned solely to localistic values. As an eager advocate of
programs to spur economic growth in the colony, Peter was closely connected with the new merchant community in England.[113] In New England,
he worked as an agent for lords Saye and Sele and Brooke, the broad-
minded Puritan leaders who had offered Underhill military employment in
Providence Island and who owned the settlement of Dover to which Underhill fled in 1639.[114] Peter, moreover, as a friend of Henry Vane, was not
wildly enthusiastic about John Winthrop's governorship; and Vane
"courted" the support of both Peter and of Thomas Dudley, albeit unsuc-
cessfully, in his campaign to embarrass Winthrop.[115] In the end, Peter
found Massachusetts to be too limiting a sphere and returned to England,
emerging in the mid-1640s as a partisan for Independency, the new model
army, and a broadened religious toleration that could never have been
accepted in the Bay. During the civil war years, Peter fiercely denounced
those English "presbyterians" who favored religious uniformity, character-
izing them as men "that never lived beyond the view of the smoke of their
chimneys."[116] In his various pro-army pamphlets and sermons, Peter argued
that "no magistrate in matters of religion [should, in an ideal polity] meddle
further than as a nursing father, and then all children shall be fed, though
they have several faces and shapes."[117]

Peter's extreme animosity toward Anne Hutchinson seems inconsistent with his later emergence as a champion of limited toleration. But
Peter, who in December 1636 had succeeded the exiled Roger Williams as
pastor of Salem, may have conflated the antinomians with the separatists
who continued for several years to trouble his church and question his
leadership. The antinomian controversy broke out at precisely the same
time when Peter was struggling to integrate eleven obstreperous "Williams-
ites" back into his congregation; one of these, a Brother Weston, went so
far as to challenge whether Hugh Peter's wife, Elizabeth, was eligible for
membership in the Salem church once she arrived in Massachusetts. Elizabeth had remained in Holland for some time after her husband's departure
for the new world, and there were rumors that she "came disorderly away"
from the Rotterdam congregation that Peter had pastored prior to his emigration.[118] The case involving Elizabeth Peter was discussed at several
disciplinary meetings, while the Salemites waited for communication from
the Dutch church; but the proceedings were interrupted by the woman's
untimely death in the spring of 1638, at roughly the same time as Hutchinson's exile. Beset by tragedy and opposition, Peter soon suffered what
would appear to have been a mental breakdown. Thus, throughout the
antinomian proceedings, Peter perceived himself as a man under siege, both

professionally and personally. It was in this frame of mind that he lamented how Hutchinson "charged us to be unable ministers of the gospel and to preach a covenant of works" and denounced her for having "stept out" of her "place" and "bine a Husband [rather] than a Wife . . . a preacher [rather] than a Hearer; and a Magistrate [rather] than a Subject."[119]

Although Peter was horrified by the disrespect and disorder that both antinomians and separatists carried in their wake, he appreciated the importance of the transatlantic world and its opportunities for trade and military conquest, and he understood that those opportunities were best pursued under a regime where a variety of voices were allowed to be heard. (It may, indeed, have been the separatists' expressed desire to cut themselves off from the outside world—a desire not shared by antinomians—that inspired Peter's hostility toward them.) Peter, like Underhill, admired the great Elizabethans, who pursued conquest under the aegis of a flexible but intense Protestantism; by 1646, he complained that England's failure to act on the world stage, and to appear "terrible" to other nations, came because contemporary Englishmen indulged in trifling internal divisions that rendered them "more effeminate than our predecessors in Queene Elizabeths time."[120]

While Peter, whom his biographer calls the "strenuous Puritan," was ill equipped to see the exile of Anne Hutchinson as a great loss to the colony, he may well have appreciated Underhill's talents, for this aggressive Puritan blended religious deviance with real military achievement and a culture of honor. Perhaps for this reason, Peter, once safely ensconced within his own Salem congregation, lent support to the Underhill-Knollys government at Dover, at least until Knollys's adulterous behavior was revealed. The career of John Underhill, who refused to believe that the recovery of his position in Massachusetts was impossible and who gained the grudging respect of so dedicated an enemy as John Winthrop, suggests that antinomians who used unorthodox religiosity to pursue important ends might win some degree of acceptance in the Bay.

DURING THE 1650s and 1660s, in the wake of the aborted war between New England and New Netherland, John Underhill made one more attempt to penetrate the ranks of the New England elite, this time by cultivating an association with John Winthrop, Jr., governor of Connecticut.[121] From 1656 through 1660 Underhill wrote Winthrop a series of letters asking for a variety of favors that would establish a patron–client relationship between the two men. In these letters, Underhill requested medical advice for the benefit of his dying wife; news and information about the affairs of the day; aid in the possible annexation of the English-dominated towns of Long Island to Connecticut (another one of Underhill's schemes to become an important man in New England, if not Massachusetts itself); and help in resolving a dispute surrounding Underhill's sale of the House of Good Hope, a trading post in Connecticut he had seized from the Dutch in the summer of 1653.[122] Around 1660, after the death of Underhill's ailing first wife, the captain attempted to draw even closer to Winthrop by marrying Elizabeth Feake, a woman whose kinship with the Winthrop family allowed Underhill to begin addressing John Winthrop the younger as "onckel." Underhill's new mother-in-law, Elizabeth (Fones) Winthrop Feake Hallett, was a Quaker whose first husband had been the unfortunate Henry Winthrop (John Jr.'s brother), a sort of prodigal son of the Winthrop family who, prior to the Great Migration, had married against his father's wishes, lost a fortune in the West Indies, and then tragically drowned at Salem in 1630, almost immediately upon arrival in the Bay Colony.[123]

Underhill's second marriage may seem ironic because it brought him into the kinship orbit of the Winthrops at the same time that it introduced him to the Hallett's community of Quakers.[124] But Underhill believed that all varieties of Puritan-derived belief properly belonged within the same "family."[125] In the first letter in which Underhill addressed his new relative as "onckel," he praised the Connecticut governor for his colony's religious moderation:

> youer slfe and Coloni [was] spred thorro the world [in a Quaker tract Underhill had read] as moderat and pittifull in youer demenyour to them [Quakers] . . . God hase prserfd you from shedding innosent blod, and cept your Coloni from acktse of cruelti to that pepel, so I trost you will be preserved to the end; that you maye not pertake in the aprochching jugsement.[126]

John Winthrop, Jr.'s reputation for religious toleration attracted Underhill and made him hope that a marriage between orthodoxy and heterodoxy, as well as a favorable alteration of the meaning of New England history, was in the offing.

It was typical of Quakers during this period to predict in menacing tones the punishments that persecutors of Friends would endure when God avenged them in a fast-approaching judgment day.[127] Underhill, who inclined naturally toward a violent rhetorical style, had read Humphrey Norton's *New England's Ensigne*, a tract that belonged to this genre, almost as soon as it came off the press.[128] Yet, while Underhill criticized what he regarded as Massachusetts' myopic stance on religion and made mention of a "judesment" from which the tolerant John Winthrop, Jr., would be "preserved," his purpose in this bridge-building letter was to find common ground between himself and the Winthrop family, a potent symbol of Bay Colony orthodoxy. In this spirit Underhill, noting the approach of the eighteenth anniversary of his forced departure from the Bay, attempted through tortuous logic to claim the elder John Winthrop as part of the same tradition to which Underhill himself had always belonged:

> Most diere and loving onckel, gife me lefe for your forther incorrgsement from percekuchon, to mind you of my farewell words from your nobell father, of happi memori, to mee, and hafe taken such imprschon [impression] throg the sperrit of God in mee, that I dare not

meddel with the pepell; but lefe them to there libberti grantted bi the gud ould Parlement of Eingland.[129]

The memory of Winthrop, Sr., could not have been a "happi" one for Underhill. Still, Underhill explained that Winthrop, Sr.—in taking leave of Underhill just prior to the latter's departure for Stamford, Connecticut— had observed how "the gret skorge of God hangse over the hedse of this pepel and land, for God is wroth with the Contri and will otter his sore displesure agaynst it." Underhill implied that while Winthrop was incapable of understanding that God was angry at the "soferings and bannishmentse" that occurred during Winthrop's own "time," he had nonetheless inspired Underhill's quest to understand the reasons for God's displesure— a quest that ended with his commitment to toleration and his belief that the "pepell" should be left to the "libberti grantted bi the gud ould Parlement of Eingland."[130] Underhill urged the younger Winthrop toward greater acts of toleration, suggesting that this would be to fulfill, rather than to reject, his father's legacy; and he hoped (vainly) that such a re-reading of the Winthrop legacy would allow Underhill himself, at least symbolically, to return to the Bay Colony pantheon of heroes.

JOHN UNDERHILL'S PERSONAL circumstances, and his behavior, were in many ways singular or unique; but even under banishment he could not help but feel himself part of New England and the greater Puritan mission in the world.[131] Conversely, the character flaws for which Underhill was condemned—the heightened concern for personal honor, the propensity to participate in a series of shifting alliances with outside forces, the distaste for a narrowly defined orthodoxy, the inclination to turn public trust to private advantage, and the manipulation of a seemingly fractured self that could be different things to different people—were not at all uncommon among the men charged with boundary-keeping functions in seventeenth-century Massachusetts.

The Massachusetts officers remaining in the Bay Colony after Underhill's departure were no less concerned with their rank and the accoutrements of office than he had been; and they often felt thwarted in their efforts in this direction. In 1651 the General Court took steps to ensure that the rank of major general, then held by Edward Gibbons, would be sufficiently exalted in power and prestige over others in the jurisdiction, proclaiming that henceforth the colony's major general, unlike any of his subordinates, would be accorded the right once per year to summon up his regiment for training upon his own authority, without a call from the council or the General Court. Had this change not been made, the prerogatives accompanying the rank of major general would not have far enough exceeded those exercised by the sergeant majors general, who commanded the colony's county regiments.[132]

But the Court could not always be so obliging when it came to the craving for honor. Bent on keeping militia companies down to manageable proportions, the General Court acted during the 1640s and 1650s to place strict limits on the number of men who could serve in each company and on the number of commands each officer could hold.[133] But because honor was thought to be directly proportional to the size of one's command, military officers were inclined to allow the companies to grow unchecked and to strive toward multiple officeholding. As early as 1637, in his history of the Pequot War, John Underhill had voiced the fear that, because colonial units were so small, English readers might not give due respect to Massachusetts captains:

> I would not have the world wonder at the great number of commanders to so few men, but know that the Indians' fight far differs from the Christian practice; for they most commonly divide themselves into small bodies, so that we are forced to neglect our usual way, and to subdivide our divisions to answer theirs, and not thinking it any disparagement to any captain to go forth against an enemy with a squadron of men, taking the ground from the old and ancient practice, when they chose captains of hundreds and captains of thousands, captains of fifties and captains of tens. We conceive a captain signifieth the chief in way of command of any body committed to his charge for the time being, whether more or less, it makes no matter in power, though in honor it does.[134]

This concern for rank, and the quality of command, persisted in the decades following Underhill's departure. The Court, despite the concessions made to Gibbons, did little to assuage officers' sensibilities. When anxious officers asked the Court in 1652 to determine the precise order of precedence for captains holding the same rank within each of the county regiments, the Court decided that seniority—"their antiquitie of being captain in that regiment"—would be the most important criterion for determining relative rank.[135] The more ambitious of the colony's military men, however, eager to enhance their prestige through more aggressive methods than amassing years of seniority, had for some years been supplementing militia service with the command of horse troops—a practice that became illegal in the early 1650s.

In 1652, the election of John Leverett to the captaincy of Boston's south regiment placed the thirty-six-year-old combat veteran on the horns of a dilemma. Massachusetts law prohibited men from holding dual commands; Leverett, who was already serving as the captain of a Suffolk horse troop that he had helped to found, was forced to choose between two very attractive offices. The militia captaincy would have made him the fourth-highest ranking military figure in the Suffolk regiment—behind Major General Edward Gibbons and captains Thomas Savage and Thomas Clark. But the command of a horse troop was a "place of greater honor"; indeed, the military wisdom of the day held that the leaders of horse troops deserved "a greater respect [than the captains of foot soldiers] from the Magistrate and more serious reverance from the common people."[136] The men of the

South Company, possibly encouraged by Leverett, composed a petition asking essentially that an exception to the law be allowed in his case. The petition was submitted and rejected on three separate occasions, the Court refusing to consider a dual command and insisting that Leverett must continue with the horse troop, where he would be "more serviceable to the country"; any other arrangement, it added diplomatically, would tend to "our loss and the discouragement of a deserving man."[137]

The persistent petitioning on Leverett's behalf reflected the myriad tensions attending the exercise of honor in a Puritan community. If Leverett chafed at the prohibition against dual commands, his men may have resented how their popular captain ultimately chose the command that would more greatly enhance his military stature. Attempts to place constraints upon the exercise of honor, however, despite the enthusiasm among the militiamen who voted for Leverett and championed his cause, would appear to have represented the will of the people.

In subsequent years the General Court continued to assume that the drive for honor might compromise basic considerations of safety; a 1658 petition from the town of Newbury, complaining that William Gerrish had officered a horse troop during his incumbency as the town militia captain, reveals that this supposition was widely shared. Arguing that only a fully committed militia captain could provide the security to which the community was entitled, townsmen requested that they might "have the bennefitt of the law that no man should have comand of the horse and foote both . . . that so they maybe exercised by him, upon whom they must depend in time of neede."[138] Leverett and Gerrish were, for different reasons, controversial figures in their respective towns; but both, very much in the tradition of John Underhill, felt constrained by the Massachusetts conviction that the pursuit of honor represented a danger to the common good.

IF JOHN UNDERHILL had difficulty disentangling himself from the Bay Colony, so too did the colony find that it would be impossible (indeed undesirable) to cut itself off completely from the values and ideas that Underhill represented. There is no question that Underhill himself was unacceptable to most people in Massachusetts. But other men closely associated with the antinomian cause were able to reintegrate themselves into the Bay; at the same time, so did antinomian-derived ideas, despite their potential dangers, find a place in the colony's official rhetoric.

Committed antinomians William Aspinwall and Edward Hutchinson, like Underhill, went into exile for their support of doctrines that Bay Colony authorities deemed "false"; unlike Underhill, both were able to redeem themselves (in Aspinwall's case only temporarily) in Bay Colony society. Despite a warning in 1641 from Thomas Hooker that Aspinwall still held heretical views, as well as the knowledge that Aspinwall had been deemed a "seditious" force in Portsmouth, Rhode Island, the Massachusetts General Court accepted his recantation of antinomianism, and allowed him to take up the official position of public notary and clerk of the writs—at least until the early 1650s, when he publicly questioned the authority of the General Court and was forced to leave the colony for good, returning to England, where he achieved notoriety as a Fifth Monarchist pamphleteer.[139]

Hutchinson, meanwhile, rose very quickly in Puritan society, remaining in Massachusetts until his death in King Philip's War and becoming a key merchant, land speculator, and military man. Bay Colony authorities must have known that in recanting antinomianism men such as Aspinwall and Hutchinson were insincere; but they valued the talents that these men possessed, both in war and commerce. Aspinwall was accounted a good "artist," or cartographer, and led an expedition into the Delaware country on behalf of a group of Boston merchants interested in the fur trade. Hutchinson, who became a General Court deputy, accompanied John Leverett in 1642 on a diplomatic mission to treat with the Narragansetts; and in 1654, he was permitted to found the Three County Troop of Horse, a prestigious cavalry unit long dominated by Hutchinson family members. Neither Aspinwall nor Hutchinson relinquished their heterodox ideas. In 1658 Hutchinson's Quaker aunt, Catherine Scott, was detained in the Boston House of Correction when she entered Massachusetts from Rhode Island; Edward Hutchinson not only paid her charges but joined Thomas Clark in speaking out against the colony's harsh law against Quakers.[140] Still, a reluctant orthodoxy was forced to admit, at least tacitly, that the talents that made such individuals useful could not be so easily separated from their attachment to religious ideas that fell well beyond the bounds of New England orthodoxy.

The antinomian ideas expressed in the ill-fated Wheelwright sermon— ideas for which the men just discussed sacrificed much—became an integral component in the rhetoric of war. To upholders of the New England Way, condemnation the Wheelwright fast-day sermon had seemed cogent and rational since the work was organized around three major themes thought to be particularly dangerous: that the "spirit acts most in the saints when they endeavour least"; that spiritual doubts plagued only the nonelect; and that saints must always be in a state of contention, or agitation, for their faith. At best, the leaders said, excessive pride and violations of morality would come of these ideas; at worst, a bloodbath. In the very act of charging Wheelwright with sedition, however, the magistrates had paid oblique tribute to the power of highly spiritualized antinomian discourse to galvanize people to action. In subsequent decades, sermons organized around the theme of war—especially the artillery election sermons preached each spring when the Artillery Company elected its officers—carefully preserved aspects of Wheelwright's original formula.[141]

Artillery election sermonists speaking in the late seventeenth century equated every Christian's endless struggle for salvation with the covenanted community's effort to purge the land of external enemies: "Every Christian when he is New Born is born a Souldier." Although warfare and the conversion process were thus framed as analogues to one another, the role ascribed to human endeavor in each case was markedly different. Orthodoxy mandated that in the context of personal salvation, it was important to stress sanctification, or godly living and inherent human grace; but no such emphasis on "preparation," or the separation between the supernatural and natural worlds, could be admitted into military rhetoric. Reflecting their audiences' interest in the providential significance of and supernatural control over war, artillery election sermonists retained Wheelwright's interpolation of spiritual and worldly ends and means, exhorting hearers to "run sin Thorow and Thorow your swords up to the very Hilts. Prick it to the Heart, else it will not die. Hit the Old Man under the fifth rib and let his bowels out, else you do nothing." The so-called liberalization of Puritan theology notwithstanding, the favorite text for artillery election sermons down to the mid-eighteenth century remained "The battle is not always to the strong."[142] If John Underhill could not find a home in Massachusetts, some elements of his proscribed faith did.

Even one so orthodox as Edward Johnson, captain of Woburn, failed to divorce antinomian-based ideas from his spiritual lexicon. In his Wonder-Working Providence, Johnson was highly critical of Anne Hutchinson; he expressed great hostility to the antinomian emphasis on justification over sanctification, and he believed in the importance of the soul's "preparation" in the process of individual conversion. But when it came to warfare, the arena in which the covenanted community struggled for salvation, this erstwhile "preparationist" positively embraced the notion, associated with antinomianism, that saints were "acted" by God. Antinomians, as I have shown, had argued that an emphasis on "preparation," by suggesting that humans had powers not wholly dependent on the divine will and strength, would detract from the glory that belonged to God alone. While Johnson could not accept this line of reasoning when applied to the trials and tribulations of the individual soul, he did adopt it in the context of war; Johnson went so far as to dismiss practical preparations for battle as not only useless but dangerous, being "but so many traps and snares to catch a people in." The supernatural aid that came directly from God, Johnson held, must be the focus of all discussions of war: "Woe be to you, when the same God that directed the stone to the forehead of the Philistine, guides every bullet that is shot at you." In describing instances where God intervened directly in the wars of his saints, Johnson was forced to contradict his own orthodox assertion that "the Lorde workes by means and not by miracle."[143]

Nowhere is evidence for the continuing importance of antinomian ideas more startling than in tributes to fallen military heroes and other societal leaders. By the end of the century, men controversial in their youth, like Thomas Savage and John Leverett, had risen to preeminent military and civil positions; when they died, preachers of funeral sermons praised them not for their submission to the moral law but for their preternatural prowess in wrestling with God and discerning his will for the colony. Great leaders stood in the "gap" or the "breech" where, it was thought, the temporal and spiritual worlds collided. There they exercised special "powers with God himself that blunt the edge of his fury, and turn by the stroke of his revenge, that it cannot light where else it would." Several decades earlier, accused antinomians had been punished for claiming to receive revelations and for deemphasizing an individual's own inherent morality. Now New England's most prominent men were revered for these very characteristics. The "mighty man, the man of war, the Judge," was, remarkably enough, expected to possess the talents of the "diviner, though not to be taken in an evil sense." These leaders were above the moral law, because they acted "not in [their] own disposal; but . . . guided by a Divine Providence, and by a secret, invisible, and unpreventable direction from above." The rectitude of leading men was "not to be understood in a legal sense, for one that is in all parts compleat, answering the Moral Law in every point," but only as they were "righteous . . . by the imputation of Christs righteousness."[144] These eulogized leaders, characterized as conjurors of sorts and placed above human or moral law in recognition of their ability to intercede with an angry God, embodied not only the virtues of John Winthrop but those of John Underhill as well.

DESPITE THE BOLD oppositions revealed during the antinomian controversy, the mental worlds of John Underhill and John Winthrop were not as dichotomous as one might suppose. Tied as it was to the attractions of "wilderness" land, of mercantile profits, and of conquest, the mystical lure of antinomianism—and its temporal benefits—remained strong, even among the orthodox. Antinomianism condoned a suspension of behavioral norms and an acceptance of boundlessness, or contingency, that at once threatened and enhanced the orthodox community. The confluence of military and economic dynamism with religious heterodoxy was not coincidental; nor was it confined to the lives of people historians have defined as marginal. Rather, these elements of belief and action were mutually supportive; as I will show, elite men entrusted with the colony's highest military ranks, as well as other public functions, possessed many of the same traits as Underhill. Still, the accommodation between the New England Way and the social values loosely associated with antinomianism remained tense. While some men would learn to live within the confines of Bay Colony orthodoxy, others would continue to be alienated by it.

3

Cosmopolitan Puritans in a Provincial Colony

In 1624 Gervase Markham, a well-known author of books on military and other practical matters, complained that England's relative peace under James I had given rise to a generation of young men who enjoyed the perquisites of rank and honor, but never had been compelled to earn them. Markham chided these "yong men . . . able men," luxuriating in chivalry and romance, for having "received honors beyond expectations, favours past hope, and wealth past merit"; and he exhorted those people who cared about England's reputation to "tell these great ones (whom hardly thunder can awaken) that when they neglect Honour, they neglect and are rebellious against God."[1]

Sixteen years after the publication of Markham's tract, the English Puritan leader Lord Saye and Sele expressed similar frustration with the isolationist bent of the Massachusetts Bay Colony, taking Governor John Winthrop to task for neglecting the responsibility to combat religiously-significant enemies, like the Spanish, whose strongholds to the south were difficult to attack from faraway New England. Hanging in the balance between isolationism and involvement, wrote Saye, was "the advancement of the gospell and the puttinge down the great adversary thearof, that man of sin, whearunto as you are now you neather are able, nor are likely to be, to putt your handes to the least wheele that is to be turned about in that worke, otherwayse then by well wishing thearunto." While Markham had fretted over how the aristocracy's enjoyment of the unearned trappings of honor weakened the country, Saye criticized New England for isolating itself from worldly conflict and refusing to provide sources of honor sufficient to motivate men to do great feats: the colony had neglected to exercise the "power in a state to reward virtue hereditarly."[2] To be sure, Saye's disdain for the colony's failure to establish an aristocracy reflected his fear that members of the Puritan gentry might lose the claim to leadership (and status) that they enjoyed in England should they decide to migrate. But Saye's broader point—that the Bay Colony denied a sufficient degree of latitude to enterprising high-ranking indviduals who might help it to fulfill its providentially appointed task—meshed, in significant ways, with contemporary criticisms leveled by certain elite Bay Colony Puritans.

The proclivity toward isolationism that Saye had detected in 1640 persisted through the civil war and commonwealth years and, arguably, through the end of the century. This isolationism reflected the colony's commitment to the aims of ordinary people; and it depended, to a large degree, on the enforcement of religious uniformity. Recent scholarship, especially Karen O. Kupperman's study of the "lords and gentlemen" of Providence Island and Robert Brenner's examination of the "new merchants" during the English Revolution, has suggested reasons why Bay Colony leaders might have had good reason to disagree with some of the priorities established by the secular leaders of the Puritan cause in England. Important gentry figures like Lord Saye and Sele, the earl of Warwick, and Lord Brooke, as well as merchants like Matthew Craddock, Samuel Vassall, and Maurice Thomson, played instrumental roles in launching the Massachusetts Bay Company and providing it with ongoing support. Yet these sorts of individuals believed that only a "dynamic military/commercial offensive" could properly serve the cause of worldwide religious reformation.[3] Such grand goals were bound to conflict with the humbler aims of the majority of New England colonists.

Drawing in part on the wide-ranging and diffuse Protestant imperialism of the Elizabethans, the English Puritan gentry and their "new merchant" allies evinced, throughout the middle decades of the century, greater concern for the spread of right religion in the world at large than the particular fate of the Massachusetts Bay colony or its specific (and in their view unduly narrow) form of orthodoxy. These Puritans, oriented to the transatlantic world and committed to a general reformation that involved striking at the Spanish antichrist, establishing England's commercial superiority, and aiding in the fight against Catholicism on the continent, accepted a greater diversity within the "light" of Puritan doctrine; not only did they criticize the persecuting ways of their coreligionists in Massachusetts but, despite their advocacy of the colony, they also called into question the providential purpose of a seemingly unproductive, geographically remote settlement disinclined to engage in the great conflict with Spain.[4]

The antinomian controversy, occurring toward the end of the first decade of settlement, had provided a vehicle through which the colony could establish its official position on a whole constellation of self-

definitional issues. The Winthrop faction envisioned the colony as a bea-
con of godliness but not a direct agent of change in the wider world. It was
to be a place where "middling" colonists could pursue lives of quiet glory
and security rather than engage in grand exploits. This New World dream
required that the colony be relatively isolated and highly unified, primarily
through religious uniformity. While a more relaxed attitude toward eccle-
siology and belief facilitated the task of Puritan "grandees" and merchants
interested in promoting their own individual and collective advancement
through trade and conquest, exactitude was vital for Massachusetts Puritans. The antinomian controversy, as well as later controversies over toleration and anabaptistry, helped New England Puritans to define themselves as inhabitants of a colony dedicated to the needs of "middling" folk
rather than grandees. It was not that grandees were thought to be heretics
in the precise religious sense of that word. Rather, antinomianism, which
was reviled in part because it would permit a wider toleration than orthodoxy, was made synonymous with all the moral failings—pride, deviance,
aggressiveness, acquisitiveness, individualism, and inconstancy—that
could conceivably detract from the centrality or cohesiveness of the Bay
Colony. An antinomian was one whose loyalties were split, whose demeanor hinted of court as well as country, whose character was prideful,
and whose deepest motives were unreadable, hidden, and complex. Antinomianism was a convenient rubric under which to represent a cultural
style, by no means limited to the "Hutchinsonian" party, that threatened
"honest husbandmen" in secular as well as theological ways.

By defining antinomianism in this way, orthodox leaders were rejecting, in a very subtle manner, the priorities of England's Puritan leaders,
whose good offices they depended on but whose schemes, which brought
conflict, greater diversity, and a more intense connection to transatlantic
capitalism, might plunge the colony into the dreaded realm of undiscipline
and chaos. If the most avid English backers of Massachusetts refused to
view it as their sole project, it became all the more important that the
colonists themselves be imbued with a sense of loyalty and a commitment
to the geographical space, as well as the emergent idiosyncratic culture, of
New England. The antinomian controversy symbolically separated the particular interests of the Bay Colony's "middling" settlers from those of high-
ranking English Puritans, such as Henry Vane, whose reputation soared
regardless of his disgrace in Massachusetts.[5] Indeed, at the time of the
antinomian controversy, Winthrop and other orthodox leaders began to
associate safety and virtue with doctrinal uniformity and commitment to
place to such an exaggerrated extent that participation in alternate colonizing enterprises, close ties to outsiders, certain concomitants of trade, and
even efforts to expand territorially could be construed as bordering on the
heretical.

But there was a dilemma here. Orthodox Bay Colony Puritans, even
as they jealously guarded their ability to take charge of their own society,
also admired transatlantic Puritans who aspired to do great things for the

cause. And they needed, for the sake of their own temporal success, to cultivate within the colony persons possessing traits suitable to the accomplishment of vital commercial and military goals.

Major figures in the military and commercial life of the colony were, like many English Puritans, attracted to grand undertakings for profit, adventure, and the advancement of a loosely defined new world order. Although these men did not share the same high status as the Puritan gentry or larger merchants, they presented a similar challenge, and a similar mixture of threats and promises, to the dominant faction in the Bay Colony. The Artillery Company indeed was an institutionalized embodiment of the vilified congery of secular traits associated with the trope of antinomianism. The key military officers who joined the company, most of whom combined their military activities with mercantile pursuits, both transatlantic commerce and Indian trade, aggressively pursued personal wealth and honor, sometimes employing duplicitous means to do so. And some of the most powerful and dynamic among them, often as a result of service in the English civil wars or participation in the imperialist plans of Oliver Cromwell, were inclined to recommend that the Bay Colony ease its religious restrictions. Although these men were perceived to pose certain dangers to the purity of the Bay Colony, their exploits, no matter how they may have violated the communal ethic, tended also to redound to public benefit.

In this chapter I will explore how a number of the Bay Colony's most vibrant military personages of the 1630s, 1640s, and 1650s—including John Humphrey, Edward Gibbons, John Leverett, Robert Sedgwick, and Nehemiah Bourne—contributed to the colony while at the same time violating in a variety of ways the territorial, religious, and jurisdictional boundaries that defined it and sustained its purity. Some of these men, like Leverett, who eventually rose to the governorship of the colony, were able to succeed despite championing unpopular policies and ideas; others, like Humphrey and Bourne, were forced out or chose to leave. All posed threats to the multifarious boundaries that separated a variety of metaphoric and real "wildernesses" from the "garden" that the Bay Colony aspired to become.

DURING THE LATE 1630s and 1640s Winthrop and other magistrates and ministers expressed their commitment to the geographical space of New England by agonizing over the attraction that some colonists felt toward opportunities outside the Bay, in Long Island and the West Indies. But this did not prevent a number of New Englanders of substance, including those normally charged with maintaining the colony's boundaries, from experimenting with alternative colonizing schemes. Nathaniel Turner, the Lynn captain and Pequot War veteran who, according to an approving Underhill, had bristled at encroachments on his personal honor, moved out of Massachusetts in 1639, helped to found New Haven, and acted as that colony's agent in unsuccessful attempts to acquire land on both sides of the Delaware River. Daniel Howe, the Lynn trainband lieutenant who served alongside Turner and Underhill in the Pequot War and who offered to pay Wheelwright's charges should it become necessary to imprison him, was instrumental in settling some forty families in Southampton, Long Island. And John Humphrey, an extremely influential magistrate in the colony who turned out to be a great disappointment to most of his peers, embarked on a scheme backed by Puritan grandees in England to resettle colonists from New England to Providence Island.[6]

Winthrop understood on one level that interest in settlement schemes outside Massachusetts were spurred on by the economic hardships accompanying the outbreak of civil war in England and a consequent downturn in out-migration from the metropolis:

> The sudden fall of land and cattle, and the scarcity of foreign commodities, and money, etc., with the thin access of people from England, put many into an unsettled frame of spirit, so as they concluded there would be no subsisting here, and accordingly they began to hasten away, some to the West Indies, others to the Dutch, at Long Island, etc. (for the governor there invited them by fair offers), and others back for England.

Still, Winthrop thought that these departures represented a direct or implied disparagement of the New England Way and a betrayal of those colonists who stayed in Massachusetts:

> Much disputation there was about liberty of removing for outward advantages, and all ways were sought for an open door to get out at; but it is to be feared many crept out at a broken wall. For such as come together in a wilderness, where are nothing but wild beasts and beastlike men, and there confederate together in civil and church estate, whereby they do, implicitly at least, bind themsleves to support each other, and all of them that society, whether civil or sacred, whereof they are members, how they can break from this without free consent, is hard to find, so as may satisfy a tender or good conscience in time of trial. Ask thy conscience, if thou wouldst have plucked up thy stakes, and brought thy family 3000 miles, if thou had expected that all, or most, would have forsaken thee there. Ask again, what liberty thou hast towards others, which thou likest not to allow others towards thyself; for if one may go, another may, and so the greater part, and so church and commonwealth may be left destitute in a wilderness, exposed to misery and reproach, and all for thy ease and pleasure, whereas these all, being now thy brethern, as near to thee as the Israelites were to Moses, it were much safer for thee, after his example, to choose rather to suffer affliction with thy brethren, than to enlarge thy ease and pleasure by furthering the occasion of their ruin.[7]

That other colonists besides Winthrop experienced this kind of uneasiness was reflected in the reaction to John Underhill's announcement that he would take up a tract of land he had been offered in the Dutch colony; the Boston church immediately interceded, advised him to accept the military employment offered him by the English settlement of Stamford, and even hired a pinnace to transport him there. Even though Underhill was familiar with Dutch culture and language from his long military stint in the Netherlands, the church thought it better that he be with people who were "our countrymen and in a church estate."[8]

Movement into territory claimed by the Dutch, whether by invitation or encroachment, threatened the Bay Colony from a variety of perspectives. In 1640 Daniel Howe's group at first ignored Dutch claims to Long Island and instead acquired title to land for a town from an agent of the English Lord Sterling (Sir William Alexander), as well as local Indians. An advance party of "Linne men," including Howe, "took down the prince's arms," which the Dutch had erected on a tree to indicate their claim, and allowed an Indian to draw "an unhandsome face" over the countenance of the Prince of Orange. The Dutch, enraged at this defacement and usurpation, sent armed men to arrest the despoilers and dispossess them of the land. Ultimately the migrants "(finding themselves too weak and having no encouragement to expect aid from the English), deserted that place" and took up a tract farther to the east, where they established a civil corporation. While Winthrop conceded that some Bay Colony magistrates helped the party acquire a minister and organize themselves for "civil combination," he worried that such settlements could stir up unwanted conflict between Dutch and Bay Colony authorities; the Bay Colony's ambiguous response to William Kieft's complaints about English usurpers on Dutch lands asserted weakly that the English could not "suffer" their compatriots to be "injured." On the other hand, it was clear that because they wished "to hold peace and good correspondency with all our neighbors" and because they "would not maintain any of our countrymen in any unjust action," they would do little or nothing to help them: "those at Long Island . . . went voluntarily from us."[9] Massachusetts evinced only token support of those who sought to ameliorate their "straitened" economic position through out-migration.

The potential dangers to be faced as a result of English usurpations of Dutch-claimed territory seemed less sinister, however, than voluntary agreements between would-be migrants and Dutch authorities. Winthrop told, for example, how in 1641 the Massachusetts magistrates and elders managed to dissuade a group of Lynn and Ipswich inhabitants from accepting a Dutch offer to settle on Long Island:

> This year divers families in Linne and Ipswich having sent to view Long Island, and finding a very commodious place for plantations, but challenged by the Dutch, they treated with the Dutch governor to take it from them. He offered them very fair terms, as that they

should have the very same liberties, both civil and ecclesiastical, which they enjoyed in the Massachusetts, only liberty for appeal to the Dutch, and after ten years to pay the 10th of their corn. The court were offended at this, and sought to stay them, not for going from us, but for strengthening the Dutch, our doubtful neighbors, and taking that from them which our king challenged and had granted a patent of, with Martha's Vineyard and other islands thereby, to the earl of Sterling, especially for binding themselves by an oath of fealty; whereupon divers of the chief being called before the general court . . . and reasons laid down to dissuade them, they were convinced, and promised to desist.[10]

The Bay Colony, gravitating toward an isolationism that would become even more pronounced as the civil war years progessed, desired neither to press English claims at Long Island by providing support to usurpers who moved there nor to acquiesce in Dutch claims by allowing colonists openly to make agreements with Dutch authorities.

John Winthrop and other magistrates viewed as selfish the would-be migrants' willingness to pursue their own economic well-being no matter what the impact on their coreligionists. But the trope of selfishness alone could not fully express the depth of the fears and insecurities that out-migration conjured up among the Bay Colony's orthodox majority. Almost inexorably the attraction to alternative colonizing ventures, raising unpleasant questions about ultimate loyalties, came to be associated with religious apostasy. Part of New Netherland's appeal, after all, lay in its more tolerant approach to religious diversity. Both John Underhill, who eventually moved to New Netherland, and the Lady Deborah Moody, a Lynn Anabaptist who founded the town of Gravesend on Long Island after being excommunicated from her church in Massachusetts, benefited from the Dutch colony's tendency to overlook the failure of important settlers to subscribe to Dutch Reformed orthodoxy.[11]

Still, the most compelling illustration of how closely religious apostasy and economic greed were linked could be found in the fate of Anne Hutchinson, killed by Indians in 1643 along with sixteen of her family members and supporters after having migrated to New Netherland from the radical community-in-exile at Aquidneck, Rhode Island. "These people," wrote Winthrop,

> had cast off ordinances and churches, and now at last their own people, and for larger accommodation had subjected themselves to the Dutch and dwelt scatteringly near a mile asunder: and some that escaped, who had removed only for want (as they said) of hay for their cattle which increased much, now coming back again to Aquiday, they wanted cattle for their grass.[12]

Winthrop suggested here that spiritual antinomianism, acting as a solvent on the bonds of loyalty among people, carried secular consequences harmful to purveyors and critics alike. Those who pursued their own course through some combination of greed, disloyalty, and religious apostasy (the three seemed always to be conjoined) not only injured church and community but also placed themselves beyond the protection of these bulwarks of safety.

EVEN MORE VEXATIOUS than the lure of New Netherland was the appeal, sanctioned by English Puritan leaders, of the West Indies, a place Winthrop believed to be "infected with familism."[13] Artillery Company member John Humphrey, an original member of the Massachusetts Bay Company and the first holder of the title sergeant major general, entered Winthrop's pantheon of antiheroes in the late 1630s, as soon as his interest in the "southern parts" was made manifest. Humphrey, who had married one of the sisters of the earl of Lincoln, entered the colony in 1634 as a promising and well-placed leader whose loyalty appeared beyond reproach. Having been elected magistrate and deputy governor of the Massachusetts Bay Company at a 1629 meeting held in London, Humphrey's actual migration was delayed for several years; but the colonists in Boston consistently elected him to the magistracy because he was "daily expected." In 1633, just one year prior to his migration, Humphrey was among a group of Puritans who did invaluable service to the colony by helping to thwart the efforts of Sir Ferdinando Gorges and Captain John Mason, English proprietors of Maine and New Hampshire respectively, who recommended to the King that the Massachusetts charter be revoked and a general governor appointed to rule the entire New England region. Finally, when Humphrey arrived in the colony, he brought much-needed military supplies, as well as a donation from the Puritan Richard Andrews of sixteen heifers intended to benefit both the clergy and the poor of the colony.[14]

Despite these auspicious beginnings, however, Humphrey soon demonstrated that he could be satisfied neither with the humble livelihood the Bay Colony had to offer nor, perhaps, with its narrow orthodoxy. Having attained freemanship and magisterial status before setting foot in New England, Humphrey unaccountably put off joining a church. In a 1636 letter to Lord Saye and Sele, John Cotton charitably attributed Humphrey's unchurched status to "the unsettledness of the congregation where he liveth"; he then employed the Humphrey example to reassure his correspondent that persons of quality were not summarily stripped of their proper rank in Massachusetts simply because they did not belong to a church:

> A godly woman, being to make choice of an husband, may justly refuse a man that is either cast out of church fellowship or is not yet received into it, but yet when she is once given to him, she may not reject him then for such defect. Mr. Humphrey was chosen for an assistant (as I hear) before the colony came over hither, and, though he be not as yet joined into church fellowship . . . yet the commonwealth do still continue his magistracy to him, as knowing he waiteth for opportunity of enjoying church fellowship shortly.

Cotton's diplomatic words emphasized how Humphrey's status was safely beyond dispute. But the letter could also be read to imply that Humphrey, like the ill-considered hypothetical bridegroom, possessed certain "defects," that, had they been perceived earlier, might have excluded him from the magistracy. The requirements for leadership, Cotton observed, were different "over hither"—a lesson whose full import the teacher of First Church Boston was only just beginning to appreciate.[15]

Humphrey did finally join the congregation of his friend Hugh Peter in Salem. But his religious intentions became a topic for speculation once he became involved in plans to entice New Englanders to Providence Island, an enterprise backed by prominent English Puritans who offered Humphrey the governorship of the island in 1640. In that year it was rumored that Humphrey would recruit to Providence Island Charles Chauncy of Plymouth, a clergyman thought by some to be Anabaptist; an alarmed Thomas Hooker reported to Thomas Shepard news he had heard that "Mr Umphry . . . invites him [Chauncy] to Providence, and that coast is most meet for his opinion and practise."[16] The interest in the Providence Island project manifested by the troublesome Thomas Lechford, whose failure to attain freemanship thwarted his efforts to succeed in the Bay Colony, and Thomas Venner, a Salem wine cooper whose religious radicalism eventually led him into the Fifth Monarchy movement, could only have reinforced the idea that the endeavor was "most meet" for those whose orthodoxy left something to be desired.[17] Humphrey, moreover, was on good terms with the Lady Deborah Moody, a prominent widow of Lynn who also joined Hugh Peter's Salem congregation and who purchased Humphrey's Swampscott farm when he left the Bay. While Moody appeared orthodox when she joined Hugh Peter's church, she was admonished soon after the remigration of Humphrey and Peter for having expressed reservations about infant baptism.[18] Whether or not these views were concealed to the eyes of Humphrey is uncertain, but the connection would be remembered when Humphrey's reputation was subsequently blackened by his involvement with the Providence Island venture.

In the eyes of John Winthrop, Humphrey's worst sin was his disloyalty to New England.[19] Although English Puritans and their New England allies intended the various Puritan-backed colonial projects to complement rather than clash with one another, Winthrop could not help but feel that these efforts represented a deliberate "disparagement" to the colony he had done so much to establish. Winthrop reported learning from "divers letters and reports, that the Lord Say did labor, by disparaging this country, to divert men from coming to us, and so to draw them to the West Indies." An angry Winthrop then wrote to Lord Saye, threatening that the hand of the Lord would be outstretched against all who questioned the destiny or divine credentials of New England:

> The governor [Winthrop] also wrote to the Lord Say about the report aforesaid, and therein showed his lordship, how evident it was, that God had chosen this country to plant his people in, and therefore

how displeasing it would be to the Lord, and dangerous to himself, to hinder this work, or to discourage men from supplying us, by abasing the goodness of the country, which he never saw, and persuading men, that here was no possibility of subsistence.

Lord Saye, nonplussed by Winthrop's anger, responded that Massachusetts might have been "appointed only for a present refuge, etc., and that, a better place being now found out, we were all called to remove thither."

Although Saye bruised Winthrop in this sharp exchange, the Massachusetts governor could nevertheless take heart that the powerful "lords and others of Providence" had begun to be swayed by the success and popularity of the Massachusetts model:

> finding that godly men were unwilling to come under other governors than such as they should make choice of themselves, etc., they condescended to articles somewhat suitable to our form of government, although they had formerly declared themselves much against it, and for a mere aristocracy, and an hereditary magistracy to be settled upon some great persons, etc.[20]

More to the point, God really did seem ready to rebuke those who had "spoken ill of this country, and so discouraged the hearts of his people . . . thinking thereby to further their own plantation." In 1640, he was able to report that a ship dispatched from England with passengers and cargo for Providence Island had been taken by Turks, and that a prize taken by Captain Thomas Newman, who conducted privateering voyages for Providence Island, was seized by "Dunkirkers" before it could reach England.[21]

While Winthrop must have been accustomed to the idea that prominent Englishmen might overlook the importance of Massachusetts, it was more difficult for him to understand why someone like John Humphrey, given his long and valuable service to New England, would adopt such an attitude. The governor therefore related with smug satisfaction the difficulties that Humphrey faced in his attempts to transport colonists to the West Indies; first, a fire, apparently set by his servants, consumed his barn and its valuable contents of corn, hay, and powder; then, in 1641, Spain's conquest of Providence Island put an end to Humphrey's attempts to set himself up as the leader of a Puritan colony intended to rival the Bay. The small band of prospective colonists Humphrey had sent out returned home, some so "ashamed" that they had begged the sailors to carry them to Florida or Virginia instead of Massachusetts so that they would not have to face those in the Bay who had tried to dissuade them from going. "This," a satisfied Winthrop wrote, "brought some of them to see their error, and acknowledge it in the open congregation, but others were hardened."[22] Forsaking New England, these prospective West Indians knew, would be regarded not simply as a wrongheaded or unfortunate decision but as a sin.

Although Humphrey himself was never suitably chastened in public, the Lord, thought Winthrop, duly punished Humphrey with a series of providential humiliations. In a 1642 voyage into England, Humphrey sailed on a ship whose passengers, including three ministers and a schoolmaster, "would needs go [back to England] against all advice." The ship experienced a safe passage until some of the passengers began to cast aspersions upon New England;

> the wind coming up against them, they were tossed up and down, being in 10ber (*December*), so long till their provisions and other necessaries were near spent, and they were forced to strait allowance, yet at length the wind coming fair again, they got into the Sleeve, but then there arose so great a tempest at S.E. as they could bear no sail, and so were out of hope of being saved (being in the night also).

Having ignored the first storm, which had abated, the prideful passengers waited until the second warning before they "humbled themselves before the Lord and acknowledged God's hand to be justly out against them for speaking evil of this good land and the Lord's people here."[23] At this point the weather calmed, and the ship reached port. Still, the Lord was not through with Humphrey.

So resentful were New Englanders of the former sergeant major general's actions that even the sexual abuse of his daughters at the hands of servants and a neighbor was regarded as divine retribution for Humphrey's neglect of his communal obligations. In describing the misfortunes that stalked those ship's passengers who had derided New England, Winthrop explained how "One had a daughter that presently ran mad, and two other of his daughters, being under ten years of age, were discovered to have been often abused by divers lewd persons, and filthiness in his family."[24] Just as Humphrey had abandoned his responsibilities to the colony, which Winthrop conceived as a mutually dependent extended family, so too had he abandoned his biological family. For Winthrop, it stood to reason that a failure to fulfill the obligations to one sort of family would lead to a similar failure to exercise due care over the other.

Humphrey's connection with the Providence Island Company caused Bay Colony residents to doubt his motives in all undertakings regarding the relationship with England. In 1641 English Puritans advised that Massachusetts send over some emissaries to "solicit for us in the parliament, giving us hope that we might obtain much." The first reaction to this suggestion was defensive:

> consulting about it, we declined the motion for this consideration, that if we should put ourselves under the protection of the parliament, we must then be subject to all such laws as they should make, or at least such as they might impose on us; in which course though they should intend our good, yet it might prove very prejudicial to us.[25]

The colonists, determined to follow an independent course, were wary of their allies in the metropolis, some of whom disapproved of the New England Way. The impulse to shrink from sending representatives soon passed, however, because, in light of the depression that hit in 1640, there was a need to explain to English creditors why many of the colony's financial obligations had not been met and to explore opportunities for trade and regional economic development. While the magistrates could agree thus far, the decision to include Hugh Peter among the representatives became controversial because of the strong influence that John Humphrey was thought to hold over his longtime acquaintance.[26]

John Endecott of Salem, a member of Peter's congregation, headed a group who opposed Peter being sent to England on the grounds that the clergyman might never return to the Bay Colony and that such a mission might give the impression that "we were in such want as we had sent to England to beg relief, which would be very dishonorable to religion, and that we ought to trust God who had never failed us hitherto." Such an eventuality, it was hinted, would be all the more likely since Humphrey intended to make a trip into England on the same ship that would take the commissioners there and since the other delegates, William Hibbens and Thomas Weld, were "well affected" toward colonizing schemes in the West Indies. In a letter to Winthrop, Endecott argued that the colony's woes were not so great as most colonists thought and that they could be solved if only people would rely on God and give up the sinful extravagances of imported "wines and liquors and English provisions of dyett and onnecessarie braverie in apparrell" that dragged the economy down. Having depicted England as the source of corrupting luxuries, Endecott also asked Winthrop to consider whether "it be not somewhat preposterous to goe from a place of safetie provided of God, to a place of danger under the hand of God to seeke reliefe for us." To Winthrop, it appeared that the "main reason . . . privately intimated" for Endecott's opposition was the "fear lest he [Peter] should be kept there, or diverted to the West Indies, for Mr Humfrey intended to go with him, who was already engaged that way by the lord Say, etc., and therefore it was feared he should fall under strong temptations that way, being once in England." As if to confirm these suspicions, an irate Humphrey, learning of the Salem magistrate's antipathy, soon fell "foul upon Mr. Endecott in the open assembly at Salem for opposing this motion."[27]

Endecott's objections ultimately went unheeded. But his worst fears were realized when the valuable Hugh Peter became caught up in the civil wars and never returned to Massachusetts. Humphrey's unsettling influence, meanwhile, continued to be felt through 1643, when he was blamed for Captain John Chaddock's voyage from the West Indies to Boston in search of colonists for Trinidad; Humphrey, according to Winthrop, had informed the earl of Warwick, who employed the troublesome Chaddock, that "he might be supplied from hence."[28]

During the civil war years in England, John Humphrey, as well as Hugh Peter, became avid supporters of Independency and participated in a series of ventures launched by leading mercantile and gentry figures whose political programs and colonizing projects relied increasingly on tolerationist ideas that contrasted sharply with the New England Way. Although Peter had been opposed to Hutchinson during the antinomian controversy, he had shown sympathy toward Knollys and Underhill, who had symbolized how religious apostasy might be channeled to support geographical expansionism and aggression. During the 1640s in England, Peter waxed positively eloquent in his defiance of presbyterian calls for religious uniformity. According to his enemy Thomas Edwards, Peter

> improved his time . . . Preaching against the Reformed Church and the Presbyteriall Government . . . and for a Toleration of all Sects . . . he preached . . . that the word Uniformity was not in all the Scripture, but the word Unity . . . that in Holland, an Anabaptist, a Brownist, an Independent, a Papist, could live all quietly together, and why should they not here? that in the Army there were twenty several opinions, and they could live quietly together.

Edwards, a presbyterian, was bound to present Peter in the worst possible light. But Peter's correspondence and writings show that he had come strongly to disapprove rigid intolerance in England and New England alike. In a 1645 letter to John Winthrop, Jr., Peter expressed simultaneously his high regard for the future remonstrant Robert Child and his reservations concerning the narrowness of the New England Way; Child, according to Peter, was "that honest man who will bee of exceeding great use if the country know how to improve him . . . let us not play tricks with such men by our jealousyes." In 1646, he warned his friends in Massachusetts that "None will come to you because you persecute. Cannot you mend it?" One year later, Peter exclaimed how a "sweet New England" would be "yet sweeter if divisions bee not among you," and he recommended that those in authority "give . . . incouragement to those that are godly and shall differ etc . . . doe what you can herein and know that your example in all kinds swayse here."[29]

In 1647, meanwhile, John Humphrey invested in a Puritan-backed scheme to establish an explicitly tolerationist colony in the Bahamas (Eleutheria), the population of which was to be drawn from a defeated and demoralized faction of Puritan settlers (which had been cultivated in the 1640s by future Bay Colony minister John Oxenbridge) living in Bermuda. Historian Robert Brenner has argued that key individuals who would later mold the Cromwellian Protectorate framed this endeavor more as a political gambit than an economic project. By touting Eleutheria as an "explicitly oligarchic republican and tolerationist project," Brenner explains, Bahamas investors were unveiling their best hopes for the Commonwealth. At the same time, they deliberately needled "presbyterian" supporters of uniformity, using the *Articles and Orders*, a tract that laid out the objectives of the proposed settlement, as a platform from which to denounce "the great inconveniencies that have happened, both in this Kingdom of England, and other places, by a rigid imposing upon all an uniformity and conformity in matters of judgement and practice in the things of Religion, whereby divisions have been made, factions fomented, persecutions induced, and the publick peace endangered."[30]

The saints, according to this document, might appear to differ because all "hath not the same place and office, nor the same measure of light"; but these apparent differences should not be used as an excuse for preventing all, both "babes and strongmen in Christ," from "walk[ing] according to what they have received, in all godliness, justice and sobriety"; "we well know that in this state of darkness and imperfecton we know but in part." The only way to avoid the "inconveniencies" of unfounded persecution, according to the *Articles and Orders*—and to ensure that "strongmen" in Christ were free to explore the "light"—was to forbid not only magisterial controls on orthodoxy but also the use of divisive sectarian descriptors:

> It is therefore ordered . . . That there shall be no names of distinction or reproach, as Independent, Antinomian, Anabaptist, or any other cast upon any such for their difference in judgement, neither yet shall any person or persons, assume or acknowledge any such distinguishing names . . . That no Magistracie or Officers of the Republike, nor any power derived from them, shall take notice of any man for his difference in judgement in matter of religion, or have cognizance of any cause whatsoever of that nature: But that their jurisdiction shall reach onely to men as men, and shall take care that justice, peace and sobriety, may be maintained among them.[31]

Though its English backers framed the Eleutheria project to gall "political presbyterians" in England, the scheme proved no less offensive to key figures in Massachusetts. In 1648 John Winthrop recorded, with no small pleasure, how the venture was, quite literally, torn apart, first through factional infighting touched off by a young man who "could not endure any ordinances or worship" and then by a providential shipwreck that destroyed the nascent colony's provisions and forced all the settlers "to lie in the open air, and to feed upon such fruits and wild creatures as the island afforded." To a disdainful Winthrop, it seemed as though the colony's "covenant and articles" contained the seeds of anarchy and destruction: "the first article was for liberty of conscience, wherein they provided, that the civil magistrate should not have cognizance of any matter which concerned religion, but every man might enjoy his own opinion or religion, without control or question." Such "liberty," Winthrop thought, could easily degenerate into godlessness: "nor was there any word of maintaining or professing any religion or worship of God at all."[32]

Winthrop's comments on Eleutheria had been prompted by a request for advice from the leaders of a small Puritan congregation on the Nansemond River in Virginia, who wondered, in light of Governor Berkeley's recent banishment of their pastor and elder, whether they should relocate their flock to the "Summers Islands." Governor William Sayle had himself invited the Virginians to settle in the Bermuda islands when he had trav- eled to the Chesapeake in search of supplies for his perishing colonists in the wake of the shipwreck. Bay Colony magistrates advised their corelig- ionists in Virginia that, because there was the "hope of a far more plentiful harvest at hand," they "should not be hasty to remove, as long as they could stay [in the Chesapeake] upon any tolerable terms." Winthrop con- ceded that the harried southern congregation had been inclined to "listen" seriously to Sayle's proposal, "but after they had seen a copy of his com- mission and articles . . . they paused upon it (for the church were very or- thodox and zealous for the truth) and would not resolve before they had received advice from us." The message from the Bay Colony was unequiv- ocal: "letters were returned to them, dissuading them from joining with that people under those terms."³³ A well-controlled environment in which congregational purity could be maintained, with a greater harvest of souls someday anticipated, was safer, both practically and religiously, the Bay Colonists seemed to be saying to their fellow Puritans, than "liberty of conscience."

Nathaniel Ward, who had served briefly in Massachusetts as a preacher in Ipswich and who emerged in civil war England as a promoter of unifor- mity, an exposer of the dangers of "polypiety," and a pamphleteer whose favorite target was Hugh Peter, similarly singled out the Bahamas project for special criticism. Massachusetts, of course, ostensibly aligned itself with Independency; but Nathaniel Ward's thinking, contoured by his exposure to the New England Way, was nonetheless very similar to that of "pres- byterian" pamphleteers like William Prynne.³⁴ Ward, whose affinity with "presbyterianism" came because of and not in spite of his devotion to the New England Way, reacted with predictable horror to the tolerationist ethos manifested in the Bahamas project:

> Here is lately brought us an Extract of a Magna Charta so called, compiled between the Sub-planters of a West-Indian Island; whereof the first Aricle of constipulation, firmely provides free stable-roome and litter for all kinde of consciences, be they never so dirty or jadish; making it actionable, yea, treasonable, to disturb any man in his Re- ligion, or to discommend it, whatever it be. We are very sorrow to see such professed profanenesse in English Professors, as industriously to lay their Religious foundations on the Ruine of true Religion; which strictly bindes every conscience to contend earnestly for the Truth: to preserve unity of spirit, faith, and Ordinances, to be all like minded, of one accord; every man to take his brother into his Chris- tian care; to stand fast with one spirit, with one minde, striving to- gether for the faith of the Gospel: and by no meanes to permit Heresies or erroneous opinions: But God abhorring such loathsome beverages, hath in his righteous judgement blasted that enterprize,

which might otherwise have prospered well, for ought I know: I pre-sume the case is generally known ere this.[35]

Styling himself the "simple cobler of Aggawam in America," Ward affected the same meekness of manner and some of the same arguments that Thomas Shepard, Peter Bulkeley, and John Winthrop had marshaled during the antinomian controversy. Charging that the Independent reli-gious milieu of the 1640s was rife with "anabaptists" and those claiming to possess a "faith that can professedly live with two or three sordid sins" (antinomianism), Ward vowed "to help mend his Native Country, lam-entably tattered, both in the upper-Leather and sole, with all the honest stitches he can take . . . willing never to bee paid for his work, by Old English wonted pay."[36] Like the orthodox critics of antinomianism in New England, Ward associated both heresy itself and the toleration of "one Religion in segregant shapes" with unnecessary complexity, dissimulation, a desire to separate spirit from embodied reality, and an ill will "bred of the Exhalations of . . . pride and self-wittednesse":

> The finer Religion grows the finer he [Satan] spins his Cobwebs, he will hold pace with Christ so long as his wits will serve him. Hee sees himselfe beaten out of grosse Idolatries, Heresies, Ceremonies, where the Light breakes forth with power; he will therefore bestirre him to prevaricate Evangelicall Truths, and Ordinances, that if they will needs be walking, yet they shall . . . not keep their path. . . . The power of all Religion and Ordinances, lies in their purity; their purity in their simplicity: then are mixtures pernicious. . . . The wisest way, when all is said, is with all humility and feare, to take Christ as him-selfe hath revealed himselfe in his Gospel, and not as the Divell presents him to prestigiated phansies. I have ever hated the way of the Rosie-Crucians, who reject things as Gods wisdome hath tem-pered them, and will have nothing but their spirits.[37]

In advocating a wider latitude in spiritual matters, men like John Hum-phrey and Hugh Peter, who identified with English Independency, never intended to institute full-blown tolerationism as we would understand that concept in the twentieth century. Rather, these men cautioned against the sharp religious disputation that might harm the cause by setting the godly against one another, and they recommended that distinctions be made between those essential truths that must never be compromised and those less crucial principles that might still be peaceably debated by reasonable people in good faith.[38] Peter, for example, who believed that too much precision caused the saints wrongfully to interpret honest differences as evidence of heresy, longed for a "union betwixt all men truly godly, that we may swim in one channel . . . with free and loving debates allowed in every county that we may convince not confound one another."[39] For Ward, Winthrop, and the orthodox party in Massachusetts, on the other hand, these views seemed to place the godly on the leading edge of a slippery slope. By giving credence to people's uncorroborated claims of having experienced different manifestations of the same "light," religious toleration, no matter how limited, would rest on the same logic as heresy. If the scales balancing word and spirit were tipped in favor of invisible spirit, and if it were conceded that some, albeit nonessential, truths might be judged differently depending on the idiosyncratic experiences of various individuals with the "light"—then people of an uncomfortably wide variety of judgments would eventually thrive, since there could be no earthly way to validate the truth or worth of their assertions.

By identifying himself as someone who had experience in "America," Ward implied that his encounter with the chaste "ordinances" of New England endowed him with a special authority to speak on matters involving purity; New England was simple and wholesome, while England in these "slippery" times was becoming complicated and corrupt.[40] Still, Ward's eager identification with the New World was by no means an out-and-out endorsement of colonization: "Englishmen, be advised to love England . . . since the pure Primitive time, the Gospel never thrived so well in any soile on earth, as in the British . . . if ye lose that country, and finde a better before ye come to Heaven, my Cosmography failes me." Bay Colony residents, because they had truly been called to New England, had been empowered to resist the temptations of the wilderness, for "if God calls any into a Wildernesse, He will be no wildernesse to them." But Ward, whose heart "naturally detested . . . Forrainers dwelling in my Countrey" and "crowd[ing] out native Subjects into the corners of the Earth," perceived there to be a danger in colonial schemes not so well controlled and principled as Massachusetts. The transformation of England into a polyglot transatlantic empire might be its undoing, Ward warned, for "it is much to be feared, that laxe Tolerations upon State-pretences and planting necessities, will be the next subtle Stratagem he [the Devil] will spread, to distate the Truth of God and supplant the peace of the Churches."[41]

Nathaniel Ward and John Winthrop were ideologically far apart on some issues; Winthrop looked with a jaundiced eye on Ward's agitation for a written code of law, and he criticized an election sermon Ward had preached that drew too heavily, in Winthrop's opinion, on secular classical sources.[42] Still, there was much that Winthrop and Ward had in common; just as Winthrop and other orthodox souls worried about the influence of people with cosmopolitan interests on New England, so too did Ward fret over the repercussions on England of social experimentation in the colonies. Ward's thinking helps us to understand the ambivalence some New England leaders felt toward the transatlantic aims of English Independency. The Ipswich minister's suspicion of "Forrainers," his longing for a strictly bounded and homogeneous English community, his preference for "simple coblers" over deceitful men of "Paracelsian parts" (such as the disruptive European-educated alchemist Robert Child), and his fear that intense contact with outsiders would somehow pollute English culture were all very much reinforced, perhaps derived from, his experience in Massachusetts.[43]

For Ward, the cosmopolitan, peripatetic lifestyle taken up by so many seventeenth-century transatlantic figures was dangerous, and the image of seemingly out-of-control mobility came easily to mind as the most fitting analogue to religious heresy:

> The good Spirit of God doth not usually tie up the Helme, and suffer passengers to Heaven to ride a drift, hither and thither, as every wave and current carryes them: that is a fitter course for . . . wandring Starres and Meteors, without any certain motion hurryed about with tempests, bred of the Exhalations of their own pride and self-wittednesse: whose damnation sleepeth not, and to whom the mist of darknesse is reserved for ever.[44]

Given these attitudes, it should not be surprising that important Bay Colony figures who developed alliances with forces outside the colony, or who attempted simultaneously to serve colony and commonwealth, were regarded with mixed feelings.

THE MASSACHUSETTS CAREERS of Underhill, and especially Humphrey, illustrate how easily ties to a more fluid transatlantic world, or a seemingly selfish pursuit of private over public goals, could be conflated with religious apostasy and disloyalty to the New England Way. Underhill and Humphrey were able to maintain good reputations in the colony only for relatively brief periods of time. Other military and mercantile elite men, however, whose highly successful New England careers spanned much longer periods of time, continued through the 1640s and 1650s to manifest the same keen desire to be enmeshed in the transatlantic community. Yet even when such desires were fulfilled by rendering service to the Parliamentary and Cromwellian armies, "jealousies" on the part of committed New Englanders could easily be aroused.

The seaman and merchant Nehemiah Bourne, who returned permanently to England in the 1640s, worried that his reputation in Massachusetts would suffer once he moved his wife and children out of the colony. In a letter written in 1648 from a merchant ship in Newfoundland, Bourne tried to reassure Governor John Winthrop that his removal and his present inability to visit Boston and "see your face" was not intended as a slight:

> I am yours in heart, though kept at a distance for the present by my lawfull and necessary imployments, and I cannot but look westward. The Lord knowes my heart reaches further then I can with my body attaine. I know I am lyable to the apprehensions and conclusions that all may conceave and conclude from my absence, and the present removall of my Family, yet do assure yow that gods providence outwent my purposes . . . ther was no designe in us either at first or last going over to pluck up my stakes or to disjoynt myself from yow.

Bourne, a prominent Boston shipbuilder who would go on to occupy a series of important military and administrative posts in the Commonwealth army and navy, had openly expressed his strong reservations toward the Bay Colony's religious restrictions in 1645, when he signed a petition in favor of tolerating Anabaptists.[45]

Bourne's disaffection toward strict "orthodoxy" came to him partially as a result of having witnessed the brutalities of civil war in England. In a tract written in 1642 describing the "battell fought on Saturday last at Acton, between the kings Army, and the Earl of Essex his forces," Bourne showed how parliamentary troops "slew on like Tygers" until they prevailed over an adversary that outnumbered and outgunned them. Still, having seen personally how war "causeth so many dead corps to lye on the ground as now doth, to the great terror and affrightment of all the beholders," Bourne was compelled to exhort people to seek a reversal of their potentially worsening fortunes not only through regeneration but also through a clearer commitment to unity and brotherhood, in which God would "unite us all in one, that we may be all of one Church, and of one Resolution, and that we may not stand in opposition one against another." His recommendation that Englishmen metamorphose into "new creatures" did not imply that converts should embrace a specific outward form of Christianity, such as the New England Way, but rather that they should embark upon a general reformation, encompassing as many of the godly as possible, prompted by seeing their plight in the context of the worldwide Protestant struggle. Bourne used the example of the Palatinate to remind readers of the price they might be called on to pay if unity could not be achieved:

we all know that was the flourishingest Kingdom in all Christendome: but the Lord sent first the Sword that devoured many a thousand, then came the pestilence, that swept away many, then came famine, so these three together hath made it a depollished Countrey, it is credibly reported that a man may travell a hundred miles and not see a Town, nor . . . man woman nor child: the first is begun here, but let us all humbly and joyntly together shew unto the Lord that he will keep the others from us which we may dayly expect continuing in our sinne and wickednesse.[46]

Bourne's advice, and his encouragement to think in international terms, went unheeded in Massachusetts. When Puritan prospects in England were dimmed by the Restoration, Bourne, writing from Hamburg in 1662, explained to John Winthorp, Jr. how some of their "friends" hesitated to flee to New England because they feared the "prickles that are neere the rose, least the one may vex more then the other refresh." Bourne was still waiting "upon the good hands of the Lord, to point out" his own "way," confessing to Winthrop that while he regarded New England with "charity" and "hope," he nonetheless had "too much cause to lament the severe and narrow spiritt amongst them who have had a large and plentifull experience of the grace of God to themselves."[47]

NEHEMIAH BOURNE'S FRUSTRATIONS were shared by a number of New England merchants and military men who had gravitated toward parliamentary and Cromwellian service in England. John Leverett and Robert Sedgwick, in particular, were able to finesse their New England careers more adroitly than Bourne; but, as in his case, these men's sympathies for religious views at odds with the New England Way had deepened or developed during their service in England, and when they returned to the Bay they spearheaded efforts to ameliorate the colony's policy of religious intolerance.[48] At the same time, they recommended an aggressive program of conquest and trade modeled on the ethos of the Protectorate but not always welcome in the eyes of wary Massachusetts magistrates. The Parliamentary cause was so identified with the New England Way that, as the Jennison episode illustrates, no criticisms of it could be voiced in Boston. Yet in practice it was sometimes difficult for Bostonians to determine whether actual participants should be hailed as returning heroes or feared as agents of cultural contamination.

John Leverett, who would preside as governor of Massachusetts in the 1670s, and Robert Sedgwick, who died while participating in Cromwell's Western Design, were dominant personalities in the mercantile and military world of mid-seventeenth-century Boston. Both men rose in Massachusetts to become regimental leaders and majors general (the highest military rank in the colony); both, often in partnership, were involved in transatlantic trade; both served in the parliamentary and Commonwealth armies; and both labored in the 1640s and 1650s to make New England's ways more consistent with those of the metropolis.[49] To the latter end, Sedgwick, along with fellow Artillery Company member Nehemiah Bourne, affixed his signature in 1645 to a failed petition requesting a relaxation of the laws against Anabaptism. And in subsequent years Leverett, as a General Court deputy, not only objected to the fining of Malden inhabitants who had supported the supposedly heterodox clergyman Marmaduke Matthews but joined Artillery Company members Thomas Clark, William Tyng, and Jeremy Houchin (among others) in opposing the move to establish the Cambridge Platform as a uniform confession of faith.[50]

The calling in 1646 of the Cambridge Synod, a gathering of ministers charged by the General Court with issuing an official statement of Bay Colony church government and discipline, had been a defensive measure taken, in part, to counteract merchant Robert Child's demand that all freeborn Englishmen receive full civil liberties regardless of church membership. It was objectionable to men like Leverett both because it appeared to be an attempt to impose on the Bay Colony a "uniformity" that would diminish the independence of individual congregations and because it asserted (though with many caveats) that magistrates should have a role in the enforcement of right religion. "The end of the Magistrates office," the synod proclaimed, "is not only the quiet and peaceable life of the subject, in matters of righteousness and honesty, but also in matters of godliness yea of all godliness." According to John Winthrop, the individuals who agitated against the calling of the Cambridge Synod opposed the coercive power it would appear to give to civil authorities:

> their objections were these, first, because therein civil authority did require the churches to send their messengers to it, and divers among them were not satisfied of any such power given by Christ to the civil magistrate over the churches in such cases; secondly, whereas the main end of the synod was propounded to be, an agreement upon one uniform practice in all the churches, the same to be commended to the general court, etc., this seemed to give power either to the synod or the court to compel the churches to practise what should so be established . . . hence was inferred that this synod was appointed by the elders, to the intent to make ecclesiastical laws to bind the churches, and to have the sanction of the civil authority put upon them, whereby men should be forced under penalty to submit to them, whereupon they concluded that they should betray the liberty of the churches, if they should consent to such a synod.[51]

Men like Leverett, Clark, Sedgwick, Bourne, and Hutchinson appreciated how English Puritans had yoked their expansive vision of Puritanism to an impressive array of religious, political, economic, and military goals; Winthrop himself complained that the "principal men" who opposed the calling of the Cambridge Synod because it would "betray the liberty of the churches" were "some of Boston, who came lately from England, where such a vast liberty was allowed, and sought for by all that went under the name of Independents . . . To these did some others of the church of Boston adhere, but not above thirty or forty in all." Both Leverett and Nehemiah Bourne, for example, served together for about a year in a parliamentary regiment commanded by Colonel Thomas Rainsborough and officered primarily by Artillery Company members drawn from New England; Israel Stoughton was lieutenant colonel, Nehemiah Bourne major, John Leverett captain, and William Hudson ensign. Thomas Rainsborough, whose brother William had joined the Boston Artillery Company during a brief period of settlement in Massachusetts, was, like many of his fellow London merchants, committed to a tolerationist course that would permit a political alliance between Puritan interests and the radical sects; he believed too that Puritans must, through trade and conquest, spread their influence throughout the world and defend the Protestant interest wherever it was challenged.[52]

Several years before Leverett, Bourne, and the other New England officers joined his regiment, Rainsborough had been involved in an enterprise that reflected these goals perfectly—the Additional Sea Adventure to Ireland. The Irish rebellion of 1641, seen as evidence of a Catholic/

royalist plot, motivated leading Puritans to put together a venture that rendered broad policy initiatives dependent on individual initiative and hopes of private gain, for in the absence of sufficient public funding, committed Puritans volunteered to invest and man an expedition in exchange for conquered Irish land. The two Rainsboroughs had served on the Additional Sea Adventure to Ireland with two former New Englanders, Captain John Humphrey and Chaplain Hugh Peter, both of whom had found Massachusetts too constraining.[53] John Leverett and Nehemiah Bourne, serving with Rainsborough in 1644, found congenial—and perhaps tried to imitate—both the tolerationist spirit and the enterprising nature manifested by this energetic Puritan.

Nowhere is Bay Colony ambivalence toward the larger Puritan mission more pronounced than in reactions to the New World exploits of Oliver Cromwell.[54] If exposure to tolerationist circles in Puritan London caused some influential New Englanders to press for the acceptance of similar principles in Massachusetts, so too was the most extreme Puritans' linking together of private gain with public service deemed worthy of emulation. In July 1652 the Protectorate, whose leaders believed that England must surpass the Dutch in trade in order to achieve national superiority, commenced the first Anglo-Dutch War.[55] John Leverett, who had consistently been attempting to press tolerationist principles upon the Bay Colony, and Robert Sedgwick, who had himself seen service in the parliamentary army, seemed determined, for their own as well as larger ends, to extend this war to New England, despite the reluctance of the dominant faction of Bay Colony magistrates. As I will show, Leverett and Sedgwick jockeyed for official positions—as commissioners to New Netherland and as messengers to England—that would allow them to hasten the drift toward a war that fellow colonists perceived as compromising the "independence" and purity of Massachusetts.

The colonies of Connecticut and New Haven had long experienced differences with New Netherland over boundaries, ship seizures, restrictions on trade, and tariffs. Early in 1653 a new and more immediate danger was added to these chronic tensions, as rumors began to spread that the Dutch, anticipating the extension of the Anglo-Dutch War to the New World, had allied themselves with Ninigret, sachem of the Narragansetts, in a plan to wipe out the English colonies. Information regarding the plot, which Ninigret vigorously denied, had originated with the Mohegan sachem Uncas, an inveterate foe of the Narragansetts. Uncas informed the Connecticut governor John Haynes that the Narragansett sachem and some of his men had spent the winter of 1652–53 at New Amsterdam, where they had entered a "league" of friendship with the Dutch by exchanging presents with Peter Stuyvesant. Ninigret, according to Uncas, then sought further allies by declaiming "against the English and Uncas and what great Injuries hee had sustained by them" both to his Dutch hosts and to a gathering of Indians "over Hudsons River." Uncas asserted too that Ninigret had paid a "Monheage" sachem to locate a powwow "skilfull in magicke workings and an artest in poisoning" for the purpose of doing away with Uncas. He knew all this, he said, because his men had apprehended seven people returning from "Manhatoes"—four Narragansetts, one Pequot, and some strangers. During questioning, two of these prisoners "freely confessed the whole plott formerly expressed and that one of there companie was that Powaugh and poisoner pointing out the man"; Uncas's subordinates immediately killed the powwow for fear "least hee should make an escape or otherwise doe either mischeife to Uncas or the English."[56] Subsequently Uncas was able to produce two other captives, a Narragansett and a Monhegan, who would testify before Haynes in Hartford as to the existence of the plot.

The English knew that the Narragansetts had reason to bear them, and their Mohegan allies, ill will. Back in 1644, the United Colonies had given their ally Uncas, sachem of the Mohegans, what amounted to a license to murder Miantonomi, the former Narragansett sachem, for having threatened to create a pan-Indian union to oust the English from Indian lands. Ten years later it seemed logical to suppose that current troubles with Ninigret were simply an extension of the earlier conflict.[57] When in the late summer of 1653 Ninigret's men attacked Long Island Indians loyal to the English, it was assumed that the sachem was taking revenge for the Long Islanders' earlier part in the downfall of Miantonomi, the events

> calling to mind the concurrant testimonies they had from the Indians in severall parts of the Countrey of Myantonimoes Treachorus plots about ten years sence to engage all the Indians by giuftes to cut of att once the whole body of the English in these parts and that the longe Island Indians were among those whoe . . . might in the Narragansetts conceite bee (with others) Instrumentall causes of theire proud Sagamors death.

The United Colonies commissioners could not forget how, in the wake of Miantonomi's killing, Ninigret had "proudly and Insolently" delivered threats against his English and Mohegan foes, and "what provocking tearmes hee sent to them Namly that if they did not withdraw theire Garrisons from Uncas hee would procure as many Mahaukes as the English should affront them with." Ninigret had promised, moreover, to "lay the English Cattle on heapes as high as theire houses and that noe English man should stirr out to pisse but hee should be killed."[58]

Although war between the English and Narragansetts had been averted in 1645, colonists feared that Ninigret was "returning" to this earlier defiant "frame." Ninigret's reported demeanor toward United Colonies emissaries Richard Waite and John Barrell, for example, appeared threatening. While Ninigret denied firmly all knowledge of plots afoot against the English, he alluded forebodingly to how he had heard from some unnamed Indians in "Manhatoes" that the "English and Duch were fighting together in theire owne countrey and that there were severall other shipps cominge with ammunition to fight against the English heer and that there would bee a great blow given to the English when they came." Maintaining steadily that he journeyed to Dutch territory solely to "take Phisicke for my health," Ninigret insisted that he did not know if these stories of Dutch strength were true; nor had he entered or been invited to join a "league" with the Dutch.[59]

From the outset, New Englanders were disinclined to believe the claims made by Ninigret and his fellow sachems Mixam and Pessacus. The Narragansett version of events must have seemed even more dubious to New England eyes when information Ninigret later transmitted through his messenger Awashaw conflicted in some details with the earlier testimony presented to Richard Waite. The United Colonies required the Narragansetts to send messengers—or preferably the sachems themselves—into Hartford or Boston to "give satisfaction" concerning the Indians' intentions and the meaning of recent events. Awashaw, the designated leader of the Narragansett delegation, reiterated Ninigret's claim that he had traveled to New Netherland for his health. But Ninigret elected at this time to provide more details that subtly changed his story; it was now learned that the healer Ninigret had sought was a Frenchman and that John Winthrop, Jr., widely regarded for his medical skills, had known of the planned journey. By invoking the Winthrop name and giving the New Englanders to understand that he was not trucking with powwows, Ninigret, although he refused to appear before the commissioners in person, clearly hoped to present himself in a better light. Still, the reference to the French could not have been comforting; and while Ninigret had claimed to Waite earlier that he had neither met with Peter Stuyvesant nor received guns in exchange for wampum, Awashaw now gave out that Ninigret indeed met with the Dutch director general and had procured coats (not guns) for his wampum; later he received two guns (not twenty) in trade with Indians (not Stuyvesant).[60]

Evidence of a Dutch–Narragansett alliance, meanwhile, came from a wide variety of sources. John Underhill, now living at Hempstead, and, as I have shown, interested in manipulating these events for his own purposes, sent word to New Haven that reliable Long Island Indians had informed him of the existence of a Narragansett–Dutch alliance; the United Colonies learned too that Underhill, having rashly accused the Dutch fiscal of plotting against the English, had been "fetched from Flushing by the fiscal with a gaurd of souldiers and confind to the Monhatoes till the Relation hee made att Hempsteed was affeirmed to his [the fiscal's] face then without triall or hearing hee was dismised and all his charges borne."[61] Underhill's release seemed to signify an admission on the part of the Dutch that the captain's accusations were true. From Long Island also came chilling accounts of how English colonists had been told they could soon expect an "East India breakfast," a reference to a thirty-year-old incident at Amboyna in the East Indies, where the Dutch had wiped out an English trading station in a most "horrid Treacherus and crewill" manner. A tract published in 1653 in England to whip up popular excitement for war warned that the "treacherous Cruelty" exhibited by the Dutch at Amboyna was now "extending itself from the East to the West Indiaes," where the Netherlanders had already manifested rank ingratitude toward John Underhill, who, "with the hazard and some loss of English Blood," had earlier aided them in their Indian wars and "resetled the Hollander in peace and safety."[62] Closer to home, Rhode Islanders reported how Pomhom and Sacononoco, two sachems estranged from the Narragansetts because of their cooperation with the English, had reconciled with Ninigret, their "Discourse" being now

> wholy in high comendation of the Duch with Disrespect to the English that the Duch promise to furnish them with comodities att the halfe the prise the English sell them; that they are furnished with powder plentifully as if it were sand; that Nimnegrett hath brought wildfier from the Duch which being shott with theire Arrowes will kindle and burne any thinge; that hee had charged his men to procure amunition of all sorts; and within that time they should drinke strong lyquors without limits.[63]

Throughout the crisis occasioned by the Anglo–Dutch War and local encounters with seemingly hostile Narragansetts, John Leverett and Robert Sedgwick worked toward goals that ran contrary to those of the majority of Massachusetts magistrates, who, regardless of damaging evidence against the Dutch and Narragansetts, preferred neutrality. In May 1653 Leverett accepted an appointment from the United Colonies to travel to New Netherland as part of a three-man committee whose ostensible purpose was to authenticate or rule out rumors of Dutch involvement with the Narragansetts. The behavior of these commissioners, and the subtly worded instructions they had received from the United Colonies, suggests that the minds of those New Englanders who took an active role in these affairs had been made up long before the commission arrived in Dutch territory.

The United Colonies directed Leverett and his companions to deliver an accusatory letter to Dutch authorities; to demand a joint investigation into the widespread allegations of a Dutch–Narragansett alliance; to collect testimony from Indian and English witnesses in the towns of western Connecticut and Long Island; to impress upon the Dutch that the United Colonies would not allow "theire Countrey men causlessly and upon such accounts to bee oppressed"; and to meet with John Underhill and receive from him "two letters . . . which you shall coseale from all such as will take advantage against him . . . himselfe and the English att Hempsteed will produce such Evidence as the case requires."[64] While Leverett and the other emissaries did make a halfhearted attempt to reach some sort of agreement with Dutch authorities as to how a joint investigation should be conducted, negotiations quickly broke down, and the Leverett commission spent most of its time gathering information on its own. This outcome by no means contradicted the spirit of the instructions provided by the United Colonies, which suggested that, while trying to come to an understanding with the Dutch, the representatives

> may by conference and observation have oppertunitie to enforme youer selves and us of sundrey things very considerable as the State of affaires which wee need not mention particulares to you if you Receive any newes waighty and Important either from Europe Verginnia or other partes you will send it hither with all possible speed.[65]

In essence, the United Colonies encouraged the commissioners to gather intelligence about the Dutch—or, more plainly, spy on them—under cover of negotiation.

As events played out, the commissioners offended their reluctant hosts not only by collecting information independently of Dutch authorities but also by rushing back to New England before the Dutch governor, Peter Stuyvesant, was able to complete his lengthy rebuttal to the charges laid against his colony. Stuyvesant deeply resented the short shrift he was given by the negotiators, and he referred in a subsequent letter to the

> sudden Departure of youer Messengers contrary to our freindly Invitation without coming to any conclusion about those weighty affaires as theire order and Comission did Import or giveing any punctuall answare to our well meaning propositions makeing soe great hast that they would not attend one halfe day to take our answare with them; unto youer honored large and considerate Message.

While adamantly denying any involvement with the Narragansetts and dismissing as preposterous any comparison between current events and the Amboyna tragedy, Stuyvesant chided the commissioners of the United Colonies for the behavior of messengers who seemed more intent on finding justification for war than grounds for peace; this, he wrote

> might cause in us thoughts of noe Real Intencions [for an amicable understanding,] how evell [however] wee have have made the best Construction of It; youer messengers Cloaking theire suddaine Departure under pretence of the day of election to bee held this weeke att Boston att which they must appeer if posible.[66]

Although Massachusetts had acquiesced for several months in the investigation of rumors about a Dutch–Narragansett alliance, Governor Simon Bradstreet, expressing his own "particular thoughts," announced categorically in the fall of 1653 that Massachusetts would not support the impending declaration of war against Ninigret pressed by the leaders of Connecticut and New Haven. There was no denying that the Narragansetts had sent raiding parties out against the English-allied Indians of Long Island or that Ninigret had behaved recalcitrantly toward a delegation sent from the United Colonies (including Massachusetts sergeants Waite and

Barrell) to question him regarding this latest affront. Still, Bradstreet maintained that the United Colonies could not compel any of its members to go to war contrary to their own judgments; further, he argued that there was

> noe agreement produced or proved whereby the Collonies are obliged to protect the Long Island Indians against Ninnigrett or others and soe no Reason to engage them in their quarrells the grounds whereof they can not well understand; I therefore see not sufficient light to assent to this vote.[67]

Many in the Massachusetts mercantile community disagreed with Bradstreet's reasoning. Those active in transatlantic affairs urged that Massachusetts do nothing to jeopardize its international image and argued that the colony was obliged to protect, and thereby to accept as bona fide New Englanders, those persons (Winthrop had thought of them almost as traitors) who had settled in territory adjacent to New Netherland. A May 1653 letter subscribed by teacher Edward Norris and many "pensive harts" in the mercantile community of Salem explained that the New England colonies must stand up strongly to the Dutch not only to ensure that the Indians did not think them weak but also to avoid being "looked att by the Parliament of England as Newters and dealt withall accordingly which may bee mischiefe to the whole countrey."[68] The New Haven governor Theophilus Eaton produced a declaration of the "case" against the Dutch that similarly emphasized the need to expand the definition of community so as to include those English warring against the Dutch abroad, as well as those English who had moved to settlements close to Dutch territory. Eaton recognized that the latter might be "Justly blamed" for their folly but that

> most of them did it before any breach betwixt the two Nations; And now they are in continuall feare not onely from the Duch but from the Indians by the Duch Instigation and the danger dayly encreaseth because they will not engage themselves by oath for the Duch against the English Nation and English Collonies.

To assume, argued Eaton, that the Anglo–Dutch War had nothing to do with the colonies was utter folly:

> The Insolency Treachery and bitter Enmity exercised by the Duch in Europe against the Commonwealth of England which they alsoe Mannifest against all the Nation abroad when they have oppertunitie and power may in Reason assure us that if onece they have leasure to send any smale fleet to the Monhatoes the Collonies can neither bee safe in theire persons or estates on shore nor in theire Trad att sea.[69]

Those individuals favorable to war feared not only the immediate dangers of a Dutch–Narragansett alliance but also the loss of face involved in a refusal to participate in a conflict that threatened their own backyard. Such diffidence, the prowar party warned, would call into question the New England Puritans' masculinity and render them as "newters" in the eyes of the world.

At this time John Underhill, recognizing that the tensions between Dutch and English colonists could work to his own advantage, added his distant voice to those in New England agitating for war. In the spring of 1653, Underhill had helped John Leverett gather incriminating evidence from "friendly" Indians about the suspected Dutch–Narragansett alliance. Elated from the experience of having collaborated with this impressive civil war veteran, who promised to return with troops from New England, Underhill, eager for glory, had overplayed his hand and opently condemned Stuyvesant's government. When the expected New England troops did not materialize, Underhill was forced to flee, ending up at Newport, where he received from Providence Plantations a commission against the Dutch. Underhill used this commission a month later, in June, to seize the House of Good Hope, a trading station that constituted the only Dutch territory left in Connecticut.[70]

While Underhill was busy dreaming of glory and exercising his Rhode Island commission against the Dutch, Leverett went off to England where, together with his father-in-law Robert Sedgwick (who was there already on business), he successfully pleaded the case of New Haven and Connecticut and procured military aid from the Commonwealth. By February 1654 Sedgwick and Leverett set sail from London at the head of a small, four-ship expeditionary force charged with "vindicating the English right and extirpating the Dutch." After a long and difficult crossing, the expedition finally arrived in Boston in June, with instructions to use New England as a staging area for the attack on New Netherland. Sedgwick and Leverett were authorized to treat with the United Colonies in order to obtain supplementary troops for the campaign; in the event that any of the jurisdictions comprising the United Colonies should refuse to provide such additional troops (this could only have been aimed at Massachusetts), the commanders were permitted to enlist volunteers.[71] Underhill hurried into Boston harbor as soon as he received word of the expedition's arrival, and Sedgwick rewarded him with a Cromwellian commission. But all hopes of glory were dashed when peace was declared in Europe before the mission could get underway. Mark Harrison, who had accompanied the expedition from England as captain of one of the ships, described the Bay Colony's recalcitrance to his superiors:

> The Assistance of the Southern colonies was not wanting for the carrying on that designe, but the Colonye of the Massachusets did not Act with that life that was Expected supposing they had not a just call for such a worke.

Hoping perhaps to have continued hostilities in the colonial theater even after peace was concluded in Europe, Harrison went on to say that all of the "Colonies disserted us" when they learned of the peace, "upon which we were forced to let the designe fall." Not to be thwarted in their ambitions, however Sedgwick and Leverett immediately formulated and successfully carried out a new plan: to capture the four forts that comprised French Acadia. In the aftermath of the Acadian victory, Sedgwick immediately accepted a commission to serve in the Western Design, the Cromwellian plan to wrest territory from the Spanish antichrist in the West Indies.[72]

Bay Colony officials could not openly condemn Leverett and Sedgwick for furthering the goals of the Commonwealth. Still, the records indicate that the arrival of the English fleet and the actions of its Bay Colony leaders, especially Leverett, were regarded ambivalently. In June 1654 John Mason informed his correspondent John Winthrop, Jr., that some in New England feared that the purpose of the Cromwellian fleet was to "settle Gouerment amongst the Colonyes," not just to "make warre upon Manhatas."[73] And in 1655 the General Court issued Leverett a "grave and serious admonition" for taking as prize and "delivering to our harbor" the Dutch ship *Prophet Samuel*. According to the complaint, Leverett lacked a "commission from the Lord Protector to make prize of the said ship" because the Anglo–Dutch War was officially at an end. But the phrasing of the charges against him suggests that the Court's main concern was that Leverett had been acting for the past two years as the agent of an extracolonial polity in schemes not approved by the majority of Bay magistrates. In the words of the Court, "such actings (without the consent or allowance of authoritie heere established) is a confronting of this government, and tends highly to the infringing of our liberties, discouraging of trade, and [is] destructive to our comfortable being heere." Still, Leverett was a "usefull" man, and the Court, in admonishing the captain, wished only to make sure that the "liberties and authoritie of this government are vindicated," not to engineer the "losse of the helpe of any usefull person." Thus, although Leverett was supposed to be suspended from the exercise of his military command, this element of the punishment was lifted once the "said Captain Leverett . . . solemnly prottest[ed] his fidellitie to this government, and the due honnor that he beares thereunto."[74] Massachusetts needed men like John Leverett; but it also feared them.

Privateering, whether authorized or not, had been proven throughout the colonial world to be a menace to successful colonization. Leverett's connection to a questionable episode of privateering, his prominent role in fomenting a war that Massachusetts authorities viewed more as an imposition than as a duty, and his well-known reservations about the New England Way powerfully symbolized the difference between his priorities and those of the majority of Massachusetts magistrates and "middling" colonists. It was ironic—and unsettling—that a man frequently entrusted with the responsibility of preventing ships from fighting in the harbor would now have to be reminded that his potentially disruptive action was "no small grievance" and that New Englanders did not want "such hostile assaults . . . [to] be suffered in our harbor."[75] While Leverett's action might enrich him personally, it could harm the "hopes of trade" entertained by other merchants who relied on a peaceful harbor.

The Western Design, meanwhile, resurrected old insecurities, for it underscored yet again that English Puritans did not acknowledge New England's primacy of place in the unfolding of the divine scheme. Sedgwick, brother-in-law of Robert Houghton, a prominent English merchant and investor in both the controversial Bahamas scheme and a New England mining project launched by the obstreperous Robert Child, was appointed governor of Jamaica in recognition of the important role he played in its conquest. Sedgwick then attempted, under the direction of the Protector, to people the island with transplanted New Englanders; to aid Sedgwick in this mission, the Commonwealth dispatched Artillery Company member Daniel Gookin, then in England on business, to Massachusetts, but these efforts toward recruitment proved fruitless.[76]

Robert Sedgwick, whose mission was to reinforce troops stationed on the recently won island of Jamaica, arrived in the West Indies on the heels of the English failure to take Hispaniola, an enterprise that cost some four to five hundred lives. Faced with rampant disease and the soldiers' predilection for privateering and raids on small towns, Sedgwick's attempts to fortify and plant Jamaica proved unsuccessful and he soon began to doubt whether God was with the English: "methinks I see little will be; yet sometimes think God may return in mercy, and yet own a poor people," he reported to the Protector, "but on the other side, sometimes am thinking he will not own his generation, but that they will die in the wilderness."[77] Sedgwick himself died in June 1656, sad, dispirited, and uncertain about the future; apparently, he had decided not to return to Massachusetts after the mission, inquiring casually of the Protector whether there might be a place for him in England. Interestingly, Sedgwick's death, and his ruminations on the problems of the Western Design, reveal how dedicated he was, despite his interest in riches, to the worldwide Puritan cause:

> I have had of late not few . . . turnings of heart . . . if we do fall upon small towns and places, it is true we may burn, and it may be destroy the estate of our enemy; but by attending such a course . . . it will be prejudicial to the great ends proposed in this design; for first we are not able to possess any place we attack, and so in no hope thereby to effect our intents in the dispersing any thing of the knowledge of the true God in Jesus Christ to the inhabitants, but rather render ourselves to the Indians and Blacks as a cruel, bloody, ruinating people, when they can see nothing from us but fire and sword, we have no opportunity to converse with them, but in such a way, as will cause them I fear to think us worse than the Spaniard, which might be otherwise did we converse with them.

Sedgwick was not adverse to privateering; like Leverett, he had indulged in the seizure of Dutch ships just prior to his involvement in the Western

Design. But he was also sensitive to the fact that such forays, especially in the West Indian context, might damage the reputation of the English among those native peoples whom they most wished to proselytize: "this kind of marooneing, cruseing, west India trade of plundering and burning of townes, though it have bin long practiced in these parts, yet it is not honorable for a princely Navy, neither was if I thinke the worke designed, though perhaps it may be tollerated at present."[78] In the end, Sedgwick's own life, and the providential life of the worldwide Puritan cause, were so tightly wired together that the putative death of the one brought on the death of the other. But Sedgwick's dedication to these larger issues, and his professed interest in spreading the Puritan message to people of other races, ran directly against the grain of the New England Way, where such concerns received little more than lip service.

If schemes that aligned Massachusetts more directly and more explicitly with the Commonwealth diluted those isolationist inclinations that helped residents stay committed to the bounded geographical space of New England, such policies also threatened the colony's religious purity. In 1654 Benjamin Saucer, an English soldier who arrived in Boston as part of the Sedgwick-Leverett expedition to New Netherland, was arrested on charges of blasphemy, a capital crime. Saucer had allegedly boasted while "in drinke" that "Jehova is the Devel, and he knew noe God but his sworde, and that should save him." At the time the case came before the Court of Assistants Edward Hutchinson, the son of Anne and William, was sitting as foreman of the jury of life and death. Saucer admitted that, while on shore leave after a long confinement aboard ship, he had been too "hasty and proud" while exchanging insults with some "fellow souldiers," and had indeed "returned unseemely, and ungodly, and as they say divelish language." He averred, however, that, while his religious education had been deficient, he "dare not speake or thinke evelly of the name of God soe farre as I know him." Hutchinson's jury decided that Saucer's blasphemous language had been uttered "willingly and prophanely" but not "wittingly and willingly," as required for conviction under the blasphemy statute. Despite magisterial protests, the jury "acquitted the prisoner upon poynt of ignorance," and before the case could come up for review in full court, Saucer escaped.[79]

The odious presence of this brazen blasphemer, who, like many religious dissenters, insisted that colonial courts had no jurisdiction over his case, would never have been felt in Boston had Sedgwick and Leverett been less forward in pressing for an attack against New Netherland. In a petition begging relief from the General Court, Saucer himself revealed that he—and presumably many of his fellow soldiers in the expeditionary force—felt little kinship with the colonists who lived in "these remote Corners of the world." Saucer viewed himself as a "true borne subject of England: a subject to his Highnesse Oliver Lord Protector: of England: Scotland: and Ireland" who had been willing to "venture" his life "in their cause and quarrell, as tendinge and mindinge the good of the English nation in generall." But he was no New Englander:

My Commanders that brought mee out desired to free mee accordinge
to that Law appoynted for mee and my fellow souldiers in any transgression that should fall out: I would have submited to it but could
not obtaine it . . . I am a free borne subject of England, and was sent
out as a servant employed in the service of his Highnesse, and the
State of England: I am noe inhabitant of this place, therefore give
mee liberty without offence . . . to appeale unto the State and Government to whom I doe belonge.

The determination on the part of many magistrates to label Saucer's ill-
considered remarks blasphemous, and then to prosecute him to the full
extent of the law, reflected the intensity of anti-war feeling in Massachusetts; Saucer's behavior, and his subsequent petition, could only have reinforced the notion that joint efforts with "Cromwell's boyes" could come
to no good end. As the product of a social polity far more religiously tolerant than Massachusetts, Saucer seemed to prove Nathaniel Ward correct
in his assertion that too much lenience in this regard was synonymous with
atheism: "He that willingly assents to the last [religious toleration], if he
examines his heart by day light his conscience will tell him, he is either
an atheist, or an Heretique, or an Hypocrite, or at best a captive to some
lust."[80] It could not have escaped the notice of authorities in Boston, moreover, that the two men most responsible for Saucer's presence had more
than a decade earlier revealed themselves as tolerationists. Nor could it be
forgotten that Edward Hutchinson, whose jury's lax decision made it possible for the offender to escape, was not only a persistent petitioner in the
cause of religious toleration but also the scion of a family whose name had
become synonymous with heresy.

IN ADDITION TO jeopardizing the jurisdictional and religious boundaries protected by close adherence to the New England Way, the activities
of men like John Leverett and Robert Sedgwick blurred the emergent
boundary between the public and private spheres. Neither the planned
assault on New Netherland nor the conquest of the French forts in Nova
Scotia would have been undertaken had these projects not dovetailed with
economic interests that ran deep in the Bay Colony's mercantile and military community. Seventeenth-century people acknowledged, of course,
that officeholders, including military officers, had the right to use their
essentially unsalaried posts for financial gain; otherwise, no one would be
willing to carry out vitally important public services. All agreed too in the
desirability of economic development. But at same time, Massachusetts,
beginning with Winthrop's *Model of Christian Charity*, had developed an
ethos that stressed private sacrifice for the public good; as Stephen Carl
Arch has suggested, Winthrop wrote the famous lay sermon with the intent
of showing how a society organized along traditional lines of hierarchy and
deference could nonetheless be capable of "restoring the Old World's misshapen forms—of man and society—to their original lineaments in the

New." While this idealism did not prevent Bay colonists at all levels from demonstrating a keen regard for their own economic gain, most seemed to recognize that a balance must be struck between the interests of self and society.[81] As always, selfish behavior was easier to detect in others than oneself. But the balance was severely strained when men like Sedgwick, Leverett, and, as I will show, Edward Gibbons, risked war not to defend or offend against a common enemy or a present danger but to obtain trade advantages whose enjoyment would be limited to the very few.

Robert Sedgwick originally became interested in Dutch-controlled territory not in his capacity as the highest ranking military man in Massachusetts—a position he held at the time Leverett began agitating for war—but rather as a merchant. In 1644 Sedgwick and partners William Aspinwall, Joshua Hewes, William Tyng, Thomas Clark, Valentine Hill, and Francis Norton sought and obtained permission from the General Court to form a "free company of adventurers" with a twenty-one-year monopoly over all sources of fur discovered along the Delaware River during the company's first three years of existence. The men were motivated by tales of the rumored Lake of the Iroquois and believed that the Delaware River would lead them there.[82]

Remarkably, virtually all of the men involved in this company could be considered outside the religious mainstream of the Bay Colony. William Aspinwall had authored the antinomian petition in favor of John Wheelwright and had reconciled himself with Bay Colony authorities just two years prior to joining the fur-trading partnership.[83] Thomas Clark, commander of the Suffolk regiment, and William Tyng, captain at Braintree, were, like Sedgwick, champions of a wider toleration. Clark would go so far in 1658 as to protest with Edward Hutchinson the harsh laws passed against the Quakers; and Tyng, with Leverett, objected to the Cambridge Platform. Valentine Hill, a landowner and trader to the "eastern parts," was connected to the Hutchinson family because his first wife, Frances Freestone, was a cousin of William Hutchinson who had emigrated to Massachusetts on the *Griffin* with the Hutchinson's huge party of extended kin. Hill's second wife, Mary Eaton, a daughter of Theophilus Eaton of New Haven, connected him through her stepmother, Anne Eaton, to David Yale (Anne Eaton's son), a Boston merchant who agitated, with Robert Child, for a more flexible form of Puritanism.[84] Francis Norton, who would rise to the captaincy of the Charlestown militia, came to the New World initially as an agent for the Mason family of New Hampshire rather than as a devoted Puritan; he gravitated toward Sedgwick's more expansive vision of Puritanism and was married to Mary Stetson, the daughter of Sedgwick's partner in a Charlestown tide mill. Joshua Hewes, nephew of the prominent English merchant and ironmonger Joshua Foote, was involved closely in business dealings with Edward Hutchinson and other tolerationist forces in the colony. Finally Robert Child himself, also an investor, became infamous as the author of the protolerationist Remonstrance of 1646.[85]

The General Court, in reviewing these mens' petition for an exclusive fur-trading concession, had been "very unwilling to grant any monopoly." But given the unfavorable economic straits in which New England found itself in the 1640s and the improbability of financing such an important venture in any other way, the petition was granted. The anticipated benefits, including greater access to much-needed imports—a result that would benefit the colony as a whole as well as the merchants—never materialized. The two expeditions sent out by the company in the spring of 1644 and the winter of 1644–45 failed miserably; the first, led by William Aspinwall and assisted by Artillery Company member Richard Collicot, was turned back by Swedish and Dutch authorities, who ignored the letter from Governor Winthrop asking that the voyage of discovery be allowed to pass. The second was set upon by Indians. In the process, at least seven hundred pounds' worth of trade goods and supplies were lost, and the company was destroyed.[86]

This failure, as well as the reversals faced by Daniel Howe and Nathaniel Turner, set the stage eight years later for the interest manifested by many merchants in Anglo–Dutch hostilities. A war would not only allow the satisfaction of revenge against Dutch officials and traders whose highhandedness had offended New Englanders but also might, if successfully concluded, yield access to valuable trading opportunities. As I have shown, John Leverett, from the first hint of trouble, had set himself against the antiwar sentiments that dominated Massachusetts counsels and worked closely with Connecticut and New Haven officials, going so far as to represent their interests, rather than the Bay Colony's, in England. Richard Collicot contributed his bit to the United Colony's collection of horror stories about the Dutch by providing an account of his experiences while on the Lake Company expedition with Aspinwall. The Dutch governor, he said, had given a verbal promise that the expedition could pass unmolested up the Delaware River. But then

> in an underhand and Injurius way hee presently sent a vessell well maned to the Duch fort att Dellaware with comaund to John Jonson his agent that rather to sink the said vessell then to suffer her to passe; by meanes wherof . . . his companie were forced to Returne and therby theire whole stocke which att lest was seaven hundred pounds was wasted and theire Designe overthrowne besids the hope of future trade and bennifitt.[87]

Even after the war failed to materialize, some of the original Lake Company investors and their associates remained interested in breaking into the Dutch trading sphere. In 1659 Thomas Clark and Francis Norton joined a new consortium, which included Artillery Company members Thomas Savage and John Richards, as well as William Hawthorne, John Pynchon, and four other men, in an attempt to establish a town halfway between Springfield and Albany, ostensibly to furnish cattle to the Dutch

Fort Orange. But the investors' most likely real intent was, as the New Netherland director Stuyvesant suspected, to break the Dutch monopoly on the fur trade in that region. In 1664 Thomas Clark, perhaps still hopeful of expanded trading opportunities, was present when authority over New Netherland passed officially into English hands.[88]

The resistance of Massachusetts to the economic schemes of men like Leverett and Sedgwick came not because Puritans feared capitalist development but rather because such development had transatlantic political implications. Trading enterprises that led to conflict always ran the risk of leading toward English intervention and the end of Bay Colony "independency." In religious terms, moreover, the promoters of these schemes seemed disturbingly at home with a religious system that lacked the fixity and the determinacy that characterized the identity-conferring New England Way.

LIKE THE PLANNED attack on New Netherland, the second foray undertaken by Leverett and Sedgwick in 1654—the takeover of the forts in French Acadia—was rooted deeply in the trading considerations of the Bay Colony's mercantile/military community. During the early 1640s, Artillery Company member Edward Gibbons, a frequent business partner of Leverett and Sedgwick and major general of the colony in 1649, convinced Bay Colony authorities to intervene in the struggle between Charles de La Tour and Charles D'Aulnay, two rival claimants to authority and profitable trading forts in French Acadia. Gibbons's personal financial involvement with the untrustworthy La Tour, whose cause Massachusetts briefly championed, eventually brought about his economic ruin and departure from the colony. But this fiasco did not blind the Massachusetts trading community to the potential worth of the Acadia trade in fish and furs. It was therefore a logical step for Leverett and Sedgwick to take it upon themselves to attack Acadia in 1654, while they had an expeditionary force ready to hand. As Sedgwick explained to authorities in England, he "thought best . . . to spend a little tyme in rangeing the coast against the French, who use tradinge and fishing hereaboute." Mark Harrison, who had accompanied the fleet from London, concurred with Sedgwick's assessment; once the "Peace with the Hollanders" became known, "it was thought good to Turne or designe toward the french and to Prosecute the same." Bay Colony magistrates viewed Sedgwick's victory over the French forts with more equanimity than his design to attack New Netherland. Still, the General Court raised questions concerning the validity of his authority to have undertaken the mission in the first place and turned down his request to publicize the new trade regulations he and Leverett sought to impose over the region.[89]

Edward Gibbons, whose activities helped spark interest in the French forts, was, like many of his colleagues, a vitally important yet potentially disruptive force in the Bay Colony. During the 1620s Gibbons with his "Jocund Temper," had lived in Thomas Morton's Merrymount, a trading settlement whose despised leader had been banished (and his house destroyed) by Puritan authorites at Plymouth—and later Massachusetts—who were discomfited by Morton's close association with the Indians, his adherence to the traditional social mores of "merrie olde England" (including the Maypole), and his supposed encouragement of servants to overthrow their masters. The freebooting young Gibbons, having chosen in his early life at Merrymount "rather to Dance about a May Pole, first Erected to the Honour of Strumpet Flora then to hear a good Sermon," would seem an unlikely candidate to become a trusted Puritan militia officer; yet this is precisely what happened. "Pricked at the heart" when he observed the 1629 gathering of the church at Salem, Gibbons made known his desire to "be one of the Society" and was admitted as a Bay Colony resident in the early 1630s. He began his military career in 1634 as ensign to John Underhill, and just prior to the outbreak of the Pequot War he rose to the lieutenancy and was dispatched on a diplomatic mission to prevent the formation of an alliance between the Pequots and Narragansetts.[90]

But old freebooting habits died hard. In 1636 Gibbons embarked for the West Indies on what was most likely a privateering voyage. The following year he arrived at Boston with a prize ship "traded" to him by an acquaintance, a former inhabitant of Piscataqua, who while captaining a French man-of-war in Caribbean waters happened to encounter the Gibbons expedition. Gibbons, whose ship had been given up for lost, explained this sudden windfall to Winthrop in a manner calculated to allay the logical suspicion that the meeting with the Frenchman had been planned in advance. As Winthrop recorded the tale in his journal, the meeting with the Frenchman, far from being contrived between partners who knew one another from the Piscataqua trade, was an act of providence: Gibbons's thirty-ton pinnace, having been blown off its course to Bermuda, ended up at Spanish-held Hispaniola, where he and his crew, carefully avoiding populated areas, lived on turtles and hogs caught in "obscure places" in the island. "At last they were forced into a harbor, where lay a French man-of-war with his prize, and had surely made prize of them also, but that the providence of God so disposed, as the captain, one Petfree, had lived at Pascataquack, and knew the merchant of our bark, one Mr. Gibbons."[91] We can never know for certain whether Gibbons planned in advance the meeting with the mysterious and strangely generous Frenchman. But the incident shows that Gibbons was at home in a world of shifting alliances and uncertain loyalties that disturbed most Massachusetts Puritans. Ironically, as with Leverett, Sedgwick, and even Underhill, it was precisely this aspect of Gibbons's character that made him both an asset and a danger to the colony.

In the years following the possible privateering venture, Gibbons provided useful services but at the same time gave notice in subtle ways that he found New England orthodoxy constraining. As I have shown, in 1638 he was called to account for his modest effort to protect Anne Hutchinson from excommunication; and in 1646 he protested the severity of the punishment meted out to remonstrant Robert Child.[92] The episcopal-minded

Samuel Maverick, always a thorn in the side of Bay Colony magistrates, touted Gibbons as one of the few men in Boston from whom he could always expect to receive civil treatment. Indeed Gibbons's reputation for moderation traveled far afield, for in 1643 Lord Baltimore, proprietor of Maryland, offered the Massachusetts resident a commission for the purpose of recruiting New England settlers "with free liberty of religion and all other privileges which the place afforded." Winthrop, reflecting on this incident, was relieved that neither "our captain" nor "our people" experienced any "temptation that way"; and he marvelled at Baltimore's promotion of what seemed like an outlandish religious mix: while Baltimore was "himself a papist, and his brother Mr. Calvert the governor there a papist also . . . the colony consisted both of Protestants and papists." This religious mixture did not seem so preposterous to Gibbons, though; years later, when his financial hopes were dashed in Massachusetts, he finally did accept Baltimore's invitation to settle in Maryland as justice of the peace, council member, and admiral.[93]

Despite any suspicions about his ultimate loyalties, Gibbons, a successful merchant trading to England, Virginia, and the West Indies, advanced steadily through the military ranks.[94] In 1643, as a commissioner from Massachusetts, he helped to establish the Confederation of New England; in 1644, as the result of a militia reorganization, he became sergeant major of Suffolk county, the most prestigious of the four new county-based regimental commands; in 1645, when Massachusetts and other English colonies felt themselves threatened by the Narragansetts, Gibbons was called to command not only the Massachusetts troops but the combined forces organized by the Confederation of New England; finally, in 1649, Gibbons attained the highest military rank in the colony, that of sergeant major general, which gave him authority over all four Massachusetts regiments.[95]

Gibbons's meteoric rise as a military leader was hindered neither by his close dealings with threatening elements outside Puritan New England nor his sympathies with nonconformist elements within. But the Massachusetts major's ongoing employment as agent to Charles de La Tour of French Acadia posed many potential hazards, some of which were realized.

English claims on the Acadian region, which Englishmen referred to as Nova Scotia in recognition of the attempt by Scots Privy Councillor William Alexander to settle a proprietary colony there in the 1620s, had officially ceased in 1632, when Charles I agreed to return the territory to France in the Treaty of St. Germain. In the late 1630s Charles de La Tour, a longtime wielder of French authority in the region, became enmeshed in a power struggle with the newly appointed lieutenant general of Acadia, Charles d'Aulnay, who refused to share trading rights with him. The two "rival chieftains" engaged in a series of violent clashes that met with the disapproval of authorities in France, who worried about the destabilizing effects of continued armed conflict. By the early 1640s d'Aulnay had convinced his superiors in France that La Tour was the main aggressor in these raids, and the Crown, inclined for some time to see La Tour as an overgreat subject, gave d'Aulnay the authority to seize his nemesis and send him across the ocean to explain his violent behavior. Beleaguered by officially sanctioned blockades and attacks on his forts, La Tour sent emissaries on three separate occasions to Massachusetts, offering trading privileges to Bay Colony merchants in exchange for military aid against d'Aulnay. Despite warnings from d'Aulnay, the magistrates finally agreed to La Tour's proposal for free trade, though they refused his request for military aid. Still, the resourceful La Tour, appealing in person to Bay Colony authorities in 1643, was able to secure permission to hire men and privately owned ships from the colony.[96]

The uncertain boundary between the public and private spheres became controversial when members of the interlocking military and mercantile elite used their considerable influence to transform their desire for access to new markets into violent and potentially dangerous public policy. It was just such a course that Gibbons and other far-from-disinterested merchants followed in the 1640s, when they agitated for the right to supply La Tour's forts and offer him other aid. To the horror of John Endecott and other magistrates who feared reprisals from d'Aulnay against the exposed northern communities of Massachusetts, Gibbons headed the group of Charlestown merchants and Artillery Company members that persuaded John Winthrop not only to permit Boston traders to supply La Tour's posts but also to countenance the interloper's hiring out of ships and men from Boston to break the blockade d'Aulnay had erected around his competitor's forts. William Tyng, an investor at about the same time in the Lake Company, and Robert Keayne, again at the center of controversy, witnessed the document registered with the Suffolk County Court wherein Gibbons and Thomas Hawkins hired out the *Seabridge*, the *Philip and Mary*, the *Increase*, and the *Greyhound*, all vessels in which they held partial ownership, for the warlike purpose of blockade-running and blockade-breaking. La Tour, allowed to place up to ten of his own soldiers aboard each of the ships, agreed to pay the equivalent of five hundred and twenty pounds in usage fees for the shipping; in addition, he was bound to provide pay and provisions for at least twenty English soldiers per ship.[97] Hawkins, who was a close associate of Nehemiah Bourne and who in 1638 had been made to acknowledge before the General Court his "indiscretion in roughly addressing a member of the court while in session," went along as leader of the mercenary force; it broke the blockade, chased d'Aulnay back to his own fort, burned his mill, destroyed his corn, and returned to Boston with eight hundred stolen moose and beaver skins as booty.[98]

John Winthrop's decision to accede to the Boston merchants' wishes had been out of character and so controversial that it cost him the governorship in 1644. La Tour, departing his blockaded fort to take passage on a 140-ton French supply ship sent out from the Huguenot port of La Rochelle, had arrived in Boston in the summer of 1643. Because the General Court was not in session at that time, the Standing Council, consisting of magistrates from Suffolk and Middlesex counties, had treated with La

Tour and made the decision allowing him to lease ships. The principal men of Essex and Norfolk—including John Endecott, Richard Saltonstall, Simon Bradstreet, and Nathaniel Ward—were incensed that they had not been consulted; and two publicly circulated letters were sent to Winthrop, accusing him of highhanded and irresponsible behavior. Historian Robert E. Wall has suggested that the Essex magistrates' anti–La Tour stance came as a result of their own desire to enter the fur trade and their consternation that the Charlestown and Boston merchants were receiving an unfair advantage.[99] But the points brought out in the letters subscribed by these men, focusing on the folly of having allowed the "Idolatrous French" to see Bay Colony fortifications, the sinfulness of engaging in an unholy war motivated by greed, the characterization of the "Spirit of warre" as "Scholastick and Jesuitical," and the rashness of risking the alienation of a powerful adversary who might decide to wreak revenge upon the far-flung communities of northern Massachusetts, seemed to reflect a popular opinion that mistrusted "strangers": as the Saltonstall letter pointed out, "He that loseth his life in an unnecessary quarrel or danger dyes the Devills Martyr," but "had they had the voyces of the people with them it had beene better then nothing but that wind seems to us to blow strong in the Teeth of their voyage." Winthrop, though generally an isolationist, had faced numerous pressures to modify his usual stance. There had been the importunities of the Boston mercantile community, including his own son and namesake John Winthrop, Jr.; there had been the considerable powers of persuasion, not to mention military strength, of Charles de La Tour; and there had been the political fact, as historian John G. Reid has pointed out, that Winthrop had "recently returned as governor to replace the more strictly isolationist Richard Bellingham." Once the decision was made, Winthrop defended it vigorously against what he regarded as an "unwarranted Protestation," for he believed that open strife among magistrates endangered all authority, "It blowes a trumpet to division and dissention amongst ourselvs, magistrats protesting against magistrats, Elders against Elders, blameing, condemning, exposing brethren to the peoples Curses, and casting them downe to hell it selfe." But Winthrop too came to acknowledge the pitfalls of allying oneself with a man like La Tour. Indeed, in August 1643, when the Hawkins expedition returned to Massachusetts, Winthrop recorded that the "report of their actions was offensive and grievous to us."[100]

In April 1645, less than a year after the Massachusetts-backed raid, d'Aulnay captured Fort St. John and regained the upper hand over La Tour; fortunately, the victorious Frenchman was willing to make peace in the fall of 1646 so long as the New Englanders would acknowledge some degree of wrongdoing in allowing La Tour to stage a raiding expedition from Boston. The Massachusetts government refused to accept any direct blame, but

because we could not free Captain Hawkins and the other voluntaries of what they had done, we were to send a small present to Monsieur

d'Aulnay . . . a very fair new sedan . . . sent by the viceroy of Mexico
to a lady his sister, and taken in the West Indies by Captain Cromwell
and by him given to our governor.[101]

La Tour, meanwhile, just months before the negotiations with d'Aulnay,
had shown his true colors when he returned to Boston from Newfoundland,
convinced merchants to fit him out with four hundred pounds worth of
trade goods, and then absconded to Quebec, having "conspired with the
master [of the pinnace] (being a stranger) and his own Frenchmen, being
five, to go away with the vessel, and so forced out the other five English,
(himself shooting one of them in the face with a pistol)." Edward Gibbons,
who had personally advanced large amounts of capital and provisions to
La Tour in this and other instances, lost upwards of two thousand pounds.
For Winthrop, La Tour's behavior only confirmed what, deep down, he
had always known: "that there is no confidence in an unfaithful or carnal
man. Though tied with many strong bonds of courtesy . . . he turned
pirate."[102]

La Tour represented a world outside the bounds of the colony where
loyalties shifted with the wind and religious, national, and even racial
identities were supple and changeable. The father of two mixed-race
(Franco-Micmac) daughters whom he sent to France to be educated in
Benedictine and Ursuline convents, La Tour was most likely Catholic. Yet
in his dealings with New Englanders the chameleonlike Frenchman
claimed not only a Huguenot identity but also a Scots baronetcy, through
his father Claude. In 1628, Claude, captured at sea and brought into England, had encountered Sir William Alexander and accepted on behalf of
himself and his son knights-baronetcies that gave them the right to create
settlements for New Scotland and to control the fur trade of southern Nova
Scotia. For political reasons, Charles de La Tour had refused to be so closely
associated with New Scotland.[103] But in the 1640s, when he needed aid
from Massachusetts, the claim on a Scottish baronetcy helped create and
sustain the illusion of a common religious identity. Knowing perhaps of
the way that New England had been criticized for hanging back from the
international Protestant struggle and recognizing the appeal that this struggle held for men like Gibbons and Hawkins, La Tour had drawn a parallel
between his own situation and the Dutch fight for independence: England
had "assisted the Hollanders with men, money and arms, notwithstanding
the confederation of Spain"; New England, he implied, should do no less
for La Tour and Nova Scotia.

Winthrop attempted through tortuous logic to explain to his critics
why aid to La Tour might indeed help the international Protestant community. But, consistent with his final assessment about the unreliability of
a "carnal" man, he focused in his journal on incidents that reflected the
dangers inherent in such schemes. The larger struggle for the faith held
great merit; yet it also held out the hope of booty, which in turn attracted
unsavory elements to the cause (and to the colony).

Winthrop ruminated, for example, upon the tale of Captain John Chaddock, who, supposedly on Humphrey's advice, had come to New England in the summer of 1643 to find settlers willing to populate Warwick's colony of Trinidad but, disappointed in his original mission, had signed his crew on for a two-month stint with La Tour, convoying to Acadia a pinnace belonging to the Frenchman and performing "other service against d'Aulnay there." Arriving in Acadia, the men found that d'Aulnay had departed for France and was unavailable to harass. The men then spent the two months of their indenture guarding d'Aulnay's new fort at Port Royal so that no trade could be conducted. When the two months were over, Chaddock and his men, grown surly during the weeks of relative idleness and no booty, returned to Boston in bad spirits. While entering the harbor, three men—one of whom, Winthrop thought, had "taken some things out of the deserted castle as they went out"—drowned after being shaken off the mainmast. Once ashore, the captain and his crew, having learned nothing from the providential deaths of their comrades, proceeded to drink, brawl, and ridicule the godly colony.

John Chaddock, Winthrop knew, was the son of a "godly gentleman," Thomas Chaddock, who had been governor of Bermuda before removing to Trinidad in Warwick's service. Nonetheless, he was a "proud and intemperate man" who "began to speak evil of the country [Massachusetts], swearing fearfully that we were a base heathen people." When the ship's master disagreed, saying that New England was "the best place that ever he came," the two men drew swords and pistols; onlookers prevented them from harming one another. Chaddock was fined twenty pounds, and the master ten shillings, although the magistrates wrote to Warwick, "who had always been forward to do good to our colony," that he could reclaim the forfeited money at any time. Soon after this incident, some of Chaddock's men, departing for Trinidad aboard a French pinnace purchased from La Tour, were blown up in the harbor when two barrels of gunpowder were accidently ignited by the firing of a pistol. Winthrop observed that "two vessels have thus been blown up in our harbor, and both belonging to such as despised us and the ordinance of God amongst us." About two weeks later, mysterious lights were seen and voices heard at the site of the explosion. Speculation ("occasion of speech") ensued that these "prodigies" could have been caused by one of the victims of the explosion, who had been known to practice the black arts. The body of the person in question had not been found, and "that man . . . professed himself to have skill in necromancy, and to have done some strange things in his way from Virginia hither, and was suspected to have murdered his master there; but the magistrates here had not notice of him till after he was blown up."[104]

The presence of Chaddock, a "proud" man who "despised us and the ordinance of God amongst us," had to be borne because of his association with Warwick; but such men were part of a world in many ways alien to the average Bay Colony resident—a world of masks and intrigue where the quest for booty, regardless of the peril in which it placed colonizing families and farms, could be equated with defense of the faith. That Chaddock would be linked to La Tour, another person of shifting loyalties and uncertain faith, was not to be wondered at. Nor was it strange that the diabolism of one of Chaddock's crew should become the talk of the town; no symbol could more powerfully express popular fears of the "other," and the unknown, than illicit magic.

Through the letters circulated by the disaffected Essex magistrates we get a sense that ordinary people in the outlying northern settlements feared that they might be forced to pay the price for the greed of some of the colony's merchants. Winthrop's journal suggests that ordinary colonists in Boston were similarly disaffected toward the La Tour mission, though for somewhat different reasons. In 1644, while the Frenchmen were in town, a Portuguese trading ship arrived in Boston with a cargo of salt and two English crew members. The Boston constable arrested one of these Englishmen for public drunkeness and put him in the stocks on his own authority, since no magistrate was available to adjudicate the situation. One of "La Tour's gentlemen," passing by, "lifted up the stocks and let him out." The constable, becoming irate when he heard about this, pursued the Frenchman, by this time "gone and quiet," and attempted to place him in the stocks:

> The Frenchman offered to yield himself to go to prison; but the constable, not understanding his language, pressed him to go to the stocks: the Frenchman resisted and drew his sword; with that company came in and disarmed him, and carried him by force to the stocks, but soon after the constable took him out and carried him to prison, and presently after took him forth again and delivered him to La Tour.[105]

The "many Frenchmen . . . in town, and other strangers," though "quiet," were incensed at the constable. When the magistrates endeavored to clear matters up the next morning, La Tour dutifully placed his employee under the power of Massachusetts officials and expressed regret over his "servant's miscarriage"; but he also communicated that he was "grieved . . . for the disgrace put upon him [the servant] (for in France it is a most ignominious thing to be laid in the stocks)." The magistrates agreed to allow bail, paid for by "two Englishmen, members of the church of Boston," even though La Tour's party was "not like to stay till the court." This was "thought too much favor for such an offence by many of the common people; but by our law bail could not be denied him."

Winthrop presented this incident as representative of the problems that arose when lowly officeholders like constables failed to go through proper channels and await instructions from magistrates, who knew better how to deal with such delicate situations. Although the constable had the authority to detain people "disturbing the peace," he was not supposed to arrest them after the fact without a warrant; there would have been no problem, Winthrop thought, had the constable "kept within his own bounds, and . . . not interfered upon the authority of the magistrate."[106] Yet just as Winthrop's defense of aid to La Tour was tempered by his later conclusion that La Tour was an untrustworthy "carnal" man, so did his account of this incident between the constable and the Frenchman reflect his understanding that the values of the image-conscious and playful "French gentleman" were at variance with those of Puritan colonists.

Historian Richard Gildrie has recently pointed out how, for certain thieves populating the Massachusetts underclass, stealing was attractive not only because it allowed the outlaws to "survive" in style, like "gentlemen," but also because it represented a "deliberate inversion of the Puritan social ethic of hard work and personal asceticism."[107] The freebooting activities with which La Tour and his "servant" involved themselves were legal in an official sense. But, as demonstrated in the behavior of Chaddock and his crew, raiding and privateering, even when officially sponsored, gave rise to a way of life, or an ethos, very similar to that indulged in by "profane" thieves; it was this perceived similarity, reinforced by the Frenchman's seemingly deliberate intent to ridicule Puritan morality by releasing a drunk, that brought forth the animosity of common "middling" people in Boston.[108] Winthrop's narrative suggests that he understood and sympathized with the apparently widespread resentment of the court's accommodation of a "foreigner" or "stranger" whose very crime manifested contempt for his hosts' desire to maintain a wholesome social environment. The constable, an "honest officer," was accordingly apprised of his mistakes in private, for fear that a public admonition would have "given occasion to the offenders and their abettors to insult over him." As was so often the case when the Bay Colony interacted with the transatlantic world, the virtuosity of honest and plain, if somewhat overzealous, persons was pitted against the vainglory of debauched "gallants."

THE EVENTS OF the 1640s, including Gibbons's financial debacle, the stinging political denunciations that rang out against Winthrop for having supported Gibbons's risk-laden scheme, and the friction between "middling" colonists and "strangers," illustrated clearly the difficulties involved in pursuing the interventionist policies necessary to break into the Acadia trade. Yet none of these untoward events or conflicts could dampen enthusiasm for the riches of Acadia. In 1650, after the drowning death of d'Aulnay, the crafty La Tour, though jailed briefly in France, gained from authorities there a new commission as lieutenant general. But despite this good fortune, enhanced by his success in contracting a marriage to the widow and heir of his former enemy, La Tour, pursued by creditors of the d'Aulnay estate, still needed to turn to Massachusetts merchants to supply his forts.[109] In 1652 and 1653, three Boston merchants, including John Leverett and Joshua Scottow, both of whom would become deeply enmeshed in Acadian affairs, petitioned for and received special permission— despite a trade ban that had been put in place "for prevention of any such trade as may be of dangerous consequence to ourselves, as the strengthening of persons in hostillitie to our nation or ourselves"—to carry flour, peas, and other provisions to the French forts.[110] One year later, with their Commonwealth-backed plans to attack New Netherland scuttled by the peace declaration, Leverett and his kinsman Robert Sedgwick decided to use their idle expeditionary force to conquer the French forts on behalf of England.

Leverett and Sedgwick failed to profit as much as they might have hoped from their conquest, for Cromwell granted Acadia and exclusive trading rights there to Thomas Temple, William Crowne, and Charles de La Tour, the latter of whom arrived in England as Sedgwick's prisoner but managed by 1656 to convince English authorities that his claim to a Scottish baronetcy lent legitimacy to England's retention of the forts. La Tour promptly sold his stake in the patent to his partners in exchange for a 5 percent interest in the profits from trade, while Thomas Temple, a poor relation of the Fiennes family (Saye and Sele), moved to Massachusetts and governed Nova Scotia from New England, where eager merchants (including Leverett, Joshua Scottow, Thomas Lake, Hezekiah Usher, and Samuel Shrimpton) encouraged the inexperienced governor to incur staggering debts for supplies.[111]

Sedgwick died while serving in the Commonwealth's Western Design soon after his foray into Nova Scotia; Leverett, who lived on for many years, was thwarted in his ultimate objectives regarding the forts. Leverett's expenditure of large sums of borrowed money to support the soldiers and sailors who held Nova Scotia during the months following the victory suggests that the captain anticipated a princely reward for his role in the venture. But in 1656, after it was decided that a patent to the Acadian territory and its trade would be awarded to La Tour, Temple, and Crowne, Leverett could do nothing but petition the Commonwealth begging reimbursement of monies already spent.

Although the government acknowledged Leverett's claims, there were seemingly interminable delays in the disbursement of the money. A disgruntled Leverett continued to write petitions, reminding authorities that he was owed almost five thousand pounds "for monyes layde out by him in Navy, and Army busynes for the Comonwealth, at the forts taken from the French in America," and was now suffering terrible hardships, being "reduced almost beyond necessityes to extremityes." Bitterly Leverett recounted how he "hath wayted almost twelve monthes from his family and calling, which are in New England, to his great losse and affliction, and is likely to suffer in his credit for not payment of such moneyes as he borrowed for the supplying that service."[112] Although Massachusetts had in 1655 instructed Leverett, who was then acting as its agent, to explore whether Cromwell might be willing to place Nova Scotia under Bay Colony jurisdiction, it is clear that Leverett, regardless of his obligation to speak for the communal interest, had pursued a personal grant. The Restoration found Leverett still petitioning the English government to recoup his losses.

He explained to the king that "your petitioner upon the takeing of severall forts from the French in Nova Scotia and coast of Accadie in America was left to command and keepe them in the year 1654, in which service your petitioner for the payment of Souldiers and seamen ran out his Estate." Leverett thought he deserved recompense because the "moneyes were expended for the Takeing of a country which is in Addition to your Majesties Dominions." In lieu of a cash payment, he was bold enough to suggest what he had most likely always desired—a grant of "the said Country for a Terme of yeares, or such part thereof to him and his heires forever as may be a just compensation for his disbursements."[113]

No one would dispute the fact that Leverett was justified in seeking to recoup his expenditures. Still, there is evidence to suggest that some New Englanders saw Leverett and Sedgwick less as public servants than monopolizing predators.[114] In 1656, Thomas Jenner, "an inhabitant of Charles Towne in New England," complained to English authorities that his vessel, the fourteen-ton *John* of Boston, had been unjustly seized in April 1655 under a "derived power from Captain Sedgwicke" for interloping the Indian trade in the environs of the newly won French forts. A committee charged by the Council of State with investigating Jenner's complaint determined that Sedgwick and a "Councell of War" had prohibited all trade with the local Indians, and commissioned subordinates to "goe rangeing about" searching for "interloping Traders with the Salvages, and such to seise and bring to the Fort Penobscot." Under this law, Jenner's boat had been captured by one John Peirce, a subordinate of Captain John Allen, commander of Fort Penobscot, Artillery Company member, and soon-to-be captain of the Charlestown militia company.[115] Jenner was then held for several days by men who refused to show their commissions, and Peirce admitted in later testimony that

> part of the goods in the said shipp were imployed and spent by the soldyers in Penobscot fort, part imployed in a way of trade with the salvages by order of the governor of the . . . fort, and part shipped for the use of Captain Leverett [probably to offset his expenses in taking and manning the forts] and put into his warehouse at Boston.

Having ascertained the facts of the case, the investigatory committee ruled in favor of Jenner because they could find "noe warrant" under the "severall instructions given by yor Highnesse [Cromwell] and Councell" for Sedgwick's and Leverett's policy of apprehending traders within the "English pale," that is, the region where Englishmen had been allowed to trade prior to the takeover of the French forts. In any event, the committee was inclined to believe Jenner's claim that he had no knowledge of these novel rules of trade, for the General Court of Massachusetts had refused Sedgwick's request to promulgate them, "saying it belonged not to them to publish the orders of other provinces." The evidence for Jenner's "disobedience to the said Order," moreover, amounted, in the eyes of the committee, to mere "hearsay" from "several salvages" who gave out that they had traded with him.[116]

Yet again, Leverett and Sedgwick, arguably the most active military officers in the Bay, could to a certain extent be viewed as potentially threatening individuals who, by virtue of their Cromwellian commissions, were in a position directly and personally to benefit from an extracolonial authority that, in some instances, propped up their decisions and possibly encouraged them to uphold a military agenda extraneous to that of the colony. In this case, Leverett and Sedgwick had so blatantly overstepped their authority, appearing to treat the entire region surrounding the French forts as personal property, that the investigatory committee ruled against their high-handed ways.

Leverett's mere presence in London as Massachusetts agent at the time when Jenner's petition arrived was indicative of his dangerous mixing of public and private business. Leverett, more than anyone, could allay suspicion on the part of the Protectorate government that the colony's diffident approach to the Anglo-Dutch hostilities indicated any hint of underlying disloyalty; he was similarly well situated to work toward trading concessions and other forms of aid coveted by the inhabitants of Massachusetts. Yet, at the same time, Leverett was clearly pursuing his own ends.[117] Indeed, in his petition to the Protector concerning the French forts, Leverett downplayed the official role that he was supposed to be playing as Massachusetts agent, and portrayed himself instead as being forced to remain in England, away from "family and calling" for almost a year, primarily because of the need to recoup his huge expenditures.

Several years later, when the monarchy was restored, Leverett himself cagily reminded Massachusetts leaders how mutually dependent were his public duties and private interests. Leverett blamed Massachusetts Governor John Endecott and the General Court for the unresolved state of his finances relative to the French forts. In 1658, Cromwell's Privy Council had made the release of Leverett's monies contingent upon an audit of his accounts to be supervised by authorities in Massachusetts; and the New Englanders, as of 1660, had not yet completed the job. Because his fellow colonists had dragged their feet, Leverett would now have to re-commence the process of drafting petitions to a new and far less friendly government. In his anger, Leverett described to Bay Colony officials how he had considered retaliating against them by shirking his duties as their agent. The callousness he had experienced during a time of need, Leverett recounted craftily

almost wrought me to a resolve of neglecting this opportunity of presenting my due respects in giveing you any account of others motions in England concerning you; but least you should have cause of chargeing me with neglect I have set pen to paper, to let you understand what I have in relation to New England.[118]

Leverett went on to provide his correspondents with important information about what plots were afoot against Massachusetts in the metropolis, and how best to counter them. In this deftly written missive, Leverett demonstrated how valuable he was to the colony, while subtly threatening his associates at home that if they continued blatantly to disregard his interests, there might be a price to pay.

JOHN LEVERETT STOOD at the center of a group of leading men who, unlike most Massachusetts magistrates, feared "uniformity" more than Puritan heterodoxy, regarding a certain level of diversity as a necessary precondition for the success of their transatlantic commitments.[119] Ever since the antinomian crisis of the late 1630s, New England orthodoxy, with its scrupulous control over doctrine and behavior, had inspired in its followers a certain dread of the outside world, where the familiar parameters observed in Massachusetts no longer obtained. In this context, the cultural purity of merchants and military officers, who in the course of their official duties and private enterprises had intense contact with all manner of outsiders, frequently came under suspicion. Yet these characteristics had to be allowed expression if the colony were to accomplish its worldly goals and remain credible in the eyes of prominent English Puritans.

Men like John Leverett, Edward Hutchinson, Robert Sedgwick, Thomas Clark, and Edward Gibbons operated effectively, but somewhat uneasily, in the Bay colony through the 1660s, evincing sympathy, at various times and in various combinations, with transatlantic actors who ran afoul of the New England Way, and openly manifesting their distaste for "uniformity" in religious practice. There existed, nonetheless, a reservoir of resentment of military men and merchants who were sworn to protect the colony's boundaries and yet all too often seemed themselves to transgress those bounds, either by flirting with tolerationist or heterodox ideas, by fraternizing with potential enemies, or both. Just as military men who doubled as merchants exposed Massachusetts to the potentially deleterious effects of a seemingly limitless frontier populated by an alien race, so too did they in their mercantile roles expose the colony to the effects of a seemingly boundless, identity-confounding and unpredictable transatlantic market.

Under the pressure of King Philip's War in 1675, these resentments, festering among the common people, were given full vent. While religious heterodoxy per se ceased to be a major issue in the war era, popular animosity began to be directed against those who refused to use religion as a boundary capable of emphatically separating self and "other"—namely, Puritans of English descent from Indians who sought to penetrate their ranks. The predilection for isolationism, and the fear of transatlantic projects (such as missionary work) that surfaced at this time had been encouraged, indeed specifically mandated, by the "orthodoxy" that had triumphed over "antinomianism" in 1638.

4

Praying with the Enemy

Daniel Gookin, King Philip's War, and the Dangers of Intercultural Mediatorship

ate on the evening of February 28, 1676, the obscure Massachusetts private Richard Scott reached an emotional breaking point. Convinced that magistrate Daniel Gookin's solicitude for the plight of Christian Indians during King Philip's War signified that the militia captain (and soon-to-be major) was little better than a traitor to his "country," Scott burst into Blue Anchor Tavern in Cambridge and launched into an impassioned diatribe against his foe. The chief witness to this incident, tavern proprietor Elizabeth Belcher, swore out a deposition several days later detailing the verbal contents of Scott's shocking tirade.[1] Not only had Scott "broak out into many hideous railing expressions against the worshipful Captain Daniel Gookin, calling him an Irish dog that was never faithful to his country, the sonne of a whoare, a bitch, a rogue, God confound him, and God rott his soul," but the disorderly soldier had also given voice to a violent fantasy involving Gookin: "if I could meet him alone I would pistoll him. I wish my knife and sizers were in his heart. He is the devil's interpreter."[2] Earlier in the day of Scott's verbal explosion at the Blue Anchor, the anonymous "society A.B.C.D.," to which Scott undoubtedly belonged, had posted handbills throughout Boston threatening the lives of both Gookin and his fellow magistrate Thomas Danforth (Elizabeth Belcher's brother) and advising readers "not to supprese this paper but to promote its designe, which is to certify . . . that some generous spirits have vowed their destruction; as Christians wee warne them to prepare for death, for though they will deservedly dye, yet we wish the health of their soules."[3]

Scott's violent rage against Gookin, erupting at one of the English colonists' darkest hours during King Philip's War, stemmed from his resentment of the captain's dogged insistence that the Christianized, or "praying," Indians, be accepted as true, albeit subordinate citizens of the Puritan commonwealth, worthy of being trusted as spies, guides, and soldiers rather than eyed warily as potential turncoats richly deserving of internment or even annihilation.[4] Fined heavily and imprisoned briefly for having "so vilely reproacht" a magistrate, Scott was extraordinarily bold in his actions; but his animosity toward Bay Colony leaders who advocated the cause of praying Indians was not unusual. Other military leaders, especially Major Thomas Savage and Captain Daniel Henchman, also experienced resistance whenever they manifested trust in their praying Indian adjuncts. Gookin, however, who had worked closely with the "apostle" John Eliot and had served more than twenty years as superintendent, or chief magistrate, of the praying Indians, bore the brunt of the abuse, fearing at one point to "go along the Streets" alone.[5] By occupying a whole series of literal and figurative "middle grounds," Gookin had set himself at odds with the isolationist thrust of late-seventeenth-century New England social culture; and, what was even more damaging, he seemed to profit, as a developer of the frontier, and as a merchant, from the manipulation of dangerous liminal space.[6]

Historians studying Puritan missionary endeavors, especially the "praying towns" that Gookin helped Eliot to create and maintain, have rightly focused on how these efforts to "reduce" Indians to "civility" destroyed Indian cultures and dashed all hopes for any sort of native autonomy.[7] But this approach elides important issues raised by the violent reaction against Daniel Gookin in King Philip's War. While scholars have shown clearly that assimilative missionary endeavors caused extensive damage to Indian societies, they have only just begun to consider why many English residents of the Bay Colony felt themselves threatened by these efforts.[8] In coming to terms with why rank-and-file Puritan colonists were so repulsed by figures like Gookin, this chapter will elucidate the contested roles that ideas about race, religion, and empire played in the conceptualization of "liberty" and the formation of colonial identity in late-seventeenth-century Massachusetts.

The harsh rejection of praying Indians represented not just a temporary "loss of control" on the part of Massachusetts elites, as one scholar has recently suggested, but rather signaled the culmination of a decades-long process in which ordinary New Englanders, not unlike their contemporaries in Virginia, came to define liberty as the right to prioritize local over transatlantic needs and to define community in racially exclusive terms.[9] The land pressures plaguing second-generation New Englanders undoubtedly exacerbated hostility toward the praying Indians; but it is important to recognize too that the missionary enterprise drew criticism because it was perceived as the intrusive project of transatlantic elites, both Puritan and Anglican, who envisioned a heterogeneously constructed empire in defi-

ance of the wishes of ordinary local residents.[10] The association of Christian
or "friendly" Indians and their advocates with unwanted transatlantic influence endured long after Bay Colony leaders reestablished control over
men like Richard Scott. Ironically, Edmund Andros, the hated royal governor overthrown during New England's Glorious Revolution, and Daniel
Gookin, whose vigorous opposition to royal intervention in the 1680s
brought him back into public favor, shared one thing in common: both, at
the height of their respective periods of unpopularity, were believed to have
shown greater "love" toward their Indian friends than their English countrymen; and both were thought capable of plotting with those allies against
the English.[11]

Daniel Gookin's contention that praying Indians should be accepted
as true converts and true allies sparked intense, class-based controversy in
a colony whose leaders had failed in the decade prior to the outbreak of
King Philip's War to provide a collective, community-affirming response
to the frightening array of political, social, and religious changes that characterized the second half of the seventeenth century. With the Restoration
of the Stuart monarchy in 1660 and the silencing of English Puritanism,
the New World's preeminent Puritan colony entered a period in which its
political and religious identity, and its future, came into serious doubt.[12]
The seemingly heavyhanded assertion of Crown authority, as embodied in
a crown commission sent in 1664 to investigate conditions in Massachusetts, led some New Englanders to fear that they would be swallowed up
by an imperial system indifferent, indeed hostile, to the needs of a pure
Bible commonwealth. Worse yet, on the domestic scene, the bonds of true
religion seemed to be unraveling as elites squared off against one another
in arguing the merits of a liberalized means of attaining church membership
known disparagingly as the "halfway" covenant. Debates over the "halfway"
covenant muddied the distinction between true "saints" and hypocrites and
revealed that leaders on both sides of the issue were experimenting with
new and frightening ways of expanding the definition of community. In
this environment of doubt and suspicion, questions about ultimate loyalties
and accusations of treachery—the same issues raised by Richard Scott—
came easily to the fore.

The combined effect of these conditions, which conspicuously eroded
New Englanders' sense of a fixed communal identity and their confidence
in the existence of a set of carefully policed communal boundaries, produced in the King Philip's War era an enhanced fear among rank-and-file
colonists of anyone whose loyalties seemed ambiguous or ill defined. Daniel
Gookin fit this description in a number of different ways: the Cambridge
captain was enmeshed in arenas outside New England, particularly the
frontier and the transatlantic market, that were believed to be fraught with
danger and vice; he embraced a missionary vision shaped more by his family's experiences as colonizers of Ireland than by his experiences in Massachusetts; he was thought to play the role of intercultural mediator even
when that role conflicted with his official military position; and, at the

conclusion of the war, he wrote a tract, *Doings and Sufferings of the Christian Indians in New England*, that placed praying Indians not only at the center of the war's dramatic action but also at the center of its providential meaning, thereby challenging the notion that God used the "rod of affliction" to speak exclusively to his English saints. At a time when transatlantic and regional events impelled ordinary English Puritans to rededicate themselves to their always latent tribalistic urges, Gookin, like other members of the mercantile and military elite, symbolized those forces working toward a polymorphous rather than an unambiguously fixed colonial identity.[13] Under the stress of war Gookin's relationship with the praying Indians came to symbolize the amalgamating tendencies of a late-seventeenth-century world that seemed bent on destroying the boundaries that kept Englishmen distinct from Indians, garden distinct from wilderness, and the Bible commonwealth distinct from a corrupt (and corrupting) metropolis.

RICHARD SCOTT, IN the heat of anger over Gookin's preferential treatment of Christian Indians, blurted out that Gookin was an "Irish dog." At first glance this imprecation appears to make little rational sense. While it was true that Gookin's father and uncle—Daniel and Vincent Gookin, respectively—had been English Protestant colonizers of Munster early in the seventeenth century, the younger Gookin, Scott's nemesis, had resided steadily in Massachusetts since 1644, when his conversion to Puritanism had made it impossible for him to remain on the extensive Gookin family holdings in William Berkeley's Virginia.[14] Despite Gookin's long absence from Irish affairs, however, Scott was correct to associate Gookin's "disloyalty," by which he meant Gookin's defense of the Christian Indians, with the captain's Irish past.

Daniel Gookin was born in 1612 to a Kentish family primed for colonial exploits. In 1617 his father and uncle acquired leaseholds in Munster from Richard Boyle, first earl of Cork, an ambitious economic "projector" who built a veritable family empire around the Munster lands he purchased from Sir Walter Raleigh.[15] The elder Daniel Gookin, not fully satisfied with opportunities in Ireland, branched out during the 1620s into other endeavors, purchasing shares in the Virginia Company and establishing extensive landed holdings in Virginia through headrights, by shipping livestock, settlers, and servants there from Ireland.[16]

Motivated, perhaps, by the Irish Rebellion of 1641, which drove many English Protestants out of Ireland, the younger Daniel Gookin decided to settle permanently on family lands in the Chesapeake.[17] He initially did well in Virginia; he acquired two plantations in New Norfolk and served in capacities of public trust, such as burgess and militia captain. But Gookin's Protestant ardor soon sealed his fate. Having grown up in the religiously charged atmosphere of Protestant Munster and having possibly fought (like Underhill) in the early 1630s to defend the Reformed religion in the Netherlands, Gookin was dissatisfied with the seeming lack of religious commitment in Virginia. In 1642 he joined with a group of intense

Nansemond Protestants who petitioned the Bay Colony "earnestly entreating a supply of faithful ministers, whom, upon experience of their gifts and godliness they might call to office." When Governor Berkeley's government responded to the arrival of three clergymen from New England by outlawing religious nonconformity, Gookin was compelled, after a brief sojourn in a Puritan region of tolerationist Maryland, to relocate to Massachusetts.[18]

Given his obvious usefulness and his stature as a man who had suffered in Virginia on account of religious scruples, Gookin received a warm welcome in the Bay Colony. He quickly attained church membership, took his place beside fellow elites in the colony's prestigious Artillery Company, and rose to high military and political office; in 1652, he was elected to the magistracy for the first time.[19] Yet while Gookin successfully integrated himself into the highest ranks of a Puritan colony determined to shelter itself from outside influence, his interest in converting New England's indigenous peoples to Christianity had, as Richard Scott hinted, been conditioned in a transatlantic environment whose pressures and priorities were in many ways disturbingly different from those of New England.

Back in Munster, the first colonizing generation of Gookins had been profoundly influenced by the distinctive colonial ethos fashioned by their patron Richard Boyle. Boyle had believed that the "new" English Protestant colonizers of Ireland, arriving from 1560 to 1660, must set about the task of significantly "improving" the Irish people and land so as to establish their identity as the rightful colonizers of Ireland and to demonstrate their superiority over both the Irish Catholic natives and "old English" settlers, who had blended almost indiscriminately with the indigenous population.[20] For Boyle, "improvement" meant transforming the "savage" and improvident Irish Catholics into good, culturally assimilated Protestant workers and subjecting the land to the newest agricultural and extractive methods.

The influence of the Boyle family and the memory of his Irish past certainly predisposed Gookin to become active in the cause of Christianizing and "civilizing" the New England Algonquians; but a voyage to London in 1655, in which the Massachusetts captain renewed his acquaintance with an Irish cousin, Vincent Gookin, proved to be the key galvanizing experience. Daniel traveled to London in 1655 for the purpose of administering the estate of his deceased older brother, Edward. At that time Vincent Gookin, then serving as one of Ireland's thirty representatives in the Protectorate parliament, was also in the metropolis, engaged, significantly, in a dispute over how Protestant colonizers should treat the Gaelic rebels who had temporarily dispossessed English colonizers in the rebellion of 1641. While many of the Cromwellian military men instrumental in the reconquest of Ireland, and expecting spoils, wanted the subject population to be relocated and concentrated in a single district supervised and controlled by an English garrison, Vincent Gookin, who continued to operate in Ireland in a cultural and political milieu still dominated by the Boyle heirs, published a pamphlet, *The Great Case of Transplantation in Ireland*

Discussed, explaining why it would make good economic, religious, and moral sense to reject this policy and to focus instead on the "uplift" and assimilation of the "wild" Irish population.[21]

In the immediate wake of his exposure to this English controversy, Daniel Gookin became more active in the missionary endeavor in New England. To be sure, Gookin in the 1640s had manifested some interest in "apostle" John Eliot's work with the indigenous peoples of Massachusetts.[22] Nonetheless, his decision in 1656 to accept the post of superintendent of the praying Indians—a position that allowed him to have a direct influence in shaping the "civilizing" process—coincided exactly with his return from the trip in which he encountered Vincent Gookin. Six years later, when the Irish-born scientist and Hartlib Circle associate Robert Boyle (Richard's son) was appointed governor of the refashioned Company for the Propagation of the Gospel in New England, it was as though the patron–client relationship obtaining between the Boyle and Gookin families of Ireland had been symbolically extended to the new world. The London-based missionary society collected and disbursed monies for the work of conversion, including a small stipend for Gookin; Gookin, in turn, prefaced his writings with cordial "epistles gratulatory and dedicatory" to Boyle.[23] In his *Historical Collections of the Indians in New England*, completed in 1674, Gookin unequivocally acknowledged his reliance on the Irish example, explaining how the American Indians were destined to remain in the same darkness and despair suffered by the Irish Catholics unless good Christians took steps to lead them toward the light.

> It hath been the observation of some prudent historians, that the changing of the language of a barbarous people, into the speech of a more civil and potent nation that have conquered them, hath been an approved experiment, to reduce such a people into the civility and religion of the prevailing nation. And I incline to believe, that if that course had been effectually taken with the Irish, their enmity and rebellion against the English had been long since cured or prevented, and they better instructed in the protestant religion; and consequently redeemed from the vassallage and affection to the Romish see; who have by this means kept the greatest part of them in ignorance, and consequently in brutishness and superstition to this day.[24]

From his Boyle-influenced cousin Vincent Gookin, who wrote exclusively on the Irish Catholics, Daniel borrowed important insights as to how the enterprise of "civilizing" an inferior people through religion should proceed and what role these people should play in colonial English society once they were reformed. New Englanders were less dependent on Indian labor than their countrymen in Ireland were on the Gaelic Irish; but Gookin readily approved the idea of transforming "savage," indolent souls into disciplined, God-fearing Christian workers, and he strove, along with John Eliot, to impart the work ethic as an initial step in the acculturating process.[25] As an investor and developer of the New England frontier, more-over, Gookin extended the definition of labor to include military service, an innovation that would have been unthinkable in the Irish context and that many New Englanders, as I have shown, staunchly resisted.

In addition to anticipating the benefits of joint Anglo-Indian military ventures and explaining how praying Indian towns might stand as a "living wall to guard the English frontiers," Gookin also speculated about ways that English capital and Indian labor could be used to expand New England's frontier trade, particularly so as to include the Mohawk bands inhabiting the environs of the Hudson River. This enterprise would be a

> costly thing; yet, in the issue, it may also be greatly advantageous unto the discoverers, not only in using means for conveying and communicating the christian religion unto so many poor, ignorant souls, which is the greater,—but also in accumulating external riches, as well as honour, unto the first undertakers and perfecters of this discovery. There would be a need, Gookin thought, for "pious and religious Indians . . . to accompany the English in their discovery; and some of them may be left behind among those Indians, if they find encouragement, to be instructing them in the knowledge of the true God, and our Lord Jesus Christ."[26]

Vincent Gookin's stance on the issue of the Catholic Irish eerily prefigured Daniel Gookin's role twenty years later as protector of the Massachusetts praying Indians; but Vincent Gookin, unlike Daniel, operated in a political context where elite factions were free to debate assimilationist policies with minimal reference to or input from ordinary men like Richard Scott. As Nicholas Canny has shown, Vincent Gookin, a political protégé of the Boyles, argued in favor of assimilationist policies as a means of preserving the rights of those elite "new" English colonizers who had established themselves in Ireland prior to the 1640s and who feared displacement at the hands of the victorious soldiers who had put down the rebellion; only the ideal of a "mixed plantation," based on the Spanish model, Canny says, could preserve their identity-confirming role as Ireland's "civilizers."[27]

Vincent Gookin, in pleading the cause of cultural assimilation, was acting as a spokesman for those with interests similar to his own. But, conscious of his political environment, he effectively demonstrated how the Ireland of his dreams, integrated at last by the "unitive principles of Christianity," would benefit not only investors but the dawning Cromwellian empire as a whole; "benevolent" policies would reduce the likelihood of future rebellions and permit Ireland, with its Catholics "swallowed up by the English and incorporated into them," to begin absorbing England's surplus population: "And what a pleasing sight will it be to England, instead of meagre naked Anatomies, which she received driven from Ireland in the beginning of a War, to empty her self of her young Swarms thither in the beginning of a Peace?"[28]

The missionary impulse, while consistent in a sense with the wider Cromwellian dream of empire, nonetheless allowed the "new" English colonizers of Ireland to retain an identity separate from and superior to that of brutal Cromwellian soldiers on the one hand, and of degenerated "old" English settlers on the other. But in Puritan Massachusetts, where ordinary people held more sway, corporate identity never did, and never would, hinge on the "uplift" of indigenous peoples.

Daniel Gookin, in Massachusetts, was every bit as hegemonic in his intentions for the local Algonquians as Vincent Gookin had been in his plans for the Gaelic Irish; but the "middling" planters and freemen of New England rejected Gookin's efforts. Ordinary colonists viewed the privileging of local over imperial affairs, and the drawing of their own tribal social boundaries as key components of their English liberty. The new roles Gookin limned out for converts as laborers and soldiers threatened to collapse the distinction between Indians and ordinary English colonists, not only exposing the latter to danger in the case of Indian treachery but also possibly denigrating the labor of Englishmen who already occupied the lower rungs of the colony's social ladder. At a time when the coveted status of landed "independency," which connoted full "manhood," increasingly eluded the best efforts of many English colonists, Gookin, by protecting Indian claims to land, appeared to be extending hopes of economic "competency" to "savages" while depriving his own people of the same benefit.[29]

Even Wait Winthrop, grandson of the former governor, believed that his family's livelihood was threatened by land grants made on behalf of the praying Indians. In 1679 Winthrop complained to the General Court that a grant made in 1660 to create the praying town of Wamesit conflicted with an earlier grant of three thousand acres, to be located between the Merrimack and Concord Rivers, promised to his grandfather—a tract his grandmother (Margaret Winthrop) had thought "might by private improvement have purchased a competency for the whole family." According to Winthrop, "some persons zealous to settle the Indian in some civil and ecclesiastical state" had successfully petitioned the General Court to grant a large tract "called I suppose Wamesit for an Indian plantation . . . ordering the like quantity or value of other lands to bee laid out to us [Winthrop heirs] in lieu thereof." But the compensatory land had never been found, and to Winthrop's horror,

> though God has pleaded our right by expelling the Indyan inhabitants and leaving the land in status quo . . . yet I have information that some English have by Addresses to this Honorable court petitioned for the same or some part thereof.[30]

Winthrop felt that his rights had been usurped, not only by the initial petitioners, including Gookin and Eliot, who had taken advantage of his absence from the colony to make their bid for his lands, but also by subsequent seekers of Merrimack grants, such as Jonathan Tyng, Thomas Brattle, and Thomas Henchman, all of whom evinced some degree of sympathy for the praying Indians. The timing of Winthrop's petition, in the postwar period, suggests that he was trying to take advantage of the widespread resentment of the praying Indians and their advocates.

In addition to threatening Bay colonists' claims to frontier lands, missionary work also—at least at a rhetorical level—called into question the primacy of Englishmen as God's chosen people. As an exhortatory device, ministers sometimes incorporated accounts of Indian conversions into their jeremiadical preaching as a warning that if Englishmen did not mend their ways, God might adopt another people, the Indians, as his chosen nation. A group of English ministers who endorsed Thomas Shepard's *Clear Sun-Shine of the Gospel Breaking Forth*, a missionary tract, warned readers that "God abides with England" not "for need but for love," and that one day his affection might turn elsewhere:

> And indeed God may wel seek out for other ground to sow the seed of his Ordinances upon . . . he may well bespeak another people to himself, seeing he finds no better entertainment among the people he hath espoused to him, and that by so many mercies, priviledges indeerments, ingagements. We have as many sad symptoms of a declining, as these poor outcasts have glad presages of a Rising Sun among them. The Ordinances are as much contemned here, as frequented there, the Ministry as much discouraged here, as embraced there: Religion as much derided, the ways of godliness as much scorned here, as they can be wished and desired there . . . if he [God] cannot have an England here, he can have an England there and baptize and adopt them into those priviledges, which wee have looked upon as our burthens. We have sad decayes upon us, we are a revolting Nation, a people guilty of great defection from God. . . . Some fall from professed seeming holynes, to sin and profanenes; who like blazing comets did shine bright for a time, but after have set in a night of darkness . . . God hath forsaken other Churches as eminent as ever England was . . . where are those ancient people of the Jews who were . . . his peculiar and chosen people of al nations? they are scattered abroad as a curse, and their place knows them no more.[31]

These ministers did not seriously believe that the Indians could replace English Puritans in God's affections; the employment of a trope that depicted Christian Indians and Christian Englishmen as spiritual rivals, however, was damaging to the Indians, whose possessions the colonists already coveted. Interestingly, too, William Hubbard's history of King Philip's War reported the alarming fact that at least one purportedly Christian Indian, the Saco sachem Squando, believed that his own people were the chosen ones, and preached that God was planning, through war, to extirpate the English colonists in favor of the Indians: "Squando doth inform them that God doth speak to him, and doth tell him that God hath left our Nation to them to destroy, and the Indians do take it for a Truth all that he doth tell them." The colonist William Harris, writing to a friend in England, similarly complained that "our enemyes" added insult to injury by "bosting that God was departed from us, and was with them."[32]

If the rivalry alluded to in missionary tracts was merely figurative, the ongoing pressure colonists were placing on Indian lands and social space was all too real. Clergymen, of course, intended their preaching and writing to spark a "reformation of manners"; these strains, however, could easily augment popular hostility toward praying Indians and their most adamant supporters.

The resentment of missionaries who played at inverting the relative positions of Indian and English Christians came to a head in 1661, when the General Court condemned *The Christian Commonwealth*, a tract authored by John Eliot. It was politic, during the Restoration, for Bay Colony leaders to dissociate themselves from a tract that proclaimed the rule of "Christ the King" as opposed to Charles II. But the tract was targeted, too, because it subtly criticized the New England Way, arguing that the Indian residents of Eliot's praying towns, living strictly in accord with biblical prescription, might achieve greater heights of social perfection than the English colonists themselves.[33] Like the members of Boyle's influential Hartlib Circle, Eliot believed that the conversion of indigenous peoples to Christianity should be regarded as a first step toward a dawning millennium of Protestant unity in which pure believers from all nations, not just one chosen locality, would accept the true religion in preparation for the prophesied thousand-year reign of Christ; to this end, Eliot looked forward to the invention of a universal language that all could understand.[34] These ideas partook more of international Puritanism than the local New England orthodoxy.

The assimilationist project may have seemed identity-affirming in Boyle's Ireland; but in Massachusetts, the concept of cultural conversion, with its inherent assumption that identity was a mutable or fluid construct, posed a direct threat to the distinct and particularistic (and now embattled) New World identity—homogeneous, roughly egalitarian, and provincially oriented—that had prevailed in Massachusetts since the 1630s. The Massachusetts merchant John Nelson, writing in the 1690s, observed that the English colonies' neglect of the Indians, both in religious and diplomatic terms, could be attributed to this provincial outlook: "they [the various colonies] are become and doe in a manner esteeme each as foraigners one unto the other." The majority of Bay colonists had long shied away from those crosscultural, transatlantic ties on which missionary work depended; and, in the late seventeenth century, despite the impending "anglicization," many turned inward in response to reversals on the world stage.[35] Under these circumstances, and particularly with the commencement of a devastating Indian war, Daniel Gookin was bound to be perceived as a traitor.

MISSIONARY WORK WAS almost by definition a cosmopolitan endeavor that many New Englanders, committed more to their own locality than to the wider world, regarded with some degree of ambivalence. The London-based societies that financed and conceptualized the goals of proselytization, whether dominated by Puritans, royalists, or some combination thereof, seemed bent on eviscerating the cultural distinctions among all the English colonial regions that they touched.[36] Missionary writings, moreover, even those produced by loyal adherents of the New England Way, always seemed to rebuke the colony's spiritual accomplishments or to threaten the cosmic place of its residents. And outside critics, from Henry Vane to Thomas Lechford, who openly condemned the New England Way from a variety of different perspectives, reiterated with striking consistency the Bay Colony's failure to do its part for the saving of Indian souls.

Thomas Lechford, who had expressed views on the millennium at odds with those of the majority in the Bay Colony and who had subsequently returned to the Anglican fold, explained that the New England church polity was flawed because, institutionally and temperamentally, it was incapable of of outreach and could meet the spiritual needs only of those who already believed. The Congregational Way, which rejected the supervisory role ascribed in biblical times to "Apostles," "Evangelists," and a unifying hierarchy, lacked the infrastructure to disseminate religious principles, set up native churches, ordain indigenous preachers, and provide for regular visitation and supervision; at the same time, the preference for "extempore" preaching "in publique" over "forms in set words and the reading of the Scriptures" boded ill for the catechizing of people new to Christianity. Introverted New Englanders, Lechford charged, had selfishly built up a church polity to suit themselves without thinking about how best to "convert and plant churches among pagans and heathens" or how to ensure that future generations were properly educated in Christian theology:

And surely it is good to overthrow heathenisme by all good wayes and meanes. But there hath not been any sent forth by any Church to learne the Natives language, or to instruct them in the Religion; First, because they say they have not to do with them being without, unlesse, they come to heare and learn English. Secondly some say out of Rev. 15. last, it is not probable that any nation more can be converted, til the calling of the Jews . . . and God knowes when it will bee. Thirdly, because all Churches among them are equall, and all Officers equall, and so betweene many, nothing is done that way. They must all therefore equally beare the blame; for indeede I humbly conceive that by their principles, no Nation can or could ever be converted. Therefore, if so, by their principles how can any Nation be governed? . . . The conversion and subduing of a Nation, and so

great a tract of ground, is a work too weighty for subjects any much
longer to labour under without Royall assistance, as I apprehend, I
think, in religious reason.

Not all advocates of missionary work insisted, as Lechford did, that "the
poor Indians" ought to be "taught by forms"—the set prayers and rituals
that Puritans so despised.[37] But Lechford's central criticism—that Massachusetts had allowed its zeal for a particularistic brand of purity to triumph
over broader religious responsibilities—resonated widely in the transatlantic world, even among Quaker dissidents like John Easton and Thomas
Maule.[38] To slight New England on its poor treatment of the Indians or
its paltry efforts at proselytization was to disparage the bible commonwealth's isolationism, its tribalism, and its rejection not only of Indians but
of other deserving outsiders.

Bay Colony residents had long resented Puritan "grandees" who questioned New England's primacy of place in the divine scheme of things and
engaged in imperialistic projects that might detract from Massachusetts.[39]
Some of the same sorts of resentments attached themselves to the Puritan-
led missionary enterprise of the 1640s and 1650s. I have shown already
how John Eliot became a controversial figure at midcentury because he
embraced a vision of the missionary endeavor that flew in the face of tribalism. After 1660, when the restored monarchy took over the New England
Company, the potential threat that it posed to New England regional culture became that much more sinister.

Daniel Gookin, despite his commitment to the New England Way,
was a man whose heart lay in the wider world. In 1655, at the same time
that he encountered Vincent Gookin in London, Daniel had quickly become embroiled in political affairs, agreeing reluctantly to carry out a mission for the Cromwellian Protectorate that he knew would be unpopular
in New England. His mission, intended to support the Western Design,
was to promote among New Englanders the idea of resettling Jamaica,
which had just been conquered from the Spanish with the help of Gookin's
Massachusetts Artillery Company colleague Robert Sedgwick. Gookin, understanding the deep reservations New Englanders harbored about such
projects, was not eager to take on the assignment.[40] Nonetheless he acceded
to the Protector's wishes, possibly out of gratitude for the recent reconquest of Ireland, which greatly benefited his Irish kinsmen.[41] While
Gookin's loyalty would never have been questioned so openly and directly
in 1675 had he not become an advocate for the praying Indians, the halfhearted efforts on behalf of the settlement of Jamaica two decades earlier
may have left some residual sense that Gookin was not fully committed to
New England—Scott, it will be recalled, had charged that Gookin was "an
Irish dog . . . *never* faithful to his country."

In 1662 the latitudinarian Robert Boyle, a member of the Council for
Foreign Plantations, rose to the governorship of the New England Company. Boyle, while a member of the established church, could work well

with Puritans; as governor, he carried forward into a new era the progressive, millennial vision that had infused the Hartlib Circle. At the same time, however, Boyle's ideas had clear imperialistic overtones far more threatening than those of Cromwell. Not only did he believe that the transformation of "savage" indolent souls into disciplined, God-fearing workers possessed an intrinsic moral good, ridding the world of paganism and papacy alike, but also he thought that the economic expansion bound to occur as these marginal peoples became productive would help to heal the residual animosities left over from the civil war years; factions that had been at odds and regional areas that had been at crosspurposes could all unite under the banner of trade and civilized prosperity.[42] New Englanders continued to look to Boyle as one of the few figures of the Restoration government who would lend a friendly ear to the concerns of dissenters; still, his larger commitments were at variance with theirs, especially those of the common people.[43] John Eliot's millennial dream, and the explicit imperial dream that Robert Boyle subsequently worked out as governor of the New England Company, were equally disturbing, for each posited a connection between the transatlantic world and the frontier, hinting darkly that the two might one day coalesce and overrun the New England center.

Both the correspondence addressed to the Bay Colony from the new king and the actions and rhetoric of the commissioners acting on his behalf in the mid-1660s tended to confirm such fears. The Crown consistently cast itself as the ultimate protector of Indian subjects, who had most likely been abused by colonial authorities. The commissioners promised that injustices visited upon indigenous peoples, particularly in the context of land claims, would be promptly redressed. They characterized the colonists' theory that Scripture warranted the appropriation of unimproved land from non-Christian people as an affront "both against the honor of God and the justice of the king," for the phrase " 'children of men' " in the Bible "comprehends Indians as well as English; and no doubt the Country is theirs till they give it or sell it, though it be not improved." On more than one occasion, the commissioners called to mind that their royal master had referred to the colony's original inhabitants as "neighbor kings and princes" and recommended that

> full reparation and satisfaction be made them for any injury or damage they have susteyned, since any violation of promise, or other violence, will discredit and call into question the faith of Christianity and disappoint or obstruct our great end of converting of infidells in those parts.[44]

The needs of the colonists were here made trifles compared with those of the Indians, whose leaders were referred to continually as "kings," "princes," and "great men" with whom royal officials might negotiate directly rather than respecting the arrangements made by colonial governments. The royal commissioners were less interested in righting wrongs done the Indians than rankling colonial leaders and asserting their authority in the starkest possible manner. But the commissioners' rhetoric, which subtly threatened the use of Indians to keep colonists in line, would have helped to cement in some colonial minds the association between missionary aims and transatlantic danger; after all, the commissioners had suggested that some sort of redistributive justice might be in order so as to keep the Christian religion in good repute among the "infidells."

Quaker critics of the New England Way, meanwhile, capitalizing on the strained relationship between metropolis and colony, similarly took to exposing the Puritans' abuse and mismanagement of the Indians as a means by which to get back at those "priest-ridden" colonists who had passed "sanguinary" laws against their sect. The Rhode Island Quaker John Easton, for example, wrote a tract about the outbreak of King Philip's War in which he not only explained how some of the Indians' grievances were justified but also suggested that war might have been averted if crown officials like Edmund Andros, then governor of New York, had been allowed to intervene:

> I see no menes lickly to procuer a sesation from arems exept the governer of new york can find a way so to intersete . . . we know no English should begin a war and not first tender for the king to be umpier and not persecute such that will not Conforem to ther worship, and ther worship be what is not owned by the king. The king not to mind to have such things redresed, sum mai take it that he hath not pouer, and that ther mai be a wai for them to take pouer in oposition to him. I am so perswaided of new Englnad prists thay ar so blinded by the spiret of persecution and to maintaine to have hyer, and to have rume to be mere hyerlings that thay have bine the Case [cause] that the law of nations and the law of arems have bine vioilated in this war, and that the war had not bine if ther had not bine a hyerling.[45]

King Philip's War came about, Easton suggested, because headstrong Bay Colony magistrates insisted on pursuing policies, both in Indian affairs and religion, that ran contrary to the will and interest of the Crown. Once the imperial will asserted itself, Easton hoped, the exclusionary New England Way, which represented the root cause of the carnage and of the persecution of his coreligionists, would perforce be uprooted.

In the years following King Philip's War, Gookin regained popularity in Massachusetts by taking a firm stand against England's political encroachments on the Bay Colony charter; but his missionary work and his economic goals had the opposite effect, connecting New England to a transatlantic web of commerce in which a unique Puritan culture would become difficult to maintain. Even Gookin's harsh stance against religious dissent, which could be interpreted as devoted commitment to the New England Way, may have been motivated by the desire to help new converts gain a firm grasp on Puritan doctrine. Vincent Gookin had, after all, denounced

> the many divisions among those who are called Protestants, and bitternesses of those who are thus divided, because by the former the Papist sees not where to fix if he should come to us, and because of the later he sees not what friends or security he could partake if he should fix.[46]

Gookin's efforts in the 1670s to integrate Algonquian and English Christians through religious, military, and economic means met with stiff resistance. Colonists, intent on retaining their own identity as a separate people, resented Gookin's efforts to replace the ties of race and kin with those of religion alone. Both Indians on the frontier and imperial or colonial officials willing to negotiate and do business with them manifested a cultural porosity that ordinary people greatly feared. While the clear, visceral expression of these resentments depended on the charged atmosphere of war, the widespread feelings of insecurity on which the hatreds fed was rooted in the previous decade's debates over religious, and therefore communal, inclusion and exclusion.

DANIEL GOOKIN'S PLANS for transforming "others" into "brothers" coincided, inauspiciously, with the controversy over the "halfway" covenant. In 1662, a ministerial synod recommended that congregations remedy the problem of declining church membership by extending an attenuated, "halfway" status to those children of the "saints" who, for a variety of reasons, were unable to make the required conversion narrative. For the ministers who supported it, the halfway covenant seemed like the best way to guarantee the survival of the colony's religious institutions in a changing world. But because the "innovation" symbolically spoke to the broad issue of corporate identity and belonging, it became the subject of acrimonious debate.[47] Scholars have not yet examined how Anglo-Indian tensions may have shaped responses to the halfway covenant; but here I will argue that Gookin's high visibility as a champion of both halfway covenant and praying Indians inhibited the people's acceptance of an innovation that, in the long run, tended to reinforce popularly based tribalistic urges. (Although we normally think of New England's indigenous peoples as living in tribes, it was the English colonists' discomfort with porous cultural bounds and their hesitancy to accept "strangers" as brothers and sisters in Christ, that marked them off as the true tribals.)[48]

The halfway covenant was disquieting because it could be read differently by different constituencies. Faced with a resistant laity, ministerial advocates of the halfway covenant tended to acquiesce in the popular tribalistic belief that some blood lines were more disposed to godliness than others: an obliging Increase Mather, for example, argued that the halfway covenant should be adopted because it simply ratified the widespread popular notion that regeneracy normally passed "through the loyns of godly parents."[49] This kind of reasoning unintentionally created an intellectual climate hostile to the acceptance within the Massachusetts fold of ethnic or cultural "others," particularly those, like the Indians, with a reputation for deceit and treachery.[50] Like witchery, heresy, or perhaps savagery, some promoters of the halfway covenant seemed to be saying, religion was a family affair. Yet, while arguments in favor of the innovation were tailored to appeal to popular sensibilities, they failed in the short run to achieve their mark, for high-ranking secular elites like Daniel Gookin, who supported the new measures, did so for reasons that ran counter to the growing consensus in favor of tribalism. Massachusetts entered King Philip's War with an elite bitterly divided over how best to redefine the parameters of the symbolic community for a new age; this divisiveness exacerbated class polarization, for neither side was able to inspire the confidence and trust of the people.

In the five years prior to King Philip's War, Bay colonists witnessed the painful rupture of First Church Boston, when a faction of "dissenting brethren" withdrew from the church and created a new Congregation (Third Church, or Old South) in protest against the majority's rejection of the halfway covenant.[51] The breakup of this prestigious congregation, which contained a fair percentage of the colony's war leaders, caused deep and long-lasting political and social turmoil; even more disturbing, from the perspective of ordinary colonists, was the fact that neither side was able (or willing) to articulate a vision of the good life that was acceptable to the commonalty. Daniel Gookin, together with leading proponents of the halfway covenant in Third Church, like Thomas Savage, showed by word and deed that they did not equate the innovation with provincial tribalism. First Church Boston, meanwhile, while retaining the old forms, represented a cosmopolitanism that comported even less well with the aims of the common folk.

In 1671, the clergyman John Oxenbridge, who had formerly been involved in the promotion of a project to Christianize the natives of Surinam, chose to accept the pulpit call of First Church Boston, which had just suffered the death of its contentious pastor John Davenport. Oxenbridge was not at all put off by the fact that First Church was deeply embroiled in controversy over its rejection of the halfway covenant. Having himself been accused of instigating a similar religious battle over pure church membership and ordinances during the 1640s in Bermuda, Oxenbridge was no stranger to acrimony.[52] What was more, he believed that he had detected a fatal flaw in the logic of the halfway covenant: the potential to underwrite a kind of racial exclusivity that would work against non-English converts by making saving grace the exclusive birthright of certain families, places, and peoples.[53] In 1670, Oxenbridge completed a manuscript "Conversion of the Gentiles," in which he implied that halfway covenant–derived tribalism was a leading cause of the anti-Indian sentiment evident in Massachusetts.

Oxenbridge warned pointedly that those Englishmen who despised or distrusted Indian converts ignored the Abrahamic covenant of grace and willfully reverted to the ideals of the Old Testament Jews, whose legalistic covenant of works necessarily confined the bonds of sacred fellowship to those within the nation and the race. The failure to recognize that regenerate souls were scattered throughout the world, rather than concentrated in one locality, was understandable among the Old Testament Israelites, Oxenbridge conceded, for they had not received the dispensation of grace; but for seventeenth-century Englishmen to deny that "true religion" was "ambulatory or moveable not fixed to any one part of the earth" and that the "church and its officers" were "redeemed to God by the blood of the lamb out of every kindred and tongue and people and nation" was not only myopic, it was a sinful rejection of the covenant of grace:

> And shall then any of the Jewish legall spirit conceited of their own (English or other) nation dare to build up a new partition wall between Gentile and Gentile and exclude and set at naught the poor Indians as once the proud Jews did all Gentiles! Let such a one take heed lest he be accused of the Lord for building that which God will have utterly destroyed . . . the same blood runs in the veins of an Indian as thine . . . God hath made of one blood all nations of men not the Indians of one blood and the English of another.[54]

The halfway covenant's implication that ethnicity or race predisposed certain peoples toward salvation would, Oxenbridge feared, artificially seal New England off not only from Indian proselytes but also from the nourishing influence of the whole multiethnic spiritual world.

Although Daniel Gookin and John Oxenbridge concurred on the issue of praying Indians, the two men were political enemies. Oxenbridge's prominent flock, which included John Leverett, Edward Hutchinson, Thomas Clark, and James Oliver, supported limited tolerationist goals that Gookin, an avid persecutor of Anabaptists and Quakers, adamantly opposed.[55] Still, while First Church Boston adhered to the rigorous standards of church membership associated with the founders, its vision of community was neither traditional nor appealing to the common people. In combining rigorous admissions procedures with tolerationist beliefs, a dominant faction within the congregation would seem to have begun to conceptualize the churches of Massachusetts as noncoercive enclaves of purity within a diverse society—a formulation that figured the realm of spirit as individualistic, private, and unconnected to a specific people or geographic location. The cosmopolitan community envisioned by First Churchers was patently unpopular, resembling to some extent that advocated earlier by the antinomians of the 1630s.[56]

Of course, there was the possibility that First Church, simply because it did retain the stringency of the founders, might become a rallying point for the popular classes if only it would reach out to them; but this was not to be. In 1675, a group of men, angry at what they perceived as the Court's lenient treatment of praying Indian defendants, attempted to rally behind James Oliver, a prominent First Church member and a foe of Daniel Gookin. But when the "crowd" came to Oliver's door, wishing him to lead a party that would visit *vigil ante* justice on a praying Indian man believed guilty of murder, Oliver refused the popular "draft" and called a neighbor, Edward Tyng, to help disperse the crowd.[57] Oliver was perceived as a potential Indian-hater because he had lambasted Gookin in the General Court for his close ties with the praying Indians; but as the signer of a petition in favor of tolerating Anabaptists, Oliver was hostile to Gookin for political reasons that went far beyond, and were indeed distinct, from the praying Indian issue.[58] While Oliver attacked Gookin on what he knew had become a sore subject with the people—telling Gookin "he ought rather to be confined among his Indians than to sit on the Bench"—he probably had no real animosity toward the praying Indians per se. Once this became clear, it contributed to the sense that the common people's worries were not taken seriously by most of their leaders.

Given the disturbing direction in which Oxenbridge's First Church contingent was moving, the promoters of the halfway covenant, who played up the importance of the "seed," might have looked like the more reliable guardians of communal identity. These champions of covenantal reform had, after all, suggested that a reinvented New England Way could still form the backbone of a provincial community defined by its homogeneous dedication to a single interpretation of Puritanism. Nathaniel Saltonstall, moreover, a member of Third Church who authored several King Philip's War tracts, attempted to make political hay out of the war by warning that an open and variegated Christian community such as that sought by First Church would bring nothing but defeat and divine disapproval. In one of his more polemical efforts, Saltonstall implied that the ambush and rout of troops serving under Captain Edward Hutchinson near Brookfield in the summer of 1675 represented God's rebuke of First Church in general and the unfortunate captain in particular. The doleful event, Saltonstall informed readers, occurred on the same day that First Church was holding a fast to propitiate divine aid, "which thing was taken especial notice of, by all those who desire to see the Hand of God in such sad Providences." Hutchinson, a frontier landowner who often employed Nipmucks to work his fields near Brookfield, was culpable for the tragedy, Saltonstall thought, because he had been overly trusting of a group of Indians who promised to negotiate but then double-crossed him.[59] The church, meanwhile, in its rejection of the halfway covenant, had forsaken the ideal of the homogenous, locally oriented Christian community; it had effectively abandoned the "seed" while embracing in its stead a variety of dangerous strangers.

Gookin, like Saltonstall, was a political enemy of First Church and a supporter of the halfway covenant; indeed, as a magistrate he had supported the push to censure Hutchinson's congregation for its shabby treatment of the "dissenting brethren." But Gookin could not agree with Saltonstall's substantive claims about the danger of intercultural contact any more than Oliver could lead the Indian-hating mob that appeared on his doorstep. Nor could Gookin acquiesce in Saltonstall's efforts to manipulate popular opinion by presenting the halfway covenant as an engine of exclusion. Unlike Saltonstall, Gookin understood the halfway covenant to be an innovation whose broad principles might inform the safe expansion, rather than the constriction, of the scope of community; and this was precisely why he became so unpopular. Gookin's patron Robert Boyle favored, in England, a comprehensive, latitudinarian Anglicanism that would harshly exclude abject heretics yet welcome all pure-hearted souls, regardless of their lack of theological sophistication.[60] Daniel Gookin, in his own colonial milieu, sought to strengthen Puritanism along the same lines, arguing that the faith should "comprehend" all would-be believers, including the Indians, who were sincere and well-behaved, while, at the same time, weeding out and persecuting heretical followers of Anabaptistry or Quakerism, in part because sectarian doctrines would confuse would-be converts.

The halfway covenant had multivalent meanings for supporters and defenders alike. The common people were primed to respond favorably to the kinds of arguments deployed by Saltonstall, who would have used the halfway covenant to justify excluding praying Indians from the religious community. But ultimately they came to understand, by observing Gookin and others like him, that the halfway covenant had other meanings and uses that would prevent it from functioning either as a bridge to the past or as a bulwark against the social changes represented by the integration of praying Indians into the Puritan polity. The halfway covenant could certainly be used to reinvigorate the New England Way and protect it from all enemies, both foreign and domestic; at the same time, however, the halfway covenant could be seen as the first in a series of adjustments— culminating with the covenant renewals, territorial churches, and "sacramental renaissance" of the late seventeenth century—that brought religious practice in New England closer to the latitudinarian, "polite," and sophisticated model of post–(Glorious) revolutionary England.[61] With or without the halfway covenant, the bonds of community would continue to expand in ways that ordinary colonists found alarming. Praying Indians, meanwhile, were etched into the New England mind as one of the most potent, and frightening, symbols of that expansion.

To be sure, Gookin never suggested that the halfway covenant be applied directly to Indian converts. The percentage of full church members among the Christian Indians remained small because John Eliot prescribed for them the full rigors of Puritan conversion. As Gookin explained to readers of *Historical Collections*,

> all those we call praying Indians are not all visible Church members, or baptized persons; which ordinance of baptism is not to be administered unto any that are out of the visible church, until they profess

their faith . . . but the infants of such as are members of the visible church are to be baptized.[62]

In demanding that colonists accept as part of their community those Indians who resolved to convert and to live in Christian settlements, Gookin did attempt to appropriate for these proselytes the same "charitable" feelings, and trust, that ministers exhorted their flocks to extend toward halfway members.

The resonant concept of "charity," as employed on the *pro* side in debates over the halfway covenant, was meant to encompass only those individuals whose parents (or at least one of them) were "visible" saints; the congregational churches, it was argued, must recognize and reward the spiritual potential of those children of the covenant who lived moral lives, understood religious tenets intellectually, and put forth a demonstrable effort to convert. In writing of Indian conversion, however, Gookin preserved the regnant commitment to "charity" but inverted the hierarchy that privileged insiders over "others," insisting instead that new converts with no historical relationship to the covenant were, precisely because of their inexperience with Christian ways, equally, if not more, deserving of latitude—or at least the benefit of the doubt.

Although Gookin clothed his ideas on Christian "charity" in the rhetoric of the local debate over the halfway covenant, his own favorable response to that debate, as well as his ideas on conversion, owed much to his Irish background. Vincent Gookin, writing about the benighted Catholics of Ireland, had minimized the dangers of hypocrisy, which New Englanders greatly feared, arguing instead that the external performance of Protestant practices, especially the saying of family prayers, even if done only to gain worldly benefits, was sufficient to place converts on the right path: "The son may be sincere, though the father be a hypocrite, and what his earthly father intended onely for the saving of his estate, his heavenly father may advance to the saving of his soul."[63] In Massachusetts, Daniel Gookin adapted this line of reasoning to a New England context; although Gookin admitted that some praying Indians, like some Englishmen, were no doubt "hypocrites" and "evil-doers," he held that the judging of "men's hearts" was up to God and not mere humans:

> we may not presently exclude them [the Praying Indians] out of visible Christianity, but rather endeavour to convince and reform them, if God please to be instrumental to correct them, and turn them to God effectually. Whilst men do externally attend the means of grace, keep the Sabbath, pray in their families morning and evening, and endeavour and desire to be instructed in Christian religion, both themselves and children, as the praying Indians do, there is charitable encouragement and good hope, through grace, that, as God hath wrought effectually upon some, so he will upon others, in his own time and according to his good pleasure, that he hath purposed in

himself. I account it my duty not to censure and judge, but to pray for them and others.[64]

If religion and the churches had always symbolically defined community for Bay Colony Puritans, Gookin's formulation threatened pollution—a risk that many colonists remained resolutely unwilling to take, even when it might benefit their own relatives and friends.[65]

Daniel Gookin recognized and welcomed the "halfway" covenant's potential to expand the bonds of community; but the majority of clergymen, better understanding the popular mood, emphasized that this innovation, based on the idea that faith ran in families, might help to ensure that Puritan New England would remain a place apart, a place specially blessed with godliness. When the purported Indian "lover" Daniel Gookin advocated the halfway covenant, the latter cause no doubt suffered by association. Still, even if the majority of ordinary colonists remained hostile to the halfway covenant, the tribal calculus, voiced and legitimated again and again in exhortatory preaching and debate, contributed to New Englanders' preexisting tendency to give their spiritual enemies the human face of a racial "other."

It was a staple of Puritan thought that Satan was most dangerous when he came in a pleasing shape, posing as a friend. The venerated Puritan author William Gurnall, for one, explained that the devil conquered more souls by "wiles" than "open force" and warned readers that they must learn to perceive aright the thin line demarking true spiritual friends from veiled enemies:

> When two men stand out one against another at the swords point
> . . . half an eye can see that they are enemies; but fraud in fellowship,
> enmity under brotherhood, is not so easily descryed . . . [the devil is]
> never so dangerous, as when he is most tame; he will give thee leave
> to defie and spit at him, to insult and tread upon him, to bridle and
> saddle him, so he may carry thee to hell.

During King Philip's War, the "back friends" of the soul, against whom William Gurnall and other traditional Puritan writers had thundered, seemed almost effortlessly to spring to life in the shape of Christian Indians. Gurnall himself explicitly characterized the Indians as evil: "I have read of a people in America, that love meat best when 'tis Rotten and Stinks. The Devil is of their diet . . . some are more the children of the Devil than others." [66] The converts might temporarily allow themselves to be "bridled" and "saddled," but eventually their pretenses would be exposed as a collective ruse undertaken with the purpose of ultimate betrayal.

With Puritan tribalism enjoying a renewed lease on life, colonists found it difficult to trust or respect Christian converts who could help the English only by betraying their own people. The majority of Bay Colony ministers, meanwhile, did little to dispel the common notion that ethnic or racial ties inspired a deeper loyalty than religious or ideological ones.

William Hubbard, for example, described the vast majority of Indians as "all hanging together, like Serpent's Eggs" and sharing an "inbred Malice and Antipathy against the English Manners and Religion"; for Hubbard, blood was thicker than water—even baptismal water.[67] In the 1670s, most rank-and-file colonists, more skeptical than ever of the idea that religious conversion could break the bonds of cultural, or racial affinity, came to view the Christian Indians as wily dissimulators who should be regarded as equally, if not more, dangerous than clearly discernible enemies. During the war Gookin explained how prevalent was the notion, especially among the "vulgar," that praying Indian adjuncts deliberately shot over the heads of the enemy and surreptitiously informed them of English plans and troop movements.[68]

IN ADDITION TO denouncing Gookin as an "Irish dog," Richard Scott also charged that the captain was the "devil's interpreter." There is no evidence to suggest that Gookin spoke any of the Algonquian languages (he seemed to have employed translators); but Gookin did attempt, figuratively and literally, to interpret the behavior of the praying Indians for his English backers and colonists alike. These acts of cultural interpretation—writing histories, providing and soliciting affidavits attesting to the loyalty of Christian Indians, and even suggesting that some backsliders who had joined Philip should be forgiven—easily shaded into advocacy, as did some of Gookin's public and private activities as negotiator and frontier broker. The popular Puritan author Samuel Crooke defined a hypocrite as a "man of both worlds" who "converseth with the living by that which he pretendeth, and with the dead, by that which he concealeth. But always that is best lov'd which is concealed, yea, only loved, for the other is exposed for the safety of this."[69] Daniel Gookin came to be regarded as a man who pretended and concealed much in his connection with the world of Indian villages. Like the "cunning" people who used methods of doubtful legitimacy to heal their neighbors and whose power to do good was uncomfortably balanced with the countervailing power to harm, so too did Gookin perform unnatural manipulations at the edge of a multivalent boundary where intercultural "magic" was as likely to produce war and destruction as prosperity and trade.[70] And just as the "cunning person" could easily transform into a witch, so could a cultural mediator turn "traitor."

Gookin played a number of different roles on the frontier. He was an engrosser of land and developer of towns, particularly Worcester; he sat on General Court committees that regulated trade and licensed traders; he negotiated differences between colonists and Indians, both praying and "profane"; he distributed implements, and sometimes arms, from the New England Company; he occasionally was authorized to sell gunpowder to Indians; and, as chief magistrate of the praying towns, he influenced the choice of civil leaders and had the authority to judge all cases except for capital crimes.[71] Some praying Indians developed a personal rapport with

Gookin and used him as an attorney of sorts. In 1680, for example, Gookin petitioned the General Court to obtain restitution for a Natick woman whose gun had been unjustly "impressed" from her by the Sudbury constable in the early months of King Philip's War; although Gookin apologized to the deputies for taking up their time with such a trivial matter, he nonetheless made sure they understood that the recompense was "justly due," explaining that "shee hath for many years solicited mee about it."[72] These multifarious roles and powers provoked anxiety among colonists. In 1675, Mary Pray of Providence twisted one of Gookin's earlier legal roles— the selling of gunpowder in 1666—into something sinister, complaining in a letter to Boston that "it is reported . . . that Captain Gucking helps them [praying Indians] to powder and they sel it to those that are imployed by Philip to bye it for him."[73] Missionary work, combined with other kinds of mediatorship, threatened the personal identity of would-be assimilators who occasionally tried to see the world through Indian eyes.

The image of Gookin as a loathsome traitor began to take definite shape in April 1671, during a period of tension between Plymouth Colony and Philip's Wampanoags. The Indians were incensed because free-ranging English livestock were destroying their unfenced cultivated fields.[74] Gookin, in an apparent attempt to mediate the conflict, had spoken about the situation with various praying Indians. Much to his horror, a story soon began to circulate, based on "some Indian testimony left upon record there" (Plymouth), that Gookin encouraged Philip's rancor. In a terse letter addressed to Governor Thomas Prince of Plymouth, Gookin categorically denied any wrongdoing:

> I understand . . . I am accused for speaking words to a Natick Indian, tending to animate Philip and his Indians against you. Sir, I look upon it favoring of as little charity as justice, to receive, record and publish Indian reports, tending to the infamy of any christian man, much more a person in public place, without any other demonstration than such figment and falsehood as usually accompany Indians' tales . . . such a thing never entered into my heart, much less into my lips; neither did I, to my remembrance, either see or speak with any Natick Indian for several months before I heard of this report; nor ever did I speak or lisp to any Indian of Natick, or other, the least word about the business, since first I heard of those differences between your colony and the Indians.[75]

Prince's courteous yet stern response to this letter held that it had never been suggested that Gookin had spoken "words to animate Philip and his Indians against us" but rather that he was said to have referred to "not fighting with Indians about horses and hogs, but as matters too low to shed blood."[76] Given the fact that Anglo–Indian disputes over land sales and animal husbandry were at the root of the war scare that gripped Plymouth colony in 1671, however, this was no trivial accusation.[77] Gookin's intervention was considered tantamount to treachery because he had criticized Plymouth's policy in front of Indians; whether his indiscreet comments had been made among Philip's people or the converts of Natick made no difference to his anonymous accusers.

It was Gookin's mediatory role, as the events just described would suggest, that made him vulnerable to criticism. In figuratively and literally representing praying Indians to the Bay Colony populace, Gookin emphasized the tremendous potential for growth in Christ, the great feats of loyalty some praying Indians performed, and the harsh pressures that gave them every reason to slide back into their old ways; at the same time, as his response to the Plymouth governor indicates, he subscribed fully to the notion that Indians were naturally mendacious. These kinds of contradictions made Gookin seem either treacherous or dangerously naive, as did evidence that some of the highest-ranking converts experienced and expressed ambivalence about Christianity.

Gookin and others involved in missionary work praised William Ahauton, for example, "teacher" at the praying town of Packemit (or Punkapoag), as one of the most devoted of praying Indians. John Eliot featured Ahauton in his "Indian Dialogues" and entrusted him in 1671 to intercede with Philip for peace as an emissary of the Natick church; Increase Mather credited Ahauton for having informed authorities that Philip had indeed ordered the murder of Christian Indian intermediary John Sassamon in one of the precipitating incidents of King Philip's War; and Gookin extolled Ahauton's bravery in military service under Major Thomas Savage.[78] But the Ahauton name was also linked with a scandal that could easily have been construed to illustrate the fragility, not the deep endurance, of Indian conversions.

Just seven years prior to the outbreak of King Philip's War, Sarah Ahauton, William's wife, had been tried in the Massachusetts General Court for the capital crime of adultery.[79] While the Court had decided to spare Ahauton's life, as it did with most English offenders of the law against adultery, it nonetheless meted out a particularly harsh sentence; the defendant was ordered not only to "stand on the gallowes [in Boston] . . . with a roape about hir necke one hower" but also, at a later date, to submit to a "severely" administered public whipping "not exceeding thirty stripes" in Natick.[80] Daniel Gookin, hoping to mitigate Sarah's sentence, had helped the defendant to construct a lengthy confession that emphasized Sarah's recognition of the seriousness of her sin, and her willingness to prostrate herself before her judges.[81] This confession, ironically, may help to account for the severity of the sentence, since it revealed that Sarah's illicit relationship, during which she ran away to Philip's Mount Hope with her partner in adultery, was more than a simple manifestation of lust.

Sarah, it would seem, in the midst of political infighting within her village, had been tempted and successfully wooed by a restive Packemit faction that had begun seriously to question its cultural accommodation.

Sarah reported in her confession that various persons had repeatedly approached the two Ahautons just prior to their difficulties, trying to convince each that the other had been unfaithful. While Sarah ignored the rumors about her husband, William had given credence to the stories about Sarah and had responded by beating her and hauling her before the local praying Indian courts. It was this "suspition of her husband without cause," Sarah confided to Gookin through an interpreter, that "did weaken and alienate her former affection to him," leading her soon to "commit folly" with a man named Joseph, whose family (particularly its elder female members, as Ann Marie Plane has pointed out) facilitated the couple's illicit relationship.[82] A troubled Sarah Ahauton fled twice from Packemit in the face of these troubles: initially, when Joseph warned her that the praying Indian court at Natick might condemn her to a whipping, Sarah sought shelter and solace from her parents at Wamesit; then, later on, after she had consummated her relationship with Joseph, the two took refuge at Mount Hope and Warwick, until God saw fit to "smite" Sarah's soul with remorse.[83]

The Ahauton trial would certainly have fed suspicions that the praying Indians' hold on "civilization," hence their loyalty, was fragile. Sarah's testimony suggested that her marriage, symbolizing the replacement of Algonquian with English mores, had been targeted by certain people in Packemit—Joseph's relatives in particular—who felt drawn to Mount Hope, where, despite the existence of a praying faction, Indians followed Algonquian, not English, precepts.[84] Gookin was well aware that in the years just prior to Sarah's trial the Massachusett sachem Josiah Chekatabutt (or Chickataubut, alias Josiah Wampatuck) had fallen away from Christianity and left the village of Packemit, taking some of his followers with him; in his *Historical Collections*, Gookin referred in a veiled manner to Chekatabutt's departure when he explained how over the past ten years some Packemit converts had "turned apostates, and removed . . . which dispensations of God have greatly damped the flourishing condition of this place." Sarah Ahauton rethought her religious and social identity in the shadow of Chekatabutt's renunciation of Puritan ways. Significantly, Chekatabutt, who soon began (against Gookin's advice) to gather a war party to fight the Mohawks, met with the greatest success in recruiting warriors at Wamesit, the praying village where Sarah Ahauton's parents lived, and to which she at one point fled during her escalating conflict with William.[85] Sarah Ahauton, unlike "Captain Josiah," returned to the Christian fold, despite, as she pointed out to her judges, the mortal "dangers" awaiting her in the court system. But Sarah's attraction to Joseph and her willingness to travel to Mount Hope indicates that she was mindful that something had been lost in the assimilative process.

This sense of loss would seem to have persisted with Sarah even as she promised, if spared the gallows, to "love her husbande and continue faithful to him . . . yea although hee could beat her againe and suspect her of falseness to him without cause . . . shee doth acknowledge it to be her duty to suffer it and to pray for her husband and to love him still." A local legend from the town of Canton (the name given to Packemit after it became a predominantly English village) holds that Sarah, deeply shamed by the court proceedings and loath to submit to the indignity of being whipped before her own neighbors, committed suicide by throwing herself off of "squaw rock."[86] To Puritans, Sarah's final act of defiance would have looked like a manifestation of the unseemly pride normally ascribed to Indians—a pride that could never be replaced with the due humility required of true Puritans. It was precisely this sort of resistance, and the more generalized forces observed to disrupt the marriage of Sarah and William Ahauton, that would obsess colonists during the King Philip's War era.

Daniel Gookin, who shaped the haunting words of Sarah Ahauton's written confession, must have known that Christian Indians would long be called on collectively to play the loving, submissive spouse to a figurative husband, the English, who would constantly suspect them of lying and continually "beat" them. But he did not foresee that in the cauldron of war, with suspicions raised to extremes, a stance of submission and virtue would fail utterly to make a favorable impression on rank-and-file colonists. At the same time, Gookin's own negative assessment of Algonquian culture prevented him from recognizing the nourishment that native peoples derived from a culture that valued reciprocity over hierarchy in all human relationships, including that of matrimony.[87] Because he saw little to value in Algonquian culture, Gookin could neither comprehend nor acknowledge the pain of tortured souls like Sarah Ahauton. This cultural blindness, combined with the limitations imposed by a social context hostile to Indians, caused him to focus attention on the seemingly uncomplicated valor of individuals like William Ahauton and to ignore the stumblings and complex feelings of those like Sarah. Ultimately, Gookin's tales of triumphal converts made him seem deceptive to an audience that had never been sympathetic toward the plight of praying Indians and that, perhaps more important, could not imagine itself making the wholesale cultural changes required of Indian converts. Most Bay Colony residents assumed that the Indians were as rigid in their definition of cultural and communal bonds as were the English themselves. In this context, any sign of accommodation was interpreted not at face value but as Indian attempts to deceive and confuse their "natural" adversaries.

In writing of King Philip's War, Daniel Gookin emphasized the heroic services performed by self-effacing Christian Indians like Job Katenanit, Joseph Tuckapawillin, James Quannapohit, Andrew Pitimee, and William Ahauton, all of whom did faithful service for the English and remained loyal, despite the internment and devastating abuse—including the deaths and endangerment of family members—that they suffered at the hands of colonists.

The immediate aftermath of the war found William Ahauton desperately petitioning to have various praying Indians freed from the slavery or servitude that was their portion if they had been unlucky enough to be captured by Englishmen who expended little or no effort in distinguishing between Indian friends and foes. In 1678–79, it even became necessary for Ahauton to intercede with the commissioners of the United Colonies to win the freedom of a sister of John Sassamon, the praying Indian whose murder Philip had probably ordered as retribution for Sassamon's having informed the English of Philip's warlike intentions. Instead of designating public funds to pay the full ten pounds required to compensate the woman's master and obtain her freedom, the commissioners decreed that half must be raised by the Sassamon family's war-impoverished friends, while the rest would be taken from the "Indian stock."[88]

Andrew Pitimee's postwar experiences were even more dispiriting, for in the summer of 1676 his wife and sister were murdered near Watertown by four English soldiers, two of whom were later tried and executed for the crime. Although Pitimee had served as a military adjunct under Thomas Savage, public opinion favored the murderers; according to a deposition gathered in the middle of September 1676, John Woodcock reported to authorities what he regarded as the "dreadfull words" one William Mash uttered in his presence, to the effect that "there was no fear of those [who killed the women] being hanged for there were three or four hundred men that would guard them from the gallows."[89]

The people of Massachusetts, already suspicious of Gookin's assurances of praying Indian loyalty, remained unmoved by the sufferings of Pitimee and Ahauton; nor were they comfortable with the work these converts were doing on the frontier. Job Katenanit's long quest to rescue his three children, captured along with all the residents of the praying town of Hassanamesitt in November 1675, seemed highly suspicious to ordinary English colonists, who could not believe that Christian Indians had anything to fear from fellow Algonquians and who were certain that Katenanit had gone "forth to give intelligence to the enemy."[90] At the same time, Englishmen knew that a number of praying Indians, including some with whom the missionaries had taken considerable pains, had turned "traitor" during the war, despite having rendered good service in its beginning stages.

The brothers Joseph and Sampson Petavit (or Petuhanit), for example, had been featured in Gookin's *Historical Collections* as exemplary converts; but in *Doings and Sufferings* they reappeared as tragic backsliders. Gookin, by his own account, had known the young men from boyhood; their father, Robin, who died before the war, had been a leader at Hassanamesitt, dutifully opposing the "sagamores, who sometimes would ruffle against religion and good order in his presence" or who brought liquor into the town. Gookin admitted that Sampson and Joseph had at times tried his patience; Sampson in particular had been a "dissolute person, and I have been forced to be severe in punishing him for his misdemeanors formerly." But by the time of their father's death, both Joseph and Sampson had become "hopeful, pious, and active men." A reformed Sampson served as teacher at Wabquissit, and Gookin regarded this transformation with wonder because it "tendeth to magnify grace, and that to a prodigal, and to declare how

God remembers his covenant unto the children of such, as are faithful and zealous for him in their time and generation."[91]

Gookin had enough regard for the Petavit family to consider the sons prodigals rather than mere backsliders or "counterfeit" Christians. In the summer of 1675, this regard appeared to have been well founded, as both Sampson and Joseph "acquitted themselves very industriously and faithfully" in the service of Captain Edward Hutchinson. When the captain's party of horsemen was ambushed by a group of Nipmucks with whom he had expected to negotiate, the two Christian Indians helped the moribund Hutchinson, his wounded lieutenant, and the rest of the party, reach Brookfield, "which was in a few hours after attacked by those [enemy] Indians, and most of it burnt." Yet within a space of months, both Sampson and Joseph, "for want of shelter, protection, and encouragement," chose to remain among the enemy Indians who had carried them off from Hassanamesitt. Whether Sampson actually took up arms against the colonists is uncertain, but he died at the hands of a praying Indian scout near Philip's stronghold of Watchusset. Joseph, meanwhile, was captured near Plymouth and was held as a servant; were it not for the intercession of John Eliot, who did not believe rumors that he aided the enemy, Joseph would have been sold as a slave in Jamaica.[92]

To the people of Boston, Gookin seemed to have vastly underestimated the Indians' fundamental dedication to their own culture and people. Gookin could no more predict which Indians would turn traitors under the stress of war than he could have divined Sarah Ahauton's susceptibility to the temptations posed by a village faction having second thoughts about its commitment to English ways. Worse yet, even when Gookin did apprehend treachery, he was inclined to argue that the English, by mistreating the praying Indians and spurning their efforts to help, had created the very conditions that made backsliding almost inevitable.[93] Gookin's reaction to the apostasy of Wuttasacomponom, alias Captain Tom, was a case in point. Captain Tom, as magistrate of the praying town of Wabquissit, had dutifully removed to Hassanamesitt in the summer of 1675, when his own town, one of the "new" Christian villages, defected to the enemy. But several months later, when Hassanamesitt itself fell to the "pagan" Indians, Captain Tom "yielded to the enemies' arguments, and by his example drew most of the rest [except for the resistant little band that pastor Joseph Tuckapawillin led back to the English], for which he afterwards suffered death, being executed at Boston, the June after." Gookin claimed that he had no sympathy for traitors like Wuttasacomponom, for "had he done as he ought, he should rather have suffered death, than have gone among the wicked enemies of the people of God." Still, Gookin softened this harsh judgment with a testimonial to Captain Tom's former character: he was "a prudent, and I believe, a pious man . . . I had particular acquaintance with him, and cannot in charity think otherwise concerning him in his life, or at his death, though possibly in this action he was tempted beyond his strength." It was the praying Indians' fear, implied Gookin, and not their untrustworthy nature, that drove them to "accompany the enemy to their quarters"; and "perhaps if Englishmen, and good Christians too, had been in their case and under like temptations possibly they might have done as they did."[94]

In the aftermath of war Gookin may have gone so far as to help Captain Tom's friends—the faultlessly loyal Andrew Pittimee, James Quannapohit, Job Katenanit, John Magus, and James Speen—to compose a petition requesting that some leniency be shown toward "those few of our poor friends and kindred, that, in this time of temptation and affliction, have been in the enemy's quarters; we hope it will be no griefe of heart to you to shew mercy, and especially to such who have (as we conceive) done no wrong to the English." That Gookin chose to include this petition in the appendix of his history of King Philip's War suggests that, even if he did not have a direct hand in writing it, he at least sympathized with its contents. The Court, however, while agreeing to spare Captain Tom's wife and children, contended that Captain Tom's presence in the enemy camp could not be overlooked because he was not only

> an instigator to others over whom he was by this government made a Captain, but also [contrary to the claims of those who petitioned on his behalf] was actually present and an actor in the devastation of some of our plantations; and therefore it cannot consist with the honour and justice of authority to grant him a pardon . . . it will not be availeable for any to plead in favour for them that they have been our friends while found and taken among our enemyes.[95]

While the argument that undue suspicion would lead to sin might buy the life of an accused adulteress, it could not save the reputations of Christian Indians, who, even in the best of times, were not fully accepted into English society.

The people of Massachusetts were uncomfortable with the practical and religious work that even the most exemplary Christians were doing on the frontier, partly because, in using Indian adjuncts, colonial forces sought not to tap the converts' newly attained Christian values but rather to exploit the particular genius for stealth, deceit, and treachery that all Indians were thought to possess as part of their natural endowment. Daniel Gookin was no different from most of his countrymen in believing Indians to be uncommonly "subtle and wily to accomplish their enterprise."[96] But the Indians' possession of special skills different from those of the English contradicted his claim that religious conversion had eliminated the cultural distinctions separating the two peoples. William Hubbard, for example, told the story of a praying Indian man who had betrayed his own father to the English. Instead of using the tale to illustrate how Christians must forsake all in order to follow God, Hubbard hinted that the betrayal of such a close relative reflected the Indians' treachery and lack of civility:

> Whereby their natural Perfidiousness even to their nearest Relations may be observed, which makes their Treachery towards us their Foreign Neighbours the less to be wondred at. And therefore till they be

reduced to more Civility, some wise Men are ready to fear Religion
will not take much Place amongst the Body of them.[97]

The nature of the Indians' special skills would seem to mark them off as
the people of the devil, the father of lies and wiles.[98] Reliance on the
trickery and deceit of an alien people, who were valued because they had
much in common with the colony's spiritual and temporal enemies, seemed
particularly dangerous, because these methods, in addition to being unholy,
could so easily be turned back upon the English themselves.

William Hubbard's history of King Philip's War conveys a sense of
what sorts of doubts people harbored about Christian Indian adjuncts. The
spies Job Katenanit and James Quannapohit, Hubbard writes, were able to
infiltrate the "Indian habitations" and receive "free Liberty of Discourse
with them" because they exploited Quannapohit's friendship with Monoco,
or One-Eyed John, "a great Captain of the Indians, that afterward led them
that spoiled Groton." Because Quannapohit had been Monoco's boon
"Companion . . . in Hunting, and Fighting against the Mohawks formerly,"
Monoco would not "suffer any of the rest to touch" his Christian friend,
despite the suspicions he excited and despite the ominous urging from at
least one warrior that Quannapohit be brought to appear before Philip.[99]
Hubbard conveyed to his readers that the successful spy mission was valuable to the English cause; but at the same time, he injected doubt into
their minds by demonstrating that this success rested not only on the spies'
willingness to betray old friendships but also on their ability to call on
bonds of loyalty that, under other circumstances, would have been difficult
for the English to understand or control and that might just as easily have
drawn Quannapohit back into the embrace of those old confederates who
"esteemed of him" so highly.[100] Although Hubbard's narrative in places
criticized the colonists for their rejection of Christian Indian helpers and
tactics, he himself harbored considerable doubt about these techniques'
wholesomeness, even their efficacy.

The common people of Massachusetts believed that the ties of blood
naturally prevailed over all other bonds; and the exercise of this inexorable
natural law demanded that all Indians be treated as enemies. This efflores-
cence of Puritan tribalism, spurred on by ministers who used such arguments to promote the halfway covenant, was injurious not just to Gookin
and the praying Indians but also to the majority of King Philip's War–era
military officers, most of whom relied on multiethnic ties not only to fight
but to do business on the frontier.

AT THE CONCLUSION of King Philip's War, Daniel Gookin produced
a war narrative, *An Historical Account of the Doings and Sufferings of the
Christian Indians in New England,* that was dramatically different from all
others produced in Massachusetts. The book, never published during
Gookin's lifetime, was a veritable paean to the "middle ground" and its
inhabitants, both English and Indian. In Daniel Gookin's version of King
Philip's War, the heroes among the English were fellow military officers

who, not unlike himself, maintained investments on the frontier, employed Indian laborers and military adjuncts, and believed that success in trading and military ventures alike rested on the crosscultural ties that many colonists viewed with alarm and disdain. Even more interesting, Gookin, unlike any orthodox writer who manifested sympathy for the praying Indians, depicted these converts as spiritually significant individuals for whom God had a message.

As already shown, Gookin's Irish roots excited unfavorable comment in certain quarters. But Gookin's status as a frontier broker, land engrosser, and facilitator of trade—a status that was not unrelated to his missionary activity and that he shared with the majority of military officers during King Philip's War—was even more clearly provocative of resentment among the common people. The King Philip's War years witnessed a generalized popular distrust of the colony's military and mercantile elite, whose profitable ties to the frontier seemed to run contrary to the public good. And major expositors of the war's cosmic meaning, such as Increase Mather and William Hubbard, did more to promote than to check the growing mistrust of secular leaders and the ad hoc relationships that characterized the frontier, a place traditionally regarded as a scene of disorder and vice.

During the 1670s, Increase Mather and William Hubbard produced rival histories of King Philip's War and competed fiercely for interpretive predominance. Historians have argued that Hubbard was the more "modern," or "rational," of the two, because he deemphasized the theme of declension and offered a detailed narrative treatment of major personalities and events of the war.[101] But when we compare the work of these two rivals to that of Gookin, the differences between them fade into near insignificance. Mather and Hubbard were united in their belief that the miseries of war were rooted in the mysterious, irregular dealings thought to take place in frontier trading posts. While Gookin, who encouraged economic exchange on the frontier, made a determined effort to view the war from the perspective of people caught in the middle, both Hubbard and Mather offered interpretations that not only reinforced aggressively the spiritual preponderance of the community of New English saints but also leveled a great deal of criticism against the frontier and all who inhabited its "middle ground." The narratives of these clergymen undermined the legitimacy of the liminal world of the frontier and tended to turn colonists ever more profoundly in upon their own culture and ideals.

Mather and Hubbard were in profound agreement when they blamed the miseries of the 1670s on the irregular dealings thought to take place in frontier trading posts. In November 1675 Increase Mather goaded the General Court to include on the list of New England's "provoking" sins the abuses associated with Indian trading posts, "whereby the Heathen have been debauched"[102] In his *Earnest Exhortation to the Inhabitants of New England*, Mather elaborated on this theme:

Is the interest of New-England indeed changed from a Religious to a Worldly Interest? that's a strange God, and if it be so, no wonder that there is War in our Gates: do men prefer their Farms and Merchandize above the Gospel? here is the reason why Armies are sent forth against us, and our Cities are burnt up. Inordinate love to this present evil World, hath been the Fountain of all that misery, that we are bleeding under at this day; Those unhappy Indian-trading-houses, whereby the Heathen have been so wofully scandalized, hath not covetousness built them, and continued them for so long a time? and was it not from the same root of all evil, that the Indians have been furnished with Arms, and Ammunition? would ever men have sold Guns, and Powder, and Shot, to such faithless and bloody creatures, if a lust of Covetousness had not too far prevailed with them?[103]

William Hubbard, in his history of King Philip's War, explained similarly that the Indian "Troubles . . . have ordinarily either begun, or have fallen heaviest upon those Places and Persons that have had most to do in the Trading with Indians."

Neither Mather nor Hubbard could decide whether traders were more culpable for mistreating the Indians in ways that inspired vengeful retaliation or for turning a blind eye to the dangers that lurked just beneath the surface of seemingly amicable crosscultural alliances or friendships. By both men's accounts, however, these middlemen appeared to be slippery figures who would deceive their own English countrymen with as little remorse as they would abuse their Indian trading partners. Hubbard went so far as to imply that the spread of Anglo–Indian hostilities to Maine could be laid at the doors of unnamed traders who had ignored signs of Indian hostility so that they might continue engaging in business as usual:

It is reported by some of the Inhabitants of Kennibeck, lately fled, or rather driven from thence, that about five Years since four Englishmen were slain by the Amoroscoggin Indians up Pegypscot River, that runs into Kennibeck; but it was concealed by the wicked Traders of those parts for fear of discovering their wicked Manner of trading with the Heathen; which if it had been duly enquired into when it was first done, much of what followed, might have been prevented.[104]

Even more revealing than Hubbard's thoughts about King Philip's War itself was his impression that the interests of trade and settlement had been opposed since the earliest encounter between colonists and Indians living in the remote regions of New England. Hubbard argued that Anglo–Indian relations in the "eastern" parts began inauspiciously in 1614, when ship master Thomas Hunt kidnapped and sold into slavery at Malago, Spain, a group of Indians whom he had tricked into boarding his ship. In all probability, Hunt undertook this dastardly deed for the sole purpose of turning a quick profit; but Hubbard argued instead that Hunt's real goal was to sour Anglo–Indian relations, frustrate plans for a settled plantation, and manipulate the situation so that "he [Hunt] and a few Merchants might wholly enjoy the Benefit of the Trade of the Country."[105] Hubbard did not explain how Hunt had expected to live down his role in the kidnappings and convince the Indians to trade with him; but this ill-framed, irrational argument about the Hunt legacy speaks volumes about Hubbard's underlying and widely shared assumption that vice-ridden trading posts were antithetical to wholesome settlements:

> If any such have as yet escaped their [the Indians'] Hands, to be sure they have been threatned, as if they had been before others, particularly lookt upon by them, as the Object of their Revenge, which makes some moderate Persons Fear, that those Men have either themselves offended in that kind, or else have connived at others under them, to carry on the Traffick with the Indians, by such Ways and Means, that have been as well offensive to God, as injurious to those they have traded with.[106]

Mather and Hubbard probably intended to aim their criticisms of unscrupulous dealings on the frontier primarily at the actions of small, unauthorized traders widely reputed to have sold proscribed or controversial trade goods, such as guns and liquor, to the Indians and to have contributed to the general disorder and lawlessness of the eastern settlements. Yet their words could be read as an indictment of all people, regardless of social status or official position, who maintained close economic ties with the Indians. Mather and Hubbard, each in his own way, contributed to the general sense that the colony's secular leaders lacked a moral compass, primarily because they put profits ahead of maintaining the colony's traditional social and cultural bounds.

William Harris, a "sojurnor at Rhode Island" who had lost a "deer son," a "Negroman," livestock, and a farm in King Philip's War, would have agreed with these clergymens' assessment of the pernicious effects of frontier exchange. In Harris's estimation, trade was at the root of the native peoples' ability and inclination to fight what he regarded as a war of aggression on their part. Trade had improved the Indians' material quality of life, Harris wrote, and made it possible for them to store up surplus provisions in preparation for war: "when they began the war" the Indians were "far more supplied and better then when the English first came for then they wear in great wants but since in great plenty." It was the new abundance indigenous peoples enjoyed as a result of contact with the English, and not any injustice at the colonists' hands, that emboldened King Philip to commit "high treason" against the king by taking the "authority and dominion and rule to himselfe": "the Indeans make war with the English rather by the prosperity they enjoyed (by the English) then by any adversity by them tempted to the war." Harris acknowledged that aid from allied Indians was instrumental in the colonists' eventual victory, and that matters would have been far worse "had the Indeans bin all our enemyes." But in the final analysis, he reasoned, both parties would have been better off had they not established such close economic ties: "prosperity hath slayne them, yea and many of us to."[107]

Early in 1676, at a time when Gookin was praising Governor John Leverett, an unlikely ally, for recognizing that a renegade officer's action against some praying Indians in the town of Concord was a "very offensive" breach of authority, Mather was openly criticizing the governor for his failure to help curb drunkenness: "He [Leverett] hath bin the principal Author of the multitude of ordinaries which be in Boston, giving licences when the townsmen would not doe it. No wonder that New England is visited, when the Head is so spirited."[108] In the spring of 1676, Mather punctuated his disdain for laxity in high places by boycotting the annual dinner held on the day when the Artillery Company, an organization with which Leverett, Gookin, and a majority of the colony's key military officers had long been closely associated, elected its officers:

> I refused to dine with souldiers because it [the dinner] was in an ordinary, contrary to the Law [on "provoking evils"] established [by the General Court after a great deal of prodding from Mather], as considering, it would not be possible to Reforme the common sort of people . . . if Leaders did not set before them a good example.[109]

While Mather's emphasis on sin and declension, especially drinking, could not have been popular, his suggestion that there was corruption in high places could be bent to other uses by those who had reason to doubt the efficacy and the public spiritedness of the colony's military elite.

Thomas Lake and John Richards, active developers of land and trade in Maine who belonged to Increase Mather's Boston congregation, took offense at their pastor for precisely this reason. Back in 1670, five years prior to the outbreak of King Philip's War, Mather had regarded it as a godsend when Lake and his close business associate, Sir Thomas Temple, governor of Nova Scotia, had joined the North Church. At a time when Mather felt keenly the burden of a seemingly ungrateful flock that refused to "looke after my comfortable subsistence," these well-heeled new members made large contributions to the church, and to the purchase of a new house for Mather.[110] In February, 1676, however, the friendship between wealthy congregants and minister was strained when, after a church meeting, Lake and Richards took their spiritual leader to task for belaboring the notion that "provoking evils" were at the root of the war. Mather later recorded the incident in his diary:

> After the church was gone Captain Thomas Lake and Mr. Richards stayed, and Captain Lake said (the other seconding him) that when ministers did lay a solemn charge upon people, it might take in the ignorant but no rational men would regard what was said the more for it.[111]

While Mather recalled that he had spoken at length on "excess in apparel" and "town dwellers being at Taverns," these merchants had probably taken greater offense at his recitation of the sins of the frontier. John Richards was a broker of Maine lands who fought against Mather's implementation of the halfway covenant in North Church and conceived of the spiritual community in the broadest possible terms. In 1651 Richards, a future sergeant major of the Suffolk regiment, had sold Arrowsick Island to Lake and his partner, Major Thomas Clark.[112] The partners, both heavily involved in the Acadia trade, had then proceeded to establish on the island an impressive outpost, including sawmills, shipbuilding facilities, a fort, a foundry, and a trading post.[113] Neither of these men could have approved of the way Mather and other clergymen cast suspicion on the activities of the investors, entrepreneurs, and developers whose trading activities connected dispersed communities of saints and who, in most cases, were the very individuals responsible for the colony's defense.

Even in death, Thomas Lake's position between two cultural worlds occasioned a controversial demand from his surviving brother, John Lake, for compromise with the enemy. In the fall of 1676, John Lake had heard rumors that Thomas had been captured rather than killed, as originally (and correctly) reported. Fearing that news of the planned execution in Boston of a particularly hated Indian leader, Sagamore Sam, would cause his brother's captors to retaliate in kind, John Lake requested not only that the General Court delay the execution but also that authorities go so far as to strike a deal with Sagamore Sam, such that "if the said Sam can be instrumental to procure the return of my brother . . . you then would be pleased to spare his life."[114] The petition was denied; but its suggestion that authorities overlook the treachery and past cruelties of a "savage" foe in exchange for something of value to an elite Bostonian was precisely the sort of thing that colonists who did not profit directly from the frontier had long resented.

With the exception of Gookin, most authors of tracts on King Philip's War fed the popular suspicion about individuals who were comfortable both in the circumscribed world of the Puritan towns and the fluid world of the frontier. Nathaniel Saltonstall wrote several accounts of wartime events in the guise of informative "letters" to associates in England; in these epistles, Saltonstall clearly expressed the worry that regular economic dealings on the frontier might desensitize men in authority to the very real hazards that stalked them. In recounting Captain Edward Hutchinson's famous debacle near Brookfield (or Quabaug), Saltonstall condemned Hutchinson's longstanding employment of Nipmucks to farm a tract of frontier land he owned in the vicinity of Brookfield. This, he suggested, had dulled the captain to the possibility of betrayal:

(For you must understand that Captain Hutchison had a very considerable Farm therabouts, and had Occasion to employ several of those Sachems there, in Tilling and Plowing his Ground, and thereby he was known by Face to many of them.) The Sachems sent this word, they would speak with none but Captain Hutchison himself; Whereupon Captain Hutchison and Captain Wheeler sent them

Word they would come to them themselves: Accordingly the Indians appointed the Meeting at such a Tree, and at such a Time.[115]

The Hutchinson family had a reputation not only for employing Indian laborers but for squeezing English tenants on its lands in western Massachusetts and the "eastern" parts. Now Saltonstall was suggesting openly that people like the Hutchinsons were not only greedy but dangerous; the besieged residents of Brookfield paid with their blood for Hutchinson's misplaced trust in friendly Indians and his pride in being the sachems' preferred intermediary.

Daniel Gookin, as I have shown, had significant political and religious differences with the First Church faction that Edward Hutchinson and John Leverett represented; yet he was aligned with them in the sense that he promoted frontier enterprise, crosscultural contact, and a view of the ideal Christian community very much at odds with that of the commonalty. Because Gookin saw the integration of indigenous peoples into the transatlantic market as a central element in the civilizing and, therefore, the conversion process, he necessarily argued that the English heroes of King Philip's War were fellow military officers who maintained investments, and crosscultural ties, on the frontier. The common people, however, demanded a different sort of hero; and chroniclers of King Philip's War responded to that need in illuminating and sometimes surprising ways.

WILLIAM HUBBARD'S ATTACHMENT to the mercantile community of Boston in general and John Leverett in particular is well known. Yet these attachments did not prevent him from constructing a history of the war that implicitly criticized both the frontier trade and the military tactics of the colony's elite. Gookin, as has been shown, gave unstinting praise in his account of the war to those officers who resolutely stood their "middle ground" and defended the integrity of praying Indians and other allies. Hubbard, on the other hand, while subtle in his criticisms of high-ranking officers, structured his history in such a manner as to undermine the legitimacy of the liminal world of the frontier and to turn colonists ever more profoundly in upon their own culture and ideals.

The men that Gookin praised in his writing as heroes or complimented for their open-mindedness on the issue of praying Indians were all, like him, involved in frontier development, trade, and land acquisition. Daniel Henchman, Thomas Brattle, Thomas Prentice, and Richard Beers, all of whom served militarily in King Philip's War and all of whom responded favorably to the use of Indian guides and spies, were fellow investors in Gookin's pet project of Worcester. Brattle, married to the daughter of the influential William Tyng, owned substantial acreage in the town of Dunstable; according to Gookin, Brattle had been moved to comment, in reference to an incident in which praying Indian refugees from Hassanamesitt (including Joseph Tuckapawillin and the Katenanit children) had been taunted and terrorized while passing through Marlborough, that "he was ashamed to see and hear" what the colonists "did of that kind, and, if he had been an Indian and so abused, he should have run away as they did."[116] Jonathan Tyng, a kinsman of Brattle and a future major of the Suffolk regiment, employed Indian labor regularly on his lands in Dunstable and Chelmsford, gained renown during King Philip's War for remaining in his Dunstable garrison after most of the town's residents evacuated, and took on the responsibility of supervising (setting to productive work) Wanna-lancet's people after the war.[117] Nicholas Paige and his wife Anna, the granddaughter of Robert Keayne, received a favorable nod from Gookin for having sheltered Joseph Tuckapawillin and other Hassanamesitt refugees after their frightening experience at Marlborough. Paige had served as an officer during the first few months of the war and was an absentee landowner in Dunstable by virtue of his wife's inheritance; interestingly, the possibly bigamous union of Nicholas Paige and Anna Keayne Lane had been much discussed in the late 1660s. Local gossip held not only that the two had traveled to England so that they could enter into matrimony prior to the death of Anna's ailing first husband, Edward Lane, but also that Paige had actually fathered the children credited to Lane. (Indeed, Anna Keayne Lane had at one point demanded that her marriage be dissolved due to her husband's sexual impotence.) That this tainted couple should welcome possible traitors into their home, refreshing "their bowels with food and other comforts," probably came as no surprise to ordinary Bostonians.[118]

Hubbard was disinclined openly to criticize societal leaders; nonetheless, he described certain scenes of the war in such a way as to delegitimize those people who blurred the boundary between English and Indian. This aspect of Hubbard's history can be most clearly discerned in his account of a tragedy in which two very different Massachusetts captains came, respectively, to represent the potential undoing, and the hope, of New England. Thomas Lathrop (or Lothrop), a figure who symbolized the secular elites' openness to change and exchange on the frontier, suffered an ignominious defeat in the war, while Samuel Mosely, a figure known for his willingness to "put into execution any thing that tended to distress the praying Indians" and his determination to establish firm cultural boundaries between English and Indian, achieved a truly redemptive victory. Mosely was the one English officer Gookin portrayed as an unmitigated villain. Yet Hubbard and other writers found in this colorful captain a fascinating subject whose exploits imparted a swashbuckling component to the war's history and whose undiscriminating attitude toward the Indians helped to confirm the superiority of Englishness over "barbarism."

The experiences and fates of captains Thomas Lathrop and Samuel Mosely presented Hubbard the historian with an irresistable study in contrasts. The flamboyant Mosely, who insisted during the war on recruiting his own volunteer company, complete with captured Dutch privateers and bloodhounds, was something of an outcast from the colony's halls of power. Mosely gained immense popularity among the common people of Massachusetts because of his resolute stance against all Indians and his fearless questioning of the decisions made by the ruling elite. Not surprisingly, these very characteristics called forth the resentments of Bay Colony leaders.[119]

Nathaniel Saltonstall, for example, recorded a curious incident that took place in June 1675, when Mosely and his unit, including pardoned pirate Cornelius Andreson, were serving at Mount Hope in a large expeditionary force commanded by Major General Thomas Savage. The Suffolk County major, impressed by the apparent willingness of Andreson, a "stout man," to "venture his Life in the Cause of the English," placed him in charge of a twelve-man scouting expedition "with Orders to return in three Hours on Pain of Death." The scouts were delayed several hours in carrying out their orders because they encountered "sixty Indians that were halling their Cannoues a-shore"; Andreson was compelled to "set on them, killing thirteen," capturing eight, and pursuing the "Rest as far as he could go for the Swamps; then he returned and Burnt all those Cannoues, about forty in Number." But Savage, true to his word, initiated a court-martial as soon as the men returned to camp:

> By this Time Cornellis and his twelve men (all being preserved) re-
> turned to the Camp, but they were eight Hours absent: Whereupon
> a Council of War was called, who past the Sentence of Death on
> him, for exceeding the Order given him. Immediately was also Par-
> doned, and received thanks for his good Service done in that Expe-
> dition; and was in a short Time sent out on the like Design, and
> brought Home with him twelve Indians alive, and two Indians Heads
> (i.e. the Skin with the Hair on it).[120]

In the little drama that Savage staged for his men's benefit, Andreson, a larger-than-life figure who only three days prior to the scouting mission had "pursued Philip so hard, that he got his Cap off his Head, and now weareth it," was an obvious stand-in for Mosely.[121] Savage used the incident with Andreson, a pirate and an outsider, as a teaching tool through which to inform Mosely, and those who admired and might wish to emulate his independent style, that, while daring deeds would meet with due reward, men whose bravado "exceeded" their commissions would be treated harshly. Even at this early date, Savage seemed to understand that Mosely's volunteer unit constituted a challenge to proper authority.

Mosely clashed directly with Savage on a later occasion, in March 1676, when he protested the order, authorized by Savage and Major General Daniel Dension, that allowed Job Katenanit to leave English forces and attempt to reunite his kidnapped family. Learning of this decision, Mosely expostulated with the common soldiers and

> made a very great stir at the head-quarters at William Ward's, in
> Marlborough, where the army was drawn up in a body in order to
> their march; and spake words reflecting greatly upon that action of

sending away Job, alleging that he would inform the enemy of the army's motion, and so frustrate the whole design.

As Gookin understood the matter, Mosely's "fair pretence" stirred up a rebellious spirit in the army;

> had this mutinous practice (that so much reflected upon the chief commander of the army and authority of the Council) been committed in some other parts of the world, it would have cost the author of it a cashiering at least, if not a more severe animadversion; for it was an action against the order and good discipline of an army, for any private captain to animadvert (in such a manner) upon the general's actions, done with consideration and prudence.[122]

Throughout the hostilities, Mosely chafed under the authority of men who sought to curb his willful exercise of authority. A General Court pronouncement of February 1676 that reminded colonists that volunteer companies were indeed subordinate to the colony's military laws and its chain of command was no doubt inspired by an incident at Concord in which Mosely, without authorization, had broken up and imprisoned the inhabitants of a workhouse that John Hoar maintained for Indians. According to Gookin, the governor and council strongly disapproved of the way Mosely had acted "without commission or some express order":

> This thing was very offensive to the Council, that a private captain should . . . do an act so contradictory to their former orders; and the Governor and several others spake of it at a conference with the Deputies at the General Court, manifesting their dissatisfaction at this great irregularity, in setting up a military power in opposition to the chief authority of the country; declaring of what evil consequence such a precedent was . . . urging that due testimony might be borne against the same, by the whole Court.

Indeed, in the resolution passed that February, the Court noted pointedly that volunteers, although they might "esteeme themselves from under the comand which is necessary for the security of the country," were in fact legally "subject to all such martiall lawes as are or maybe provided for the well ordering of the forces of this jurisdiction."[123] Mosely would have to wait until the very last stages of the war, when authorities sensed the colony's impending victory and were eager to conclude hostilities, to receive a legal grant of authority that gave him a greater degree of independence in the field and conferred on his company the full "benefit that may accrew by captives or plunder that maybe divided among themselves."[124] Still, the wayward Mosely in most narratives of King Philip's War is the one English officer whom the Indians knew and feared rather than taunted.

Unlike Samuel Mosely, Thomas Lathrop, a veteran of the Pequot War and of Robert Sedgwick's seizure of four French forts in 1654, had a history of operating within the parameters of acceptable action laid down by the colony's leaders. Despite this experience—or perhaps because of it—Lathrop suffered one of the most ignominious defeats of King Philip's War. In September 1675, Lathrop's company of eighty "choice . . . young men" of Essex County was ambushed and decimated while transporting provisions from Deerfield to Hadley for the supply of garrisons in the western towns. Hubbard blamed the unfortunate Captain Lathrop, killed along with many of his men, for the carnage, arguing that it was the officer's stubborn insistence on using Indian tactics that spelled his doom. According to Hubbard, the tragic defeat

> came to pass by the unadvised Proceeding of the Captain . . . having taken up a wrong Notion about the best Way and Manner of fighting with the Indians (which he was always wont to argue for) viz. that it were best to deal with the Indians in their own Way . . . by skulking behind Trees, and taking their Aim at single Persons . . . but herein was his great Mistake, in not considering the great Disadvantage a smaller Company would have in dealing that way with a greater Multitude . . . which gross Mistake of his, was the Ruine of a choice Company of young Men, the very Flower of the County of Essex, all called out of the Towns belonging to that County. . . . For had he ordered his Men to march in a Body . . . they had not lost a Quarter of the Number of those that fell that Day by the Edg of the Sword.[125]

If Lathrop symbolized all that was wrong with the Massachusetts officer corps, Mosely, in Hubbard's view, represented a possible cure. Mosely appears in Hubbard's history as a hero who, while arriving "too late" on the scene of Lathrop's destruction to save the day, was able to provide ample proof of English fortitude. If Lathrop's fatal error had been the decision to adopt Indian martial strategies, the "valiant and successful Captain Mosely" reversed that error by eschewing Indian strategies and proving how effective English techniques could be. Not only, wrote Hubbard, did Mosely mass his troops in English fashion, rather than separating them into smaller groups as Lathrop had done, but he

> marched through and through that great Body of Indians, and yet came off with little or no Loss in comparison of the other [Lathrop]. And having fought all those Indians for five or six Hours upon a March, lost not above two Men all that while, nor received other Damage except that eight or nine were wounded.

The presence of a tireless Mosely, "almost melted with labouring," brought forth, moreover, what Hubbard regarded as a near miracle:

> As Captain Mosely came upon the Indians in the Morning, he found them stripping the Slain [of Lathrop's men], amongst whom was one Robert Dutch, of Ipswich, having been sorely wounded by a Bullet

that rased to his Skull, and then mauled by the Indian Hatchets, was left for dead by the Salvages, and stript by them of all but his Skin; yet when Captain Mosely came near, he almost miraculously, as one raised from the Dead, came towards the English, to their no small Amazement; by whom being received and cloathed, he was carried off to the next Garrison, and is living and in perfect Health at this Day. May he be to the Friends and Relations of the Rest of the Slain an Emblem of their more perfect Resurrection at the last Day to receive their Crowns among the Rest of the Martyrs that have laid down and ventured their Lives, as a Testimony to the Truth of their Religion, as well as Love to their Country.[126]

Mosely was depicted here as the agent of rebirth. A bloodied English host could rise again, if they trusted in their own ways and the "Truth of their Religion."

William Hubbard was not the only writer who found favorable depictions of Mosely to be an effective way to respond to the widespread need on the part of chastened New Englanders to redeem their confidence in the superiority of English over Indian ways. Nathaniel Saltonstall too included many scenes of Mosely's valor, but none so evocative as the account of the captain's behavior in an encounter of August 1675 when the English pursued Philip's people out of Pocasset Swamp, near Mount Hope. In preparation for a battle pitting sixty Englishmen against a much larger force of Indians, Mosely, says Saltonstall, pocketed his periwig so that he would not be encumbered by it in combat.

[As] soon as the Indians saw that, they fell a Howling and Yelling most hideously, and said, 'Umh, Umh me no stawmerre fight Engismon, Engismon got two Hed, Engismon got two Hed; if me cut off un Hed, he got noder, a put on beder as dis'; with such like Words in broken English, and away they all fled and could not be overtaken, nor seen any more afterwards.

Through his use of the Indians' "broken English" and their credulous fear of a man with two heads, Saltonstall conveyed the notion that the English were superior to these backward foes.[127] Emphasizing the differences between barbarous "savages" and the "civilized" English colonists, Saltonstall attempted to show why it was appropriate that the two groups fight against one another as separate peoples.

In castigating Lathrop and praising Mosely, Hubbard and other writers subtly called attention to the dangers of venturing too far into the "middle ground." Mosely gained heroic stature both because of his deeds and because his wider reputation as a hater of Christian as well as "pagan" Indians guaranteed him a clear and unambiguous English identity. Lathrop's downfall, meanwhile, which occurred in part because he valued Indian over English ways, hinted at the greater risks many Massachusetts officers ran by trusting Indian allies too much or allowing their English identity to become diluted on the edges of settlement.[128] The frontier, in peace or war, was a place where the boundary between Indian and English could become disturbingly blurred, and people who crossed it, however heroic, benign, or even pedestrian their motives, could become the targets of popular opprobrium.[129]

The fear of intercultural mediatorship reflected in the writings of Hubbard and Saltonstall had consequences in "real" life not only for Gookin but for others who operated, whether voluntarily or involuntarily, in the liminal space "between worlds." In the eastern theatre, where fighting dragged on after 1676, doubts centered around the figure of Captain Walter Gendall of Scarborough, a captive of the notorious Mugg. During his captivity, Gendall had carried messages back and forth between his captors and colonists; at the Indians' direction, he attempted to convince defenders of Wells to surrender their garrisons; later he was apparently set at large to negotiate the ransoms for himself and other captives with authorities at Portsmouth. Upon his release, Gendall's neighbors suspected that his cooperation with the Indians had exceeded the bounds of propriety. These rumors eventually translated into a treason trial before the Court of Assistants, which charged Gendall with "perfidious and treacherous" behavior in seeking to "betray them into the ennemyes hands by his Indeavor and Counsell."

Animosity toward Gendall on the part of Boston magistrates and the military establishment probably stemmed from Gendall's disruptive attempts to undermine fellow officers at Black Point—particularly by encouraging rumors among the local populace that Bay Colony military officers were misappropriating the services of local people and their goods, under cover of protecting them. Just months before the treason trial, for example, Major General Daniel Denison had been compelled to explain how it came to pass that an unsealed letter of his, addressed to Sergeant Bartholomew Tippen of the Black Point garrison, had touched off a "mutiny" among the local soldiery. Denison explained that Gendall was at the root of this affair, for Gendall had deceitfully convinced Denison that his fellow officer Tippen (or Tipping), a sergeant recently dispatched to Maine by the General Court, was guilty of misconduct. Denison had then dutifully written a letter to Tippen, "blaming him for detaining major Pendletons men and boate, and telling him he mistooke his errand if he thought they were sent only to serve themselves, for certainely it was to secure the place and assist any inhabitants in the recovery of their owne etc." In retrospect, Denison realized that Tippen was probably not guilty of wrong doing; that Gendall had manipulated him into reprimanding Tippen; and that the crafty Gendall then had gone on to reveal the contents of the damning letter to the soldiery rather than delivering it to Tippen, thereby causing the "mutiny." Embarrassed at his own carelessness in having sent the letter unsealed, Denison underscored that he never "imagined my letter to him [Tippen] should have beene published to his souldiers, which I beleive was Gendals artifice to obtaine his owne Ends or to reveng himself of Tipping."

It could not have boded well for Gendall that he had alienated one so powerful as Denison. This incident, moreover, as interpreted by Denison, called Gendall's loyalty into question, showing that he willingly provoked dissent at a time when all should have been united against the enemy.

At any rate, Gendall was sentenced to

> Runn the Gantelop thro the millitary Companyes in Boston on the 10th Instant with a Roape about his necke that he forfeit all his lands to the Country and be banished out of this Jurisdiction to be gonn by the 6th of October next on poenalty of perpetuall Imprisonment if he Returne Againe and dischardgning the Costs and charges of the prosecution.

This draconian punishment—highly uncharacteristic of the Court—was never carried out because he escaped from prison and ended up being compelled only to pay a fine. Gendall regained his high public repute, continuing to serve as a military officer in North Yarmouth, where he was eventually killed at the hands of Indians.[130] Gendall might never have had to endure court proceedings had his machinations not so alienated men of high rank in Boston. Still, this mysterious episode illustrates how the contact implied even in adversarial relations with Indians fed the fear of treachery.

Walter Gendall was not the only prominent figure on the Maine frontier to raise the suspicions of his fellow colonists. Just a few months before Gendall's capture in September 1676, Captain Joshua Scottow of Black Point, who had been a close trading partner of La Tour, also came under scrutiny, though for selfish behavior rather than perfidy. In the summer of 1676 several witnesses—including Walter Gendall, who was apparently eager to impugn Scottow in the same way he would soon impugn Tippen—testified that Scottow stood by and refused to aid a besieged group of colonists at Winter Harbor, even though he commanded enough reinforcements to make the difference between life and death for nine young men hopelessly outnumbered by hostile Indians. A horrified local settler, Miles Edgecomb, age twenty-five, remembered having seen how

> sundrie Men [came] to Mr. Scottow importuning and profesing themselves that he would send over some Ayde to those poore distresssed Men . . . being within soe small Compass that they plainlie did see that the Number of the Heathen was farr exceeding the English; notwithstanding all this Mr. Scottow would not suffer a Man to goe to help them . . . boathe talkeing and haveing in his View that sad Sight, would not moove Mr. Scottow to releife those poore English, whoe for Want of Helpe weare found slaine.[131]

Although Scottow was not formally censured for his behavior, a General Court committee did investigate his actions. Scottow, who was perceived by some as being too slow to provide help and supplies but too forward in

demanding compensation for his mens' military services, had gained a reputation for refusing to arm or defend local residents. According to the
testimony of one wrathful Maine inhabitant, John Jackson, Scottow had
refused to give powder to a local garrison, saying that "if the Boston Soldiers
wanted Powder, they could have it, but if the Inhabitants wanted it they
must buy it."[132]

Interestingly, back in 1656, Scottow had been involved in another
controversy that pitted plain folk against the trading elite when he made
an unsuccessful bid to defend Ann Hibbens, the widow of merchant William Hibbens, from charges of witchcraft. Scottow had at Hibbens's trial
introduced into court a "writing" that impugned the testimony of one
Philip Wharton, one of Hibbens's accusers. Threatened with a censure from
the General Court for the "unseasonable presenting of the said writing,"
Scottow had quickly retreated from the cause. But the apologetic letter he
sent to the General Court suggested that there had been talk of the captain's possible involvement in some sort of conspiracy to save Hibbens:

> As for the apprehension of any that it might be a plotted buysiness
> between some and myselfe, that it should be soe ordered that Phillip
> Wharton's testimony should bee first produced and my writing soe to
> follow to the attayning of the evill ends above mentioned, I should
> humbly beg further favour, and doe hereby solemnly and seriously
> professe and protest, that I never communicated with any person
> whatsoever about the said writing, nor that I did ever discourse with
> Mrs. Hibbins or any other about the premises except the Secretary
> after the lecture yesterday was ended, immediately upon the sitting
> of the court and my writing being ended, only telling him I had
> something to say about Phillip Wharton's testimony. I am cordially
> sorry that anything from mee eyther by word or writing should any
> way tend to the hardening of Mrs. Hibbins in her sinfull and abom-
> inable courses or that I should give offence to the Honoured Court,
> my deare brethren in the church, or any others.[133]

Hibbens, who was soon executed for witchcraft, had become the target of
ill-wishers in the colony because of her overbearing, proud behavior and
her powerful social position as the middle-aged recipient of a large inheritance from her husband's estate.[134] By 1676, Scottow himself was in a
position where his manipulation of dangerous outside forces could be construed as a kind of witchery; interestingly, it was through his agency that
George Burroughs, who would be executed as a witch at Salem in 1692,
had been installed as a minister in Maine.[135]

In the fall of 1675, Lieutenant Thomas Gardiner of Pemaquid created
a stir when he offered some controversial advice to officials in Boston: if
Bay colonists did not want the northern Abenakis to join in hostility
against the English, Gardiner argued, then they should take steps to reverse
the local policy of seizing the guns of peaceful Indians and allowing "wild

fishermen" to terrorize them. In a letter to Governor John Leverett, Gardiner described in scathing terms how, only a few months after hostilities had begun at Mount Hope, local inhabitants of Maine had taken it upon themselves to abuse their Abenaki neighbors in ways that would give them no choice but to starve for the lack of guns with which to hunt or to appeal to the French for aid:

> Sir I Conceive the Reason of our Troubles hear may be occationed not only by som southern Indianes which may Com this way But by our owne Acctings and Because I much doubt of such Accting do ernestly desiere Advice and ordere. Sir upon the first Newes of the wares with the Indianes at Plimouth divers persone from Kenibek and Shepscott gott togeather makeing them selves officers and went up Kenibeke River and demanded the Indianes armes who Came downe Quiettly and Brought and delivered thear Armes how thay wear Treatted with Captain Thomas Lake Can Better Inform you then my self . . . my doubt is seing these Indianes Amongst us live most by Hunting as your Honnor well Knoweth how we Can Take Away their Armes whose livelyhood dependeth of it. And seeing these Indianes in these parts did never Apeare dissatisfied untill their Armes were Taken Away I doubt of such Acctions whether they may not be forced to go to the french for Reliefe or fight Against us having nothing for their suport Almost in these parts but their guns. . . . Sir, I do not find by Any thing I can discerne that the Indianes East of us ar in the least our Ennimies only fly for fear from Any boats or English thay se and good Reason for thay well Know it may Cost them their Lives if the wild fishermen meet with them . . . Most persone think fitt to go into the woods and Kill or sease on All Indianes thay find but for my part I hearing they ar fled from their forte and live in the woods think such procedings will not only be frutles but overbalanced with Abundance of Danger but do think best to get our selves into as defensive A posture as we Can.[136]

Gardiner, like Gookin, attempted to see things from the Indian perspective; but he was viewed as an untrustworthy figure because his trade with the Indians and the French gave him a vested interest in their well-being. It was no accident that soon after Gardiner sent this letter, reports began to surface of "Lieutenant Thomas Gardiners still tradeing with the french and Indians, to the great dainger and trouble of the English and encouragement of the barbarous natives now in Hostillity." The Massachusetts Council, faced at the same time with the public outcry against praying Indians, was compelled to investigate these reports, authorizing the constable at Pemaquid to "Inquire into the said Complaint examining all persons" who may have seen "certeine frenchmen to Come ashoare at Pemacquid and Carry up theire moose and bevar to Leiutenant Gardiners house as also such fishermen as did disarme the said Frenchmen."[137] Despite the intricacy of the rumors that swirled around Pemaquid, however, Gardiner was able to prove his innocence.

To the eyes of many rank-and-file Bay colonists, it looked as though an unlikely combination of wishful thinking, misplaced benevolence, and greed had rendered their traditional leaders dangerously undiscerning when it came to judging Indian claims of friendship or cultural conversion. The specter of military officers/investors colluding with potential or actual enemies to the seeming detriment of Englishmen continued to haunt colonists in the aftermath of the war, when it became evident that some English elites were helping Indians accused of war crimes to prepare exculpatory petitions in their defense.

In September 1676, William Awannuckhow, also known as William Jackstraw, and members of his family were charged with participating in February 1676 in a raid on a frontier dwelling in which members of Sudbury's Thomas Eames family were killed or captured. On first being questioned in August 1676, Jackstraw, formerly of the praying town of Magunkaquog, confessed to Thomas Danforth that he had been present at the raid, which was "occasioned by their necessity of corne"; while admitting that he "himself carried away on his back one of Eames sonnes," Jackstraw held also that he "kept at a distance" during the worst violence. Two weeks after this initial confession, Jackstraw and his codefendants submitted a petition for clemency. The petition explained that Jackstraw and members of his family had been bullied into participating in the raid by other Indians, most of whom were now dead. Although Jackstraw denounced the violence of the raid, he suggested that its aim, the recovery of corn that had been stolen from Magunkaquog, was at least partially justifiable; and, far from harming the Eames children, he and others who now stood accused of heinous crimes had actually been "instrumental" in saving the youngsters' lives, for the men "carried one boy upon our backs rather than let him be killed." Most important, Jackstraw claimed that Massachusetts authorities could not execute him in good conscience, since he had surrendered to Captain Thomas Prentice in keeping with Massachusetts' offer of amnesty to enemies who voluntarily "came in" during the summer of 1676.

Jackstraw probably had help in writing this well-argued (but unsuccessful) petition. Thomas Prentice, an associate of Gookin in the Narragansett and Worcester ventures, readily vouched for the good faith of the Indians' surrender. The petition's final sentences—similar in many ways to Vincent Gookin's defense of Irishmen who got caught up in but did not lead the rebellion—reminded the English that combatants in wars were not supposed to be punished simply for revenge:

> Besides it was a time of warre when the mischief was done and though it was our unhappy portion to be . . . enemies yet we conceive that depradation and slaughter in warr are not chargeable upon particular persons, especially such as have submitted themselves to your honour upon promise of life as we have done.[138]

The irony of this statement could not have been lost on readers familiar with English criticisms that Indians fought their wars for narrow, dishonorable, and vengeful reasons. But it was an irony that could not withstand the pressure of a war-torn populace.

THE WRITINGS OF Increase Mather, unlike Hubbard or Saltonstall, were notable for their extensive criticisms of colonists who needlessly harmed praying Indians and cast doubt upon their conversions. Mather, who would himself become a New England Company commissioner, no doubt felt genuine pangs of remorse for the colony's treatment of praying Indians. Yet, no less than any other New England Puritan author, Mather reinforced the concept of the racially closed Christian community; strangely, his criticisms of English cruelty were one means by which he accomplished this rhetorical goal.

To his diary Mather confided his conviction that New England's mistreatment of the Christian Indians warranted punishment. He was particularly concerned about the implications of an incident in which some men at Chelmsford had plotted to massacre the praying Indians of nearby Wamesit, managing to wound five women and children and kill a twelve-year-old boy: "It is to be feared that there is guilt upon the Land in respect of the Indians yea Guilt of blood in respect of the Indian so treacherously murdered at Chelmsford."[139] Addressing this theme publicly in *An Earnest Exhortation to the Inhabitants of New-England*, Mather harshly excoriated those readers who "slighted, scorned, and vilified" the "Indian work" and wrote that his heart "doth ake and bleed within me" to think of the intended massacre at Wamesit. Mather, it would seem, echoed Gookin almost word for word in his admonitions against those who callously rejected and abused Indian converts:

> And what though some of them may be Hypocrites? are not some Praying English as perfidious, as hypocritical, in heart as profane as some Praying Indians? Shall we therefore condemn all? Is there such a spirit in this Generation, as that they are ready to destroy? . . . the righteous with the wicked? . . . Now from the Lord I Exhort and beseech you, whoever you be that have been guilty of murmurings in any respect, or of casting a stumbling Block before the Indians, go to God in secret places, confess your sin before him, pray that it may not be imputed to you or to your Families, or to the Land for your sakes.[140]

But this view of praying Indians as objects of sympathy did not signify that Mather regarded the Indians as centrally important in their own right.

Daniel Gookin, in *Doings and Sufferings*, did two things that no other mainstream writer of the era dared or, more likely, wished to do: first, Gookin moved praying Indians from the margins of Puritan society into the center of the war's dramatic action, suggesting that in certain instances

Christian Indian contributions had actually altered its course; second, and more important, he placed Christian Indians at the center of the war's providential meaning. In writing this text, Gookin effected a jarring reversal of the roles traditionally ascribed to Englishmen and Indians. While most Puritans were accustomed to think of adversity and affliction as crucial elements of a dialogue between God and his chosen people from which Indians, praying or "profane," were firmly excluded, Gookin argued emphatically that God used the hardships of war to test and strengthen the spiritual mettle of Indian as well as English saints. Recognizing that long-suffering individuals like Job Katenanit, Andrew Pitimee, and Joseph Tuckapawillin found acceptance neither among the unconverted Algonquian peoples nor the English, Gookin framed their experiences in what would become the time-honored style of the captivity narrative, where God tests and ultimately strengthens an individual's faith through adversity and separation from the godly.[141] This narrative strategy necessitated that certain mean-spirited Englishmen must approach the unaccustomed role of pawns of Satan, preying on the embattled souls of regenerate Indian saints and goading them on to greater spiritual exertions:

> This cruel frame of spirit [hostility and doubt toward Christian Indians] (for I can give it no gentler denomination) arose I apprehend from a double ground, first, the malice of Satan against Christ's work among those Indians and to hinder their progress in religion; for they finding Englishmen, professing Christian religion, so enraged against them, and injurious to them without cause, as they well knew in their own consciences, whatever others thought or spake to the contrary, this was a sore temptation to such weak ones and little children as it were in the ways of Christianity, and hereby to incline them to apostasy, and if the devil by this stratagem could have prevailed, then the whole work of Christ among them, so spoken of, blessed and owned by the Lord, would have been utterly overthrown; this would have gratified Satan and his instruments greatly.[142]

In this inversion of the classic captivity narrative, tainted Englishmen, succumbing to the doubts that Satan placed in their minds, played exactly the same role for praying Indians as the famous Mary Rowlandson's "barbarous" Indian captors did for her. In such a formulation, there could be no firm boundary between sheltered English communities of saints and the perilous frontier.

If Gookin's text had the effect of blurring the boundary separating English from Indian saints, Mather contended that the war's spiritual meaning, and its opportunities, were reserved for the English. Mather wove the praying Indians into his war narratives only to demonstrate the consequences to the English of abusing them or of slighting the time-honored importance of the missionary enterprise, which was to be revered not so much on its own merits as on the first generation's supposed dedication to it; the "publick Seal of the Country will be a witness against this and succeeding Generations, if that design be not prosecuted; for we know the publick Seal of this Colony represents an Indian with these words '*Come and help us.*'"[143] By cleaving faithfully to the Indian work, Mather suggested, New Englanders might preserve the founders' legacy and retain their distinct provincial culture in a changing world:

> We are the Children of the good old Non-Conformists: and therefore we are under the deepest engagement, not only to reject Inventions Humane in the things of God, but to come up to the practice of Institutions Divine . . . It was worthily spoken by blessed Mr. Mitchel in a Lecture Sermon, that there is much of the Kingdome of Christ in our Civil Constitution: and it will be sad for those who shall put their hands to alter it. Such dash themselves against that stone, that whoso falls upon it, shall be broken to shivers.[144]

Mather's complaint that New Englanders were "full of murmurings and unreasonable Rage" against both the enemy and praying Indians was rooted in his fear that they were not "Humbled and Reformed" and that they failed to apprehend their own sinful culpability. Like most Puritan ministers, Mather wanted to impress upon the people of New England that the harms they suffered had less to do with forces outside themselves, like Satan, or apparent perpetrators, like the Indians, and more to do with their own vile shortcomings. To blame the war on the enemy Indians was almost like doubting Providence; to lump the praying Indians together with the "profane" and then harm them needlessly, could be regarded as a "provoking sin" of God and as yet another break with the purity of the founders:

> and I doubt one of the great sins which the English have been guilty of, that no more hath been done in order to the conversion of the Heathen: how great then is their sin, who do wholly despise and decry that work, and those beginnings of the Kingdome of the Lord Jesus, which is to be seen amongst them, our Fathers were of another Spirit.[145]

It might be objected that both Increase Mather and his son Cotton demonstrated genuine zeal for the Indian work as commissioners of the New England Company. But these clergymen seemed less interested in spending time with the colony's Indians than gaining valuable contacts among the "enlightened" members of the company in England.[146] In a gesture that communicated eloquently the colony's unwillingness to accommodate the special needs of Indians, Cotton Mather recommended that Bibles and religious tracts cease to be published in the written Algonquian language devised by John Eliot and his praying Indian informants. Increase Mather, regardless of his concern for the victims of the Chelmsford massacre, warned colonists to be wary of Indian diabolism passing as Christianity.

Mather must have known, for example, that the Saco sachem Squando had much cause to hate the colonists, for in the summer of 1675 a "rude and indiscreet" group of English fishermen had deliberately overturned a canoe carrying Squando's wife and infant son so as to test the theory that indigenous children "could swim as naturally as any other creatures"; the child had subseqently died. Despite accounts of how Squando nonetheless attempted to avoid unnecessary "Acts of Cruelty" while prosecuting the war, Mather, in his writings, was interested primarily in showing that Squando's unsupervised brand of Christianity was false and dangerous:

> A principle Actor in the destruction of Sacoe was a strange Enthu-
> siastical Sagamore, called Squando, who some years before pretended
> that God appeared to him, in the form of a tall Man, in black Cloaths,
> declaring to him that he was God, and commanded him to leave his
> Drinking of Strong Liquors, and to pray, and to keep Sabbaths: and
> to go hear the Word Preached, all which things the Indian did for
> some years, with great seeming Devotion and Conscience observe.
> But the God which appeared to him, said nothing to him about Jesus
> Christ: and therefore it is not to be marvelled at, that at last he
> discovered himself to be no other wise then a Childe of him, that
> was a Murtherer and a Lyar from the beginning.[147]

It is possible that Squando had ultimately been converted by French Cath-
olics, despite his earlier exposure to what Mather evidently regarded as right religion; this would certainly account for Mather's ire.[148] Still, Mather's warning that Christian conversion did not necessarily wash away the Indians' underlying predisposition to diabolism and perfidy contributed to the climate of opinion that made life so precarious for the Bay Colony's Puritan Indians.

Hubbard drew an even more extreme conclusion from the story of Squando, suggesting that in the last stages of the war in Maine, colonists must now regard with deep suspicion all Indians, particularly those who disguised their deviltry as Christianity and behaved in a humane manner:

> Satan hath lately changed himself into an Angel of Light, under that
> Shape, making this his last Attempt, to the Eastward. For the chief
> Leader of those Indians is a Sagamore called Squando, who hath (as
> is said by them that lately escaped from their Hands) familiar Con-
> verse with the Prince of Darkness, though under the Notion of a good
> Deity, putting him upon a Form of Religion, and forbidding any Acts
> of Cruelty and Murther to be used against any they oppose, if they
> be willing to yeild, and in that Way promising great Success to his
> followers.[149]

Once again, Hubbard stresses the Indians' seemingly innate skill at dressing up diabolism as Christianity and lies as truth. More telling, he suggests that a civil relationship with Indians was to be feared as much as one characterized by violent confrontation.

While sympathetic toward the praying Indians, Mather, like the majority of his peers, found it impossible to view these converts as being of central importance to the war's providential meaning. At most, Christian Indians represented an opportunity for the Puritans to live up to the expectations of the founders and to mollify an angry God. The colonists, in Mather's judgment, must win the war on their own terms and in their own interest; not until they had "prayed the bullet into Philip's heart" could they claim the victory.[150]

GOOKIN'S ABILITY TO write a decentered account of King Philip's War came not from his innate humanitarianism but rather from his experiences on New England's cultural margins. Hubbard and Mather were by no means hostile to the wider world; but each of these authors knew—as they had during the controversy over the halfway covenant—how to offset the threat of this wider world by sounding the tribal themes that motivated and comforted New Englanders.

In the earlier controversy over the halfway covenant, John Oxenbridge, unlike Gookin, had correctly sensed the dangers implicit in the majority faction's manner of popularizing its views. As Massachusetts leaders gradually came to enjoy the "delights" of the "new learning" and to pursue ways of connecting themselves with religious networks in the metropolis, they also emphasized countervailing images and practices capable of endowing religion with a domestic, communal feel.[151] Ministers stumbled, perhaps unwittingly, upon this manner of rendering new forms of association nonthreatening during the framing of the halfway covenant—a truly ambivalent "innovation," which could be read alternately as the very quintessence of provincialism or as an incomplete adaptation to nascent "latitudinarian" demands for "comprehensive" churches. At the same time, the emphasis on domesticity reinforced the notion that religion was a family affair noninclusive of cultural "others," like the Indians, who increasingly came to symbolize all sorts of real and imagined enemies, from crafty courtiers to conspiratorial witches.[152] Ironically, as the early Enlightenment dawned in colonial Massachusetts, so too did an enhanced sense of racial difference, and a desire for exclusivity.

THE CLASH IN late-seventeenth-century Massachusetts over whether the various bands of Algonquians inhabiting New England should be treated as a unitary people inclined always to support those of their own kind or as a series of distinct peoples and individuals capable of entertaining loyalties that went well beyond those of race resembled in some ways the internal conflict accompanying the contemporaneous Bacon's Rebellion in colonial Virginia. In Massachusetts, unlike the Chesapeake colony, antipathy toward constituted authority never spiraled into internecine violence; still, inhabitants of the two colonies, feeling strongly the need to redefine themselves in response to internal and external change, turned almost in-stinctively to popular leaders (like Mosely or Bacon) identified with in-flexible Indian policies—a pattern that would endure down to the Amer-ican Revolution and beyond.[153]

The Bay Colony's adjustment to empire forced ministers eager to pre-serve a Puritan identity in the face of a compromised (and later an absent) Puritan state to make certain accommodations with a popular culture just beginning to recognize its own power. If the clearer emphasis on tribal religiosity in the late seventeenth century denoted a coming of age for some New Englanders, it represented a diminishment of possibilities for others. The same social tensions that emerged during the King Philip's War era resurfaced in virulent form at least twice more in late-seventeenth-century Massachusetts. As already shown, in the Glorious Revolution of 1689 Edmund Andros was accused of "crimes" similar to Gookin's. And at Salem in 1692, ordinary New Englanders demonstrated, now with deadly accusations of traffic with the devil, their ongoing fear of people who trod too close to frontier and transatlantic boundaries. With this we come full circle, for Gookin himself was regarded as the "devil's interpreter."[154]

5

Epilogue and Conclusion

On May 28, 1692, with King William's War raging on the frontier and a deadly witchcraft epidemic beginning to infect Salem village, Captain John Alden, Sr., a merchant and mariner of Boston, learned that he was suspected of trafficking with the devil. His principal accuser, one of the "afflicted" girls of Salem—whom Alden collectively dismissed as "Wenches . . . who plaid . . . jugling tricks"—wavered while identifying her tormentor, thinking at one point that it might be a Captain Hill. After some prompting from another man present, however, she fastened her gaze on the unfortunate son of Pilgrims, crying out "there stands Aldin, a bold fellow with his Hat on before the Judges, he sells Powder and Shot to the Indians and French, and lies with the Indian Squaes, and has Indian Papooses."[1] Alden's gender and high status would normally have shielded him from being singled out as a witch; indeed, even after his arrest, such prominent figures as Samuel Sewall and Cotton Mather prayed for him. But at a time when the hostile activities of Indians, Frenchmen, Quakers, and grasping English officials like Edmund Andros were thought to be coordinated components of a single diabolic plot against New England, Alden had become a vulnerable figure.[2]

It is unlikely that Alden fathered "Indian Papooses"; nor is there evidence to suggest that this member of Old South Church was a Quaker, as the reference to his refusal of hat honor would suggest.[3] But Alden traded frequently to French Acadia, often in association with the Anglican merchant John Nelson.[4] And by marrying the widow Elizabeth Phillips Averill in 1660 he had incorporated himself into a family with a strong heretical tradition. Alden's mother-in-law by this marriage was none other than Bridget Hutchinson Sanford Phillips, the daughter of Anne and William Hutchinson, the widow of exiled antinomian John Sanford, and the third wife of successful Boston wine merchant and Maine land broker William Phillips. The Phillipses presided over a family enclave in Maine that provided land for Bridget's large network of Hutchinson and Sanford kin, which included numerous Quakers.[5] Like Anne Hutchinson, there is evidence to suggest that Bridget Phillips, with the connivance of her husband, had sought to carve out a life of religious freedom in the "wilderness" surrounding the Bay Colony. Bridget Phillips resembled her mother too in the possession of a strong will, as reflected in the petitions she wrote after her husband's death to ensure that the family retained clear title to its properties in Maine.[6]

If Alden's kinship with the Phillips clan of Boston and Saco was damaging to his reputation, so was his decision to exploit French and Indian trade networks in company with the Anglican merchant John Nelson. During the King Philip's War era, Nelson had barely escaped an investigation into charges that he had violated a wartime trade embargo by shipping gunpowder to his trading partners in New France; in the period of the late 1680s and early 1690s, encompassing King William's War and the witchcraft eruption that followed, Nelson maintained ties with Baron de Saint-Castin of Pentagouet, the hated organizer of raids against English villages in Massachusetts and New York. And while neither Nelson nor Alden appeared to cohabit with Indian women, as the 1692 accusation implied, Saint-Castin had married the daughter of the much-feared Penobscot sachem Madockawando, whose adaptation of Christian principles to indigenous lifeways made him, in the New England mind, all the more fearsome and potentially satanic.[7]

John Alden, as an insider to the New England Way who nonetheless aligned himself with dangerous forces outside the wall of purity, was precisely the sort of individual who could be seen as a "witch." Scholars have shown that Samuel Parris, minister at Salem, reiterated time and again in his preaching that the "witch" conspiracy was perpetrated by an enemy within, a fifth column of conspirators who appeared to be part of the community but were actually working subversively toward its destruction.[8] Alden had contact with Indians, Frenchmen, Anglicans, and Quakers, all of whom possessed communal networks extraneous, and sometimes hostile, to Puritan Massachusetts. These networks could easily be conflated with the countercultural witch community that Satan was trying to erect on the ruins of Puritan Massachusetts.[9] With tracts on witchcraft routinely representing the spectral plane as a kind of staging area for spiritual attacks on the New England soul, it took no great leap of conjecture to regard the very real, but no less shadowy, world of Maine and Acadia—already sources of controversy in Bay Colony politics—as this spectral world's geographical equivalent.

Cotton Mather theorized that the

> Prodigious War, made by the Spirits of the Invisible World upon the People of New-England, in the year 1692 [witchcraft] . . . might have some of its Original among the Indians, whose chief Sagamores are well known . . . to have been horrid Sorcerers, and hellish Conjurers and such as Conversed with Daemons.[10]

In an effort to link warfare, witchcraft, and French-allied Indians more closely, Mather reprinted clergyman Ebenezer Bapson's account of how in Gloucester, just before the outbreak of King William's War, the devil had sent "Spectres" "in the Shape of Armed Indians and Frenchmen" to torment the residents with phantom attacks stretching out over a month; it had not been long, he explained pointedly, before real attacks commenced along the perimeter of settlement.[11] While Cotton Mather's much-discussed disavowal of spectral evidence may have helped to put a stop to popularly-based trials having to do with *maleficium*, his rhetoric concerning the concrete damage presaged by these spectral intruders—captivity, death, and burned-out villages—would certainly have done much to keep the terror alive, reinforcing how high the stakes of witchcraft toleration could be. By associating witchcraft with the Quakers, the frontier, the unpopular Governor Edmund Andros, and the many forms of diversity existing within the English empire, Mather effectively worked to preserve New England's purity, and its separate identity, even as he accepted some aspects of a dawning, anglicized enlightenment. Although Mather prayed for Alden, his rhetoric had helped to bring the wolves to the captain's door.

I have shown already, by examining the case of Daniel Gookin, that Bay colonists during King Philip's War manifested greater hostility toward actual or perceived turncoats than outright enemies. Gookin, closely involved in the activities of a missionary society oriented toward the needs of the transatlantic trading and religious community, had been denounced as the "devil's interpreter," and ordinary people had proved willing to believe that the prominent captain might, perhaps unknowingly, have trucked with the devil. During the frontier wars of the 1680s, the logic linking witchcraft with those who had commerce with the French or Indian enemy, with the Anglican trading community, or with religious apostasy became far more explicit and potentially deadly. The case of John Alden, who was accused of tempting and tormenting his victims in spectral form, demonstrates that New Englanders were prepared to view as witches not only marginalized women or racial and ethnic outsiders but also illicit traders from prominent Puritan families. The lore of witch detection held that any accused person who survived the "ordeal" of dunking must have received life-saving aid from the "invisible world" and therefore must be guilty of witchcraft; by the same token, merchants who not only survived close contact with threatening outside forces but, worse, prospered, were thought somehow to have allied with them.[12] These "others," like the "familiars" who sucked on witches' "teats," offered favors and wealth in exchange for the opportunity occasionally to spill the blood of innocents.

JOHN ALDEN WAS a fitting target for witchcraft accusations not solely because of his own activities but also because of his close connections with powerful yet controversial figures in Massachusetts, such as John Nelson and William Phillips. The mildly Anglican Nelson was a religious moderate who, in the late 1690s, wrote a letter on behalf of Boston's Brattle Street church inviting the latitudinarian clergyman Benjamin Colman to minister to the controversial new congregation on the condition that Colman would "procure your ordination in England," and then proceed, once in place, to carry on "the service of God in publique . . . as is customarie in all other reformed churches, except those in this country, to say, by reading of the holy Scripture unto the People [as opposed to the New England focus on sermons] . . . as I remember your selfe very much approved."[13]

Out of step with both the traditional Puritan hierarchy and the royal office holders who crowded into the colony in the 1680s, Nelson, a facilitator of Alden's ventures into the "eastern partes," had migrated to New England in the 1660s, hoping to make his way by managing the interests of his kinsman, Thomas Temple, in Nova Scotia. Trained in the art of navigation by John Rhoades, one of the pirates captured by Samuel Mosely in 1674, Nelson soon became deputy governor of Nova Scotia. Although he suffered a setback in 1667 when the English ceded Port Royal back to the French, he quickly learned that this fort, as well as other French installations, such as the Baron de Saint-Castin's Pentagouet, still needed to trade with New England in order to provision themselves. Nelson accordingly fashioned himself into an intermediary between French and English interests. In 1682 he worked out an arrangement whereby French authorities allowed him to sell licenses to New England merchants, like John Alden, who wished to sail, trade, or fish unmolested in French waters. Nelson was considered so much the master of events on the eastern frontier that in 1687, when a fishing boat belonging to Samuel Sewall's brother was seized by French privateers, Sewall appealed to Nelson "to see, if Brother might have his ketch again." At the same time, Nelson occasionally helped Frenchmen with legal problems they might encounter in Massachusetts, serving as attorney at one point for the Baron de Saint Castin and even offering to include the Frenchman in some of his enterprises. All the while, however, Nelson was busily gathering as much useful information about French operations as he could so that, in his own recollection, "my long acquaintance in these partes made them deeply Suspitious of me."[14]

In working constantly to keep open the fragile lines of commerce and communication between New England and French Acadia, Nelson was a truly liminal figure. His predecessors in Nova Scotia, John Leverett and

Robert Sedgwick, had generated resentments when they attempted essentially to devise and follow their own foreign policy in the region; but Leverett and Sedgwick, if sometimes controversial, had possessed the backing of a strong Puritan regime in England, while Nelson, a non-Puritan, entered the field solely on his own account. Nelson held no public offices in Massachusetts and was not a freeman; his Artillery Company membership, begun in 1681, was his only claim to some semblance of a public role. But if Nelson was at odds with Puritan Massachusetts, viewing its regime as imposing unnecessary constraints on trade, he was still, like orthodox New Englanders, disaffected by the regime of Edmund Andros, the crown-appointed governor sent in 1686 to rule the Dominion of New England in the wake of the revocation of the Massachusetts charter. Interestingly, Andros supporters Francis Foxcroft and Samuel Ravenscroft viewed the self-interested John Nelson and "Mr Cotton Madder the Great Pulpitt Buffoune" as equally injurious, albeit in different ways, to England's national interest in North America.[15]

Nelson's antipathy for Andros stemmed from the latter's determination, both during his short term of office in Massachusetts and his earlier days as governor of New York, to assert imperial authority over the frontier in ways that undercut the position of intermediaries such as himself. Andros's fortification of an English installation at Pemaquid, for example, and his raids on Pentagouet gradually drove the French and Abenaki, who had long been in conflict with English residents of Casco Bay, into an alliance.[16] Nelson's disdain for these policies motivated him to emerge as one of the major leaders of Massachusetts' Glorious Revolution against Andros on April 18, 1689; he, along with merchants David Waterhouse and John Foster, both Anglicans and members of the Artillery Company, gained seats on the provisional Council of Safety at a time when other members of the Bay Colony's small Anglican community were being seized and imprisoned. Still, Nelson fell quickly out of favor and lost his Council seat because he opposed the resumption of charter rule pressed by the popular party and because he appeared too conciliatory toward the defeated Andros. Indeed, in 1695, Nelson wrote a letter to Charles Talbot, duke of Shrewsbury, arguing that English policies toward the Indians were inconsistent, disorganized, and less effective than those of the French because of the "number and independency the one from the other of so many small governments." English weaknesses could be remedied, in Nelson's opinion, if the "colonies of New England, Hamshire, Road Island, Plymouth, Conneticut and New York" were to be joined into one, so as to facilitate an "entire conquest" of French Acadia:

> to which enterprize, if the security of our Interest in America, or if honour, profit or facility in the undertaking could be arguments to induce we are thereby oblig'd to be no longer negligent herein.

Although Nelson had been personally adverse to the Andros regime, he continued to advocate a form of government similar in structure to the one that he had just helped to overthrow—a structure that the vast majority of his fellow New Englanders continued to abhor.[17]

It was in the immediate wake of the Glorious Revolution, in the two years prior to the Salem witchcraft outbreak, that the activities of Nelson and Alden seemed most threatening. Andros, by mobilizing the Massachusetts militias in the winter of 1688–89 and attempting to make incursions into French territory, had succeeded only in infuriating the Baron de Saint Castin and touching off a mutiny among English troops resentful of Andros's importation of officers from New York. Indeed, the New England militiamen, who regarded Andros himself as a kind of witch bent on stealing their land and polluting true religion, feared that he planned to sacrifice the colony to the French: "abundance of odd Stories [about Andros] then buzz'd about the Country," wrote Cotton Mather, and "made 'em to imagine, that he had carried 'em out only to Sacrifice 'em." The royal governor's style of rule, moreover, "Arbitrary as the Great Turk," had reduced virtuous colonists to the "Condition of persons possessed with Evil Spirits, which will go an Hundred Leagues in less time than others can Ten; but at the Journeys End find themselves to be so Bruised that they never can recover it"—a telling analysis indeed, given the events to follow.[18]

The eventual overthrow of Andros brought relief to stalwarts like Mather, but it did not solve the Bay Colony's military problems: Baron de Saint-Castin had launched devastating raids against frontier villages, and the Massachusetts government, with no new charter as yet from William and Mary, was too unstable to take decisive action. In these uncertain and desperate times, Nelson, along with a group of merchants that included John Alden, Sr., suggested a solution that was workable yet self-serving: the merchants would pay for an expedition to retake Port Royal in exchange for monopoly trading rights, plunder, and a guarantee that the government would repay them their expenditures in the event that the French recaptured Acadia before they were able to turn a profit.[19]

Like plans pursued formerly by Leverett, Sedgwick, and Gibbons, this scheme would incur considerable public risk while primarily benefiting the private interests of a small but important segment of the mercantile population. The Massachusetts government, however, balked at the guarantees demanded by the merchants and in the end launched the attack at public expense with soon-to-be-governor William Phips, not John Nelson, at its head. According to the Anglican diarist Benjamin Bullivant, Nelson was excluded from command because the "Country Deputies said he was a Merchant and not to be trusted"; too proud to serve under Phips, he refused "with scorn and contempt" a position as Phips's lieutenant.[20] In the aftermath of the conquest of Port Royal, Nelson quarreled vehemently with Phips over what Nelson saw as Phips's dishonorable behavior toward the French captives, especially Governor Meneval, one of Nelson's former associates, whose personal effects Phips had seized contrary to the rules of honor.[21]

While Nelson made a spectacle of himself by openly siding with French captives in Boston, his partner John Alden, Sr., received permission to voyage northward for the ostensible purpose of supplying English frontiersmen, surveying the region, and working toward the release of English captives. Despite these worthy goals, it was well known that the profit motive was uppermost in Alden's mind. Nelson's adversary Samuel Ravenscroft enclosed in a letter to Francis Nicholson, an Andros henchman, the damaging affidavit of Mark Emerson, a common soldier and Indian captive who, disgruntled because Alden had refused to take an aggressive role in his rescue, quoted the latter as "saying he came to Trade and not to Redeem Captives." In the course of his testimony, Emerson eagerly described Alden's questionable dealings on the frontier, and held that New England's enemies viewed Alden as a great ally:

> last winter and spring both French and Indians were forced to eate their Doggs and some of thier Captives, for haveing noe Powder and shott could not kill a Fowle . . . till the arrival of Mr. Alden . . . [who] brought them all supplyes as Powder and shott, Rumm . . . Bread with other Necessaries, or they had all perished. The Indians have a saying, that Mr. Alden is a good man and loves Indians very well for Beaver, and hath been with them often since the warr, to their great Releif.

Ravenscroft's purpose in including this testimony in his letter was to convey to English authorities how Bay Colony Puritans refused to take action against members of their own leading families, even self-interested men like Alden who so blatantly "assist our Enemies to kill our Friends." But the common people living in exposed areas—as well as residents of Essex county, from which Emerson hailed—would have been incensed by news of Alden's demeanor and his friendly dealings with frontier Indians. Alden's attempts to arrange a truce with the Indians in Maine, moreover, was thought somehow to have led to the subsequent raid, in January 1692, on the settlement of York, in which about fifty English colonists were killed.[22]

In the summer of 1691, John Alden, Sr., and his son, John Alden, Jr., subscribed as investors to a final scheme, launched by Nelson and other traders interested in Acadia, that provided the immediate context for Alden's arrest on charges of witchcraft. In exchange for a five-year monopoly on trade, the merchants offered to garrison Port Royal, with Colonel Edward Tyng, a longtime expert on dealings with the Abenaki, as governor. According to Nelson's political enemy Francis Foxcroft, this "sham company" shortchanged the public interest; they hired only "20 sentinells" to guard Port Royal, and "carryed noe more than force sufficient to guard their Traffick."[23]

Tyng, the commander on whom the merchants insisted, was not a particularly beloved figure. In 1688, he had experienced difficulty in mediating conflicts between colonists and local Indians. And, while describing the Saco Indians' resentment at the incursions of English livestock—an ever-present problem whenever the two groups lived in close proximity— he passed on the unpopular opinion, gathered from one of his colleagues, that English colonists might be at fault:

> I have . . . Recived an account from Captain Blackeman that upon the 6 of this month the Saco Indians four or five times fired up on some Cattle which got in to there Corne and wounded sume with small shot and that thay gave very threatning words to the English of Shooting them though he feares the English ware much to blame in not keeping out their Creatures which had Bin In once or twice be fore.

At about the same time, during the Andros administration, Tyng, a Council member, land engrosser, and military officer who exercised extensive powers on the eastern frontier, alienated the inhabitants of Falmouth. In a petition written after Andros's overthrow, the townsmen expressed the wish that "those men [Tyng and two of his associates] be in noe power for if theay be the most part of our Inhabitance will leave the Towne." In the minds of the Falmouth dwellers, "Corenell Tinge" was a man who "can terne his coate when he please, when he was with the Army he could Dominear with the wost, but now we heare he can comply and profess like the best and all for profett." They well remembered how Tyng "did in forme Sir Edmond Andrews that the peopell of our Towne whear an unsubdewed peopell . . . and that he [w]ould take som spedy course with them." And they charged that Tyng, with the permission of the tyrannical governor, had exacted excessive military service as a way of punishing them for their defiance of his authority. Frequent guard duty ruined the townsmen's health, they claimed, and made it more difficult to find time to earn their livelihood. The requirement that they

> should be upon the wach Every third night and day hath bine the lost of many of our men, being thine cloathed and lying upon the hard floar this long wintear nights . . . and then beinge in our Arms as often as theay please to call us som tyms every other day . . . hath soe desabelled us about our Implyment in providinge for our familys that it hath very much Impoverished our towne.

The Falmouth residents complained further that Tyng's associate Captain Sylvanus Davis had charged excessive rates for drawing up land patents so as to "make the Inhabetance poor" and that he had refused to "subscribe to pay to our ministear sence Sir Edmond came." Still, the leaders of the interim Bay Colony government, not considering Tyng, the scion of a powerful merchant family, to be a disloyal figure, retained him in high rank.[24]

Understandably, Nelson's plan, perceived as yet another attempt to generate private profits at the risk of the public safety, was unpopular; not only did Nelson admit Jean Martel, the son-in-law of Joseph Robinau de Villebon, the governor of New France, as an investor but he also planned to resume ties with the Baron de Saint Castin, whose Penobscot relatives would be important for the revival of old trading arrangements with the Indians. As events unfolded, however, it became apparent that French officials, including Governor Villebon and the baron himself, were more interested in reasserting French authority in the region than allowing it to return to its old liminal status. In August 1691, when an English force, including John Nelson, Edward Tyng, and the two Aldens, sailed into French waters and began to trade and fortify Port Royal, they were intercepted and captured by Governor Villebon, who had just returned from France. The French, hoping to exchange these high-ranking English prisoners for the French captives that Phips had taken a year earlier, granted Alden a parole to make the necessary arrangements.

But the elder Alden, despite the fact that his son was at risk, appeared to prefer commerce over captives. Not only was Alden dilatory in returning to the region, taking eight months when the French had expected him in no more than three, but he also brought with him only six of the approximately thirty soldiers that the French wished to redeem. According to Nelson's later account of the dispute that "arose . . . between the French governor and our peopel," Alden offered the unlikely excuse that those left behind had refused to "come with them, but the Contrarie was maintained by those six that were delivered." The enraged French negotiators threatened to "detaine" Alden, "who was then ashoare . . . untill a full performance" of what had been promised was delivered. But the fast-talking Alden reminded his counterparts that he still held the agreed-upon ransom money for the ship, "which the French governor was very desierous to receive." The French therefore permitted him "to returne unto his vessell, Accompanied with two French men to settle it," and Alden took this opportunity to flee:

> Instead of paying the money, he detained the two French men that went with him, soe sett saile and returned to Boston, leaving me under the miserable reproach of what had hapened, wherein I had nothing to defend my selfe by, but by pleading rashness and indiscretion in the whole matter on booth sides, whereby through feare of being detained, occationed the [untimely] returne [to Boston] of our Comander [Alden] with the money etc. For reparation of which all that I had to say was to offer the payment of the money at Quebec, which divers Gentlemen were so kinde as to lende me on this Occation.

To be sure, making arrangements for the exchange of captives was always a long, complicated process, and even people with the best of intentions suffered long delays and missed opportunities.[25] But with Alden things appeared in a more sinister light, for in addition to absconding with the ransom money, Alden opportunistically seized a French ship, while sailing under a safe conduct the French had granted him for purposes of the exchange. Alden's actions, occurring on the eve of his accusation for witchcraft, prevented the immediate redemption of any of his former business partners; Nelson, Alden, Jr., and Tyng, while kept in Quebec for some time, all ended up in prisons in France, where Tyng perished. It took many years of intermittent negotiations—involving English officials and merchants, as well as depositions from Elisha Hutchinson and David Waterhouse on the dispersal of the French captives—to procure the release of the other two English colonists.[26]

Alden's seemingly perfidious role in this botched exchange of captives—in addition to rumors that his machinations on the Maine frontier had caused a raid on York that resulted in the death of the beloved minister Shubael Dummer (a kinsman of Samuel Sewall)—undoubtedly played a role in his witchcraft accusation. In May 1692, when Alden was called to answer charges of witchcraft, it was common knowledge that the captain had just weeks before been forced to beat a hasty retreat back to Boston, his mission to rescue his son and business associates having failed as a result of his own greed.

IN THE POPULAR mind witches shared with merchants the willingness to defile and endanger the Puritan community in exchange for wealth and ease; confessing "witches" had related time and again how the devil had enticed them with promises of such coveted goods as "new clothes," and, revealingly in one case, "a pair of French fall shoes." As compensation for meddling with dangerous outside forces, Alden had received much more than a taste of French fashion. And while his recent flight from the "eastern partes" might suggest that he had finally lost control of his "familiars" in that world, the young women "afflicted" with witchcraft told a different story, suggesting that Alden continued to hold high rank in an invisible, spectral community—an inverted eastern-based counterculture—that Satan had created to corrupt Puritan New England from within and supplant it. The most damaging testimony against Alden came on August 3, 1692, when Mary Warren described before a jury of inquest Alden's connection with the convicted witch George Burroughs, a former pastor of Salem village who had departed under a cloud of anger and suspicion to serve a settlement in Wells, Maine:

> Sometime in July last mr Burrougs pinched mee very much and choaked me almost to death: and I saw and hard him sound a Trumpett and Immediatly I saw severall com to him as namely Capt Allding . . . and severall others and they urged me to goe along with them to their sacremental meeting and mr Burroughs brought to me bread to eat and wine to drink which I refuseing he did most greviously torment me urging me vehemently to writ in his book.[27]

That Alden's specter had been "observed" in such close proximity to that of the doomed Burroughs indicates how dangerous Alden was thought to be. Recent scholarship has shown that the trial and conviction of Burroughs was a pivotal incident at Salem because it spoke to the elite fear of pacts with Satan that could endanger the civil state, as opposed to the popular classes' concern with *maleficium*, or the personal harms that witches could inflict on their enemies.[28] In the years prior to the witchcraft outbreak, moreover, there was talk that the Wells pastor might have succumbed to Anabaptist belief: Burroughs had neglected to have his children baptized, and on visits to Salem and Charlestown he had refused to partake in the Lord's Supper, a method of protest Baptists used to manifest their unwillingness to commune with churches that practiced infant baptism. In the context of 1692, these behaviors might have opened up speculation as to whether the more compelling fellowship Burroughs sought might be satanic in nature. It was this lurid possibility, scholars have suggested, that intrigued and alarmed elites, inspiring them to give credence to accusations that they might otherwise have ignored or discouraged.[29] On their own, the female "witches," lacking a competent male leader, might have been thought incapable of creating a viable anticongregation in the wilderness. But after Burroughs was brought in for questioning, evidence of the inverted satanic baptism was frequently sought by interrogators and cited by people confessing to witchcraft or describing their temptation at the hands of a distinguished "black" man.[30]

If the popular classes were nonplussed by references to satanic pacts, they were nonetheless primed to fear and revile people of indeterminate loyalty who inhabited the frontier. During the King Philip's War era, men like Richard Scott acted on such fear in defiance of authority. And it was precisely this kind of anxiety, fanned to some extent by the hyperbolic rhetoric of Cotton Mather, that surfaced in accusations against both Alden and Burroughs, comprising a deadly convergence of popular and elite antipathy. Burroughs, referred to as a "lettell black menester," was thought to have received as a gift from Satan the prodigious frontiersman's strength of which he often boasted.[31] At the same time, tainted by religious imposture, he was thought on a number of occasions to have administered a mysterious "sacrament," perhaps a Catholic one conformable with the expectations of Satan's French minions and their Indian converts. While it was true that Bay Colony Puritans experienced a "sacramental renaissance" of their own in the late seventeenth century, their sacraments were designed and understood to fortify and unite the Christian community in trying times. Burroughs's rituals, in contrast, were meant to divide the godly and tempt them away from the proper path. Burroughs's former servant, Mercy Lewis, reported that an apparition in the shape of the minister, "whom i very well knew," had by turns enticed and threatened her to sign a strange book:

> he brought to me a new fashon book which he did not use to bring
> and tould me I might writ in that book: for that was a book that was
> in his studdy when I lived with them: but I tould him I did not beleve
> him for I had been often in his studdy but I never saw that book their:

but he tould me that he had severall books in his studdy which I never saw in his studdy and he could raise the divell.

When she refused to sign after the specter tortured her, she testified, he "caried me up to an exceeding high mountain and shewed me all the kingdoms of the earth and tould me that he would give them all to me if I would writ in his book and if I would not he would thro me down and brake my neck." While the swarthy, silver-tongued Burroughs distributed the spiritual weapons needed to tear down the kingdom of Christ, Alden, his confederate, who "lies with the Indian squaes," was delivering to New England's enemies the temporal weapons, "powder and shot," that could hasten its physical destruction.[32]

Burroughs was executed for his "crime" in August 1692; Alden, who wisely broke out of prison after "observing the manner of Tryals," lived on to his eightieth year. But the same dynamics that led to Burroughs's execution were also at play in the accusation against Alden. Both men spent time on the frontier, where they appeared to have entered alternative communities capable of incorporating people of diverse religious, racial, and ethnic backgrounds. These communities, seen ironically both as beachheads of savagery and of the transatlantic world, threatened to engulf Puritan New England and rob it of its unique identity. Alden and Burroughs, as societal elites, were supposed to protect New England bodies and souls from destruction and pollution; instead they succumbed to temptation and joined a society whose unnaturalness and illegitimacy could only be expressed through the metaphor of miscegenation and other "crimes" against the family. George Burroughs was rumored to have abused and murdered two of his former wives, acts that symbolized not only his rejection of the Puritan community—itself an extended family—but also his initiation into a burgeoning counterculture that parodied and inverted all the virtues of the godly community. Alden, meanwhile, had proved himself none too solicitous toward his son's plight in Quebec. Not only had Alden rejected his "own" people by failing to respect their bounds but, with his alleged Indian consorts and mixed progeny, he was establishing and arming a kind of antifamily capable of destroying them. It was all the more revealing that Alden's relatives—Phillipses, Sanfords, and Hutchinsons—embraced or tolerated Quakerism, for this sect, according to Cotton Mather, was prone to align itself with Indians, some Quakers endeavoring to "Defend the Indians in their Bloody Villanies, and Revile the Countrey for Defending it self against them."[33]

GEORGE BURROUGHS WAS made vulnerable to charges of witchcraft because of the implication that he dissented from Puritan orthodoxy, and its accompanying ideas about the proper bounds of community. But John Alden's kinship ties with the Phillipses and Quakerism were deeper and all the more incriminating.

John Alden's father-in-law, William Phillips, had begun his career in Massachusetts as a tavern owner and wine merchant. Fully integrated into the colony's mercantile community, he was designated on several occasions as a tax farmer to collect the custom on wines. Although there is no direct evidence that Phillips himself was a religious dissenter during his years in Boston, his name did appear in the business records of John Bowne, the future Quaker and brother-in-law of John Underhill whose stay in the Bay Colony was cut short because of the unfavorable religious climate there. Several years later, around 1655, Phillips married the widow Bridget Sanford, whose credentials as an antinomian, and later a Quaker were, to put it mildly, unambiguous. It was in 1660, just a few years after his marriage to Bridget, that Phillips decided to move to Maine. Interestingly, in 1661, Phillips entrusted his "honored and Beloved friend" Thomas Clark, one of only two magistrates (the other was Edward Hutchinson) who had openly counseled toleration of Quakers, to "appear in my behalf iff any thing be further desired" in the presentation of a petition to the General Court in which Phillips asked for outright ownership of the Maine lands associated with his nascent mining enterprise; soon after its submission, the request was granted by a committee that included Edward Tyng and Daniel Gookin.[34]

Phillips was a wildly successful frontiersman; in addition to becoming a land broker, selling huge tracts to such eminent Bostonians as John Leverett and Richard Russell, Phillips also built sawmills, employed tenants, and attempted to mine silver at Saco on land previously owned by Robert Child.[35] The mining venture, while potentially lucrative, was also, it would seem, part of a strategy to get permanent title to land.

Phillips, in the aforementioned 1661 petition, explained to the General Court that he would need a greater inducement to invest in mining than was allowed under the Massachusetts law that granted (grudgingly) a twenty-one-year monopoly on profits and lands to the developers of important projects, "and also liberty . . . to purchase the Interest of any Indian in such Land where such Mine shall be found."[36] The petitioner Phillips, "having beene at a Considerable Charge to search out a place where he hath some ground to Conceive there is a mine and hath likewise purchaseed the Land of the trew Indian proprietors," worried that "the said Law seemeth to leave matters something doubtfull (as to perpetuall proprietie) notwithstandin such purchass." Phillips and his go-between Clark, because of their earlier experiences with fur-trading and iron-mining monopolies, recognized that the General Court, which usually refused to grant land for any purpose other than town-building, might be willing, given the remoteness of the region and the desirability of development, to secure Phillips's land titles in perpetuity and not just for twenty-one years. The petition therefore contained a veiled threat that Phillips might not go forward with mining activities unless he were guaranteed permanent possession of the land he had purchased from Indian owners,

> [the mine] being remote from the sea and wages of men and every thinge else beinge at such a high rate that the Improvement thereof would rather undoe then enrich your said petitioner in case he should

be in any hazard of the Loss of his disbursements after the tearme of twenty one yeares.

The petition suggested that in order to make continued investment worth his while, Phillips would need guaranteed ownership of tracts of land "both where the minerall lieth; and the land adjoyning to it bought of the same Indian being noe way meete for a plantation"; in addition, the petition made "bold" to "begg A Confirmation of another purchase of Land bought of an Indian sachem which is likewise noe way convenient for any English plantation, and may bee of use for accomodation of the said mine."[37] It is difficult to determine how serious William Phillips was about the mining enterprise; but there is no denying that it provided him a fitting pretext for his demands.

Phillips's decision actually to relocate to the frontier rather than to manage his lands on an absentee basis was probably motivated at least in part by Bridget Phillips's desire to practice her religion where she would be less easily observed (and disciplined) by stern Boston magistrates. Kittery and Scarborough, the two main settlements in York county, both offered active Quaker meetings.[38] If this were not enough to engender suspicion of the Phillipses, it would soon become evident that William Phillips, despite his pivotal position as land broker to the great men of Bay Colony society, had succumbed not only to feminine Quaker wiles but to the closely associated spirit of "royalism" and "episcopacy" thought to infect the region.

William and Bridget Phillips arrived in Saco during a period of political turbulence, when Bay Colony authority over Maine foundered as a result of the Restoration. The prominent Quaker Nicholas Shapleigh, major of the York County militia, stood at the head of a faction of disaffected inhabitants pressing to reject Bay Colony authority in favor of a more tolerant government that might be formed under the auspices of the heir of Ferdinando Gorges. Meanwhile, the arrival of the royal commissioners under Randolph several years later generated yet another royalist faction, which existed from 1665 until 1668, when Bay Colony authority resumed.[39] During this period, William Phillips, though holding the rank of major in the Massachusetts militia, began to see the advantages of a less doctrinaire government. For the brief spate of years when the royal commissioners dominated Maine affairs, Phillips remained a man of note. And in the summer of 1668, when Massachusetts was finally able to reassert its power over Maine, a defiant Phillips deliberately tried to obstruct the efforts of his former colleague, Captain Brian Pendleton, to organize elections in York and Scarborough.

Pendleton, in a letter to John Leverett, who was then supervising the submission of Maine towns, described just how forceful an adversary Phillips could be. Pendleton complained that when he had gone to York in the summer of 1668—"endea[v]ouring . . . in a loving and peaceable way" to "obtaine [their] subjection to the Massachusetts Governement"—William Phillips had opposed him at every turn. Phillips had urged the inhabitants in threatening tones not to attend Pendleton's meetings, claiming that Pendleton was "no legall associate" and making a "very large speech" after church services on a sabbath day to "render mee [Pendleton] as odious to the people as he could, and as his great Enemie." County Court depositions (gathered by Pendleton) attested further to Phillips's disruptive behavior, relating how when Pendleton

> did set up a warant on the meting house for all the inhabitance to mete to gether to chuse ofisors to atend the Contrys service . . . maigor phillips pulid it downe . . . and said if there was a hundred he wold pull them all downe and furdar he said it mite be as much as his neck was worth.

In September 1668, Phillips was jailed briefly for his recalcitrance but was released when he agreed to pay a five-hundred-pound bond to ensure that "I will not acte in any place of Authority in the pvince of Mayne,—nor oppose the Authority of the Masethusetts, but Reest quiett accordinge to the Writtinge I sett my hand unto with others in Comition with me, at Yorke."[40] Despite this episode, Phillips remained an important man. In his history of King Philip's War, William Hubbard continued to refer to Phillips as major; and during the war, Phillips helped to garrison Maine settlements, returning to Boston only after his mills and house at Saco were destroyed.[41]

Phillips died in 1683, well before the outbreak of witchcraft at Salem. But Cotton Mather may have been thinking of the Phillips clan, particularly its matriarch, in pointing out the similarities among Indians, witches, and Quakers:

> If the Indians have chosen to prey upon the Frontiers and Out-Skirts, of the Province, the Quakers have chosen the very same Frontiers, and Out-Skirts, for their more Spiritual Assaults; and finding little Success elsewhere, they have been Labouring incessantly, and sometimes not unsuccessfully, to Enchant and Poison the souls of poor people, in the very places, where the Bodies and Estates of the People have presently after been devoured by the Salvages.[42]

As a man of high rank, Phillips should have acted to prevent the spread of Quaker religion and to project godly Massachusetts authority in Maine. Instead, in marked similarity to William Hutchinson, he had acquiesced in his wife's heretical beliefs and might even have been willing to submit to royalist authority to further protect her.

In addition to all this, Phillips transmitted through sale and inheritance large tracts of land to Bridget's children by John Sanford and her Hutchinson kin, few of whom were known for their religious orthodoxy.[43] Bridget's daughter, Eliphel Stratton, was arrested on many occasions for attendance at Quaker meetings; and Phoebe Phillips, William's daughter, married Zachariah Gillam, whose family, like that of his bride, was associated both with the frontier and Quakerism.[44] The Gillam family was well acquainted with the displaced ex-antinomian Hugh Gunnison, the former proprietor of a disorderly Boston tavern who moved to the frontier and served as a General Court deputy from Maine in 1654 only to be declared "unmeet" for this or any other judicial service by 1657.[45] During the 1670s and early 1680s, Zachariah Gillam, along with Bridget's son Esbon Sanford, worked for the Hudson Bay Company, where both were cited unfavorably for having traded on their own accounts and where both lost their lives in 1682 while company censure against them was pending in London. Interestingly, the two had also had dealings with Charles Bayly, one of the Hudson Bay Company's first overseas governors and an extremely flamboyant Quaker who had traveled to Rome in an effort to convert the pope to right religion.[46]

IN THE PURITAN mind, both Indian "savagery" and witchcraft were simultaneously abhorrent and enticing, each offering freedom from the suffocating sense of sin that plagued the godly and drove some to distraction. William Barker, a confessed witch of Andover, admitted that he had been attracted by the devil's promise to relieve both his spiritual terrors and his economic woes; in addition to helping Barker pay off his debts, Satan's "design" was to create a new society in which "all his people should live bravely that all persones should be equall; that their should be no day of resurection or of judgement, and neither punishment nor shame for sin."[47] Quakerism, with its doctrine of the inner light and the ideal of equality implied by the rejection of that honor, was thought to be seductive in exactly the same ways. Cotton Mather compared Quaker doctrines to fruit trees

> which bear Apples of such an Odour and Colour as invites people to Eat thereof; but it is horribly Dangerous to do so; for there is no Antidote that can secure a man from speedy Death, who hath once tasted of them. The Leaf of the Trees makes an Ulcer on any place touched with it; the Dew that falls from them fetches off the Skin; the very Shadow swells a man, so as to kill him, if he be not speedily helped.

Because Quakerism was so seductive, Mather viewed it as a "special Favour of God, that the Number of Quakers is no Greater; for if they should multiply, not only would Christianity be utterly Extinguished, but Humanity it self Exterminated."[48]

Quaker tracts were vexatious because they frequently insisted that the Indian wars were visited upon orthodox New England as a punishment for its persecuting ways and because they expressed sympathy for the position of indigenous people. I have already shown how John Easton needled Bay Colony leaders not only by sympathizing with King Philip's forces but also by predicting that the magistrates' ineptitude would (or should) lead to greater imperial intervention in the colony. During the 1690s, Thomas Maule, an irascible Quaker of Salem, similarly chided Bay Colony leaders by ridiculing both the witchcraft trials and the colony's policy toward the Indians. Not surprisingly, Maule's writings inspired a devastating response from an infuriated Cotton Mather:

> One Tom Maule, at this Time living in Salem, hath exposed unto the Publick a Volumn of Nonsensical Blasphemies and Heresies, wherein he sets himself to Defend the Indians in their Bloody Villanies, and Revile the Countrey for Defending it self against them.

Maule contested the idea that Indians were evil, Mather raged, and suggested that witchcraft was an illusory concept since "all men who have a Body of Sin remaining in them, are Witches." This kind of thinking was threatening because it would make it impossible for New Englanders to detect witches and to maintain their traditional boundaries between good and evil. According to Mather, "the Devil, Sin, Death, and Hell" were, in Maule's view, "but Nothing, they are but a non-Entity."[49] Although his denunciation of Maule did not appear in print until several years after the witchcraft trials were concluded, Mather's hostility was surely expressed in other ways before publication.

If Quakers, like Indians, stalked the perimeters of settlement, seeking to pollute the true ordinances of God and inviting the rebukes of heaven, then the Phillips family, to which Alden belonged, was a catalyst of New England's defilement and ruin. Side by side with Phillipses, Hutchinsons, and Sanfords, Alden accepted his tainted legacy of frontier land while at the same time trading with the enemy, sometimes in partnership with Anglican merchants whose rights were protected by a home government that made it impossible to punish religious dissent. While Alden had not fully entered into the camp of the enemy, he was a conduit of pollution, guilty, like the "witch," of bringing the "other" into the heart of New England.

HISTORIANS HAVE TENDED to view the witchcraft tragedy at Salem as an anomalous event in New England history. Yet while the size and scope of the trials were abnormal in the annals of New England witchcraft, the prosecution of "witches" such as Alden and Burroughs drew on fears about the transatlantic world and the frontier that had been expressed as early as the antinomian controversy of the 1630s and that had deepened, with a finer point being placed on race, both during King Philip's War and the Massachusetts version of the Glorious Revolution. The significance of the prosecutions of Alden and Burroughs cannot be fully appreciated unless we recognize that hostility against such seemingly unconnected (and opposed) antecedents as Daniel Gookin and Edmund Andros fed on the same anxieties as were called forth at Salem during the last decade of the seventeenth century. One function of witchcraft accusations was to punish those individuals who had close dealings with Quakers, Indians, or Anglicans at a time when altered imperial circumstances made it increasingly awkward to act against any one of these groups.[50]

Scholars have long understood that the loss of the Massachusetts charter in 1684 and the installation of the imperious Edmund Andros as governor two years later exacerbated the sense—fundamental to the outbreak of witchcraft accusations—that New England was under siege. Andros threatened the colonists' sense of security, it has often been said, by challenging their land titles, constraining their exercise of local government, curtailing the influence of their elected assemblies, and instituting formal Anglican worship at the center of their godly commonwealth.[51] Andros's actions, which New Englanders perceived as a crypto-Catholic assault on their English liberties, were never repudiated by the new monarchs. And at the onset of the witchcraft epidemic, the authority of the Massachusetts government and its courts was in doubt because Increase Mather had not yet returned with the new charter from William and Mary.

The scholarly fixation on how the rebellion against Andros called forth a defense of civil liberties—especially the right to be secure in the ownership of private property and free from arbitrary taxation—has been long and productive, demonstrating how closely the concerns of New Englanders accorded with the Whiggish principles motivating the Glorious Revolution in England.[52] Still, in focusing on issues related to land and taxes, scholars have neglected to analyze seriously the shrill charges levied against Andros's handling of frontier-related issues. When anti-Andros polemicists rushed into print to justify their revolution and to reveal the manifold abuses perpetrated by their former governor, they included the charge that Andros, a crypto-Catholic, was in league with the Indians and French and that, once his royal master James II had fled to France he planned to "betray them [New England] into the power of the French king."[53] It was in placing this heavy emphasis on race that the New England colonists began to speak in a distinctively American accent.

Nathaniel Byfield, in his *Revolution in New England Justified*, reprinted testimonies that well illustrate how Andros, French Catholicism, and Indians were linked in the colonial mind. A group of inhabitants of Sudbury, a town known during King Philip's War for its baiting of praying Indians, swore out depositions testifying to what they had heard on January 2, 1688/9, from one "Solomon Thomas, Indian," concerning Andros's boasts about what would happen once "the fight at the Eastward should" commence:

> if the Indians had the better of it, as the English did retreat, the Friend Indians were to shoot them down, but if the English get the day, we say nothing, and that in the Spring French and Irish would come to Boston, as many, and all won [one] Indians, for that was the first place that was to be destroyed, and after that the Countrey Towns would be all won [one] nothing. And further . . . the said Solomon said, that

the Governour had given him a Book, which the said Governour said was better than the Bible, and all that would not turn to the Governours Religion, and own that Book, should be destroyed. In which Book the said Thomas said was the Picture of our Saviour and of the Virgin Mary and of the Twelve Apostles; and the Governour said, when we pray, we pray to the Virgin Mary; and when the Fight should be at the Eastward, the Governour would sit in his Wigwam, and say, O Brave Indians.[54]

Byfield, who had kinship ties with both John Leverett and Thomas Clark, was socially situated among those who, in an earlier era, would have approved of alliance-making and missionary work among the Indians. But in this later period such men easily cast their lot with the "multitude" that Daniel Gookin had so adamantly disdained to "join."[55] The conflict with Andros pushed New Englanders of all classes closer together, giving the ideas of the popular classes more play.

The conviction that the Stuarts and their officials harbored "papist" principles and made secret alliances with Catholic powers was common enough among political thinkers in England, for whom Catholicism had long been synonymous with tyranny.[56] But the colonial emphasis on Indian involvement in heretical, tyrannous schemes was something different, suggesting that colonists were protesting not just one deplorable governor or king but an imperial system that, even in the hands of figures friendly to the dissenting cause, like Robert Boyle, would destroy their identity as a people, forcing them—in what New Englanders considered to be the most egregious example of imperial amalgamation—to be blended with inferior "savages," a theme that reappeared during the witchcraft trials.

As Massachusetts representatives at Whitehall labored to secure a charter from William and Mary that would allow the colony to preserve as many of its former liberties as possible, it was vital for pro–New England polemicists and their supporters to prove that the Bay Colony's revolt against Edmund Andros implied no disloyalty to the royal authority of the new sovereigns.[57] But New Englanders who endeavored to make this case were forced to contend with enemies who constantly cited the Bay Colony's history of religious intolerance and its ill treatment of the natives as evidence that Massachusetts was self-absorbed, self-righteous, and unwilling to brook outside intervention. The colony's internal enemies, then, recognized how distinct notions about race and religion were coalescing to forge a separate American identity.

The pro-Andros pamphlet *New England's Faction Discovered*, for example, which may have been authored by Joseph Dudley, the royalist son of Thomas Dudley, pointed out that far from being the champions of English "Religion, Liberty, and Property" New Englanders had taken the

opportunity [of the late revolution] to make themselves Persecutors of the Church of England, as they had before been of all others that did not comply with their Independency, whom they punished with Fines, Imprisonment, Stripes, Banishment and Death; and all for matters of meer Conscience and Religion only.

While the Mathers pretended to accommodate themselves to the latitudinarian Anglicanism that was to become the glue of empire, Dudley charged, they had spread "scandalous Libels . . . up and down the Country insinuating into the Common People" that not only were the discredited Stuart king and the governor secretly practicing Catholicism but that "all of the Church of England were Papists and Idolators." There could be no other reason, Dudley continued, for Bay colonists' habit of referring to the frontier towns as "Heathenish English Plantation[s]" than that "many in those parts have been differently educated from those of Boston, and are of the Church of England, whose Forefathers for that cause only were forced to remove so far to escape the lash of their Persecutors in the Massachusets Colony."[58] Here Dudley cleverly inverted the logic that privileged the Puritan center over a "barbarous" frontier.

Dudley emphasized the Bay colony's ill treatment of the Indians and its religious intolerance in an effort to prove that the "rebels' " ostensible loyalty to the reconstituted government of William and Mary was mere pretense and that the popular party was still bound to hold itself aloof from the empire, especially when it came to policies regarding Indians and religion. Dudley managed to draw these two themes together by claiming that the persecution of Anglicanism ultimately injured the Indians, for, given the Puritans' inept and insincere efforts at proselytization, the Church of England represented the Indians' only real hope of conversion to Protestantism:

> But it must be admitted, that with those Mohawks and other Indians several French Priests and Jesuits have dwelt and inhabited, and endeavoured to propagate their Religion amongst them, which is more than any of our English Priests or Teachers have done; for altho by the Piety of our Forefathers considerable Sums of Money have been given, and a Corporation erected for the Evangelizing of the Indians, in New England, a very small progress hath been hitherto made therein; and now scarce any Endeavours or proper Means used at all for their Conversion, the large Sums of Money are annually sent over and disposed of amongst the Brotherhood on that pretence, which the Government or those chiefly concerned therein, would do well to enquire after . . . that so good and pious an Undertaking may be neither neglected nor perverted.[59]

Puritan New Englanders, the pamphlet pointed out, in addition to their failure to proselytize effectively, had constantly mistreated the indigenous peoples, failing to distinguish friend from foe and operating under the assumption that "if one Indian commits an Offence, all must be blamed or punished for it." A recent application of this philosophy had occurred in the summer of 1688, when, during the absence of Edmund Andros in New York, colonists decided to avenge the deaths of six Englishmen at North-field by seizing a group of Abenakis in faraway Saco:

> The noise of these Murthers soon spread throughout the Country, and notice was given thereof to all the Frontier or out-parts, advising them to be vigilant and careful to prevent Surprize by any strange or suspected Indians; and soon after this news came to Saco, (a Town and Rever . . . three hundred miles distant . . .) five Indian Men, and sixteen Women and Children, who had always lived and planted on that River were seized on, and sent by Water to Boston, some of whom were so old and feeble they were forced to be carried when ashore, on others backs.[60]

This wrongful seizure helped to touch off war on the frontier, causing the "Indians of Ambroscoggen and Kennebeque River" to respond in kind by capturing some English colonists from the Casco Bay region. While Andros was widely criticized for having eventually allowed the Saco Indians to go free, there was no way that these unfortunate captives, who were brought back to prison when conflict erupted, could have committed the "mis-chiefs" charged against them, for these, Dudley pointed out, occurred "ei-ther . . . while they were in custody or since the Rebellion and Subversion over the Government, from whence begins the date of our miseries."[61] In Dudley's formulation, it had been New Englanders' own misguided cruelty, and not their governors' alleged alliance with hostile Indians and French, that caused frontier wars and misery; Andros, indeed, could have prevailed in the conflict that occurred during the winter of 1688–89 had he not been forced to contend with an incipient rebellion.

The anti-Andros tracts, in contrast, told a very different story, making the reviled governor over into the image of the elite frontiersman whose collusion with the enemy endangered plain folk in exposed communities. In his previous role as governor of New York, Andros had dealt skillfully with the Mohawks, enlisting their aid to deliver the final blow against the New England Algonquians at the end of King Philip's War.[62] But Andros's success in frontier dealings only served to fuel the suspicions that swirled around him, just as it had for so many other Massachusetts merchants (and missionaries). There were, it was true, some prominent individuals in Maine, including Joshua Scottow's son Thomas, willing to attest to the former governor's skill in frontier negotiations and war.[63] But more fre-quently Andros was accused of crimes such as manifesting more "love" and respect for his Indian friends than English colonists; berating colonists for their unauthorized attempts to fortify English towns against Indian attack; creating a situation in which "Bloody Indians whom the English had se-cured, were not only dismissed, but rather courted than punished"; "tam-pering to engage" his old Mohawk friends to fight against Massachusetts; and delivering ammunition to a group of Abenaki women that included Madockawando's sister.

The depositions of young militiamen who had accompanied "Sir Edmund" to the frontier in the winter of 1688–89 and who attested to this last accusation are particularly revealing in this respect. According to one twenty-five-year-old soldier serving at Pemaquid,

> there came to the Fort where Sir E. A. then was, two Squaws, the one Madocowandos Sister, and the other Moxis wife (as was said) and two other Indian Women that went along with them; they were in the Fort with Sir Edmund two days, and when they came forth they seemed to be half drunk, this Deponent and Peter Ripley was commanded to Guard these Squaws from Pemyquid to New Harbour, being in distance about two Miles, and as we passed on the way Madocowandos Sister laid down her Burden in the Snow and commanded the Deponent to take it up, whereupon the Deponent looked into the Basket, and saw a small Bag which he opened, and found it to be Gunpowder, which he judged five pounds weight, and a Bag of Bullets of a greater weight, and the weight of the Basket I took up, was as much as the Deponent could well carry along, and the other three Squaws had each one of them their Baskets, which appeared Rather to be of greater than lesser burden, than that the Deponent carried and Madocowandos sister said she had that Powder of Sir Edmund, and added, that she was to come again to him within four days.[64]

Andros was probably trying to tempt Madockawando's band away from Saint-Castin by showing them that the English, who in the past had seized Indian guns and refused to trade in ammunition, could now be good allies. But his reluctant troops saw things very differently. To these young men, Andros's drinking with the "squaws" hinted at illicit relations, and his use of colonial soldiers to escort the women back to their camp was not only wasteful but humiliating, putting the privates in an inverted position where they were obliged to take "commands" from scheming female foes.

Dudley's pamphlet, like other pro-Andros tracts, was a piece of propaganda designed to enhance his own reputation while depicting the majority of New Englanders as disloyal subversives. But in arguing that the colonists' persistent mistreatment of Indians reflected a hard core of resistance to imperial goals, he had hit upon an important insight—one that allows us to discern a pattern in the seemingly diverse events of the late seventeenth century. Bay colonists throughout this period were wary of plans that entailed cooperation with or integration of racial "others"; and they were ever ready to believe that such plans had their origins in malevolent outside influences, even when embraced by such undeniably loyal figures as Daniel Gookin.

Although the colonists had good reasons for ridding themselves of the authoritarian Edmund Andros, criticisms relating to his frontier activities were probably unjust; more interesting, they matched the myriad criticisms leveled before and after the Glorious Revolution against powerful New England merchants, most of whose loyalties were never openly questioned. In this sense it could be said that Andros was scapegoated as a warning to others who could not be punished but who continued to push against New England's boundaries in ways that discomfited rank-and-file colonists. The expression of antipathy toward cosmopolitan elites who had cooperative dealings with Indians was by no means limited to New England; it showed up both in New York during Leisler's Rebellion and in Virginia and Maryland during corresponding events surrounding the Glorious Revolution in those colonies.[65] Throughout Britain's North American colonies a racial consensus, which associated liberty with homogeneity and the roughly egalitarian local community and which shunned the transatlantic British empire's efforts to incorporate all subject peoples into one ordered hierarchy, was beginning to harden, and no amount of anglicization could change this basic fact.

In the concluding paragraph of his book *The Radicalism of the American Revolution*, Gordon Wood holds forth, in compelling prose, his vision of the changes wrought by that momentous event:

> America . . . would find its greatness not by emulating the states of classical antiquity, not by copying the fiscal-military powers of modern Europe, and not by producing a few notable geniuses and great-souled men. Instead, it would discover its greatness by creating a prosperous free society belonging to obscure people with their workaday concerns and their pecuniary pursuits of happiness—common people with their common interests in making money and getting ahead . . . The American Revolution created this democracy, and we are living with its consequences still.[66]

The conditions that Wood identifies with the late eighteenth century, had already begun to emerge in seventeenth-century Massachusetts, long before anyone could have dreamed of the independence movement. Ever since the condemnation and exile of Anne Hutchinson, individuals who pursued "great-souled" schemes rather than "workaday" pragmatism—even people like Daniel Gookin, who believed in religious persecution—found themselves steamrolled by the New England Way. The Puritans were, of course, no democrats. But largely through their conceptualization of orthodoxy, they had created a social order that anticipated basic republican values—a rough egalitarianism for householding patriarchs, a suspicion of distant centers of authority, and a desire for cultural homogeneity.[67] Historians who have focused on the "oligarchic" nature of the New England Way have remarked on the extent to which it imposed on people a "culture of discipline" that sought to reign in popular culture and popular passions; but as I have shown, the nature of that discipline, whether in the age of Winthrop and Hutchinson or of Mather and Gookin, was very much shaped by, and contoured to, the interests of the ordinary "middling" folk who constituted the Bay Colony majority.[68]

To be sure, early America was more than Massachusetts writ large; but it is important to recognize that New England went through stages of development similar to those found in other regions of British North America.[69] Although historians have been quick to suggest that New England's religious culture rendered it unique, I have tried to show in this book that orthodox Puritanism expressed, enforced, and reinforced values common to ordinary people, Puritan and non-Puritan alike, throughout the Anglo-American world; communalism, cultural homogeneity, parochialism, and patriarchalism emerged everywhere, particularly in frontier regions, as potent signifiers of "liberty."

In the very first decade of settlement the orthodox party of Massachusetts stigmatized as feminine a whole series of characteristics—a commitment to private fulfillment over public goals, an interest in subjective experience rather than objective performance, a desire to adhere to cosmopolitan rather than localistic standards—that could be associated with powerful male merchants just as surely as they could be equated with the heretical delusions of a wicked woman.[70] This tendency to denounce as effete, effeminate, and elitist those traits—individualism, privacy, dissimulation, cosmopolitanism, diversity—that one would associate with market capitalism and administrative "centers" was broadly shared, quite apart from religious commitments, in many colonial contexts; but the pattern did not remain unbroken.

During the early national period, New England itself, as a region, was destined to become the target of aspersions similar to those the Winthrop party had cast upon the antinomians.[71] Just as the theological antinomianism of the 1630s had been rejected in Puritan Massachusetts, so too the evangelical reform culture that took root in the industrializing Northeast two centuries later was denounced as effeminate and elitist by detractors who believed that manly virtue and "independency" had fled New England for points south and west. By the nineteenth century, then, a secularized antinomianism would have its day. The original dialogue set in motion during the "antinomian" controversy was, in every all-encompassing sense of the word, an American dialogue—one whose themes will never die as long as we continue to debate the nature of the American identity.

Notes

ABBREVIATIONS

AC   David D. Hall, ed., *The Antinomian Controversy, 1636–38: A Docu-
        mentary History* (1968; reprint, Durham, N.C.: Duke University Press,
        1990).
MBR   Nathaniel B. Shurtleff, ed., *Records of the Governor and Company of the
        Massachusetts Bay in New England*, 5 vols. in 6 (Boston: William White,
        1853–1854).
MHSC   *Massachusetts Historical Society Collections*
NEQ   *New England Quarterly*
WMQ   *William and Mary Quarterly*
Winthrop,   *Winthrop's Journal, "History of New England, 1630–1649,"* in *Original
Journal   Narratives of Early American History*, ed. James K. Hosmer, 2 vols. (New
            York: Scribner's, 1908).

INTRODUCTION

1. Winthrop, *Journal*, I:260. On private military companies in the metropolis,
see Lindsay Boynton, *The Elizabethan Militia, 1558–1638* (London: Routledge,
1967), 215–6, 263–9. The charter appears in *MBR*, I:250–1.

Nineteenth-century histories of the company provide membership rosters and
biographical sketches illustrating the centrality of the organization to the Massachusetts military establishment. See Oliver Ayer Roberts, *History of the Military
Company of the Massachusetts Now Called the Ancient and Honourable Artillery Company of Massachusetts, 1637–1888*, 4 vols. (Boston: A. Mudge, 1895–1909); and

Zechariah Whitman, *An Historical Sketch of the Ancient and Honorable Artillery Company: From its Formation in the Year 1637 to the Present Time* (Boston, 1820).

2. This is the interpretation of Winthrop's displeasure put forth by T. H. Breen, "The Covenanted Militia of Massachusetts Bay: English Background and New World Development," in *Puritans and Adventurers: Change and Persistance in Early America* (New York: Oxford University Press, 1980), 24–45. On Puritan disaffection toward the military see also William Hunt, *The Puritan Moment: The Coming of Revolution to an English Country* (Cambridge: Harvard University Press, 1983); and Stephen Saunders Webb, *The Governors-General: The English Army and the Definition of the Empire, 1569–1681* (Chapel Hill: University of North Carolina Press, 1979).

3. Winthrop, *Journal*, I:260.

4. On Puritanism and the "new merchants" see Robert Brenner, *Merchants and Revolution: Commercial Change, Political Conflict and London's Overseas Traders, 1550–1653* (Princeton, N.J.: Princeton University Press, 1993). For Brooke's understanding of his military role see Karen Ordahl Kupperman, *Providence Island, 1630–1641: The Other Puritan Colony* (New York: Cambridge University Press, 1993), 209–10.

5. Winthrop, *Journal*, II: 254; Breen, "Covenanted Militia," 38. For biographical sketches of these founders see Robert E. Wall, *The Membership of the Massachusetts Bay General Court, 1630–1686* (New York: Garland, 1990), 261–2, 377–80, 491–92, 506.

6. Winthrop's journal indicates that the bid to create an artillery company was being debated in February and March 1638, March being the month in which Hutchinson began her exile. The Artillery Company "charter," however, does not appear in the colony records until one year later, in March 1639. According to historians of the Artillery Company, a roster existed as early as 1637. See Winthrop, *Journal*, I: 260; Shurtleff, *MBR*, I: 250–51; and Roberts, *History of the Military Company*.

7. Six of the twenty-four individuals appearing on the first roster were disarmed and/or banished for having signed a petition in favor of John Wheelwright, an "antinomian" preacher and brother-in-law of Anne Hutchinson, judged guilty of sedition. Four others were called before the Court in March 1638 because they had "declared themselves favorers of the famistical persons and opinions." And two more would in later years come under suspicion for heterodox religious beliefs. Disarmed were John Underhill and his father-in-law Richard Morris, Thomas Savage (Anne Hutchinson's son in law), John Oliver, Edward Hutchinson, and Samuel Cole. The four called before the Court in 1638, all of whom escaped punishment, were Edward Gibbons, Thomas Cakebread, William Jennison, and Robert Harding. Harding, although he recanted, moved toward anabaptism, leaving the Bay for Aquidneck, Rhode Island, in 1641 and finally returning to England in 1646. As a merchant in the metropolis, he maintained business ties with Artillery Company members in the Bay. The tavernkeeper Nicholas Upshall was a member unscathed by the antinomian controversy, but he emerged at mid-century as a Quaker. See Rufus M. Jones, *The Quakers in the American Colonies* (London: Macmillan, 1923), 28–39. Upshall's will, which provided for Quakers, is printed in "Abstracts of Early Wills," *New England Historical and Genealogical Register* 15 (1861): 250–51. Other original members who must have appeared dangerous to leaders of the orthodox faction include Israel Stoughton, Stephen Greensmith, and Thomas Hawkins. Stoughton in 1634 wrote a pamphlet attacking magisterial powers; as a result he

was banned from public office and enjoined to burn his book. On this episode, see Frances Rose-Troup, *The Massachusetts Bay Company and Its Predecessors* (1930; reprinted, Clifton, N.J.: A. F. M. Kelley, 1973), 117–27. Greensmith was fined for declaring that of the colony's ministers only Cotton and Wheelwright preached a true covenant of faith. And Hawkins was in 1638 made to acknowledge before the General Court "his indiscretion in roughly addressing a member of the court while in session." See Joseph B. Felt, *The Ecclesiastical History of New England Comprising Not Only Religion but also Moral and Other Relations*, 2 vols. (Boston: Congregational Library Association, 1855–62), I:326.

8. In the years following 1638, the company accepted thirteen more individuals who had been punished as a result of the antinomian controversy: William Aspinwall, John Button, Richard Cooke, Richard Fairbanks, Thomas Marshall, John Biggs, Richard Gridley, Zacheus Bosworth, James Johnson, John Odlin/ Audlin, Edward Bendall, Hugh Gunnison, and Richard Waite. In addition, it attracted a wide range of others disaffected with the New England Way, many unconnected to the events of 1636–38. Among the most well known were Thomas Venner and Wentworth Day, both of whom appeared in London in the 1650s as Fifth Monarchists. The Fifth Monarchy movement sought immediately to usher in (by violence, if necessary) the one-thousand-year reign of saints prophesied to precede the Second Coming of Christ. On Dunster see William G. McLoughlin, *New England Dissent, 1630–1833: The Baptists and the Separation of Church and State*, 2 vols. (Cambridge: Harvard University Press, 1971), I: 21–23; and Jeremiah Chaplin, *Life of Henry Dunster, First President of Harvard College* (Boston: J. R. Osgood, 1872). It was not uncommon for other, less well-known company members to reveal their dissatisfaction with the New England Way through such acts as signing petitions in favor of toleration for Anabaptists and Quakers or renting property to Anabaptists seeking a meeting place.

9. On these events, see chapter 3.

10. Technically, Samuel Maverick was a freeman, since he had sworn a loyalty oath to the colony prior to the full establishment of the New England Way. His writings, however, show clearly that he felt excluded from the rights he should have been able to enjoy as a prominent Englishmen. On the close relationship between church and state covenants see T. H. Breen, *The Character of the Good Ruler: A Study of Puritan Political Ideas in New England, 1630–1730* (New Haven: Yale University Press, 1970), 35–8, 43–8.

11. Edward Roberts to President Dunster, May 1655, MHSC, 2nd ser., 4 vol. 1854): 196–7. On Dunster see Chaplin, *Life of Henry Dunster*; and McLoughlin, *New England Dissent*, I: 21–23.

12. For interpretations that emphasize the gendered dimension of the antinomian controversy see Marilyn J. Westerkamp, "Anne Hutchinson, Sectarian Mysticism, and the Puritan Order," *Church History* 59: 4 (December 1990): 482–96; and "Puritan Patriarchy and the Problem of Revelation," *Journal of Interdisciplinary History* 23: 3 (winter 1993): 571–595; Ben Barker Benfield, "Anne Hutchinson and the Puritan Attitude toward Women,"*Feminist Studies* 1: 2 (1973): 65–76; Ann Kibbey, *The Interpretation of Material Shapes in Puritanism: A Study in Rhetoric, Prejudicce, and Violence* (New York: Cambridge University Press, 1986); and Lyle Koehler, "The Case of the American Jezebels: Anne Hutchinson and Female Agitation during the Years of Antinomian Turmoil, 1636–1640," *WMQ* 31: 1 (January 1974): 55–78.

Philip Gura, *A Glimpse of Sion's Glory: Puritan Radicalism in New England,*

1620–1660 (Middletown, Conn.: Wesleyan University Press, 1984), sees the radical challenge as proto-"democratic." Richard S. Dunn, *Puritans and Yankees: The Winthrop Dynasty of New England, 1630–1717* (Princeton, N.J.: Princeton University Press, 1962), 18, likewise refers to "antinomianism" as "levelling and anti-intellectual."

Emery Battis, *Saints and Sectaries: Anne Hutchinson and the Antinomian Controversy in the Massachusetts Bay Colony* (Chapel Hill: University of North Carolina Press, 1962), provides a sustained treatment of the close association between "antinomianism" and the trading community. I explain my differences with Battis's interpretation of this association in chapter 1.

13. On economic "competency" see Daniel Vickers, "Competency and Competition: Economic Culture in Early America," *WMQ* 47: 1 (January 1990): 3–29.

14. Karen Ordahl Kupperman, "Errand to the Indies: Puritan Colonization from Providence Island through the Western Design," *WMQ* 45: 1 (January 1988): 70–99, argues that English Puritans' "vision of empire reached back to the great Elizabethans and pointed forward to enthronement as national policy with Oliver Cromwell's Western Design" (72).

15. Theodore Dwight Bozeman, "The Puritans' 'Errand into the Wilderness' Reconsidered," *NEQ* 59: 2 (June 1986): 231–51, questions the classic understanding of the Puritan mission laid out in Perry Miller, *Errand into the Wilderness* (Cambridge, Mass.: Belknap Press, 1956).

16. For the isolationist tendencies of Puritan Massachusetts see Andrew Delbanco, "The Puritan Errand Re-Viewed," *Journal of American Studies* 18 (1984): 343–360.

On Puritan "tribalism," see Edmund S. Morgan, *The Puritan Family: Religion and Domestic Relations in Seventeenth-Century New England* (New York: Harper and Row, 1966); Sacvan Bercovitch, *The Rites of Assent: Transformations in the Symbolic Construction of America* (New York: Routledge, 1993); and Gerald F. Moran, "Religious Renewal, Puritan Tribalism and the Family in Seventeenth-Century Mulford, Connecticut," *WMQ* 36: 2 (April 1979): 236–54.

17. Sydney Strong, ed., *Roger Clap's Memoirs, with an Account of the Voyage of the 'Mary and John'* (Seattle: Pigott-Washington, 1929), 21. On Clap's embrace of a "quasi-mystical" conversion experience at odds with the "American experience" of orthodoxy see Patricia Caldwell, *The Puritan Conversion Narrative: The Beginnings of American Expression* (New York: Cambridge University Press, 1983), 164–8.

18. Winthrop, *Journal*, I: 225; Samuel Maverick, "A Brief Description of New England and the Severall Townes therein, together with the Present Government thereof," *Massachusetts Historical Society Proceedings*, ser. 2, vol. 1 (Boston, 1884–85): 242. Winthrop, back in 1633, had regarded Maverick as "worthy of a perpetual remembrance" for taking care of Indians stricken with smallpox (I:115).

19. Thomas Lechford, "Plain Dealing: Or, Newes from New-England," *MHSC*, 3rd ser vol. 3 (1833), 116, 121.

Richard Gildrie, *The Profane, The Civil, and the Godly: The Reformation of Manners in Orthodox New England, 1679–1749* (University Park: Pennsylvania State University Press, 1994), has argued that the "profane" culture of truculent individualism, comprising the determination to achieve economic "independency," represented a kind of challenge to orthodoxy. While Gildrie has provided us with a glimpse of an underworld that truly was "profane," I do not think that a desire for household independency, compatible with that described in Alan Macfarlane, *The Origins of English Individualism: The Family, Property and Social Transition* (Oxford: Blackwell, 1978), was in any way adverse to Massachusetts orthodoxy. Indeed I believe that orthodoxy made such independency possible.

20. Perry Miller, *The New England Mind: The Seventeenth Century* (New York: Macmillan, 1939); and *The New England Mind: From Colony to Province* (Cambridge: Harvard University Press, 1953).

21. The classic town study, arguing that early Dedham was a "Christian Utopian Closed Corporate Community," is Kenneth Lockridge, *A New England Town: The First Hundred Years: Dedham, Massachusetts, 1636–1736* (New York: Norton, 1970). For synthetic treatments that examine the huge outpouring of similar works and link the social history provided in town studies with the theory of religious declension, see Jack P. Greene, *Pursuits of Happiness: The Social Development of Early Modern British Colonies and the Formation of American Culture* (Chapel Hill: University of North Carolina Press, 1988), 55–80; and James A. Henretta, "The Morphology of New England Society in the Colonial Period," *Journal of Interdisciplinary History* 11 (1971–72): 379–98.

Harry S. Stout, in explaining the problems that town studies have created for understanding religious communities in nineteenth- and twentieth-century urban spaces, demonstrates how the "narrative line taken in virtually all of these demographic [town] studies was, ironically, borrowed from the very intellectual historian they hoped to displace: Perry Miller. When told as a story, each of these historians told the tale of social 'declension.' " See Harry S. Stout et al., "Forum: The Place of Religion in Urban and Community Studies,"*Religion and American Culture: A Journal of Interpretation* 6 (Summer 1996): 114–18.

22. Studies that argue for the leading men's singularity of opinion on doctrinal issues include Charles Cohen, *God's Caress: The Psychology of Puritan Religious Experience* (New York: Oxford University Press, 1986); Charles Hambrick-Stowe, *The Practice of Piety: Puritan Devotional Discipline in Seventeenth-Century New England* (Chapel Hill: University of North Carolina Press, 1982); E. Brooks Holifield, *The Covenant Sealed: The Development of Puritan Sacramental Theology in Old and New England, 1570–1720* (New Haven: Yale University Press, 1974); and Francis Bremer, *Congregational Communion: Clerical Friendship in the Anglo-American Puritan Community, 1610–1692* (Boston: Northeastern University Press, 1994).

For the argument that the success of Puritan orthodoxy stemmed from its ability to absorb, or co-opt, the majority of challengers, see Stephen Foster, "New England and the Challenge of Heresy, 1630–1660: The Puritan Crisis in Transatlantic Perspective," *WMQ* 38:4 (October 1981): 624–660; and *The Long Argument: English Puritanism and the Shaping of New England Culture, 1570–1700* (Chapel Hill: University of North Carolina Press, 1991); and Timothy H. Breen and Stephen Foster, "The Puritans' Greatest Achievement: A Study of Social Cohesion in Seventeenth-Century Massachusetts," *Journal of American History* 60 (1973): 5-22 Although Philip Gura, *Glimpse of Sion's Glory*, has successfully challenged the view of New England Puritanism as a homogenous expression of the New England mind, he nonetheless emphasizes how discordant voices were co-opted and subsumed within an emergent orthodoxy.

23. Stephen Innes, *Creating the Commonwealth: The Economic Culture of Puritan New England* (New York: Norton, 1995); and *Labor in a New Land: Economy and Society in Seventeenth-Century Springfield* (Princeton, N.J.: Princeton University Press, 1983). John Frederick Martin, *Profits in the Wilderness: Entrepreneurship and the Founding of New England Towns in the Seventeenth Century* (Chapel Hill: Uni-

versity of North Carolina Press, 1991), similarly goes too far in depicting Massachusetts Puritans as full-scale capitalists. For a study that takes account of openness toward the market while still showing that Massachusetts Puritans were uneasy with it, see Virginia Anderson, *New England's Generation: The Great Migration and the Formation of Society and Culture in the Seventeenth Century* (New York: Cambridge University Press, 1991). The desire to achieve "independency," as defined in Greene, *Pursuits of Happiness*, and Vickers, "Competency and Competition," was not equivalent to an embrace of full-scale market capitalism and all its social consequences. For an excellent corrective to the extreme views of Innes and Martin see Mark Valeri, "Religious Discipline and the Market: Puritans and the Issue of Usury," *WMQ* 54: 4 (October 1997): 746–68.

24. Earlier studies that have emphasized conflict rather than consensus in the first generation include Darrett Rutman, *Winthrop's Boston: Portrait of a Puritan Town, 1630–1649* (Chapel Hill: University of North Carolina Press, 1965); and Bernard Bailyn, *The New England Merchants in the Seventeenth Century* (Cambridge: Harvard University Press, 1955).

25. Janice Knight, *Orthodoxies in Massachusetts: Rereading American Puritanism* (Cambridge: Harvard University Press, 1994), argues that the doctrinal stance taken by Richard Sibbes, John Preston, John Cotton, John Davenport, and Henry Vane, while understood as antinomian in Massachusetts, was actually well respected in the transatlantic world and no less orthodox than what emerged as the New England Way. Massachusetts, in Knight's view, had two orthodoxies, one of which, propounded by William Perkins, William Ames, John Winthrop, Thomas Shepard, and Peter Bulkeley, became locally dominant. This interpretation is compatible with the one put forth in this book and in Louise Breen, "Religious Radicalism in the Puritan Officer Corps: Heterodoxy, the Artillery Company and Cultural Integration in Seventeenth-Century Boston," *NEQ* 68: 1 (March 1995): 3–43. While Knight's study focuses predominantly on clerical figures, mine focuses mostly on secular elites. Karen Ordahl Kupperman, *Providence Island*, has examined the differences between elite English Puritans and the leaders of Puritan Massachusetts, suggesting that each group interpreted differently the concept of "liberty" and the nature of their responsibilities.

26. Max Weber, *The Protestant Ethic and the Spirit of Capitalism*, trans. Talcott Parsons (New York: Scribner, 1958). The notion that antinomian spirituality would cause people to withdraw from the "real" world and thus the process of getting and spending, is forcefully advanced in Edmund Morgan, *Visible Saints: The History of a Puritan Idea* (Ithaca, N.Y.: Cornell University Press, 1963); and Edmund Morgan, *The Puritan Dilemma* (Boston: Little, Brown, 1958).

Studies that have begun to examine the ascription of trickster-like, even magical, characteristics to the market rather than simply focusing on its disciplined rationalism include Jean-Christophe Agnew, *Worlds Apart: The Market and the Theater in Anglo-American Thought, 1550–1750* (New York: Cambridge University Press, 1986); Lyndal Roper, "Stealing Manhood: Capitalism and Magic in Early Modern Germany," *Gender and History* 3 (Spring 1991): 4–22; Pamela H. Smith, *The Business of Alchemy: Science and Culture in the Holy Roman Empire* (Princeton, N.J.: Princeton University Press, 1994); and John L. Brooke, *The Refiner's Fire: The Making of Mormon Cosmology, 1644–1844* (New York: Cambridge University Press, 1994).

27. Robert Child to Samuel Hartlib, 24 December 1645, in G. H. Turnbull, "Robert Child," *Transactions of the Colonial Society of Massachusetts*, vol. 38 (Boston: Colonial Society of Massachusetts, 1959), 51–2.

28. Frederick W. Gookin, *Daniel Gookin, 1612–1687* (Chicago: R. R. Donnelley, 1912), 153–4.

29. Greene, *Pursuits of Happiness*, relies on the declension model to make this assertion, emphasizing that the Chesapeake colonies were more mainstream in American culture because of their early dedication to market imperatives. Recent work on the Chesapeake region has shown that this region was more communally oriented, and more religious, than formerly thought. See Lois Green Carr, Philip D. Morgan, and Jean B. Russo, eds., *Colonial Chesapeake Society* (Chapel Hill: University of North Carolina Press, 1988); and Lois Green Carr, Russell R. Menard, and Lorena S. Walsh, *Robert Cole's World: Agriculture and Society in Early Maryland* (Chapel Hill: University of North Carolina Press, 1991).

30. See Daniel H. Usner, *Indians, Settlers and Slaves in a Frontier Exchange Economy: The Lower Mississippi Valley before 1783* (Chapel Hill: University of North Carolina Press, 1992); Daniel K. Richter, *The Ordeal of the Longhouse: The People of the Iroquois League in the Era of European Colonization* (Chapel Hill: University of North Carolina Press, 1992); James Merrell, *The Indians' New World: Catawbas and their Neighbors from European Contact through the Era of Removal* (Chapel Hill: University of North Carolina Press, 1989); Richard White, *The Middle Ground: Indians, Empires and Republics in the Great Lakes Region, 1650–1815* (New York: Cambridge University Press, 1991); and Eric Hinderaker, *Elusive Empires: Constructing Colonialism in the Ohio Valley, 1673–1800* (New York: Cambridge University Press, 1997).

For the notion, derived from Frederick Jackson Turner, that frontier history repeated itself continually in American history see William Cronon, George Miles, and Jay Gitlin, "Becoming West: Toward a New Meaning for Western History," in *Under an Open Sky: Rethinking America's Western Past*, ed. William Cronon, George Miles, and Jay Gitlin (New York: Norton, 1992), 6.

31. For classic expositions of the republican synthesis see Bernard Bailyn, *The Ideological Origins of the American Revolution* (Cambridge, Mass.: Belknap Press, 1967); J. G. A. Pocock, *The Machiavellian Moment: Florentine Political Thought and the Atlantic Republican Tradition* (Princeton, N.J.: Princeton University Press, 1975); Gordon Wood, *The Creation of the American Republic, 1776–1787* (Chapel Hill: University of North Carolina Press, 1969); and *The Radicalism of the American Revolution* (New York: Knopf, 1992). Bernard Bailyn has insisted that "republicanism" was wholly secular; but a number of historians have, for different reasons, suggested the importance of religious cultures in paving the way to its acceptance. See, for example, Gildrie, *The Profane, The Civil and the Godly*; Harry S. Stout, *The New England Soul: Preaching and Religious Culture in Colonial New England* (New York: Oxford University Press, 1986); and J. C. D. Clark, *The Language of Liberty, 1660–1832: Political Discourse and Social Dynamics in the Anglo-American World* (New York: Cambridge University Press, 1994).

32. See Stephen Nissenbaum, "New England as Region and Nation," in *All Over the Map: Rethinking American Regions*, ed. Edward L. Ayers et al. (Baltimore: Johns Hopkins University Press, 1996), 38–61; and Peter S. Onuf, "Federalism, Republicanism and the Origins of American Sectionaliism," in the same volume, 11–37.

CHAPTER I

1. "The Examination of Mrs. Anne Hutchinson at the Court at Newtown," in *AC*, 326.

2. John Winthrop, "A Short Story of the Rise, Reign, and Ruine of the Antinomians, Familists, and Libertines," in AC, 211, 274.

3. "Examination of Mrs. Anne Hutchinson," in AC, 337–8.

4. Winthrop, "Short Story," in AC, 250.

5. Ibid., 266.

6. Ibid., 274; and "Examination of Mrs. Anne Hutchinson," in AC, 343.

7. Frank Thistlethwaite, Dorset Pilgrims: The Story of Westcountry Pilgrims Who Went to New England in the Seventeenth Century (London: Barrie and Jenkins, 1989), 50, 52, 84, 85, 87, 93, 100–1, 129. For the argument that the region from which Stoughton emigrated produced more moderate Puritans than the Hutchinsons' native Lincolnshire, see Cedric B. Cowing, The Saving Remnant: Religion and the Settling of New England (Urbana: University of Illinois Press, 1995).

8. "Examination of Mrs. Anne Hutchinson," in AC, 338.

9. Winthrop, "Short Story," in AC, 265, 275.

10. "Examination of Mrs. Anne Hutchinson," in AC, 345.

11. Ibid., 347.

12. Ibid., 346.

13. Winthrop, "Short Story," in AC, 283, 294, 284.

14. Winthrop, "Short Story," in AC, 348. On Jennison see also Robert E. Wall, The Membership of the Massachusetts Bay General Court, 1630–1686 (New York: Garland, 368–9); Emery Battis, Saints and Sectaries: Anne Hutchinson and the Antinomian Controversy in the Massachusetts Bay Colony (Chapel Hill: University of North Carolina Press, 1962), 232; Winthrop, Journal, II: 178–9; and Joseph B. Felt, The Ecclesiastical History of New England Comprising Not Only Religion but also Moral and Other Relations, 2 vols. (Boston: Congregational Library Association, 1855–62), I: 325–6.

15. "A Report of the Trial of Mrs. Anne Hutchinson before the Church in Boston, in AC, 366–7.

16. Oliver Ayer Roberts, History of the Military Company of the Massachusetts Now Called the Ancient and Honorable Artillery Company of Massachusetts, 1637–1888, 4 vols. (Boston: A. Mudge, 1895–1909), I: 77, points out that Saltonstall failed to become a freeman "probably because he was not disposed to conform to the rigid discipline of the Puritan church"; on his payment of the fine see 62. Saltonstall was the son of Sir Richard Saltonstall, who in 1652 wrote a letter to John Cotton and John Wilson castigating the Bay Colony for its failure to tolerate any level of diversity. See Sir Richard Saltonstall to John Cotton and John Wilson, 1652, in The Saltonstall Papers, 1607–1815, Robert E. Moody, ed. 2 vols. (Boston: Massachusetts Historical Society, 1972–74), 148–9.

17. Wall, Membership of the General Court, 321–2; Felt, Ecclesiastical History, I: 326.

18. On this incident see Selma Williams, Divine Rebel: The Life of Anne Marbury Hutchinson (New York: Holt, Rinehart and Winston, 1981), 193–4; and Winthrop, Journal, II: 39–40. Stoddard's behavior did not prevent his later marriage to Mary Downing, Winthrop's niece, or a subsequent marriage to Joseph Weld's widow, Barbara Weld. Interestingly, however, Anthony Stoddard's son, Solomon, enraged a later generation of orthodox stalwarts by advocating open church membership.

19. The best analysis of the theological issues at stake in the 1630s remains William K. B. Stoever, "A Faire and Easie Way to Heaven": Covenant Theology and Antinomianism in Early Massachusetts (Middletown, Conn.: Wesleyan University Press, 1978).

20. For the argument that New England was "sacred space" for Massachusetts Puritans see Avihu Zakai, *Exile and Kingdom: History and Apocalypse in the Puritan Migration to America* (New York: Cambridge University Press, 1992), 67–8.

21. On the connection between the mercantile elite and the "Hutchinsonian" movement, see Battis, *Saints and Sectaries*; and Bernard Bailyn, *The New England Merchants in the Seventeenth Century* (1955; reprint, Cambridge: Harvard University Press, 1982), 40.

22. For the argument that orthodoxy and antinomianism were "polemically constructed" in relation to one another see Janice Knight, *Orthodoxies in Massachusetts: Rereading American Puritanism* (Cambridge: Harvard University Press, 1994). On the understanding of the market as "boundless" see Jean-Christophe Agnew, *Worlds Apart: The Market and the Theater in Anglo-American Thought, 1550–1750* (New York: Cambridge University Press, 1986).

23. On this incident see Winthrop, *Journal*, I:147; and Frances Rose-Troup, *The Massachusetts Bay Company and Its Predecessors* (1930; reprint, Clifton, N.J.: A. F. M. Kelley, 1973), 117–27.

24. Israel Stoughton to John Stoughton, 1635, in *Letters from New England: The Massachusetts Bay Colony, 1629–1638*, ed. Everett Emerson (Amherst: University of Massachusetts Press, 1976), 149. For the official record of Stoughton's penalty see *MBR*, I:135.

25. *MBR*, I:175. For the rejection of the Dorchester petition see Winthrop, *Journal*, I:150. Wall, *Membership of the Massachusetts General Court*, 519–21, offers the plausible explanation that there was a desire to prevent Stoughton's emigration.

26. On Ludlow see Thistlethwaite, *Dorset Pilgrims*, 98–117.

27. On Stoughton's membership in the premigration church see James Blake, *Annals of the Town of Dorchester* (Boston: D. Clapp, 1846); and Thistlethwaite, *Dorset Pilgrims*.

28. *MBR*, I:195, 207.

29. Wall, *Membership of the Massachusetts General Court*, 519–21, asserts that Stoughton was "violently opposed to the teachings of Ann Hutchinson."

30. Winthrop, "Short Story," in *AC*, 249.

31. Ibid., 282.

32. Ibid., 290.

33. Ibid., 293.

34. John Lassiter, "Defamation of Peers: The Rise and Decline of the Action for Scandalum Magnatum, 1497–1773," *American Journal of Legal History* 22 (1978): 216–36, explains how prosecution for defamation increased in England during periods when lines of authority were blurred.

35. Winthrop, "Short Story," in *AC*, 285.

36. Ibid., 255.

37. Ibid., 292.

38. Ibid., 290–1, 295.

39. Ibid., 254–5.

40. Ibid., 253–4, 298–9, 293–4.

41. Israel Stoughton to John Stoughton, 1635, in Emerson, *Letters from New England*, 148, 151.

42. Israel Stoughton to John Stoughton, 1635, in ibid., 149.

43. Ibid., 147–8.

44. Mary Beth Norton, *Founding Mothers and Fathers: Gendered Power and the Forming of American Society* (New York: Knopf, 1996), 359–99, emphasizes how effectively Hutchinson defended herself, particularly when she argued that distinc-

tions must be made between statements made in public and those made in private. Jane Kamensky, *Governing the Tongue: The Politics of Speech in Early New England* (New York: Oxford University Press, 1997), 78–81, suggests that magistrates were thrown off balance by Hutchinson's ability to defend herself in a manner that was perceived as masculine. See also Ann Fairfax Withington and Jack Schwartz, "The Political Trial of Anne Hutchinson," *NEQ* 51: 2 (June 1978): 226–40. All of these studies emphasize how Hutchinson presumed to "teach" the Court.

45. "Examination of Mrs. Anne Hutchinson," in *AC*, 327. On the scruples Puritans held in regard to the taking of oaths see E. Brooks Holifield, *Era of Persuasion: American Thought and Culture, 1521–1680* (Boston: Twayne, 1989), 114–20.

46. "Examination of Mrs. Anne Hutchinson," in *AC*, 319.

47. Ibid., 327.

48. Ibid., 327–8. Richard Brown of Watertown argued that the use of oaths would reduce the case to a mere dispute between parties.

49. John Underhill to John Winthrop, 1636/37, *MHSC*, 4th ser., vol. 7 (Boston, 1865), 172. For Greensmith's punishment see *MBR*, I:189.

50. Israel Stoughton to John Stoughton, 1635, in Emerson, *Letters from New England*, 148, 150.

51. This incident is discussed in Edmund Morgan, *Visible Saints: A History of a Puritan Idea* (1963; reprint, Ithaca, N.Y.: Cornell University Press, 1965), 99–105; and Winthrop, *Journal*, I:177–8. Shepard quoted in Knight, *Orthodoxies*, 178.

52. "Examination of Mrs. Anne Hutchinson," in *AC*, 332.

53. On Puritan attitudes toward justice see John M. Murrin, "Magistrates, Sinners, and a Precarious Liberty: Trial by Jury in Seventeenth-Century New England," in *Saints and Revolutionaries: Essays on Early American History*, ed. David D. Hall, John M. Murrin, and Thad W. Tate (New York: Norton, 1984).

54. Still, according to Perez Zagorin, *Ways of Lying: Dissimulation, Persecution and Conformity in Early Modern Europe* (Cambridge: Harvard University Press, 1990), 231, Protestants, rejecting casuist logic, "relied chiefly on legal obstruction" to extricate themselves from difficult circumstances.

55. "Examination of Mrs. Anne Hutchinson," in *AC*, 331. In regard to Hutchinson's conversations with the ministers, Winthrop noted: "This speech was not spoken in a corner but in a public assembly, and though things were spoken in private yet now coming to us, we are to deal with them as public" (319).

56. William Prynne, *Histrio-Mastix: The Player's Scourge or, Actor's Tragedy*, 2 vols. (1633; reprint, New York: Johnson Reprint, 1972), 159. On Prynne's life, see William Lamont, *Marginal Prynne, 1600–1669* (London: Routledge, 1963). For the "crisis of representation" affecting the early modern world see Stephen Greenblatt, *Renaissance Self-Fashioning: From More to Shakespeare* (Chicago: University of Chicago Press, 1980).

57. Stephen Foster, "New England and the Challenge of Heresy, 1630–1660: The Puritan Crisis in Transatlantic Perspective," *WMQ* 38: 4 (October 1981): 624–60, criticizes Stoever, *"Faire and Easie Way to Heaven,"* and Dewey D. Wallace, *Puritans and Predestination: Grace in English Protestant Theology, 1525–1695* (Chapel Hill: University of North Carolina Press, 1982), 112–57, because these authors have pointed out the similarities between the opinions of Cotton and Wheelwright and those of "real" antinomians in England. Foster suggests that this line of reasoning stigmatizes Cotton in the same way that seventeenth-century "heresiographers" like Robert Baillie and Stephen Denison did. Foster's criticism, I believe, is

too inflexible. That Cotton was never called to account for the more extreme positions found in the work of the Eatonite circle does not prove that there were no real or perceived similarities.

For treatments that focus on clerical divisions, especially the distinctiveness of John Cotton, see Knight, *Orthodoxies;* Andrew Delbanco, *The Puritan Ordeal* (Cambridge: Harvard University Press, 1989); Teresa Toulouse, *The Art of Prophesying: New England Sermons and the Shaping of Belief* (Athens: University of Georgia Press, 1987); John S. Coolidge, *The Pauline Renaissance in England: Puritanism and the Bible* (New York: Oxford University Press, 1970); Norman Grabo, "John Cotton's Aesthetic: A Sketch," *Early American Literature* 3 (spring 1968): 4–10; James Maclear, " 'The Heart of New England Rent': The Mystical Element in Early Puritan History," *Mississippi Historical Review* 42: 4 (March 1956): 621–52; and Geoffrey Nuttall, *The Holy Spirit in Puritan Faith and Experience* (Oxford: Basil Blackwell, 1946).

58. On English Antinomianism see Christopher Hill, "Antinomianism in Seventeenth-Century England," in *The Collected Essays of Christopher Hill: Religion and Politics in Seventeenth-Century England,* 2 vols. (Brighton, Sussex, England: Harvester Press, 1986), II:162–84; Christopher Hill, "Dr. Tobias Crisp, 1600–43," in the same volume, 141–61; T. D. Bozeman, "The Glory of the 'Third Time': John Eaton as Contra-Puritan," *Journal of Ecclesiastical History* 47: 4 (October 1996), 628–54; and Gertrude Huehns, *Antinomianism in English History with Special Reference to the Period, 1640–1660* (London: Cresset Press, 1951).

59. "Mr. Cottons Rejoynder," in AC, 135.

60. "The Elders Reply," in AC, 65–6.

61. Michael McGiffert, ed., *God's Plot: The Paradoxes of Puritan Piety; Being the Autobiography and Journal of Thomas Shepard* (Amherst: University of Massachusetts Press, 1972), 74.

62. Winthrop, "Short Story," in AC, 254.

63. Ibid., 287, 297–8.

64. Ibid., 300, 287, 298.

65. "Mr. Cottons Rejoynder," in AC, 119–20, 128.

66. Ibid., 116. On the juxtaposition of Adam and Christ in the antinomian controversy see Jesper Rosenmeier, "New England's Perfection: The Image of Adam and the Image of Christ in the Antinomian Crisis, 1634 to 1638," *WMQ* 27:3 (July 1970): 435–59.

67. "The Elders Reply," in AC, 68.

68. John Cotton, *A Treatise of the Covenant of Grace, As it is Dispensed to the Elect Seed* (1655; reprint, London, 1671), 82.

69. Thomas Shepard, *The Sound Believer: A Treatise of Evangelical Conversion Discovering the work of Christ's Spirit, in Reconciling of a Sinner to God* (1645; reprint, Boston, 1736), 41. See also Peter Bulkeley, *The Gospel-Covenant; or the Covenant of Grace Opened* (London, 1651), especially 324.

70. John Cotton, "Sixteene Questions of Serious and Necessary Consequence," in AC, 57.

71. John Winthrop, "A Short Story," in AC, 273.

72. "The Elders Reply," in AC, 65–6.

73. Michael Ditmore, "Preparation and Confession: Reconsidering Edmund S. Morgan's Visible Saints," *NEQ* 67: 2 (June 1994): 298–319, argues convincingly that Shepard was far more interested than Cotton in imposing uniformity on the churches of New England and that he, rather than Cotton, should be seen as the

primary architect of the New England Way. Knight, *Orthodoxies*, argues that Cotton's use of conversion narratives was intended more to help the communicant recall the moment of conversion than to evaluate his or her spiritual fitness. In contrast, Shepard tried to impose a uniformity on his congregants by carefully circumscribing appropriate speech for public occasions. On the different roles that conversion narratives played in the divergent thinking of Shepard and Cotton see Patricia Caldwell, *The Puritan Conversion Narrative: The Beginnings of American Expression* (London: Cambridge University Press, 1983).

74. Thomas Shepard, *The Sincere Convert: Discovering the small Number of True Believers, and the Great Difficulty of Saving Conversion* (1640; reprint, Boston, 1742), 108, 112.

75. Cotton, *Treatise of Covenant of Grace*, 49.

76. John Cotton, "Sixteene Questions of Serious and Necessary Consequence," in AC, 50.

77. "Letters between Thomas Shepard and John Cotton," in AC, 31–2.

78. Prynne, *Histrio-Mastix*, 87.

79. Ibid., 85.

80. Shepard, *Sincere Convert*, 131–2. The antinomian synod similarly accused the "opinionists" of holding that "we are not to pray against all sinne, because the old man is in us, and must be, and why should we pray against that which cannot be avoyded?" John Winthrop, "Short Story," in AC, 227.

81. Thomas Shepard, *Theses Sabbaticae, or The Doctrine of the Sabbath.* (1649; reprint, London, 1655), 68–9. This passage suggests both that Shepard was acquainted with the ideas of antinomians like John Eaton, famous for his assertion that the sins of the elect were hidden from the sight of God by the "wedding garment" of Christ, and that he was prepared to see stylistic links, however imprecise, between these ideas and those held by people in Massachusetts. Far more than Cotton, however, Eaton rendered godly walking suspect and sin an unfortunate yet unavoidable presence. The genuine saint possessed two identities, according to Eaton, one visible to the "eie of faith" and the other to the eye of flesh, so that "it is no matter that we feele sinne and death still in us, as if Christ had not taken them away; because God thus stablisheth the faith of his power: and therefore that there may be place for faith, we feele the contrary . . . the feeling of the great imperfection of his [the Christian's] righteousnesse, which is subject to sense, and visible, sharpneth his faith to cling by faithfull prayer the faster to that perfect righteousnesse wherewith hee is cloathed above sense and feeling, and invisibly." God, in other words, left sanctification incomplete in his saints so that they would be forced to live by faith alone. See John Eaton, *The Honey-Combe of Free Justification by Christ Alone* (London, 1642), 114, 136–7, 83, 268, 25, 48.

82. Prynne, *Histrio-Mastix*, 94.

83. Cotton, *Treatise of Covenant of Grace*, 46, 49.

84. Ibid., 43–4, 39. On Cotton's "chilling" doctrine of "temporary faith" see R. T. Kendall, *Calvin and English Calvinism to 1649* (New York: Oxford University Press, 1979), 167–83.

85. Winthrop, "Short Story," in AC, 215.

86. Shepard, *Theses Sabbaticae*, 13, addresses this point by arguing that it was wrong to emphasize the extraordinary times when God set aside normal morality in order to accomplish his own particular purposes, for this was not the usual way of the world.

87. David D. Hall, "The Uses of Ritual," in *Worlds of Wonder, Days of Judg-*

ment: *Popular Religious Belief in Early New England* (Cambridge: Harvard University Press, 1990), 177–8; David Leverenz, *The Language of Puritan Feeling: An Exploration in Literature, Psychology and Social History* (New Brunswick, N.J.: Rutgers University Press, 1980), 28, likens much of the Puritan audience to "arriviste[s] . . . just in from the provinces or just up from the peasantry."

88. Toulouse, *Art of Prophesying*, 13–45, for example, emphasizes the liberating aspects of the individuating tendencies in Cotton's preaching. Rather than driving toward the "uses" of the sermon, as many of his colleagues tended to do, Cotton was interested, Toulouse says, "not in limiting the possibilities of a text, but in displaying a variety of possible, logical, physical, psychological and spiritual meanings for it . . . clearly suggesting the richness of God's revelation, not rigidly controlling its interpretation" (33). Other scholars associate the positive valuation placed on the bridal analogy with protofeminist concerns. Marilyn J. Westerkamp, "Anne Hutchinson, Sectarian Mysticism, and the Puritan Order,"*Church History* 59: 4 (December 1990): 482–96; and Ben Barker-Benfield, "Anne Hutchinson and the Puritan Attitude Toward Women," *Feminist Studies* 1 (1973): 65–96, both argue that the majority of ministers rejected bridal imagery because they felt uncomfortable with the idea that women were more naturally suited by gender to be "brides of Christ." But see Richard Godbeer, "Love Raptures: Marital, Romantic and Erotic Images of Jesus Christ in Puritan New England, 1670–1739," *NEQ* 68: 3 (September 1995): 355–84.

89. As Margo Todd, *Christian Humanism and the Puritan Social Order* (New York: Cambridge University Press, 1987), has shown, Puritans drew their social thinking not only from the Reformed tradition but also from a renaissance Christian humanism that enjoined people to support the common good and emphasized the merits of activism, pragmatism, and virtue. By endowing with spiritual meaning even the most mundane of human activities and institutions—civil society, marriage, and the secular "calling"—humanist-informed Puritans endorsed a religiosity that could be practiced and understood by the "priesthood of all believers."

90. Bulkeley, *Gospel-Covenant*, 326.

Those with antinomian tendencies argued that the two covenants were qualitatively distinct, both in terms of the parties involved in contracting them and in terms of the benefits to be derived from them. On the distinctive terminologies used by the two parties to the antinomian controversy see Knight, *Orthodoxies*, especially 88–93. On the other hand, Charles Cohen, *God's Caress: the Psychology of Puritan Religious Experience* (New York: Oxford University Press), 53–5. 68–9, believes that these shadings of meaning were used by virtually all Puritan ministers at various times based on "homiletic demands" and that they did not connote internal divisions.

91. Daniel Vickers, *Farmers and Fishermen: Two Centuries of Work in Essex County, Massachusetts, 1630–1850* (Chapel Hill: University of North Carolina Press, 1994), 25–7; and Stephen Innes, *Creating the Commonwealth: The Economic Culture of Puritan New England* (New York: Norton, 1995), 160–91, downplay the notion that the prosecution of Robert Keayne denoted disaffection with market capitalism.

92. Bernard Bailyn, ed., *The Apologia of Robert Keayne* (Gloucester, Mass.: Peter Smith, 1970), 1–2, 27.

93. For English antinomians' disdain for substituting the "will" for the "deed" see Hill, "Antinomianism in Seventeenth-Century England," in *Collected Essays*, II:165–7.

94. Wallace, *Puritans and Predestination*, 110, explains how "extreme" Calvinists introduced "the Antinomian language of justification before actual faith, thereby pushing justification itself back into election." Hill, "Antinomianism in Seventeenth-Century England," 165, explains the problem of Keayne's formulation, from an orthodox perspective, as follows: "Because the elect are saved from all eternity, they are uninfluenced by what conservatives saw as the main social function of religion, the maintenance of standards of conduct by fear of penalties or hope of rewards in the afterlife."

95. Patricia Caldwell, "The Antinomian Language Controversy," *Harvard Theological Review* 69: 3–4 (1976): 345–67.

96. Bailyn, ed., introduction to *Apologia*, vii–xii, emphasizes Keayne's efforts to fit his actions into an orthodox framework; but Hall, "Uses of Ritual," 185–6, points out that Keayne repudiated the earlier confession he had made before the church by "making a distinction between conscience and the ritual."

97. Andrew Delbanco, "Thomas Shepard's America: The Biography of an Idea," in *Studies in Biography*, ed. Daniel Aaron, Harvard English Studies 8 (Cambridge: Harvard University Press, 1978), 184.

98. Winthrop, *Journal*, I:210.

99. Winthrop, *Journal*, II:39–40.

100. On Puritan "primitivism," see Theodore Dwight Bozeman, *To Live Ancient Lives: The Primitivist Dimension in Puritanism* (Chapel Hill: University of North Carolina Press, 1988).

101. On Anne Hutchinson's "mortalist" thought see James F. Maclear, "Anne Hutchinson and the Mortalist Heresy," *NEQ* 54: 1 (March 1981): 74–103. For the multifaceted appeal of mortalism in a variety of contexts see Norman T. Burns, *Christian Mortalism from Tyndale to Milton* (Cambridge: Harvard University Press, 1972).

102. "Trial of Mrs. Anne Hutchinson before the Church," in AC, 365–6. Cotton challenged Savage on this point.

103. Ibid., 386–8. John Wilson disagreed with Cotton on the reason for which Hutchinson should be excommunicated. Cotton insisted that it be for her lying and stubborn "pride of Harte," while Wilson argued that "it should be for her Errors in Opinion as well as for poynt of Practise." Cotton rejected Wilson's maneuverings to have "opinions" listed as grounds for excommunication, chiding Wilson for his efforts to "delay": "for poynt of Doctrine . . . we must suffer her with Patience."

104. Ibid., 356–7.

105. Ibid., 366–7.

106. Ibid., 361.

107. Ibid., 365.

108. Ibid., 369.

109. Ibid., 363, 372–3.

110. Ibid., 364–5.

111. Ibid., 367.

112. Pertaining to this, the antinomian synod claimed the dissenters held the following errors: that "no Minister can teach one that is anoynted by the Spirit of Christ, more then hee knowes already unlesse it be in some circumstances"; and that "no Minister can bee an Instrument to convey more of Christ to another, then hee by his own experience hath come unto." John Winthrop, "Short Story," in AC, 233–4.

113. Ibid., 241–2 (Error 80). Also described as erroneous was the belief that

"if a member of a Church be unsatisfied with any thing in the Church, if he expresse his offense, whether he hath used all meanes to convince the Church or no, he may depart" (Error 79).

114. See, ibid., Error 22: "None are to be exhorted to beleeve, but such whom we know to be the elect of God, or to have his Spirit in them effectually" (p. 225). Error 70: "Frequency or length of holy duties or trouble of conscience for neglect thereof, are all signes of one under a Covenant of workes" (p. 238). Error 49: "We are not bound to keepe a constant course of Prayer in our Families, or privately, unlesse the Spirit stirre us up thereunto" (p. 232).

115. John Winthrop, "Short Story," in AC, 253, denounced this tendency: "As first, in the Church, hee that will not renounce his sanctification, and waite for an immediate revelation of the Spirit, cannot bee admitted, bee hee never so godly: hee that is already in the Church, that will not do the same, and acknowledge this new light, and say as they say, is presently noted, and under-esteemed, as savouring of a Covenant of works." The antinomian synod also deplored how church membership would be affected. See, for example, Error 31: "Such as see any grace of God in themselves, before thay have the assurance of God's love sealed to them are not to be received members of Churches" (p. 227); and Error 65: "The Church in admitting members is not to looke to holinesse of life, or Testimony of the same." (p. 236).

Morgan, *Visible Saints*, 109, emphasizes that "God enabled them to tell with absolute certainty whether a man had saving grace or not. They therefore proposed to make their own discernment of this quality the only basis for admission to the church." The synod certainly did complain that antinomians believed that "He that hath the seale of the Spirit may certainly judge of any person, whether he be elected or no." Winthrop, "Short Story," in AC, 226—error 24. But Hutchinson, as far as the record shows, claimed only the capability of judging which ministers properly preached the covenant of grace.

116. Winthrop, "Short Story," in AC, 239 (Error 73). Error 10: "That God the Father, Son, and Holy Ghost, may give themselves to the soule, and the soule may have true union with Christ, true remission of sins, true marriage and fellowship, true sanctification from the blood of Christ, and yet bee an hypocrite" (p. 222). Error 16: "There is no difference between the graces of hypocrites and beleevers, in the kinds of them" (p. 223). Error 18: "The Spirit doth worke in Hypocrites, by gifts and graces, but in Gods children immediately" (p. 223). Error 29: "An hypocrite may have these two witnesses . . . that is to say, the water and bloud" (p. 227). Error 13: "That there is a new birth under the covenant of workes, to such a kind of righteousnesse, as before is mentioned, from which the soule must bee againe converted, before it can bee made partaker of Gods Kingdome." These "errors" exaggerate and distort Cotton's original formulation. Cotton had never argued that there was no difference between hypocrites and saints; rather, that it was impossible for humans to discriminate between the two on the basis of evidence of sanctification alone. Whether the distortions came from the "Hutchinsonians" or those who condemned them is uncertain. Still, there is no doubt that the ideas were inspired by Cotton and possibly repeated by Anne Hutchinson. Indeed, as I have shown, Cotton had argued that there was available to hypocrites under the "covenant of works" a type of faith, that, while inconstant, could not, while it lasted, be distinguished from the true saving grace that belonged to the elect under a "covenant of grace."

117. The meaning of the "halfway" covenant is discussed in more depth in

chapter 4. On the one hand, this innovation's effort to make an attenuated form of church membership available to the children of members was tribal, pointing backward to the communalistic concerns of the orthodox party during the anti-nomian controversy. On the other hand, however, it can be seen as the first of a series of moves toward more liberal admissions, culminating in "pope" Solomon Stoddard's scandalously open measures in Northampton. Solomon Stoddard, interestingly, was the son of Anthony Stoddard; and, according to his biographer, though Solomon Stoddard instituted synods, he did not do so to enforce uniformity of belief, reserving "matters of doctrine for the individual's own conscience." Ralph J. Coffman, *Solomon Stoddard* (Boston: Twayne, 1978), 115–6.

118. "Report of the Trial of Mrs. Anne Hutchinson before the Church," in *AC*, 372, 373. Thomas Shepard recognized that many of the members of the church were reluctant about proceeding to excommunication, and would have preferred a second admonition instead.

119. Ibid., 368; and Battis, *Saints and Sectaries*, 182.

120. "Robert Keayne's Report of Boston Church Action," in *AC*, 390–5.

121. Ibid., 391–2. Inexplicably, John Cotton, in summarizing the report made by John Oliver, said that the Portsmouth antinomians would not receive the message from First Church unless it were presented in their church, "which had bine to have acknowledged them a Lawfull church which they [the messengers] had no Comission to doe" (392). Oliver's statement, however, indicated the opposite—that the Portsmouth congregants wanted to avoid meeting as a group to avoid any hint of submission.

122. Ibid., 392.

123. Ibid., 392–3.

124. Raymond D. Irwin, "Cast out from the 'City upon a Hill': Antinomian Exiles in Rhode Island, 1638–1650," *Rhode Island History* 52: 1 (February 1994): 2–19, suggests that the antinomians were not all that radical since many were rechurched in Massachusetts, returned to England, or created congregations of their own in Rhode Island. Yet this begs the question of what would have constituted acting radical. It is my contention here that antinomianism was a multifaceted movement that attracted a wide range of believers whose social goals were neither consonant nor well articulated. Antinomians were not adverse to living in civil or church fellowship; but they harbored strong resentments concerning the inflexibility of the New England system. On the confused conditions in Rhode Island see Bruce C. Daniels, "Dissent and Disorder: The Radical Impulse and Early Government in the Founding of Rhode Island," *Journal of Church and State* 24: 2 (spring 1982): 357–78.

125. John Winthrop, "A Short Story," in *AC*, 218.

126. Winthrop, *Journal*, I:219.

127. McGiffert, *God's Plot*, 42. Delbanco, *Puritan Ordeal*, 142, suggests that Shepard's early attraction to Grindletonian thought contributed to his rigidity throughout the controversy.

128. Rodger Brierley, *A Bundle of Soul-Convincing, Directing and Comforting Truths* (London, 1677), 172.

129. Ibid., 1.

130. Ibid., 231–2.

131. See especially Knight, *Orthodoxies*; and Caldwell, *Puritan Conversion Narrative*.

132. John Wheelwright, "A Fast-Day Sermon," in *AC*, 162.

133. Cotton, *A Treatise of the Covenant of Grace*, 177–8, advised that "there is need of greater light, then the word of itself is able to give; for it is not all the promises in Scripture, that have at any time wrought any gracious change in any soul, or are able to beget the faith of God's elect." In *The Covenant of Grace: Discovering the Great Work of a Sinners Reconciliation to God* (London, 1655), 56–7, Cotton argued that "there is no Condition before Faith, but a condition of misery, a lost condition, or if a gratious Condition, it is a Condition subsequent, not pre-existent, no Condition before it, whereby a man can close with Jesus Christ."

134. Michael Zuckerman, "Identity in British America: Unease in Eden," in *Colonial Identity in the Atlantic World, 1500–1800*, ed. Nicholas Canny and Anthony Pagden (Princeton, N.J.: Princeton University Press, 1987), 115–57; and Michael Zuckerman, "Pilgrims in the Wilderness: Community, Modernity, and the Maypole at Merry Mount," *NEQ* 50: 2 (June 1977): 255–77.

135. On these individuals see Wall, *Membership of the General Court*, 143–4, 316; James F. Maclear, "New England and the Fifth Monarchy: The Quest for the Millennium in Early American Puritanism,"*WMQ* 32 (1975): 223–60; John T. Hassam, "Early Recorders and Registers of Deeds for the County of Suffolk, Massachusetts, 1639–1735," *Massachusetts Historical Society Proceedings*, 2d ser., vol. 12 (Boston, 1898), 203–49; Battis, *Saints and Sectaries*, 102, 232; Sybil Noyes, Charles Libby and Walter Davis, *Genealogical Dictionary of Maine and New Hampshire* (1928–39; reprint, Baltimore: Genealogical, 1972), 292; Charles H. Pope, *The Pioneers of Maine and New Hampshire, 1623 to 1660* (1808; reprint, Baltimore: Genealogical, 1989), 86–7; *Notebook Kept by Thomas Lechford Esq., Lawyer . . . from June 27, 1638 to July 29, 1641*, American Antiquarian Society, *Transactions and Collections* 8 (Cambridge, Mass.: John Wilson, 1885): 48–9, 277, 436–7; and Philip Gura, *A Glimpse of Sion's Glory: Puritan Radicalism in New England, 1620–1660* (Middletown Conn.: Wesleyan University Press, 1984), 130–1.

136. Shepard, *Theses Sabbaticae*, 67, see also Bulkeley, *Gospel-Covenant*, 323–25. Richard Godbeer, *The Devil's Dominion: Magic and Religion in Early New England* (New York: Cambridge University Press, 1992), 47–9, argues that some turned to magic in order to alleviate spiritual anxieties created by Puritanism itself. At the same time, it was common to equate magic with Catholicism and conjurors with priests. See Keith Thomas, *Religion and the Decline of Magic: Studies in Popular Beliefs in Sixteenth and Seventeeth Century England* (London: Weidenfeld and Nicholson, 1971).

137. For the "romantic" view of mysticism see Evelyn Underhill, *Mysticism: A Study in the Nature and Development of Man's Spiritual Consciousness* (1955; reprint, New York: Times-Mirror, 1972). A more recent perspective on mysticism as potentially elitist is discussed in Sarah Beckwith, *Christ's Body: Identity, Culture and Society in Late Medieval Writings* (New York: Routledge, 1993). Beckwith argues that mysticism can be "democratically universal, whole and available to all in the innermost recesses of their spirits, whilst also allowing its esoteric qualities to function in mysteriously elitist ways."

138. Wallace, *Puritans and Predestination*, 117, 146.

139. Bulkeley, *Gospel-Covenant*, 326.

140. "Report of the Trial of Mrs. Anne Hutchinson before the Church," in *AC*, 365.

141. The conviction that antinomianism could shade off into Arminianism, its seeming opposite, may also have been abetted by the clergyman William Twisse's accusations, just prior to Cotton's 1633 migration, that the Boston-bound divine

had been circulating a manuscript that spouted Arminian doctrine. In this manuscript, Cotton shrank from the doctrine of reprobation, suggesting that God was responsible for the election of the regenerate but not for the damnation of the reprobate. Cotton's manuscript was published along with Twisse's rejoinder in William Twisse, *A Treatise of Mr. Cottons, Clearing Certaine Doubts Concerning Predestination. Together with an Examination Thereof* (London, 1646). Cotton had argued that "It is a greater honour to a Prince to be gratious and just, then to be wise and powerful; power and wisedome may bee found in a vitious Prince, not grace and justice: if then grace and justice doe more set forth the glory of their sovereignty, surely God (who aimeth at his highest glory) . . . aimed chiefly at the manifestation of his grace and justice, above the manifestation of his power and domininon."

Jon Pahl, *Paradox Lost: Free Will and Political Liberty in American Culture, 1630–1760* (Baltimore: Johns Hopkins University Press, 1992), 19–41, argues, incorrectly I believe, that Cotton underwent a rapid sea change upon his arrival in America, apparently going "from gentle (i.e. Arminian-leaning) to rigorous Calvinism overnight." But it would seem that Cotton was more complex than this, tending to conserve all the various, seemingly inconsistent elements of his spirituality and to rearrange them over and over again in a variety of contexts. For more on the Twisse incident see Everett Emerson, *John Cotton* (1965; reprint, Boston: Twayne, 1990), 83–4; and Larzar Ziff, *The Career of John Cotton: Puritanism and the American Experience* (Princeton, N.J.: Princeton University Press, 1962), 42.

142. Caroline Walker Bynum, *Holy Feast and Holy Fast: The Religious Significance of Food to Medieval Women* (Berkeley: University of California Press, 1987), describes how holy women in the medieval period called attention to their bodies, and endowed them with worth, even as they mortified their flesh by fasting. The New England antinomians certainly did not engage in such mortification, but they would appear to have gained a tremendous sense of power proportional to their own estimation of their dependency on God.

143. Shepard, *Theses Sabbaticae*, 113.

144. "Peter Bulkeley and John Cotton: On Union with Christ," in *AC*, 41.

145. Hill, "Antinomianism in Seventeenth-Century England," 167, explores the charge that some antinomians believed in liberty of conscience and universalism. He quotes Samual Rutherford's complaint that "sundry antinomians say Irish Papists ought to have liberty of conscience."

146. Cotton, *Treatise of the Covenant of Grace*, 52, 47.

147. The link between antinomianism and the merchant community was first noted by Battis, *Saints and Sectaries*. But Battis's causal explanation for the relationship—that antinomianism assuaged the guilt of merchants who regretted their sharp dealing—is unsatisfying.

148. Wilson reiterated at Hutchinson's church trial that "we should speake the Truth playnly one to another." "Report of the Trial of Mrs. Anne Hutchinson before the Church," in *AC*, 384.

149. On the blending of magical and pragmatic properties in coinage see Stephen J. Greenblatt, *Marvellous Possessions: The Wonder of the New World* (Chicago: University of Chicago Press, 1991). Jean-Christophe Agnew, *Worlds Apart: The Market and the Theater in Anglo-American Thought, 1550–1750* (New York: Cambridge University Press, 1986), utilizes the concept of "boundlessness" to describe the threatening, destabilizing implications of a placeless, "protean" market.

150. *MBR*, III:193, 252; Gerard Malynes, *Consuetudo: vel, Lex Mercatoria, or the Ancient Law-Merchant* (London, 1656).

Joyce O. Appleby, *Economic Thought and Ideology in Seventeenth-Century En-*

gland (Princeton, N.J.: Princeton University Press, 1978), 24–51, has shown how Malynes held forth against the free traders Thomas Mun and Edward Misselden. But the *Lex Mercatoria* contained enough information about the crafty dealings of merchants to engender pride in those merchants who read it. In addition, the tract conceived of economic evolution in terms of increasing abstraction in the medium of exchange, from bartered commodities to money to bills of exchange, with each increment of abstraction transforming and giving "life" to the market. If this were the way merchants constructed their mental universe, it was similar to the way antinomians saw religious progress as a movement from reliance on a tangible works-righteousness to reliance on the intangible infusion of grace received during justification; and just as religious radicalism was dangerous because its mystical abstractions threatened to dispense with the need for public religious authorities, so did its analogues in the economic world threaten to undermine public controls on the market.

151. Calvinist doctrine did not forbid usury, but in New England certain ministers, especially John Cotton, were wary of acquisitive behavior and attempted to enforce in Boston such conventions as the "just price." On this issue see Jesper Rosenmeier, "John Cotton on Usury," *WMQ* 47: 4 (October 1990): 548–65. Interestingly, Delbanco, "Thomas Shepard's America," 173, describes Shepard's disillusionment with the new world as follows: "The tragedy lies in the failure of the journey; it is the force of that realization, the shock of finding the new social landscape too familiar, with only the single new twist that money-lust now breeds antinomian anarchy rather than Arminian moralism."

152. Malynes, *Lex Mercatoria*, 4, 217.

153. Appleby, *Economic Thought and Ideology*, describes the antiauthoritarian biases of pre-Smithian free-market economists, especially in their views on exchange rates. Like Agnew, Appleby also finds that as the market expanded in the sixteenth and seventeenth centuries, apprehensions grew. According to Appleby, "As long as the principal elements in the economic structure remained visible and tangible, the understanding of the system was the possession of the whole society. All of this changed with the expansion of trade in the sixteenth and seventeenth centuries. . . . Barriers of local markets broke down. . . . No longer visible and tangible, the economy became generally incomprehensible" (pp. 25–6).

154. Malynes, *Lex Mercatoria*, 105, 180, 251–3.

155. Innes, *Creating the Commonwealth*.

156. Social historians of Puritan Massachusetts, including Stephen Innes, *Labor in a New Land: Economy and Society in Seventeenth-Century Springfield* (Princeton, N.J.: Princeton University Press, 1983); and *Creating the Commonwealth*; and John Frederick Martin, *Profits in the Wilderness: Entrepreneurship and the Founding of New England Towns in the Seventeenth Century* (Chapel Hill: University of North Carolina Press, 1991), have been too quick to proclaim that Puritan New Englanders were at ease in the market. In many cases, this comes from a tendency to equate the eager pursuit of individual family "competencies" with acquiescence in all aspects of transatlantic market capitalism. Indeed, Alan Macfarlane, *The Origins of English Individualism: The Family, Property and Social Transition* (Oxford: Basil Blackwell, 1978), has pushed such an analysis far back into the English past. For a more balanced view that still fails sufficiently to distinguish between individual experiences and attitudes toward the larger transatlantic market see Daniel Vickers, *Farmers and Fishermen: Two Centuries of Work in Essex County, Massachusetts, 1630–1850* (Chapel Hill: University of North Carolina Press, 1994).

157. Agnew, *Worlds Apart*; see also J. E. Crowley, *This Sheba, Self: The Con-

ceptualization of Economic Life in Eighteenth-Century America (Baltimore: Johns Hopkins University Press, 1974), for an interpretation that stresses how doubts about the morality of the market continued through the eighteenth century.

158. This, of course, derives from Max Weber, *The Protestant Ethic and the Spirit of Capitalism*, trans. Talcott Parsons (New York: Scribner, 1958).

159. Robert Child, "Large Letter concerning the Defects and Remedies of English Husbandry written to Mr. Samuel Hartlib," in *Samuel Hartlib his Legacie of Husbandry* (London, 1651), 52.

160. Ibid., 40. For a different interpretation that aligns Child almost wholly within the "culture of discipline" see Margaret Newall, "Robert Child and the Entrepreneurial Vision: Economy and Ideology in Early New England," *NEQ* 68: 2 (June 1995): 223–56.

161. On "republican" values see Bernard Bailyn, *The Ideological Origins of the American Revolution* (Cambridge, Mass.: Belknap, 1967); and J. G. A. Pocock, *The Machiavellian Moment: Florentine Political Thought and the Atlantic Republican Tradition* (Princeton, N.J.: Princeton University Press, 1975).

162. See Rosenmeier, "Cotton on Usury;" and Mark Valeri, "Religious Discipline and the Market: Puritans and the Issue of Usury," *WMQ* 54: 4 (October 1997): 746–68.

163. "A Remonstrance and Petition of Robert Childe, and Others," in *Hutchinson Papers*, 2 vols. (Albany, N.Y.: Publications of the Prince Society, 1815), I: 214–23, quoted 215–6, 217–220.

164. See, for example, Timothy D. Hall, *Contested Boundaries: Itinerancy and the Reshaping of the Colonial American Religious World* (Durham, N.C.: Duke University Press, 1994); Susan O'Brian, "A Transatlantic Community of Saints: The Great Awakening and the First Evangelical Network, 1735–1755," *American Historical Review* 91: 4 (October 1986): 811–32; and Harry Stout, *The Divine Dramatist: George Whitefield and the Rise of Modern Evangelicalism* (Grand Rapids, Mich.: Eerdmans, 1991).

165. T. H. Breen, " 'Baubles of Britain': The American and Consumer Revolutions of the Eighteenth Century," *Past and Present* 119 (May 1988): 73–104.

166. Jay Fliegelman, *Declaring Independence: Jefferson, Natural Language and the Culture of Performance* (Stanford: Stanford University Press, 1993), explains how bonds based on sensibility could be used just as much to exclude people as to include them.

Paul Boyer and Stephen Nissenbaum, *Salem Possessed: Social Origins of Witchcraft* (Cambridge: Harvard University Press, 1974), argue that, as late as 1692, witchcraft accusations flowed in part from ambivalent feelings toward the growing importance of the market. That late-seventeenth-century inhabitants of Salem would express their concerns about the market through a crisis that focused on what was traditionally regarded as a female crime speaks volumes about the perceived connection between feminine wiles and trade. For the association of women, magic, and the market in a very different early modern setting see Lyndal Roper, "Stealing Manhood: Capitalism and Magic in Early Modern Germany," *Gender and History* 3 (spring 1991): 4–22. According to Ruth Bloch, "The Gendered Meanings of Virtue in Revolutionary America," *Signs* 13:1 (fall 1987): 37–58, it was not until the late eighteenth century that rational self-interest began to be valued positively and gendered male.

167. Zuckerman, "Identity in British America."

168. Benedict R. Anderson, *Imagined Communities: Reflections on the Origin and Spread of Nationalism* (London: Verso, 1994).

CHAPTER 2

1. David Pulsifer, ed., *Acts of the Commissioners of the United Colonies of New England, 1643–1679*, vols. 9–10, in *Records of the Colony of New Plymouth, in New England*, ed. Nathaniel B. Shurtleff, 12 vols. in 9 (Boston: W. White, 1855–61), X:52.

2. On Underhill's provocative activities see Oliver Rink, *Holland on the Hudson: An Economic and Social History of Dutch New York* (Ithaca, N.Y.: Cornell University Press, 1986), 251–2.

3. For analyses of the Jephthah story see Jonathan Kirsch, *The Harlot by the Side of the Road: Forbidden Tales of the Bible* (New York: Ballantine Books, 1997), chs. 10–11; and Barry Webb, "The Theme of the Jephthah Story," *Reformed Theological Review* 45 (1986): 34–43.

4. Judges 10:6–12:7. Apparently Underhill was unconcerned about the tragedic elements of the Jephthah story—namely, that Jephthah's daughter, whose name was never given in the text, ended up being sacrificed as a consequence of an unnecessary vow Jephthah made to assure his victory. In addition, Jephthah's judgeship over Gilead was unsuccessful, for he plunged his people into war with their fellow Israelites, the Ephraimites. See J. Cheryl Exum, "The Tragic Vision and Biblical Narrative: The Case of Jephthah," in *Signs and Wonders: Biblical Texts in Literary Focus*, ed. J. Cheryl Exum, Society of Biblical Literature Semeia Studies (Atlanta, Ga.: Scholars Press, 1989), 59–83.

5. On the parallels made between the deformed "monsters" to which Anne Hutchinson and Mary Dyer gave birth and their illicit religious opinions, see Anne J. Shutte, " 'Such Monstrous Births': A Neglected Aspect of the Antinomian Controversy," *Renaissance Quarterly* 38 (1985): 85–106; and Valerie Pearl and Morris Pearl, eds., "Governor John Winthrop on the Birth of the Antinomians' 'Monster': The Earliest Reports to Reach England and the Making of a Myth," *Massachusetts Historical Society Proceedings* 52 (1990): 21–37.

6. I examine these factional splits more closely in chapter 3.

7. MBR, IV:1:186.

8. Henry C. Shelley, *John Underhill: Captain of New England and New Netherland* (New York: Appleton, 1932), 360–4.

9. Pulsifer, *Acts of the Commissioners*, X:52.

10. See, for example, Marilyn J. Westerkamp, "Anne Hutchinson, Sectarian Mysticism, and the Puritan Order," *Church History* 59: 4 (December 1990): 482–96; and "Puritan Patriarchy and the Problem of Revelation," *Journal of Interdisciplinary History* 23: 3 (1992–93): 571–95. However, Richard Godbeer, "Love Raptures: Marital, Romantic, and Erotic Images of Jesus Christ in Puritan New England, 1670–1739," *NEQ* 68: 3 (September 1995): 355–84, has argued convincingly that seventeenth-century men would not be put off by playing the "feminine" role in hierarchical relationships, for this was a common conceptual tool. The marriage to Christ, moreover, was of a spiritual nature, and Puritans would not have understood one gender to have been better qualified to play the spouse than the other.

11. John Winthrop, "A Short Story of the Rise, Reign, and Ruine of the Antinomians, Familists, and Libertines," in *AC*, 265.

12. Ibid., 275.

13. Underhill's exclusion from the ranks of "public" men was brought home at his disfranchisement: "Againe, in our cause, the Captain was but a private man, and had no calling to deale in the affaires of the Court, therefore no warrant from hence. Hee insisted much upon the liberty which all States do allow to Military Officers, for free speech, etc., and that himself had spoken sometimes as freely to Count Nassaw." Ibid., 277. On Hutchinson's offense in adopting the "rhetorical pose of an aggressive male in a culture that valued the submissive female" see Michael G. Ditmore, "A Prophetess in Her Own Country: An Exegesis of Anne Hutchinson's 'Immediate Revelation,' " *WMQ* 57:2 (April 2000): 349–88, especially 375.

14. Susan D. Amussen, " 'The Part of a Christian Man': The Cultural Politics of Manhood in Early Modern England," in *Political Culture and Cultural Politics in Early Modern England: Essays Presented to David Underdown*, ed. Susan D. Amussen and Mark Kishlansky (Manchester, England: Manchester University Press, 1995), 214, argues that in early modern England "Not all men were independent, nor were all equally independent; therefore there were different ways of asserting independence, of acting 'as a man.' "

15. Winthrop, "Short Story," in *AC*, 277.

16. On the proto-"democratic" tendencies of New England church government see James F. Cooper, "Higher Law, Free Consent, Limited Authority: Church Government and Political Culture in Seventeenth-Century Massachusetts," *NEQ* 69: 2 (June 1996): 201–22 ; and *Tenacious of their Liberties: the Congregationalists in Colonial Massachusetts* (New York: Oxford University Press, 1999). On the importance of "consensus" in all public affairs see T. H. Breen, *The Character of the Good Ruler: A Study of Puritan Political Ideas in New England, 1630–1730* (New Haven: Yale University Press, 1970).

17. Anne Kibbey, *The Interpretation of Material Shapes in Puritanism: A Study of Rhetoric, Prejudice, and Violence* (New York: Cambridge University Press, 1986) suggests that violence against the Indians during the Pequot War was enhanced by the soldiers' hostility toward the upstart women of Boston who had embraced antinomian principles and who were somehow equated in the mens' minds with the Indians. But given Underhill's affiliation with the antinomians, his central role in the war effort, and his use of antinomian principles to enhance his fighting ability, this interpretation seems highly dubious. On the importance of consensus in all public affairs see Breen, *Character of the Good Ruler*.

18. On Underhill's role in the Pequot War see Alfred A. Cave, *The Pequot War* (Amherst: University of Massachusetts Press, 1996).

19. On this point see Mary Beth Norton, *Founding Mothers and Fathers: Gendered Power and the Forming of American Society* (New York: Knopf, 1996); and Breen, *Character of the Good Ruler*.

20. Michael Zuckerman, "The Social Context of Democracy in Massachusetts," in *Almost Chosen People: Oblique Biographies in the American Grain* (Berkeley: University of California Press, 1993), 55–76, argues that New England "towns could no more condone a competing minority by their norms and values than they could have constrained it by their police power. Neither conflict, dissent, nor any other structured pluralism ever obtained legitimacy in the towns of the Bay before the Revolution" (59). Regardless of social status, people were expected to abide by consensus once a decision was made.

21. In the eighteenth-century "Real Whig" tradition, the seeking of minis-

terial preferments and "luxury" were branded as feminine. See Bernard Bailyn, *The Ideological Origins of the American Revolution* (Cambridge, Mass.: Belknap, 1967).

22. Some scholars have argued that the Jephthah story had embedded within it a strong patriarchal bias. Interpreters who have examined the biblical account from a feminist perspective have commented on the expendability of female virgins in Judges and the thoughtlessness of male protagonists like Jephthah, who made the vow even though the spirit was already upon him and the victory was assured. On this point see especially Cynthia Baker, "Pseudo-Philo and the Transformation of Jephthah's Daughter," in *Anti-Covenant: Counter-Reading Women's Lives in the Hebrew Bible*, ed. Mieke Bal (Sheffield, England: Almond Press, 1989), 195–209; Esther Fuchs, "Marginalization, Ambiguity, Silencing: The Story of Jephthah's Daughter," in *A Feminist Companion to Judges*, ed. Athalya Brenner (Sheffield, England: Sheffield Academic Press, 1993), 116–30; and J. Cheryl Exum, "On Judges 11," in the same volume, 131–44. On the other hand, scholars have also suggested that the fault may not have been Jephthah's, for he made the vow while under direct spiritual influence—an eventuality that raises uncomfortable questions about the differences between divine and human senses of righteousness. See Kirsch, *Harlot*, chs. 10 and 11. The emphasis on the disparity between the human and the divine may have been precisely what attracted Underhill to the story.

23. Laurence M. Hauptman, "John Underhill: A Psychological Portrait of an Indian Fighter, 1597–1672," *Hudson Valley Regional Review* 9 (1992): 101–11.

24. On Vane see J. H. Adamson and H. F. Folland, *Sir Harry Vane: Life and Times* (Boston: Gambit, 1973).

25. For the Underhill genealogy see Shelley, *Underhill*, 1–106; and L. Effingham DeForest and Anne C. DeForest, *Captain John Underhill, Gentleman-Soldier of Fortune*, in *Bulletin of the Underhill Society of America* (1934; reprint, New York: Underhill Society of America Education and Publishing Fund, 1985).

26. This episode was disastrous, as Leicester alienated the queen in 1586 by accepting the position of Supreme Governor of the United Provinces. Alan Kendall, *Robert Dudley: Earl of Leicester* (London: Cassell, 1980), 204–27.

27. For the circumstances of the birth see Kendall, *Dudley*, 130–51.

28. On this voyage see George F. Warner, ed., *The Voyage of Robert Dudley, Afterwards Styled Earl of Warwick and Leicester and Duke of Northumberland, to the West Indies, 1594–1595, Narrated by Capt. Wyatt, By Himself, and By Abram Kendall, Master* (1899; reprint, Nendeln/Liechtenstein: Kraus Reprint, 1991). On Raleigh see Stephen Greenblatt, *Sir Walter Raleigh: The Renaissance Man and His Roles* (New Haven: Yale University Press, 1973).

29. Dudley's life is treated by George F. Warner, preface to *Voyage*. While in Florence Dudley published navigational treatises and waged a long and ultimately unsuccessful campaign to return to England and regain his holdings and honor.

30. Winthrop, *Journal*, I:63, 69, 91–2; and Robert Wall, *The Membership of the Massachusetts Bay General Court, 1630–1686* (New York: Garland, 1990), 543–5.

31. John Underhill to John Winthrop, 1636/37, MHSC, 4th ser., vol. 7 (Boston, 1865), 173–4. For the militia law that placed the regiments under the control of John Winthrop, Thomas Dudley, John Haynes, and John Endecott see MBR, I: 186–7. Francis Markham, *Five Decades of Epistles of Warre* (London, 1622), 121–2, mentions that some soldiers saw muster-masters as "pen-men" rather than "sword-men."

32. John Underhill to John Winthrop, 1636/37, 174.

33. On the adoption of a citizen militia see T. H. Breen, "The Covenanted Militia of Massachusetts Bay: English Background and New World Development," in *Puritans and Adventurers: Change and Persistence in Early America* (New York: Oxford University Press, 1980), 24–45.

34. Petition of John Underhill to the Governor and Assistants of Massachusetts, 1637, *MHSC*, 4th ser., vol 7 (Boston, 1865), 175.

35. Underhill was not the only one to complain about these conditions. See Winthrop, *Journal*, I:78, for a description of a 1632 dispute in Watertown between the constable, John Clark, and Daniel Patrick, a hired military expert like Underhill, over who should have control over the town watch.

36. Petition of John Underhill to the Governor and Assistants of Massachusetts, 1637, 175–6.

37. Underhill to Winthrop, 1636/37, 174; and Winthrop, "Short Story," in *AC*, 276–7.

38. Norton, *Founding Mothers and Fathers*, has argued that New Englanders followed a "Filmerian" system in which the analogy between family and governmental control was particularly strong.

39. David Leverenz, *The Language of Puritan Feeling: An Exploration in Literature, Psychology and Social History* (New Brunswick, N.J.: Rutgers University Press, 1980), 9.

40. Winthrop, *Journal*, I:77–8, 84–9.

41. Breen, *Character of the Good Ruler*, 61, shows that "their feud [Winthrop and Dudley] represented a rift within the discretionary ranks and not a division between discretion and delegation." See also Edmund Morgan, *The Puritan Dilemma: The Story of John Winthrop* (Boston: Little, Brown, 1958), 104–7.

42. Winthrop, *Journal*, I:77.

43. Ibid., I:169–72. Norton, *Founding Mothers and Fathers*, 218–20, shows how this episode "led to the adoption of a formal policy (by concurrence among the assistants and the clergy) outlining procedures for minimizing conflict within the ranks of the colony's rulers" (p. 218).

44. Winthrop, *Journal*, I:77.

45. Israel Stoughton to John Stoughton, 1635, in *Letters from New England: The Massachusetts Bay Colony, 1629–1638*, ed. Everett Emerson (Amherst: University of Massachusetts Press, 1976), 151.

46. A Defence of an Order of Court made in the Year 1637 in *Hutchinson Papers*, 2 vols. (Albany, N.Y.: Publications of the Prince Society, 1865), I: 81.

47. "A Brief Answer to a Certain Declaration Made to the Intent and Equitye of the Order of the Court that None should be Received to Inhabit," in *ibid.*, 84, 88. See Gura, *Glimpse of Sion's Glory*, 187–8.

48. "A Brief Answer," 90, 96, 88.

49. Emery Battis, *Saints and Sectaries: Anne Hutchinson and the Antinomian Controversy in the Massachusetts Bay Colony* (Chapel Hill: University of North Carolina Press, 1962), 232. See also Wall, *Membership of the General Court*, 368–9.

50. *MBR*, I:132.

51. Winthrop, *Journal*, II:178–9.

52. On the petition see Battis, *Saints and Sectaries*, 150–1. For an account of how Cotton tried to persuade Wheelwright to make his peace with "orthodoxy," as Cotton himself had, see Sargent Bush, "Revising What We Have Done Amisse': John Cotton and John Wheelright, 1640," *WMQ* 45: 4 (October 1988): 733–50.

On Wheelwright's life see Charles Henry Bell, *Memoirs of John Wheelwright* (Cambridge, Mass.: J. Wilson, 1876).

53. John Wheelwright, "A Fast-Day Sermon," in *AC*, 165–6.

54. John Underhill, *Newes From America: Or, a New and Experimentall Discoverie of New England* (1638), *MHSC*, 3rd ser.,vol. 6 (Boston, 1837): 19–21.

55. For an analysis of English ideas on honor, see Mervyn James, "English Politics and the Concept of Honor, 1485–1642," in *Society, Politics and Culture: Studies in Early Modern England* (New York: Cambridge University Press, 1986), 308–415.

56. Francis Bacon, *Considerations Touching a Warre with Spaine* (London, 1629), 2.

57. Gervase Markham, *Honour in His Perfection: or, a Treatise in Commendations of the Vertues and Renowned Vertuous Undertakings of the Illustrious and Horoyicall Princes* (London, 1624), 5.

58. *A Discourse Made at Large of the Late Overthrowe given to the King of Spaines Army at Turnhaut* (London, 1597), n.p.

59. Francis Markham, *The Booke of Honour, or, Five Decades of Epistles of Honour* (London, 1625), 33; and *Five Decades of Epistles of Warre.*

60. Underhill to Winthrop, 1636–7, 171–2; and Wheelwright, "Fast-Day Sermon," in *AC*, 163.

61. On the importance in the English Protestant tradition of God's direct intervention in the wars of his people, see David Cressy, *Bonfires and Bells: National Memory and the Protestant Calendar in Elizabethan and Stuart England* (London: Weidenfeld and Nicolson, 1989).

62. Markham, *Honour in his Perfection*, 5; and Markham, *Five Decades of Epistles of Warre*, 10.

63. *The Navall Expedition of the Right Honourable Robert, Earle of Warwick (Lord High Admiral of England) against the revolted ships* (London, 1648), 11.

64. Markham, *Five Decades of Epistles of Warre*, 10–2.

65. James, "English Politics and the Concept of Honour," 406.

66. Peter's tract, published in Rotterdam in 1631 and entitled *Digitus Dei* (Finger of God), is discussed in Raymond Phineas Stearns, *The Strenuous Puritan: Hugh Peter, 1598–1660* (Urbana: University of Illinois, 1954), 61–3.

67. Pulsifer, *Acts of the Commissioners*, X:52.

68. Winthrop, *Journal*, I:220.

69. Ibid., 240–1.

70. Karen O. Kupperman, *Providence Island, 1630–1641: The Other Puritan Colony* (New York: Cambridge University Press, 1993), 212–3, shows that the Providence Island Company offered Underhill a yearly stipend amounting to more than three times as much as the salary he received in Massachusetts.

71. Petition of John Underhill to the General Court of Massachusetts, *MHSC*, 4th ser., vol 7 (Boston, 1865), ca. September 1638, 177.

72. Winthrop, *Journal*, I:275–77. That Underhill used his antinomian principles for purposes of seduction is revealed in Jane Holmes's confession of faith in George Selement and Bruce C. Woolley, eds., *Thomas Shepard's Confessions* (Boston: Colonial Society of Massachusetts, 1981), 76–80.

73. Oliver Ayer Roberts, *History of the Military Company of the Massachusetts Now Called the Ancient and Honourable Artillery Company of Massachusetts, 1637–1888*, 4 vols. (Boston: A. Mudge, 1895–1909), I:7, 12.

74. Underhill, *Newes From America*, 21–2.

75. Ibid., 19, 15–6. Stone was one of the organizers of the antinomian synod (Battis, *Saints and Sectaries*, 162).

76. On this point see Peter N. Carroll, *Puritanism and the Wilderness: The Intellectual Significance of the New England Frontier, 1629–1700* (New York: Columbia University Press, 1969).

77. Thomas Hooker to John Winthrop, December 1638, *Winthrop Papers, 1498–1654*, ed. Allyn B. Forbes et al., 6 vols. to date (Boston: Massachusetts Historical Society, 1929–) IV: 75–84.

78. Copy of a letter from Captain Israel Stoughton to the Governor of the Massachusetts, 1637, *Hutchinson Papers*, I:69–70.

79. Winthrop, *Journal*, I:275–6.

80. Ibid., 276.

81. Ibid., 276.

82. Ibid., 276–7.

83. On Underhill's activities in Dover, see John Scales, *History of Dover, New Hampshire* (Manchester, N.H.: Printed by authority of the City Council, 1923); George Wadleigh, *Notable Events in the History of Dover, New Hampshire* (Dover, N.H.: Tufts College Press, 1913); Jere R. Daniell, *Colonial New Hampshire: A History* (Millwood, N.Y.: KTO Press, 1981); and David E. Van Deventer, *The Emergence of Provincial New Hampshire 1623–1741* (Baltimore: Johns Hopkins University Press, 1976).

84. For accusations against Underhill see Richard B. Pierce, ed., *Records of the First Church in Boston* (Boston: Colonial Society of Massachusetts, 1961), 18, 31, 35.

85. Winthrop, *Journal*, I:280–1, 295–6.

86. Ibid., I:279–80. On Wiggin and Hilton, and for a detailed account of the patents in New Hampshire and Maine held by Ferdinando Gorges and John Mason, as well as events at Dover, see Charles E. Clark, *The Eastern Frontier: The Settlement of Northern New England, 1610–1763* (New York: Knopf, 1970), 8, 16–20, 39–49, 52–3.

87. George Burdett had settled originally at Salem; but disliking the church discipline there, he removed to Dover, where, prior to Underhill's arrival, he had managed to oust Wiggin as governor. Winthrop complained that he provided sanctuary for Bay Colony miscreants and fulminated over his having engaged in correspondence critical of the Bay Colony with Archbishop Laud. Underhill managed to gain power as governor after Burdett fled to Agamenticus, having been found guilty of adultery. On Burdett see Stearns, *Strenuous Puritan*, 144; and Clark, *Eastern Frontier*, 40.

88. Winthrop, *Journal*, I:285, 295–6.

89. John Underhill to the Governor and Deputy Governor of Massachusetts, *MHSC*, 4th ser., vol. 7 (Boston, 1865), 178–9.

90. Winthrop, *Journal*, I:309.

91. John Underhill to John Winthrop, 22 January 1639–40, *MHSC*, 4th ser., vol. 7 (Boston, 1865), 179–80.

92. Winthrop, *Journal*, I:328. Knollys, although he eventually emerged as an Anabaptist in England, was perceived as an antinomian in Massachusetts and therefore had been "denied residence." His preaching efforts in New Hampshire were met with resistance by George Burdett; but Underhill readily allied with him after Burdett's departure. For the religious views of this Underhill ally see Hanserd Knollys, *A Glimpse of Syons Glory, or the Churches Beautie Specified, Published for the*

good and Benefits of All Those whose Hearts are Raised up in the Expectation of the Glorious Liberties of the Saints (London, 1651).

93. Winthrop, *Journal*, I:329–30. The record of Underhill's excommunication and reconciliation with the Boston church appears in Pierce, *Records of the First Church in Boston*, 18, 31, 35.

94. Winthrop, *Journal*, I:329–30.

95. Ibid.

96. John Underhill to John Winthrop, 20 April 1640, *MHSC*, 4th ser., vol. 7 (Boston, 1865), 180–1.

97. Winthrop, *Journal*, II:27–8.

98. Winthrop, *Journal*, II:12–4. On these events see Stearns, *Strenuous Puritan*, 144–8.

99. For the formulation that Underhill's radical religiosity was a ploy see Battis, *Saints and Sectaries*. Yet like many former antinomians Underhill continued to gravitate toward religious heresy long after he departed New England: in the 1660s he was attracted to Quaker depictions of adversity and itinerancy. He read and remarked favorably on Humphrey Norton, *New England's Ensigne: It Being the Account of Cruelty, the Professor's Pride, and the Articles of their Faith* (London, 1659). The journal of Underhill's brother-in-law John Bowne, a persecuted Quaker in New Netherland, similarly emphasizes these themes. See Herbert Ricard, ed., *Journal of John Bowne, 1650–1694* (New Orleans: Friends of the Queensborough Community College Library and Polyanthos, 1975).

100. Underhill, *Newes From America*, 21.

101. Winthrop, *Journal*, II:12–4. Underhill's confession is analyzed in David D. Hall, "The Uses of Ritual," in *Worlds of Wonder, Days of Judgment: Popular Religious Belief in Early New England* (Cambridge: Harvard University Press, 1990), 172–4.

102. Winthrop, *Journal*, II:12–4.

103. Ibid. Interestingly, Amussen, " 'Part of a Christian Man,' " 213–33, argues that sexual bravado was not a key criterion of masculinity in early modern England.

104. According to Winthrop the Court specified that Underhill would not be subject to the death penalty for the adultery, since the law stipulating that punishment had been passed after to his commission of the act. See *Journal*, II:12–4.

105. Ibid., II:28.

106. For a detailed account of Hugh Peter's efforts at negotiation in Dover see Stearns, *Strenuous Puritan*, 144–8.

107. Winthrop, *Journal*, II:57, 95, 154, 161.

108. Ibid, II:28; Hall, *Worlds of Wonder*, 80, discusses how "disorders of the moral order were [thought to be] mirrored in the physical disorder of monster births."

109. Winthrop, *Journal*, II:41–2.

110. Hall, *Worlds of Wonder*, 72, has discussed the popular belief that "supernatural forces intervened to indicate the guilty. The earth could open up and swallow persons who told lies." For an analysis of why Anne Hutchinson "confessed" that she had experienced direct revelations even though she knew the probable consequences of such an admission, see Ann Fairfax Withington and Jack Schwartz, "The Political Trial of Anne Hutchinson," *NEQ* 51: 2 (June 1978): 226–40. These authors suggest that despite Hutchinson's conviction that actions in the world held no spiritual importance, she ultimately decided that it was morally right to voice

her true opinions and thereby give witness to the truth of God. But by making this decision, Hutchinson allowed the trial to play the role that her persecutors intended. "By rejecting the legal process and deciding to defy the state in her own religious terms rather than in the legal terms of the governors, Hutchinson allowed the trial to fulfill its fuction as a cleansing ritual" (238).

111. Hall, "Uses of Ritual," 172–4. Jane Kamensky, "Talk Like a Man: Speech, Power and Masculinity in Early New England," *Gender and History* 8: 1 (April 1996): 22–47, has described how men guilty of the crime of "slighting" the reputation of others were required ritually to "eat" their words.

112. Hugh Peter to John Winthrop, 6 September 1640, *MHSC*, 4th ser., vol. 6 (Boston, 1863), 103–4. On Peter's interactions with Knollys and Underhill see Stearns, *Strenuous Puritan*, 144–6, 148. Peter advised the Court that Knollys "may be useful without doubt, hee is well gifted, you may do well to heare him at Boston" (quoted at 147).

113. Robert Brenner, *Merchants and Revolution: Commercial Change, Political Conflict, and London's Overseas Traders, 1550–1653* (Princeton, N.J.: Princeton University Press, 1993), 263–5, 499–508, 405–7.

114. On these gentlemen's purchase of Dover, for which they were unable to provide religious and civic leadership see Clark, *Eastern Frontier*, 39–40.

115. Janice Knight, *Orthodoxies in Massachusetts: Rereading American Puritanism* (Cambridge: Harvard University Press, 1994), 23, points out Vane's attempts to reach out to Peter yet places Peter irrevocably in Winthrop's camp, ignoring the later part of his political and religious career.

116. Peter quoted in Brenner, *Merchants and Revolution*, 508.

117. Ibid., 518.

118. Stearns, *Strenuous Puritan*, 126–8. For a full treatment of the implications for church government of Brother Weston's bold challenge to Peter's authority, see Cooper, "Higher Law, Free Consent, Limited Authority," especially 215.

119. "A Report of the Trial of Mrs. Anne Hutchinson before the Church," in AC, 331, 382–3.

120. Hugh Peter, *Mr Peters Last Report of the English Wars* (London, 1646), 9.

121. On Winthrop, Jr., see Robert C. Black, *The Younger John Winthrop* (New York: Columbia University Press, 1966).

122. For Underhill's letters to Winthrop, Jr., see *MHSC*, 4th ser., vol. 7 (Boston, 1865), 182–94. Rebecca Tannenbaum, " 'What Is Best to Be Done for These Fevers': Elizabeth Davenport's Medical Practice in New Haven," *NEQ* 70: 2 (June 1997): 265–84, has shown that Winthrop asserted his authority by dispensing powerful purgative drugs, sometimes through the agency of elite women like Elizabeth Davenport (the wife of John Davenport)—a practice that allowed him to be a great expert on healing without himself having to attend the sick. While Underhill was certainly interested in getting aid for his wife during her illness, he also probably understood how Winthrop extended his patronage through his medical practice.

123. On this marriage see De Forest and DeForest, *Underhill*, 76; and Shelley, *Underhill*, 395–6. On Henry Winthrop see Edmund S. Morgan, *The Puritan Dilemma: The Story of John Winthrop* (Boston: Little, Brown, 1958), 35–7, 58.

124. Meredith Baldwin Weddle, "Conscience or Compromise: The Meaning of the Peace Testimony in Early New England," *Quaker History* 81: 2 (fall 1992): 73–86, has discussed the varied compliance of Quakers with the peace testimony,

showing that it was not out of the ordinary for some in Rhode Island to accept military roles and positions of authority.

125. Geoffrey Nuttall, *The Holy Spirit in Puritan Faith and Experience* (Chicago: University of Chicago Press, 1946), argues that Quakerism was essentially an exaggerated form of Puritanism, where the role of the spirit was enlarged ever further than it was in Puritan doctrine. Other scholars, such as Carla Gardina Pestana, *Quakers and Baptists in Colonial Massachusetts* (New York: Cambridge University Press, 1991), have argued that Quakers' abjuration of *sola scriptura* and their acceptance of the "inner light" rendered them anti-Puritan in doctrine. Underhill and other lay Puritans who turned Quaker, however, especially the Hutchinsonians, did not see themselves as cutting themselves off from the Puritan tradition but instead as improving it. In a strictly theological sense, there was a pronounced ideological difference between Puritans and Quakers; in the experience of individuals who were not well schooled in theology and who were attracted to Quakerism, the transition did not seem so stark.

126. Underhill to John Winthrop, Jr., March 21, 1660, MHSC, 4th ser., vol. 7 (Boston, 1865), 186–7.

127. See Carla Gardina Pestana, "The Quaker Executions as Myth and History," *Journal of American History* 80: 2 (1993): 441–69.

128. Norton, *New England's Ensigne*.

129. Underhill to Winthrop, Jr., March 21, 1660, 186–7.

130. Ibid.

131. Breen, "Covenanted Militia," 33, argues that "Daniel Patrick and John Underhill, both fresh from campaigns in the Netherlands, lasted longer in the Bay Colony than did any of the other Company appointees, but neither man was a Puritan." But John Underhill's church membership, his understanding (both doctrinal and social) of how he should go about trying to repair the breech with Massachusetts authorities, and his ongoing attempts into the 1650s to impress Bay Colony authorities with his usefulness, all suggest that he identified himself as a Puritan. Underhill's failure to fit into the Bay Colony's definition of orthodoxy did not, I would argue, render him a non-Puritan.

132. MBR, III:236; IV:1, 56.

133. Technically, a sergeant major could have one thousand men under his command for training and a captain anywhere from sixty-four to one hundred men. But in actual wartime conditions, where honor was earned, neither of these officers would have had occasion to lead groups of soldiers whose total numbers approached those of entire companies or regiments; soldiers were requisitioned from the various towns in piecemeal fashion and did not go into combat with the units with which they trained. In addition to this, the Court limited the numbers of soldiers allowed to serve in any given troop or company; militias were required to divide in two once their numbers reached two hundred, and horse troops were capped off at seventy. There were also minimum numbers to which companies or troops were required to attain before they could elect their highest officers (captain, lieutenant, ensign). Companies and troops falling below the minimum could select only sergeants and corporals. These regulations against large and unwieldy regiments were designed to prevent status conscious men from taking on multiple commands whose responsibilities they could not realistically fulfill (MBR, IV.1:86–8, 257–56; III: 265).

134. Underhill, *Newes From America*, 4.

135. *MBR*, IV:1:106.

136. Markham, *Five* Decades of *Epistles of Warre*, 138, 141. This mindset posed a problem for a New England polity bent upon keeping its military under strict control; captains of horse troops might refuse to show due deference to regimental sergeant majors. Accordingly, the Court solemnly advised horse troop officers that they must observe due subordination to their sergeant majors and must not take it upon themselves to undertake privileges not granted even to their sergeant-major superiors, such as training beyond county limits; "no troop shalbe drawne out of the countyes by the . . . officers thereof upon nay occasion or pretence whatsoever, not for exercise only, or at the regimentall meetings, but by order from the major generall and by his command." On horse troops see *MBR* IV:1:58, 155, 183; III: 127–8, 397–8.

137. *MBR*, III:285, 291, 296, 299. On Leverett's life see Charles E. Leverett, *A Memoir, Biographical and Genealogical, Of Sir John Leverett, Knt, Governor of Massachusetts . . .* (Boston: Crosby, Nichols, 1856).

138. *MBR*, III:286; IV:1:107, 341. The animosity toward Gerrish in Newbury was related to a controversy within the church; the General Court eventually had to send arbitrators to deal with the disruptive situation. See Joshua Coffin, *A Sketch of the History of Newbury, Newburyport, and West Newbury from 1635 to 1845* (Boston, 1845); and Wall, *Membership of the General Court*, 300–3. It would stand to reason, however, that the residents would couch their reservations about Gerrish's dual command in terms conformable with contemporary views on appropriate military service.

139. On Aspinwall's career see Joseph B. Felt, *The Ecclesiastical History of New England Comprising Not Only Religion but also Moral and Other Relations*, 2 vols. (Boston: Congregational Library Association, 1855–62), I:462, 466; John T. Hassam, "Early Recorders and Registrars of Deeds for the County of Suffolk, Massachusetts, 1639–1735," *Massachusetts Historical Society Proceedings*, ser. 2, vol. 12 (Boston, 1898): 203–49; James F. Maclear, "New England and the Fifth Monarchy: The Quest for the Millennium in Early American Puritanism," *WMQ* 32:2 (April 1975): 223–60; and B. S. Capp, *The Fifth Monarchy Men: A Study in Seventeenth-Century Millennarianism* (London: Faber and Faber, 1972), 56–65. Aspinwall's later writings include *A Brief Description of the Fifth Monarch that Shortly is to Come into the World* (London, 1653).

140. On Hutchinson see "Three County Troop of Horse," *New England Historical and Genealogical Register* 24 (April 1871): 138–40; *MBR*, IV:1, 369; IV: 2:82. Interestingly, Hutchinson ended up a creditor of the Winthrop estate, see *Aspinwall Notarial Records, 1644–51*, in *Records Relating to the Early History of Boston*, 39 vols. (Boston: Registry Department, 1876–1909), XXXII:277–8. For Edward Hutchinson's investment activities in Wickford, Rhode Island, see Eben Putnam, *Lieutenant Joshua Hewes: A New England Pioneer and Some of his Descendants* (Boston: J. F. Tapley, 1913), 78–84. On the Catherine Scott episode see Felt, *Ecclesiastical History*, II: 205, 253; and Stephen F. Peckham, "Richard Scott and His Wife Catherine Marbury," in *Genealogies of Rhode Island Families: From the New England Historical and Genealogical Register*, ed. Gary Boyd Roberts 2 vols. (Baltimore: Genealogical, 1989), II: 147–55. George Bishop, in denoucing the punishment of Catherine Scott, reminded Bay colonists of her exalted station in life: "some of you knew her Father, and called him Mr. Marbery, and that she had been well-bred."

141. These differences have been limned out in chapter 1; see also William K. B. Stoever, "*A Faire and Easie Way to Heaven: Covenant Theology and Antino-*

mianism in Early Massachusetts (Middletown, Conn.: Wesleyan University Press, 1978), and James F. Maclear, "The Heart of New England Rent: The Mystical Element in Early Puritan History," Mississippi Valley Historical Review 42 (1956): 621–52. For a description of Artillery Election Day protocol and pageantry see Zechariah Whitman, An Historical Sketch of the Ancient and Honorable Artillery Company: From its Formation in the Year 1637 to the Present Time (Boston, 1820), 113–21. On military preaching see Marie Ahearn, The Rhetoric of War: Training Day, the Militia and the Military Sermon (New York: Greenwood Press, 1989).

142. Urian Oakes, The Unconquerable, All-Conquering, and More than Conquering Soldier . . . Preached 1672 (Cambridge, Mass., 1674), 4; Joshua Moodey, Souldiery Spiritualized (Cambridge, Mass., 1674), 11, 17.

143. [Edward] Johnson's Wonder-Working Providence, 1628–1650 (1654), ed J. Franklin Jameson (New York: Scribner's, 1910), 150, 151, 155, 233. On the cross-fertilization of "orthodox" and "radical" ideas in the language of "declension" see Sacvan Bercovitch, The American Jeremiad (Madison: University of Wisconsin Press, 1978); and The Puritan Origins of the American Self (New Haven: Yale University Press, 1975).

144. Samuel Willard, The Righteous Man's Death a Presage of Evil Approaching: A Sermon Occasioned by the Death of Major Thomas Savage, Esq. (Boston, 1682), 147, 150; and A Sermon . . . Occasioned by the Death of the Much Honored John Leverett, Esq., Governor of the Colony of the Massachusetts, N.E. (Boston, 1679), 5; and William Hubbard, The Benefit of a Well-Ordered Conversation, as it was Delivered in a Sermon . . . Occasioned by the Death of the Worshipfull Major General Dennison (Boston, 1684).

CHAPTER 3

1. Gervase Markham, Honour in his Perfection; or, a Treatise in Commendations of the Vertues and Renowned Vertuous Undertakings of the Illustrious and Heroyicall Princes (London, 1624), 38. For an analysis of the validity of viewing England's pre-civil war years as a "halcyon" period of romance and chivalry see Barbara Donagan, "Halcyon Days and the Literature of War: England's Military Education before 1642," Past and Present 147 (May 1995): 65–100.

2. Lord Saye and Sele to John Winthrop, 9 July 1640, MHSC, 5th ser., vol 1 (Boston, 1871), 297–303.

3. See Robert Brenner, Merchants and Revolution: Commercial Change, Political Conflict and London's Overseas Traders, 1550–1653 (Princeton, N.J.: Princeton University Press, 1993); and Karen Ordahl Kupperman, Providence Island, 1630–1641: The Other Puritan Colony (New York: Cambridge University Press, 1993).

4. On this point see Karen O. Kupperman, "Errand to the Indies: Puritan Colonization from Providence Island through the Western Design," WMQ 45: 1 (January 1988): 70–99.

5. On the importance of the religiously defined community see Michael Zuckerman, "Identity in British America: Unease in Eden," in Nicholas Canny and Anthony Pagden, Colonial Identity in the Atlantic World, 1500–1800 (Princeton, N.J.: Princeton University Press, 1987), 115–57. On Vane's life see J. H. Adamson and H. F. Folland, Sir Harry Vane: His Life and Times (Boston: Gambit, 1973).

6. Nathaniel Turner's activities as land agent for New Haven are discussed in E. B. Huntington, History of Stamford, Connecticut, 1641–1868 (1868; reprint, New York: Harbor Hill Books, 1979), 15. See also Edward R. Lambert, History of the

Colony of New Haven Before and after the Union with Connecticut (1868; reprint, Milford, Conn.: Rotary Club, 1976), 51.

On the roles played by Howe and Turner in Lynn, see Alonzo Lewis and James R. Newhall, *History of Lynn* (Boston, 1865), 124, 128, 129, 135, 140, 143, 146–7, 167–9, 171, 177–8, 192–3. Howe was also a founder of Easthampton and involved himself in business ventures in several colonies; see James Trunslow Adams, *History of the Town of Southampton* (New York: J. S. Friedman, 1962). On Howe's offer to pay Wheelwright's charges see Joseph B. Felt, *The Ecclesiastical History of New England Comprising Not Only Religion but also Moral and Other Relations*, 2 vols. (Boston: Congregational Library Association, 1855–62), I:322.

7. Winthrop, *Journal*, II: 82, 83–4.

8. Ibid., II: 57–8. On Underhill's brief stay in Stamford see Huntington, *History of Stamford*; L. Effingham DeForest and Anne C. DeForest, *Captain John Underhill, Gentleman-Soldier of Fortune*, in *Bulletin of the Underhill Society of America* (1934; reprint, New York: Underhill Society of America Education and Publishing Fund, 1985); and Henry C. Shelley, *John Underhill: Captain of New England and New Netherland* (New York: Appleton, 1932).

9. Winthrop, *Journal*, II: 4–5.

10. Winthrop, *Journal*, II: 35.

11. On Moody's life see Linda Biemer, "Lady Deborah Moody and the Founding of Gravesend," *Journal of Long Island History* 17: 2 (1981): 24–42.

12. Winthrop, *Journal*, II: 138.

13. Winthrop's own son, Samuel, had become a Quaker in the West Indies. See Larry D. Gragg, "A Puritan in the West Indies: The Career of Samuel Winthrop," *WMQ* 50: 4 (October 1993), 768–86.

14. Winthrop, *Journal*, I: 79, 100–1, 127–8. For a complete account of Humphrey's career see Frances Rose-Troup, "John Humfrey," *Essex Institute Historical Collections* 65 (1929): 293–308.

15. John Cotton to Lord Say and Sele, 1636, in *Letters from New England: The Massachusetts Bay Colony, 1629–1638*, ed. Everett Emerson (Amherst: University of Massachusetts Press, 1976), 190–94, quotation on 192. Oliver Ayer Roberts, *History of the Military Company of the Massachusetts Now Called the Ancient and Honourable Artillery Company of Massachusetts, 1637–1888*, 4 vols. (Boston: A. Mudge, 1895–1909), suggests that Humphrey's wife may have been dissatisfied with the "privations of the wilderness" and being "so far from the elegant circles in which she had delighted." Arthur P. Newton, *The Colonizing Activities of the English Puritans: The Last Phase of the Elizabethan Struggle with Spain* (New Haven: Yale University Press, 1914), 286, writes that Humphrey "had always stood to a certain extent aloof from the rest of the ruling group." For Humphrey's activities in Lynn see Lewis and Newhall, *Lynn*, 56, 147, 149, 152, 164–5, 168, 169.

16. Quoted in Felt, *Ecclesiastical History*, I:443.

17. On the interest of Venner and Lechford in the project see Kupperman, *Providence Island*, 323. See also James F. Maclear, "New England and the Fifth Monarchy: The Quest for the Millennium in Early American Puritanism," *WMQ* 32: 2 (April 1975): 223–60. Interestingly, Humphrey was criticized in Winthrop, *Journal*, II: 69–70, for publishing in London an unauthorized "book of Mr. Cotton's sermons upon the seven vials," a millennialist sermon series. The book had been compiled from listener's notes, and Winthrop reported that Cotton was unhappy that he did not have the opportunity to proofread and edit the copy before publication.

18. Biemer, "Lady Deborah Moody," 26. Thomas Lechford, "Plain Dealing:

or Newes from New-England," *MHSC*, 3rd ser., vol. 3 (Boston, 1833), 97, was well acquainted with Moody's situation, writing that "shee is (good Lady) almost undone by buying Master Humphries farme, Swampscot, which cost her nine, or eleven hundred pounds."

19. Darrett B. Rutman, *Winthrop's Boston: Portrait of a Puritan Town, 1630–1649* (Chapel Hill: University of North Carolina Press, 1965), 101, points out that in 1630 Humphrey had written letters to Winthrop expressing reservations concerning recommendations being made about the religious settlement.

20. Winthrop, *Journal*, I: 334–5.

21. Ibid., II:11–2.

22. Ibid., II:34–5; on Humphrey's recruitment efforts see Kupperman, *Providence Island*, 146–7.

23. Winthrop, *Journal*, II:82–3.

24. Ibid., 83. Mary Beth Norton, *Founding Mothers and Fathers: Gendered Power and the Forming of American Society* (New York: Knopf, 1996), 107–8, sets this case in the context of a larger discussion about the obligation of householders to discipline and protect wives, children, and servants.

25. Winthrop, *Journal*, II:24–5.

26. These events are described in Raymond Phineas Stearns, *The Strenuous Puritan: Hugh Peter, 1598–1660* (Urbana: University of Illinois Press, 1954), 150–53; and Hugh Peter to John Winthrop, April, 1639, *MHSC*, 4th ser., vol. 7 (Boston, 1865), 200–1.

27. John Endecott to John Winthrop, February 1641, in *Winthrop Papers*, ed. Allyn B. Forbes et al., 5 vols. (Boston: Massachusetts Historical Society, 1929–47), IV:315; Winthrop, *Journal*, II:25–6.

28. Winthrop, *Journal*, II:150–1.

29. Thomas Edwards, *The First and Second Part of Gangraena* (London, 1646), I:106–107; Hugh Peter to John Winthrop, Jr., 23 June 1645, *Winthrop Papers* V: 30–1; Hugh Peter to John Winthrop, Jr., 4 Sept. 1646, *MHSC*, 4th ser., vol. 6 (Boston, 1863), 109; Hugh Peter to John Winthrop, 5 May 1649, Ibid., 111. See also Hugh Peter, *A Word for the Armie and Two Words to the Kingdom* (London, 1647), 11–4; *Mr. Peters Last Report of the English Wars* (London, 1646); and Stearns, *Strenuous Puritan*, 287–9.

30. Fulmer Mood, ed., "A Broadside Advertising Eleutheria and the Bahama Islands," Publications of the Colonial Society of Massachusetts, *Transactions* 32 (1933–37), 81–2. For an extended discussion of the Eleutheria project and the identity of its backers see Brenner, *Merchants and Revolution*, 523–8. In addition to analyzing the political meaning of the proposals regarding Eleutheria in England, Brenner also explains how "the longer-term origins . . . are to be found in the series of sharp religious conflicts that wracked the colony of Bermuda during the 1640s, provoked largely by the group of militant Puritan ministers that was attempting to impose on the colony a pure, congregational-type church structure" (523). On Bermuda see also Alison Games, *Migration and the Origins of the English Atlantic World* (Cambridge, Mass.: Harvard University Press, 1999). For biographical information on the investors, including Humphrey, see John T. Hassam, "The Bahamas: Notes on an Early Attempt at Colonization," *Massachusetts Historical Society Proceedings*, ser. 2, vol. 13 (Boston 1899): 4–58. For the Presbyterian denunciation of Bermuda's Puritan faction, out of which would be drawn the population for the Bahamas project, see William Prynne, *A Fresh Discovery of Some Prodigious New Wandering-Blasing Stars and Firebrands* (London, 1645).

31. Mood, ed., "Broadside," 81–2.

32. Winthrop, *Journal*, 351–3.

33. Ibid.

34. On the identification of Nathaniel Ward as a "presbyterian" and his pamphlet war with Hugh Peter, see Stearns, *Strenuous Puritan*, 303–14. Peter was a target because he adamantly defended the New Model Army, advocated religious toleration, and maintained close ties with prominent Commonwealth figures. For an argument that contrasts Ward with "younger Puritans" who "completely abandoned England when they reached the shores of New England," see Simon P. Newman, "Nathaniel Ward, 1580–1652: An Elizabethan Puritan in a Jacobean World," *Essex Institute Historical Collections* 127:4 (October 1991): 313–26.

35. Nathaniel Ward, *The Simple Cobler of Aggawam in America* (1647), ed. Lawrence C. Wroth (New York: Scholars' Facsimilies and Reprints, 1937), 4. Despite all his concern for simplicity and honesty, Ward, originally a lawyer, wrote under the pseudonym Theodore de la Guard. Bruce C. Daniels, *Puritans at Play: Leisure and Recreation in Colonial New England* (New York: St. Martin's Press, 1995), 36–7, emphasizes the use of humorous expression in Ward's *Simple Cobler*, demonstrating that Puritans had no objection to displays of wit so long as these were intended to buttress the faith.

36. Ward, *Simple Cobler*, 16; the description of Ward's purpose comes from the tract's frontispiece.

37. Ibid., 19, 2, 5, 17.

38. See Blair Worden, "Toleration and the Cromwellian Protectorate," in *Persecution and Toleration: Papers Read at the Twenty-Second Summer Meeting and the Twenty-Third Winter Meeting of the Ecclesiastical History Society*, ed. W. J. Sheils (Padstow, England: Blackwell, 1984), 199–233.

39. Peter quoted in Brenner, *Merchants and Revolution*, 518.

40. While other presbyterian pamphleteers, like Robert Baillie, saw New England as a font of all corruption, Ward tried to show that New England society was carefully constructed to gain a cohesiveness similar to what English presbyterians desired. On the English preference for contrived societies rather than naturally derived ones see Karen O. Kupperman, "The Beehive as a Model for Colonial Design," in *America in European Consciousness, 1493–1750*, ed. Karen Kupperman (Chapel Hill: University of North Carolina Press, 1995), 272–92.

41. Ward, *Simple Cobler*, 23, 5, 4.

42. Samuel Eliot Morison, *Builders of the Bay Colony* (Boston: Houghton Mifflin, 1930), 217–43; and Frederick S. Allis, Jr., "Nathaniel Ward: Constitutional Draftsman," *Essex Institute Historical Collections* 120: 4 (October 1984); 241–63.

43. Nathaniel Ward was principle author of the Bay Colony's *Body of Liberties*, and Winthrop had been opposed to having a law code, believing that magistrates should have more latitude to exercise their "prerogative." In 1641 Winthrop was annoyed at the choice of Ward to give a sermon before the Court, especially because "they had no great reason to choose him . . . seeing he had cast off his pastor's place at Ipswich. . . . In his sermon, he delivered many useful things, but in a moral and political discourse, grounding his propositions much upon the old Roman and Grecian governments, which sure is an error, for if religion and the word of God makes men wiser than their neighbors, and these times have the advantage of all that have gone before us in experience and observation, it is probable that by all these helps, we may better frame rules of government for ourselves than to receive others upon the bare authority of the wisdom, justice, etc. of those heathen commonwealths." Winthrop was discomfited too that Ward recommended that the people "keep all their magistrates in an equal rank." See Winthrop, *Journal*, II:36–7.

On Child's participation in alchemical circles see William R. Newman, *Gehennical Fire: The Lives of George Starkey, An American Alchemist in the Scientific Revolution* (Cambridge: Harvard University Press, 1994), 41–2.

44. Ward, *Simple Cobler*, 19.

45. Nehemiah Bourne to John Winthrop, 12 August 1648, *Winthrop Papers*, V:243–5. On Bourne's life see William Robert Chaplin, "Nehemiah Bourne," *Colonial Society of Massachusetts Transactions* 42 (1952–56): 28–155.

46. Nehemiah Bourne, *An Exact and true Relation of the Battell Fought on Saturday last at Acton, between the kings Army, and the Earl of Essex his Forces, with the Number that were slain on both sides* (London, 1642), 3, 4, 6. On the devastation wrought during the Thirty Years War see Philip Vincent, *The Lamentation of Germany* (London, 1638).

47. Nehemiah Bourne to John Winthrop, Jr., 19 April 1662, *MHSC*, 4th ser., vol. 7 (Boston, 1865), 305–6.

48. On New Englanders' enjoyment of political and military preferment in revolutionary England see William L. Sasche, *The Colonial American in Britain* (Madison: University of Wisconsin Press, 1956); and Charles Firth and Godfrey Davies, *The Regimental History of Cromwell's Army*, 2 vols. (Oxford: Clarendon Press, 1940), I:175, 178–85, 191–2, 198, 235; and II: 576–82, 640, 417–8.

49. For short biographies see Roberts, *History of the Military Company*, I:21–3, 91–3. Henry D. Sedgwick, "Robert Sedgwick," *Transactions of the Colonial Society of Massachusetts* 3 (Boston, 1900): 155–73; and Charles E. Leverett, *A Memoir, Biographical and Genealogical, of Sir John Leverett, Knt., Governor of Massachusetts* (Boston: Crosby, Nichols, 1856).

It was not unusual for these men to share interest in ships and do business together. John Leverett and Anthony Stoddard shared a one-sixteenth interest in the *Defense*, which they purchased from Nehemiah Bourne. Bourne sold a one-sixteenth interest in the *Margaret* to Edward Gibbons, which the latter then reassigned to Robert Sedgwick. John Leverett bought a one-third interest in the *Unicorn* from Edward Gibbons. And Gibbons sold to Bourne a one-sixteenth interest in the *Welcome* of Boston. *Aspinwall Notarial Records, 1644–51*, in *Records Relating to the Early History of Boston*, 39 vols. (Boston: Registry Department, 1876–1909), XXXII: 15, 122, 151.

50. The Anabaptist petition is described in Isaac Backus, *A History of New England with Particular Reference to the Baptists*, 2 vols. in 1 (1871; reprint, New York: Arno Press, 1969), 145 and MBR III: 51. For Leverett's activities see *MBR*, III:235–6, 240, 250–1. On Matthews see Deloraine P. Corey, *The History of Malden, Massachusetts, 1633–1785* (Malden, 1899), 126–64. The charge that Matthews failed sufficiently to denounce "sin in persons under the gospel" suggests that he was perceived as tending toward antinomianism. *MBR*, IV:1:42–3.

51. Winthrop, *Journal*, II: 274, 279. Williston Walker, *The Creeds and Platforms of Congregationalism* (Boston: Scribner, 1893), 166, 236, observes that the conflict over the Child petition formed the context for the calling of the Cambridge Synod. On the context for summoning the synod see also Robert E. Wall, *Massachusetts Bay: The Crucial Decade, 1640–1650* (New Haven: Yale University Press, 1972), 225–8.

52. Winthrop, *Journal*, II: 278–9. In a similar vein, Winthrop described one of the major concerns agitating those, like Leverett, who opposed not only the results of the synod but also the fact that such a synod should be called, and sponsored in the first place, by the civil government: "the main end of the synod was propounded to be, an agreement upon one uniform practice in all the churches,

the same to be commended to the general court, etc., this seemed to give power either to the synod or the court to compel the churches to practise what should so be established" (274). Firth and Davies, *Regimental History*; Brenner, *Merchants and Revolution*, 400–9.

53. Stearns, *Strenuous Puritan*, 187–201; Kupperman, *Providence Island*, 344–5; and Karl S. Bottigheimer, *English Money and Irish Land: The "Adventurers" in the Cromwellian Settlement of Ireland* (Oxford: Clarendon Press, 1971).

54. Francis Bremer has presented a much more collegial view of the relationship. See his "In Defense of Regicide: John Cotton and the Execution of Charles I," *WMQ* 37: 1 (January 1980): 103–24; and *Puritan Crisis: New England and the English Civil Wars, 1630 to 1670* (New York: Garland, 1989).

55. Brenner, *Merchants and Revolution*, 628–32.

56. David Pulsifer, ed., *Acts of the Commissioners of the United Colonies of New England, 1643–1679*, vols. 9–10, in *Records of the Colony of New Plymouth in New England*, ed. Nathaniel B. Shurtleff, 12 vols. in 9 (Boston, 1855–61), X:11–2. On the longterm differences between New Netherland and the New England colonies see Oliver A. Rink, *Holland on the Hudson: An Economic and Social History of Dutch New York* (Ithaca: Cornell University: Press, 1986), 214–63.

57. On these earlier events see Neal Salisbury, *Manitou and Providence: Indians, Europeans, and the Making of New England, 1500–1643* (New York: Oxford University Press, 1972), 231–5; and Karen O. Kupperman, *Indians and English: Facing off in Early America* (Ithaca: Cornell University Press, 2000), 235–9. On Ninigret's testimony, taken by Richard Waite, former antinomian, see Pulsifer, *Acts of the Commissioners*, X:8–9.

According to the treaty signed at the end of the Pequot War, Mohegan and Narragansett allies Uncas and Miantonomi received eighty surviving Pequots each and Ninigret twenty; "Tribute payments from the Mohegans, Narragansetts, and Niantics," writes Alden Vaughan, "were based on the assignment of Pequots to those tribes by the Hartford treaty of 1638. The new masters supposedly collected the specified amounts of wampum from the Pequots, then turned it over to the Commissioners, as reparations for the atrocities committed by the Pequots prior to the war and the cost of the war itself." Ninigret was accused continually of being in arrears for this tribute; see Alden T. Vaughan, *New England Frontier: Puritans and Indians, 1620–1675* (Boston: Little, Brown, 1965), 170. On the Pequot war see Alfred A. Cave, *The Pequot War* (Amherst: University of Massachusetts Press, 1996).

58. Pulsifer, *Acts of the Commissioners*, X:96–7. For an analysis of Ninigret's political strategies, and his eventual alliance with the English colonists during King Philip's War see Timothy J. Sehr, "Ninigret's Tactics of Accommodation: Indian Diplomacy in New England, 1637–1675," *Rhode Island History* 36: 2 (1977): 43–53.

59. Pulsifer, *Acts of the Commissioners*, X: 8–9.

60. Ibid., X:9–10. Ninigret, in his earlier denial of having met with Stuyvesant, had nonetheless revealed his intention to do so: "It was winter time and I stood a great parte of a winter day knocking att the Governor's dore and he would neither open it nor suffer others to open it to lett me in I was not wont to find such carriage from the English my frinds."

61. Ibid., X:24.

62. Ibid., X:23; and *The Second Part of the Tragedy of Amboyna* (1653; reprint, New York: Bartlett, 1915), 4. The "Amboyna breakfast" referred to an incident

that occurred in 1622, when representatives of the Dutch East India Company tortured, mutilated, and executed on trumped-up charges English settlers who encroached on a trading station at Ambon Island in Dutch Indonesia. In 1624, the English East India Company published an account of Dutch atrocities that was reprinted in the 1650s and 1670s, when hostilities broke out between England and the Netherlands; see *A True Relation of the Unjust, Cruell, and Barbarous proceedings against the English at Amboyna in the East Indies* (London, 1624).

63. Pulsifer, *Acts of the Commissioners*, X:23.

64. Ibid., 30–2.

65. Ibid., 30–40.

66. Ibid., 59–65.

67. Ibid., 99. On the experiences of Richard Waite and John Barrell, who had been sent to Ninigret a second time, see 94–5. Waite claimed that the Narragansetts might have made an alliance with the Mohawks: "The English in the meantime delivering theire Message to Ninnegrett his men were soe Tumultuos in speaking espetially one whoe they said was a Mohauke that they were much disturbed."

68. Ibid., 58.

69. Ibid., 53–4.

70. On Underhill's activities see Shelley, *Underhill*, 365–83.

71. "Instructions to the Commander of an Expedition against the Dutch Settlements in the Manhattoes, 8 February 1654, in *A Collection of the State Papers of John Thurloe Esq.*, ed. Thomas Birch, 7 vols. (London, 1742), I:721; and "The Protector to the governors of the English colonies in America," in the same volume, 721–2. See also Harry M. Ward, *The United Colonies of New England, 1643–90* (New York: Vantage, 1961), 178–96; and Sedgwick and Leverett to the Governors, June 5, 1654, Miscellaneous Bound Manuscripts, Massachusetts Historical Society.

72. Mark Harrison to Navy Commissioners, 1 July 1654, Sedgwick Papers in Frederick Lewis Gay Transcripts, Massachusetts Historical Society, 60–1; and Sedgwick, "Robert Sedgwick." For correspondence relating to French Acadia see "Leverett Papers," *MHSC*, 4th ser., vol. 2 (Boston, 1854), 221–5, 230–3.

73. John Mason to John Winthrop, Jr., 11 June 1654, *MHSC*, 4th ser., vol. 7 (Boston, 1865), 417–8. See also John Mason to John Winthrop, Jr., 27 May 1654, in the same volume, 416–7, for the account of an apparent conflict between the Boston watch and "Cromwell's boyes;" "It is heere reported that some of the soldiers, belonging to the fleet at Boston, fell upon the watch; after some bickering they comanded them to goe before the Governour, they retorned that they weare Cromwells boyes, telling them that when the Governour was come on shoare they would."

74. *MBR*, IV:1:229, 234.

75. Massachusetts Archives Collection at Columbia Point (SC1, 45x), 60: 187, 188. On this point see Karen O. Kupperman, *Roanoke: The Abandoned Colony* (Totowa, N.J.: Rowman and Allanheld, 1984).

76. Frank Cundall, *The Governors of Jamaica in the Seventeenth Century* (London: West India Committee 1936), xxii–xxxviii; Sedgwick, "Robert Sedgwick"; and Daniel Gookin to Thurloe, January 1656, in Birch, *State Papers*, IV:440.

On the roles of Sedgwick and Gookin in Jamaica, see Stephen S. Webb, *The Governors-General: The English Army and the Definition of the Empire, 1569–1681* (Chapel Hill: University of North Carolina Press, 1979), 153–67. Evidence of elders' and magistrates' discomfort over the Protector's suggestion that New Englanders relocate is evident in a "Letter From Certain Ministers and Others of New England to Oliver Cromwell," in *MHSC*, 4th ser., vol. 2 (Boston, 1854), 115–7; and The governor of New England, etc. to the Protector, October 23, 1656, in Birch, *State Papers*, V:510. For correspondence between Gookin and the Protectorate government see Frederick W. Gookin, *Daniel Gookin, 1612–1687, Assistant and Major General of the Massachusetts Bay Colony* (Chicago, Donnelly, 1912), 89–91, 93–103.

77. Major R. Sedgwick to Secretary Thurloe, 12 March 1655, in Birch, ed., *State Papers* IV:605.

78. Major R. Sedgwick to Secretary Thurloe, 12 March 1655, in Birch, ed., *State Papers*, IV:604–605; Sedgwick to Commissioners of Admiralty, 14 November 1655, Sedgwick Papers in Frederick Lewis Gay Transcripts, Massachusetts Historical Society, 90; Major R. Sedgwick to the protector, 5 November 1655, in Birch, *State Papers*, IV:151–5; and Sedgwick to John Winthrop, Jr., 6 November 1655, *MHSC*, ser. 5, vol. 1 (Boston, 1871), 380–1.

While en route from London to New England in the immediate aftermath of the Anglo-Dutch War, Sedgwick had seized the *John Baptist*, a Dutch ship laden with French goods, in order to defray expenses relating to the French forts. Sedgwick "did make sale of the lading at New England," and, although he claimed that he had done this in exchange for "carrying on the publique service," having "accompted for the same since his comeing to England as also for the fraight of the Merchandize brought home in the said shipp," Dutch merchants succeeded in forcing Sedgwick to show bond for their property in a case they were bringing against him in Admiralty Court. The English Council of State rapidly came to Sedgwick's aid, ordering the Admiralty judges to "forthwith deliver up to the said Major Sedgwick or his Assignes the bond so by him entred into he being not personally concerned therein but as he was a publique instrument imployed by the State in that expedition." See Orders of Council of State, 9 May 1955, Sedgwick Papers in Frederick Lewis Gay Transcripts, 1–2, Massachusetts Historical Society; and Bond of Sedgwick, 19 July 1655, Sedgwick Papers in Frederick Lewis Gay Transcripts, 3, Massachusetts Historical Society.

79. John Noble, ed., *Records of the Court of Assistants of Massachusetts Bay, 1630–1692*, 3 vols. (Boston: 1901–28), III: 34–38; and *MBR*, IV: 1:213. The blasphemy statute applied to those in the jurisdiction who "wittingly and willingly presume to blaspheme . . . either by wilfull or obstinate denying the true God, or his creation or government of the world, or shall curse God, or reproach the holy religion of God, as if it were but a politicke device to keepe ignorant men in awe." See *MBR* II:176–7.

80. Noble, ed., *Records of the Court of Assistants*, III: 34–38; and Ward, *Simple Cobler*, 5.

81. Stephen Carl Arch, *Authorizing the Past: The Rhetoric of History in Seventeenth Century New England*(DeKalb: Northern Illinois University Press, 1994), 14–5. On the perpetuation of such ideas into the eighteenth century see J. E. Crowley, *This Sheba, Self: The Conceptualization of Economic Life in Eighteenth-Century America* (Baltimore: Johns Hopkins University Press, 1974).

82. Winthrop, *Journal*, II: 164; *MBR*, II: 60, III: 53–4; and Bernard Bailyn, *The New England Merchants in the Seventeenth Century* (1955; reprint Cambridge; Harvard University Press, 1982), 51–3.

83. On Aspinwall see John T. Hassam, "Early Recorders and Registers of Deeds for the County of Suffolk, Massachusetts, 1639–1735," *Massachusetts Historical Society Proceedings*, ser. 2, vol. 12 (Boston, 1898): 203–49; and Maclear,

"New England and the Fifth Monarchy." See also B. S. Capp, *The Fifth Monarchy Men: A Study in Seventeenth-Century Millenarianism* (London: Faber and Faber, 1972), 56–65; and Roberts, *History of the Military Company*, I: 126–7.

84. Roger Thompson, *Mobility and Migration: East Anglian Founders of New England, 1629–1640* (Amherst: University of Massachusetts Press, 1994), 64, 197. On Hill's family connections see also Rosamond Allen, *Valentine Hill Genealogy* (Mandarin FL, 1973), 1–6. Anne Eaton, Hill's mother-in-law and the mother of David Yale, was admonished in New Haven for her Anabaptist views and for irregularities in her household management, including clashes with stepdaugher Mary Eaton (Hill's wife). On Eaton's experiences in New Haven see Mary Beth Norton, *Founding Mothers and Fathers*, 165–74; and Lilian Handlin, "Dissent in a Small Community," *NEQ* 58:2 (June 1985): 193–220. Thomas Clark, along with other business associates of Hill, petitioned in 1661 to replace Mary Eaton Hill as administrator because she was in a "great measure deprived of her understanding at times, and so nott capable of managing her interest in the estate." Petition to General Court, 4 June 1661, Photostats, Massachusetts Historical Society; and MBR IV.2:83. Yale, together with Gibbons, Sedgwick, and Fowle extended credit in 1646 to Nehemiah Bourne, who sailed as master and merchant aboard the *Tryall*, conveying goods and bills of exchange to mercantile contacts in London, including Richard Hutchinson and Joshua Foote; *Aspinwall Notarial Records*, 15. In 1652, when David Yale departed Massachusetts, he designated Thomas Clark and Thomas Lake as his attorneys.

85. Eben Putnam, *Lieutenant Joshua Hewes: A New England Pioneer and Some of His Descendants* (Boston: J. F. Tapley, 1913). On Child see George L. Kittredge, "Dr. Robert Child the Remonstrant," *Colonial Society of Massachusetts Transactions* 21 (Boston, 1920): 21–8; Morison, *Builders of the Bay Colony*, 244–68; and Margaret E. Newell, "Robert Child and the Entrepreneurial Vision: Economy and Ideology in Early New England," 68:2 (June 1995): 223–56.

86. Stephen Innes, *Creating the Commonwealth: The Economic Culture of Puritan New England* (New York: Norton, 1995), 235, emphasizes how Puritans in Massachusetts were inclined to reject monopolies as an impediment to free trade; but in this case, he argues, they realized that the investors would not go ahead with the project without such encouragement. Innes, however, does not give any consideration to the threats to Bay Colony "independency"—in all its multilayered meanings—implicit in these activities. On the fate of the venture see Bailyn, *New England Merchants*, 51–3.

87. Pulsifer, *Acts of the Commissioners*, X:15.

88. See Arthur H. Buffinton, "New England and the Western Fur Trade, 1629–1675," *Transactions of the Colonial Society of Massachusetts* 18 (Boston, 1915–16): 160–92; and Roberts, *History of the Military Company*, I:56.

89. Mark Harrison to Navy Commissioners, 1 July 1654, Sedgwick Papers in Frederick Lewis Gay Transcripts, Massachusetts Historical Society, 60–1. On these events, the Sedgwick quotation, and the "angry questioning" to which Sedgwick was subjected, see John G. Reid, *Acadia, Maine and New Scotland: Marginal Colonies in the Seventeenth Century* (Toronto: University of Toronto Press, 1981), 135–41; and George A. Rawlyk, *Nova Scotia's Massachusetts: A Study of Massachusetts-Nova Scotia Relations, 1630 to 1784* (Montreal: McGill-Queen's University Press, 1973). For the trade restrictions see Application of Sedgwick, Leverett and others to the General Court, 20 October 1654 *Hutchinson Papers*, I:286–7.

90. Joshua Scottow, *A Narrative of the Planting of the Massachusetts Colony* (Boston, 1694), 10–2. Michael Zuckerman, "Pilgrims in the Wilderness: Commu-

nity, Modernity, and the Maypole at Merry Mount," *NEQ* 50:2 (June 1977): 255–77, argues that the Puritans found Morton's "lush prose inscrutable, his sensual adventurism abhorrent, and his festivities almost demoniacal." Morton initially seized control of Captain Wollaston's establishment by appealing to servants who feared being sold as indentured servants in Virginia. For another full account of Morton's Merrymount see John Cannup, *Out of the Wilderness: The Emergence of an American Identity in Colonial New England* (Middletown, Conn.: Wesleyan University Press, 1990), 105–25. On Gibbons's career see Roberts, *History of the Military Company*, I: 38–40; and *MBR* I:129, 134, 165, 190–1, 201, 225, 254, 260, 262, 271, 276, 279.

91. Winthrop, *Journal*, I: 222. Samuel Eliot Morison, *Builders of the Bay Colony*, 147, comments on Winthrop's real or pretended innocence in recording Gibbons's "cock and bull story . . . as though it were no business of his to bring out the obvious fact that Gibbons had been receiving stolen goods from the buccaneers of Hispaniola. One did not like to look too closely into the Major's private business, for there was no doubt of his superior military ability."

92. For evidence that Gibbons sympathized with Child see Kittredge, "Child the Remonstrant," 51–54. For the charges against Child and the other petitioners see *MBR* III: 90–1.

93. Winthrop, *Journal*, II: 150. Roberts, *History of the Military Company*, I: 38–40, contends that Gibbons never went to Maryland. But see John Leeds Bozeman, *The History of Maryland*, 2 vols. (Baltimore: James Lucas and E. K. Deaver, 1837), II: 411–2, which shows that "Edward Gibbons, esq. major general of New England" received a Maryland commission on January 20, 1650. It is possible that Gibbons returned to Massachusetts in 1654, the year prior to his death.

94. Gibbons had a kinsman, perhaps a son, named Jotham Gibbons, a mariner who lived in Bermuda and contracted a mortgage with Joshua Scottow, the Boston merchant and military officer who, after Gibbons's death, took over his role as agent for La Tour. See Julia E. Mercer, *Bermuda Settlers of the Seventeenth Century: Genealogical Notes from Bermuda* (Baltimore: Genealogical, 1982), 67.

95. *MBR* II:23, 27, 39, 45, 74, 116, 122–23, 256, 265; and III: 39–42. For Gibbons's 1645 commission from the United Colonies in the abortive Narragansett war see Pulsifer, *Acts of the Commissioners*, IX: 37–41.

96. Reid, *Acadia, Maine and New Scotland*, 27–57; "Papers Relative to the Rival Chiefs, d'Aulnay and La Tour, Governors of Nova Scotia," *MHSC*, 3d ser., vol. 7 (Boston, 1838), 90–121; and William Jenks, "Notice of the Sieur D'Aulnay of Acadie," *MHSC*, 4th ser., vol. 4 (Boston, 1858), 462–70.

97. William B. Trask, *Suffolk Deeds*, 14 vols. (Boston: Suffolk County Commissioners, 1880–1906) I:7–10.

98. Winthrop, *Journal*, II: 136–7; Roberts, *History of the Military Company*, I: 63–4; and Felt, *Ecclesiastical History*, I:326.

99. Robert E. Wall, *Massachusetts Bay: The Crucial Decade, 1640–1650* (New Haven: Yale University Press, 1972), 64–77.

100. John Endecott to John Winthrop, 19 June 1643, *Winthrop Papers*, IV: 394–5; Richard Saltonstall et al. to the Governor, Deputy Governor, Assistants and Elders, 14 July 1643, *Winthrop Papers*, IV: 397–401; John Winthrop to Richard Saltonstall and Others, 21 July 1643, *Winthrop Papers*, IV:403; and Winthrop, *Journal*, II:136. Reid, *Acadia, Maine, and New Scotland*, 96. See also Pulsifer, *Acts of the Commissioners*, IX: 58–9, for a discussion of Hawkins's action, where it was determined that Hawkins did not have proper commission to "at-

tempt any hostile act against Monsr De Aulney, nor to enquire after wronges" done to La Tour; "but Captaine Hawkins being now absent, they leave him to answere for himself." The commissioners condemned Hawkins's actions but carefully asserted that these actions had not been taken under official orders, thereby absolving the English colonies from blame and referring the matter to "due course of Justice."

101. The final negotiations with emissaries from d'Aulnay are described in Winthrop, *Journal*, II:284–5. Captain Thomas Cromwell was a Boston seaman who had served on West Indian privateering missions with Captain William Jackson, who sailed for Warwick. In June 1646, Cromwell presented the sedan chair to Winthrop upon entering Boston, perhaps as a good will gesture, since he and one of his crewmen had recently created a disturbance by their brawling in Plymouth (272–3). For a detailed treatment of the provisions of the peace and d'Aulnay's willingness to coexist with New England see Reid, *Acadia, Maine and New Scotland*, 97–9. On the career of William Jackson, who sailed often for the Earl of Warwick, see W. Frank Craven, "The Earl of Warwick: A Speculator in Piracy," *Hispanic American Historical Review* 10: 4 (November 1930): 457–79.

102. Bozeman, *History of Maryland*, II:411–2; Winthrop, *Journal*, II:275.

103. Reid, *Acadia, Maine and New Scotland*, 32–3; and Marjorie A. MacDonald, *Fortune and La Tour: The Civil War in Acadia* (New York: Methuen, 1983). On La Tour's parentage of these girls see Natalie Zemon Davis, *Women on the Margins: Three Seventeenth-Century Lives* (Cambridge: Harvard University Press, 1995), 269, n. 63.

104. Winthrop, *Journal*, II:150–1, 153, 156.

105. Ibid., II: 191–3.

106. Ibid.

107. Richard P. Gildrie, *The Profane, the Civil, and the Godly: The Reformation of Manners in Orthodox New England, 1679–1749* (University Park: Pennsylvania State University Press, 1994), quoted at 47–8; and " 'The Gallant life': Theft on the Salem-Marblehead, Massachusetts Waterfront in the 1680s," *Essex Institute Historical Collections* 122:4 (1986): 284–98. For studies that examine how various forms of brigandage, including piracy, conflicted with nascent "bourgeois" values see Christopher Hill, *Liberty against the Law: Some Seventeenth-Century Controversies* (New York: Penguin, 1996); and Marcus Rediker, *Between the Devil and the Deep Blue Sea: Merchant Seamen, Pirates and the Anglo-American Maritime World, 1700– 1750* (New York: Cambridge University Press, 1987).

108. On drunkenness as a symbol of lack of control and chaos that was anathema to Puritans see William Hunt, *The Puritan Moment: The Coming of Revolution in an English County* (Cambridge: Harvard University Press, 1983); Keith Wrightson, "Alehouses, Order and Reformation in Rural England, 1590–1660," in *Popular Culture and Class Conflict, 1590–1914: Explorations in the History of Labour and Leisure*, ed. Eileen Yeo and Stephen Yeo (Sussex, England: Harvester Press, 1981), 11–7; and Peter Clark, "The Alehouse and the Alternative Society," in *Puritans and Revolutionaries: Essays in Seventeenth-Century History Presented to Christopher Hill*, ed. Donald Pennington and Keith Thomas (New York: Oxford University Press, 1982), 47–72.

109. Reid, *Acadia, Maine and New Scotland*, 101, 110, 127–31.

110. MBR, IV.1:120, 146.

111. Reid, *Acadia, Maine and New Scotland*, 135–43; Arthur H. Buffinton, "Sir Thomas Temple in Boston: A Case of Benevolent Assimilation," Colonial

Society of Massachusetts, *Publications* 27 (1932): 308–19; Trask, *Suffolk Deeds*, V: 508; and Thomas Lake to John Leverett, 1657, Photostats, Massachusetts Historical Society.

112. Petition of Captain John Leverett, 18 November 1656, Sedgwick Papers in Frederick Lewis Gay Transcripts, Massachusetts Historical Society; and Petition of Captain John Leverett, 2 December 1656, Sedgwick Papers in Frederick Lewis Gay Transcripts, Massachusetts Historical Society.

113. "Leverett Papers," *MHSC*, ser. 4, vol. 2 (Boston, 1854), 222–3. Thomas Savage petitioned the Crown, at about the same time, for title to a tract of land in Portsmouth that he had been promised during his brief antinomian exile. See Thomas Savage Petition, 1672, State Papers in Frederick Lewis Gay Transcripts, Massachusetts Historical Society.

114. Leverett's reputation as a sharp dealer, at least in some quarters, was already established. In 1648, for example, John Jarvis sued John Leverett and Isaac Addington for malfeasance in their partnership with him in the ship *Unicorn*. Jarvis claimed that Leverett and Addington had concealed from him the ship's profits and even its itinerary. All three partners, Jarvis said in his complaint, had agreed to a series of voyages with ports of call at Boston, Virginia, and London. But fraud ensued when Addington, who sailed as master, began, with Leverett's knowledge, to make unauthorized voyages from London to Malaga and the Canary Islands. When Jarvis requested before the Suffolk County Court a "true account" of his one-third share in the *Unicorn*, Leverett and Addington, through their attorney Edward Bendall (an Artillery Company member and former antinomian), insisted that Jarvis could not have been ignorant of the ship's movements: "Mr. Addingtons design for Malago was publicly spoken of upon the exchange and therefore will Mr. Jarvis be ignorant." Jarvis's adversaries firmly asserted also that Jarvis had sold them his interest in the ship prior to the time the contested voyages took place. For Jarvis the bond between Leverett and Addington, hardened by kinship and strengthened by the advocacy of their associate Edward Bendall, became an insuperable barrier to an equitable partnership. The sense of having been taken advantage of, even conspired against, comes through in Jarvis's description of his second response to Edward Bendall as "a reply to the prevaricating answer of Edward Bendall unto a protest against Isaac Addington and Captain John Leverett"; *Aspinwall Notarial Records*, 351–4, 363–5. Leverett had purchased his third of the ship from Edward Gibbons (49).

115. This may have been the same Thomas Jenner who had formerly been a clergyman at Saco, Maine. See Thomas Jenner to John Winthrop, 1640 *MHSC*, 4th ser., vol. 7 (Boston, 1865), 355–6. For a biographical sketch of Allen see Roberts, *History of the Military Company*, I:85

116. Petition of Thomas Jenner, 4 July 1656, Sedgwick Papers in Frederick Lewis Gay Transcripts, Massachusetts Historical Society, 8; and Report of Cock et. al., 8 July 1656, Sedgwick Papers in Frederick Lewis Gay Transcripts, Massachusetts Historical Society, 9–12.

117. For Leverett's appointment and instructions as agent see *MBR*, IV.1: 251; and Copy of the General Courts Commission to Captain John Leverett, November 1655, in *Hutchinson Papers*, 2 vols. (Albany, N.Y.: Prince Society, 1865), I:305–7.

118. Copy of a Letter from Mr. John Leverett to Governor Endecott and the General Court, 13 September 1660, *Hutchinson Papers*, II:40–2. On the stipulation that an audit be performed to square Leverett's accounts with Thomas Temple's see Copy of a Letter from John Leverett to Governor Endecott, 16 April 1658, in the same volume; and Order Concerning Accounts of John Leverett, 6 April 1658,

Sedgwick Papers in Frederick Lewis Gay Transcripts, Massachusetts Historical Society.

119. Elite men from a variety of religious perspectives resented the imposition of "uniformity." I have shown that some individuals who had sympathized with the antinomians also disagreed with the harsh treatment of Robert Child; Child, in turn, complained about the ill treatment of religious dissenters. Robert Pike of Salisbury, who, like Robert Child, has been identified as a "presbyterian" by some historians, protected Quakers in his community and was fined and temporarily disfranchised when he refused to ask the Court's pardon for his actions. See Roland Leslie Warren, *Loyal Dissenter: The Life and Times of Robert Pike* (Lanham, Md.: University Press of America, 1992); and James S. Pike, *The New Puritan: New England Two Hundred Years Age: Some Account of the Life of Robert Pike, the Puritan who defended the Quakers, resisted clerical domination, and opposed the witchcraft persecution* (New York: Harper, 1879).

CHAPTER 4

1. The Blue Anchor Tavern had belonged to Elizabeth Belcher's husband, Andrew Belcher, a frontiersman like Gookin. For biographical information on Andrew Belcher, see Oliver Ayer Roberts, *History of the Military Company of the Massachusetts* (Boston: A. Mudge, 1895), I:120; for genealogical information on the Belcher family, see Lucius Paige, *History of Cambridge, Massachusetts, 1630–1877, with a Genealogical Register* (Boston: Houghton, 1877), 486.

2. The deposition is printed in Frederick W. Gookin, *Daniel Gookin*, 1612–1687 (Chicago: R. R. Donnelley, 1912), 153; and Paige, *History of Cambridge*, 394.

3. Society A.B.C.D., Manuscript handbill threatening death to Thomas Danforth and Daniel Gookin, February 28, 1675/6, Photostats, Massachusetts Historical Society.

4. For Scott's appearance before the Court of Assistants see John Noble, ed., *Records of the Court of Assistants of the Colony of the Massachusetts Bay, 1630–1692*, 3 vols. (Boston: County of Suffolk, 1901–1928), I: 60–1. Scott was assessed a fine of two hundred pounds.

On the use of Indian adjuncts in New England, see Richard R. Johnson, "The Search for a Usable Indian: An Aspect of the Defense of Colonial New England," *Journal of American History* 64: 3 (December 1977): 623–51. James Drake, "Restraining Atrocity: The Conduct of King Philip's War," *NEQ* 70: 1 (March 1997): 33–56, notes but does not analyze the treatment of Indian allies and converts.

5. [Nathaniel Saltonstall], "The Present State of New England with Respect to the Indian War(1675)," in *Narratives of the Indian Wars, 1675–1699*, ed. Charles H. Lincoln (1913; reprint, New York: Barnes and Noble, 1959), 41.

6. Richard White, *The Middle Ground: Indians, Empires and Republics in the Great Lakes Region, 1650–1815* (New York: Cambridge University Press, 1991), X, defines "middle ground" as the "place in between: in between cultures, peoples, and in between empires and the nonstate world of villages."

7. See, for example, James P. Ronda, " 'We are Well as We Are': An Indian Critique of Seventeenth-Century Missions," *WMQ* 34: 1 (January1977): 66–82; and "Generations of Faith: The Christian Indians of Martha's Vineyard," *WMQ* 38:3 (July 1981): 369–94; Neal Salisbury, " 'Red Puritans': The 'Praying Indians' of Massachusetts Bay and John Eliot," *WMQ* 31: 1 (January 1974): 27–54; and William S. Simmons, "Conversion from Indian to Puritan," *NEQ* 52: 2 (June 1979): 197–218.

Another set of scholars has stressed the Indians' ability to salvage some form of independent identity out of the missionary experience and to use religious conversion to Christianity as a coping strategy. For variations on this interpretation see Robert J. Naeher, "Dialogue in the Wilderness: John Eliot and the Indian Exploration of Puritanism as a Source of Meaning, Comfort, and Ethnic Survival," *NEQ* 62 (1989): 346–68; Harold W. Van Lonkhuyzen, "A Reappraisal of the Praying Indians; Acculturation, Conversion, and Identity at Natick, Massachusetts, 1646–1730," *NEQ* 63: 3 (September 1990): 396–428; Elise M. Brenner, "To Pray or To Be Prey, That is the Question: Strategies for Cultural Autonomy of Massachusetts Praying Town Indians," *Ethnohistory* 27: 2 (spring 1980):135–52; and Jean M. O'Brien, *Dispossession by Degrees: Indian Land and Identity in Natick, Massachusetts, 1650–1790* (New York: Cambridge University Press, 1997).

Gookin himself is one of the most under-studied persons of the colonial era. The one full-length biography is Gookin, *Daniel Gookin*; see also J. Wingate Thornton, "The Gookin Family," *New England Historical and Genealogical Register* 1 (1847): 345–52. Alfred Cave, "New England Puritan Misperceptions of Native American Shamanism," *International Social Science Review* 67: 1 (winter 1992):15–27, focuses on both Gookin and Roger Williams, explaining and condemning how each entertained a skewed, widely shared vision of Indian religion as devil worship; and Hans Galinsky, *"I Cannot Join with the Multitude": Daniel Gookin (1612–1687), Critical Historian of Indian–English Relations* (Erlanger, 1985), provides, as his title suggests, a too-generous assessment of Gookin's attitudes toward indigenous peoples.

8. See especially Richard Slotkin, *Regeneration through Violence: The Mythology of the American Frontier, 1600–1860* (1973; reprint, New York: Harper Perennial, 1996), 81–2; Jenny Hale Pulsipher, "Massacre at Hurtleberry Hill: Christian Indians and English Authority in Metacom's War," *WMQ* 53: 3 (July 1996): 459–86; and Michael Kammen, *People of Paradox: An Inquiry Concerning the Origins of American Civilization* (New York: Knopf, 1972),

9. Pulsipher, "Massacre."

10. On 1676 as the end of colonial "independence" see Stephen Saunders Webb, *1676: The End of American Independence* (New York: Knopf, 1984). Jill Lepore, *The Name of War: King Philip's War and the Origins of American Identity* (New York: Knopf, 1998), contends that colonists were trying to establish their own "civility," and to distinguish themselves from the "barbarity" evinced in the New World by Spanish colonizers on the one hand and Indians on the other. I would argue, that a desire to maintain an identity separate from England was also at play in these events.

11. See, for example, "The Revolution in New-England Justified (1691)," in *The Andros Tracts*, ed. William H. Whitmore, 3 vols. (1868–74; reprint, New York: Burt Franklin, 1967), I: 103.

12. On the daunting series of challenges to the "city upon a hill" and the tortuous intellectual adjustments made by late seventeenth-century clergymen see Francis J. Bremer, *The Puritan Experiment: New England Society from Bradford to Edwards* (New York: St. Martin's Press, 1976), 125–68; Robert G. Pope, *The Halfway Covenant: Church Membership in Puritan New England* (Princeton, N.J.: Princeton University Press, 1969); Michael P. Winship, *Seers of God: Puritan Providentialism in the Restoration and Early Enlightenment* (Baltimore: Johns Hopkins University Press, 1996); and Richard R. Johnson, *Adjustment to Empire: The New England Colonies, 1675–1715* (New Brunswick, N.J.: Rutgers University Press, 1981).

13. The concept of Puritan "tribalism" was introduced in Edmund S. Morgan, *The Puritan Family: Religion and Domestic Relations in Seventeenth-Century New England* (New York: Harper and Row, 1966).

14. Gookin, *Daniel Gookin*; and Galinsky, *"I Cannot Join with the Multitude."*

15. On Boyle see Nicolas Canny, *The Upstart Earl: A Study of the Social and Mental World of Richard Boyle First Earl of Cork* (New York: Cambridge University Press, 1982).

16. On the Gookins in Virginia see Edmund S. Morgan, *American Slavery, American Freedom: The Ordeal of Colonial Virginia* (New York: Norton, 1975), 119, 167. For John Smith's account of the elder Gookin's independence of spirit in refusing to settle in a centralized location after the "massacre" of 1622, see Thornton, "The Gookin Family."

17. Gookin, *Daniel Gookin*; and Galinsky, *"I Cannot Join With the Multitude."*

18. On the Puritans in Maryland see Daniel Richard Randall, *A Puritan Colony in Maryland* (1886; reprint, New York: Johnson Reprint, 1973).

19. For Gookin's career see Robert E. Wall, *The Membership of the Massachusetts General Court, 1630–1686* (New York: Garland, 1990), 309–11.

20. On the centrality of cultural conversion to planter identity see Nicholas Canny, "Identity Formation in Ireland," in *Colonial Identity in the Atlantic World, 1500–1800,* ed. Nicholas Canny and Anthony Pagden (Princeton: Princeton University Press, 1987), 159–212.

21. T. C. Barnard, "Lord Broghill, Vincent Gookin and the Cork Elections of 1659," *English Historical Review* 88 (1973): 352–65, examines Gookin's efforts to get out from under the political domination of the Boyle family; but he argues that this did not imply any disagreement on the issue of "transplantation."

22. On Eliot's program of assimilation in the praying towns see Neal Salisbury, " 'Red Puritans' "; and Kenneth M. Morrison, " 'That Art of Coyning Christians': John Eliot and the Praying Indians of Massachusetts," *Ethnohistory* 21: 1 (winter 1974): 77–92. For the argument that the image of John Eliot was used in later centuries to justify removal see Joshua David Bellin, "Apostle of Removal: John Eliot in the Nineteenth Century," *NEQ* 69: 1 (March 1996): 3–32. The traditional laudatory account of Eliot's work is Ola Elizabeth Winslow, *John Eliot, Apostle to the Indians* (Boston: Houghton Mifflin, 1968).

23. For the history of this London-based missionary society and its revival during the Restoration, see William Kellaway, *The New England Company, 1649–1776: Missionary Society to the American Indians* (London: Longmans, Green, 1961). For an account of how Boyle's interests in economic "projecting," millennialism, and science came together in missionary work see J. R. Jacob, "The New England Company, the Royal Society, and the Indians," *Social Studies of Science* 5 (1975): 450–5. On the Bay Colony's creation of the post of superintendent see Richard W. Cogley, *John Eliot's Mission to the Indians before King Philip's War* (Cambridge: Harvard University Press, 1999), 224–8.

24. Daniel Gookin, *Historical Collections of the Indians in New England (1674),* ed. Jeffrey H. Fiske (1792; reprint, Boston: Towtaid, 1970), 129. For the ways in which experience with Irish "savages" informed Englishmen's views of "barbarous" peoples in America see Nicholas Canny, "The Ideology of English Colonization: From Ireland to America," *WMQ* 30: 4 (October 1973): 574–98.

25. For one of Gookin's reports concerning how on court days he tried to instill labor discipline along with the colony's ordinary laws see Daniel Gookin to Commissioners of the United Colonies, 27 August 1664, in *Acts of the Commissioners of the United Colonies of New England, 1643–1679,* ed. David Pulsifer, vols.

9–10, in *Records of the Colony of New Plymouth, in New England*, ed. Nathaniel B. Shurtleff 12 vols. in 9 (Boston: W. White, 1855–61), X: 381–2.

26. Daniel Gookin, "An Historical Account of the Doings and Sufferings of the Christian Indians in New England, in the Years 1675, 1676, 1677," *Archaeologia Americana: Transactions and Collections of the American Antiquarian Society* 2 (Cambridge, 1836): 436; and Gookin, *Historical Collections*, 28–30.

27. For this interpretation of the motives of the Boyle faction see Canny, "Identity Formation." A different view of the tensions between "old Protestants" and Cromwellian soldiers is presented in Karl S. Bottigheimer, "Kingdom and Colony: Ireland in the Westward Enterprise, 1536–1660," in *The Westward Enterprise: English Activities in Ireland, the Atlantic and America, 1480–1650*, ed. K. R. Andrews, N. P. Canny, and P. E. H. Hair (Liverpool: Liverpool University Press, 1978), 45–64.

28. Vincent Gookin, *The Great Case of Transplantation in Ireland Discussed* (London, 1655), 30–31.

29. On the centrality of "independency" and "dependency" as crucial "social categories" in British North America see Jack P. Greene, *Pursuits of Happiness: The Social Development of Early Modern British Colonies and the Formation of American Culture* (Chapel Hill: University of North Carolina Press, 1988), 186–9, 195–7. For an exposition of the analogous concept of "competency" in New England, see Daniel Vickers, "Competency and Competition: Economic Culture in Early America," *WMQ* 47: 1 (January 1990): 3–29.

30. Petition of Wait Winthrop, 9 June 1679, Photostats, Massachusetts Historical Society.

31. Thomas Shepard, *The Clear Sun-Shine of the Gospel Breaking Forth upon the Indians in New-England; or, An Historicall Narration of Gods Wonderfull Workings upon Sundry of the Indians, both Chief Governors and Common-people, in bringing them to a willing and desired Submission to the Ordinances of the Gospel* (London, 1648), in *MHSC*, 3rd ser., vol. 4 (Boston, 1834), 32–4.

32. William Hubbard, *A Narrative of the Troubles With the Indians in New England (1677)*, in *The History of the Indian Wars in New England*, ed. Samuel Drake, 2 vols. in 1 (1865; reprint, New York: Kraus Reprint, 1969), II:203; William Harris to Sir Joseph Williamson, 12 August 1676, State Papers in Frederick Lewis Gay Transcripts, II, Masachusetts Historical Society.

33. On the response to Eliot's tract see James F. Maclear, "New England and the Fifth Monarchy: The Quest for the Millennium in Early American Puritanism," *WMQ* 32:2 (April 1975): 223–60; and Theodore Dwight Bozeman, *To Live Ancient Lives: The Primitivist Dimension in Puritanism* (Chapel Hill: University of North Carolina Press, 1988), 263–86. Bozeman insists that Eliot sought the "fossilization of consensual themes"; still, Eliot operated within a missionary society explicitly oriented toward progress, trade, and the transatlantic world, not the closed communities of early-seventeenth-century Massachusetts. Constance Post, "Old World Order in the New: John Eliot and 'Praying' Indians in Cotton Mather's *Magnalia Christi Americana*," *NEQ* 66: 3 (September 1993): 416–33, suggests that Cotton Mather, by lionizing John Eliot in the *Magnalia*, was essentially claiming for himself the transatlantic mantle that Eliot had carried and that had earned Mather little appreciation.

34. Timothy J. Sehr, "John Eliot, Millennialist and Missionary," *Historian* 46: 2 (February 1984): 187–203, analyzes Eliot's avid tracking of the fruits of the "new science" and his interest in international Puritanism and the invention of a uni-

versal language; Sehr points out too that Eliot pressed during the 1660s for a "comprehension" of congregational and presbyterian churches, publishing to this end a tract called *Communion of the Churches* in 1665. Charles Webster, *The Great Instauration: Science, Medicine and Reform, 1626–1660* (London: Duckworth, 1975), connects the "new science" with millennial thought and emphasizes the impulse to recapture the pure knowledge and powers of Adam before the Fall. On the Irish antecedents of the Hartlib Circle see Canny, *Upstart Earl.*

35. John Nelson, Letter to Charles Talbot, 1695, John Nelson Collection, Massachusetts Historical Society. On the attenuation of ties to England among the ordinary colonists see Virginia Anderson, *New England's Generation: The Great Migration and the Formation of Society and Culture in the Seventeenth Century* (New York: Cambridge University Press, 1981), 211–2.

36. John Eliot was sometimes resented for appealing over the heads of colonial authorities to his English backers. See, for example, Pulsifer, *Acts of the Commissioners*, X: 121–3.

37. Thomas Lechford, "Plain Dealing: or Newes from New-England," *MHSC*, 3rd ser., vol.3 (Boston, 1833), 80, 92; and *Notebook Kept by Thomas Lechford Esq., Lawyer . . . from June 27, 1638 to July 29, 1641*, American Antiquarian Society, *Transactions and Collections* 8 (Cambridge, Mass.: John Wilson, 1885): 276.

38. John Easton, *A Relacion of the Indyan Warre* (1675), in *Narratives of the Indian Wars*, ed. Charles H. Lincoln (1913; reprint, New York: Barnes and Noble, 1959), 7–17. The voluminous writings of Thomas Maule are reprinted in James E. Maule, *Better That 100 Witches Should Live: The 1696 Acquittal of Thomas Maule of Salem, Massachusetts, on Charges of Seditious Libel and its Impact on the Development of First Amendment Freedoms* (Villanova, Pa.: Jembook, 1995).

39. On the tensions generated by these competing projects see Karen O. Kupperman, *Providence Island, 1630–1641: The Other Puritan Colony* (London: Cambridge University Press, 1993); and "Errand to the Indies: Puritan Colonization from Providence Island through the Western Design," *WMQ* 45:1 (January 1988): 70–99.

40. On Sedgwick see Henry D. Sedgwick, "Robert Sedgwick," *Transactions of the Colonial Society of Massachusetts* 3 (Boston, 1900): 155–73. For the roles of Gookin and Sedgwick in the Jamaica business see Stephen S. Webb, *The Governors-General: The English Army and the Definition of the Empire, 1569–1681* (Chapel Hill: University of North Carolina Press, 1979), 153–67. For John Underhill's curiosity about Gookin's Caribbean exploits see John Underhill to John Winthrop, Jr., 12 April 1656, *MHSC* 4th ser., vol. 7 (Boston, 1865), 182–3.

41. For Cromwellian plans to repopulate Ireland and Jamaica see Charles M. Andrews, *The Colonial Period of American History*, 4 vols. (New Haven: Yale University Press, 1934), I:499.

42. See J. R. Jacob, "Restoration, Reformation and the Origins of the Royal Society," *History of Science* 13 (1975): 155–76; and "The Ideological Origins of Robert Boyle's Natural Philosophy," *Journal of European Studies* 2 (1972): 1–21.

43. See, for example, Governor Leverett and Others to Robert Boyle, 10 May 1673, in Gookin, *Daniel Gookin*, 119–22. According to Richard S. Dunn, *Puritans and Yankees: The Winthrop Dynasty of New England, 1630–1717* (Princeton, N.J.: Princeton University Press, 1962), 161–2, 117–42, Boyle was a "prerogative" man who helped John Winthrop, Jr., secure a charter for Connecticut but responded in a less-than-cordial manner when Massachusetts asked in 1665 that he work to convince authorities to recall the Randolph commission.

44. *MBR*, IV.2: 190, 158–61, 176, 198, 211–3.

45. Easton, *A Relacion of the Indyan Warre*, 17.

46. Vincent Gookin, *Transplantation*, 3. In like manner, Daniel Gookin's hostility to religious dissent flowed in part from his belief that strange inconsistent doctrines might confuse and discourage converts. See, for example, Gookin, *Historical Collections*, 68–9; 99–100.

47. The classic treatment of the halfway measures, which stresses lay resistance, is Pope, *Halfway Covenant*. But David D. Hall, "The Meetinghouse," in *Worlds of Wonder, Days of Judgment: Popular Religious Belief in Early New England* (Cambridge: Harvard University Press, 1990), 153, demonstrates how, in the long run, more "lay people favored than opposed the halfway covenant because of how it fit into their thinking about baptism and children. Theirs was an instinctive response, a projection of their concern for the welfare of their families."

48. For the importance of family in colonial America see Helena M. Wall, *Fierce Communion: Family and Community in Early America* (Cambridge: Harvard University Press, 1990).

49. Increase Mather, *Prayer for the Rising Generation* (Boston, 1679), 12, quoted in Hall, *Worlds of Wonder*, 152.

50. On English views of Indian treachery see Karen O. Kupperman, "English Perceptions of Treachery, 1583–1640: The Case of the American 'Savages,' " *Historical Journal* 20 (1977): 263–87. For an analysis of the difference between European and Indian conceptions of lying in a wide variety of colonial settings see Gerald Sider, "When Parrots Learn to Talk, and Why They Can't: Domination, Deception and Self-Deception in Indian–White Relations," *Comparative Studies in Society and History* 29: 2 (April 1987): 3–23.

51. On this event see Hamilton Hill, *History of the Old South Church, Boston, 1669–1884*, 2 vols. (Boston: Houghton Mifflin, 1890); Pope, *Halfway Covenant*, 152–84; and Perry Miller, *The New England Mind: From Colony to Province* (Cambridge: Harvard University Press, 1953), 93–118.

52. John Oxenbridge, *A Seasonable Proposition of Propagating the Gospel by Christian Colonies in the Continent of Guiana* (London, n.d.). For efforts to colonize Surinam during the 1660s see Carl and Roberta Bridenbaugh, *No Peace beyond the Line: The English in the Caribbean, 1624–1690* (New York: Oxford University Press), 198–200. On the disputes arising from religious innovations introduced by Oxenbridge and his colleague Nathaniel White in Bermuda see J. H. Lefroy, *Memorials of the Discovery and Early Settlement of the Bermudas or Somers Islands, 1515–1685*, 2 vols. (London: Longmans, Green, 1877–79), I: 569–85, 615–22; William Prynne, *A Fresh Discovery of Some Prodigious New Wandering-Blasing Stars and Firebrands* (London, 1645); and Nathaniel White, *Truth Gloriously Appearing From Under The Sad and Sable Cloud of Obloquie* (London, 1646).

53. For the argument that English observers during the contact period judged native peoples on the basis of their perceived level of civility and not anachronistic concepts of racial difference see Karen O. Kupperman, "Presentment of Civility: English Reading of American Self-Presentation in the Early Years of Colonization," *WMQ* 54: 1 (January 1997): 193–228.

54. Oxenbridge, "Conversion of the Gentiles," 1670(?), Ms. SBd.56 Massachusetts Historical Society.

55. On the divisions between First and Third Church partisans see Richard C. Simmons, "The Founding of the Third Church in Boston," *WMQ* 26: 2 (April 1969): 241–52; E. Brooks Holifield, "On Toleration in Massachusetts," *Church His-*

tory 38: 2 (1969): 188–200; and Stephen Foster, *The Long Argument: English Puritanism and the Shaping of New England Culture, 1570–1700* (Chapel Hill: University of North Carolina Press, 1991), 175–230. The faction that formed Third Church, which included Major Thomas Savage, was opposed to religious toleration. Yet the leading men of both these opposing churches were of a piece on the issue of praying Indians; and it may be that, as far as the issue of extending the bonds of community was concerned, these elites had more in common than they thought.

56. For the argument that the halfway covenant helped to reinforce the new orthodoxy, and the association of First Church with antinomian beliefs, see Janice Knight, *Orthodoxies in Massachusetts: Rereading American Puritanism* (Cambridge: Harvard University Press, 1994).

57. Saltonstall, "Present State," 40–1.

58. Holifield, "Toleration in Massachusetts," 192, points out that James Oliver was one of a number of individuals fined or admonished in 1668 for petitioning the General Court to free some Anabaptists who had been imprisoned.

59. Saltonstall, "Present State," 38, 35.

60. See Jacob, "Restoration, Reformation and the Origins of the Royal Society"; "The Ideological Origins of Robert Boyle's Natural Philosophy"; and "The New England Company, the Royal Society, and the Indians."

61. See Adam B. Seligman, *Innerworldly Individualism: Charismatic Community and its Institutionalization* (New Brunswick, N.J.: Transactions, 1994), on the ultimate continuity between the halfway covenant and a wide range of late-seventeenth-century changes in church polity, including Stoddardarianism and the Brattle Street Church. On the "sacramental renaissance" see E. Brooks Holifield, *The Covenant Sealed: The Development of Puritan Sacramental Theology in Old and New England, 1570–1720* (New Haven: Yale University Press, 1974), 197–224.

62. Gookin, *Historical Collections*, 68. On the difficulty of trying to inculcate among Indians crucial Puritan doctrines, especially that of original sin, see Charles L. Cohen, "Conversion among Puritans and Amerindians: A Theological and Cultural Perspective," in *Puritanism: Transatlantic Perspectives on a Seventeenth-Century Anglo-American Faith*, ed. Francis Bremer (Boston: Northeastern University Press, 1993), 233–56.

63. Vincent Gookin, *Transplantation*, 4–5.

64. Gookin, "Doings and Sufferings," 515. Gookin would here seem to be recommending a "civil" connection with the Indians, as he did when reminding colonists that "The reason, why the English government is concerned with the Indians' affairs in point of rule and order, is because all those praying Indians in Massachusetts colony did long since, before they began to worship God, actually and solemnly submit themsleves unto the jurisdiction and government of the English in the Massachusetts, as the records do declare"; Gookin, *Historical Collections*, 62. On the distinction between the "godly" and the "merely civil" see Richard Gildrie, *The Profane, the Civil and the Godly: The Reformation of Manners in Orthodox New England, 1679–1749* (University Park: Pennsylvania State University Press, 1994).

65. Hall, "The Meetinghouse," 144–5, has shown that some "halfway" members of Puritan congregations actually admitted that they turned to witchcraft for a release from religious demands they felt unable to fulfill—particularly the demand to move toward full membership. Given these circumstances, it would have been easy for them to believe that Indians' temptation-fraught spiritual journeys might similarly lead to devilish practice.

66. William Gurnall, *The Christian in Compleat Armour* (London, 1679), 70, 64, 95.

67. Hubbard, *Narrative*, I:120.

68. Gookin, "Doings and Sufferings," 444, 449–54, 494.

69. Samuel Crooke, *Ta Diapheronta, or Divine Characters . . . Accurately Distinguishing the More Secret and Undiscerned Differences Between . . . the Hypocrite in his best Dresse of Seeming Virtues and Formal Duties and the True Christian in his Real Graces and Sincere Obedience* (London, 1658), 7–11.

70. On the "cunning" people see John Demos, *Entertaining Satan: Witchcraft and the Culture of Early New England* (New York: Oxford University Press, 1982).

71. On Gookin's entrepreneurial land acquisition see John Frederick Martin, *Profits in the Wilderness: Entrepreneurship and the Founding of New England Towns in the Seventeenth Century* (Chapel Hill: University of North Carolina Press, 1991), 23–8. For Gookin's official position on committees that controlled trade and on sales of guns and ammunition, see MBR, IV:2, 329–30, 366; for his role in developing Worcester and Sherborne see MBR, V:10, 83, 216–7, 228–30, 460.

72. *Massachusetts Archives* 30:258a.

73. Mary Pray to James Oliver, 20 October 1675, MHSC, 5th ser., vol. 1 (Boston, 1871), 106.

74. On the role of husbandry-related disputes in the tensions preceding King Philip's War see Virginia Anderson, "King Philip's Herds: Indians, Colonists and the Problem of Livestock in Early New England," *WMQ* 51: 4 (October 1994): 601–24; and Joshua Micah Marshall, " 'A Melancholy People': Anglo-Indian Relations in Early Warwick, Rhode Island, 1642–1675," *NEQ* 68: 3 (September 1995): 402–28.

75. Daniel Gookin, Letter to Governor Thomas Prince, 17 April 1671, Miscellaneous Bound, Massachusetts Historical Society; and Thomas Prince, Letter to Daniel Gookin, 26 April 1671, Miscellaneous Bound, Massachusetts Historical Society. Both letters are printed in MHSC, 1st ser., vol. 6, (Boston, 1779), 198–201.

76. This correspondence is reprinted in Gookin, *Daniel Gookin*, 138–40.

77. For an in-depth treatment of how the 1671 crisis was averted see Philip Ranlet, "Another Look at the Causes of King Philip's War," *NEQ* 61: 1 (March 1988): 89–95.

78. See "Instructions from the Church at Natick to William and Anthony," 1 August 1671, MHSC, 1st ser., vol. 6 (Boston; 1799), 201–3; Increase Mather, "A Brief History of the Warr With the Indians in New England," in *So Dreadfull a Judgment: Puritan Responses to King Philip's War, 1676–77*, ed. Richard Slotkin and James K. Folsom (Middletown, Conn.: Wesleyan University Press, 1978), 87; and Gookin, "Doings and Sufferings." For Eliot's idealized view of how Ahauton might have behaved in encounters with Philip see his rendition of the ill-disguised character "William Abahton" in *John Eliot's Indian Dialogues: A Study in Cultural Interaction*, ed. Henry W. Bowden and James P. Ronda (Westport, Conn.: Greenwood Press, 1980).

79. For a full-length exposition of this case see Ann Marie Plane, " 'The Examination of Sarah Ahhaton': The Politics of 'Adultery' in an Indian Town of Seventeenth-Century Massachusetts," in *The Algonkians of New England: Past and Present*, ed. Peter Benes, Dublin Seminar for New England Folklife, Annual Proceedings (Boston: Boston University Press, 1993), 14–25. Although war was still far off, Increase Mather, "Brief History," 124–5, explained that supernatural signs had begun to presage its coming as early as 1667.

80. *MBR*, IV: 42, 407–8. On laws pertaining to adultery in Massachusetts, where the death penalty was imposed only once for this crime, see Mary Beth Norton, *Founding Mothers and Fathers: Gendered Power and the Forming of American Society* (New York: Knopf, 1996), 72–6, 342.

81. Daniel Gookin, "The Examination of Sarah Ahhaton, Indian Squa Wife Unto William Ahhaton of Pakemit alias Punquapauge taken the 24th of October 1668 Before Daniel Gookin," Massachusetts Archives collection at Columbia Point (SC1, 45x), 30:152. The name "Ahhaton" is spelled variously as Ahauton, Ahaton, Nahaton.

82. Plane, "Examination."

83. Gookin, "Examination."

84. On Philip's move to curtail religious efforts in Mount Hope and for the suggestion that missionaries' injunctions against spousal abuse may have been attractive to female converts, see Lonkhuyzen, "Reappraisal of the Praying Indians," 420. According to Samuel G. Drake, *The Book of the Indians, or, Biography and History of the Indians of North America From its First Discovery to the Year 1841* (1841; reprint, New York: AMS Press, 1976), bk. 2, p. 113, missionaries prescribed at Natick that if "any man shall beat his wife, his hands shall be tied behind him, and he shall be carried to the place of justice to be severely whipped." Sarah's husband, however, was never punished for beating her.

85. On Chickataubut and for a description of Wamesit, the town in which Sarah's parents lived, see Gookin, *Historical Collections*, 72, 74, 40–1. Chekatabutt met his end in 1669 while serving as the "chiefest general" in a war against the New York Mohawks. For evidence that William Ahauton and his father, "Old Ahauton," had recently served as "wise men" on Chekatabutt's council, see Drake, *Book of the Indians*, bk. 2, pp. 42–5. By toeing the English Puritan line, the Ahauton men perhaps hoped to augment their power, assuming the vacuum left by Josiah Chekatabutt. On relations between the Mohawks and the Algonquian peoples of New England see Neal Salisbury, "Toward the Covenant Chain: Iroquois and Southern New England Algonquians, 1637–1684," in *Beyond the Covenant Chain: The Iroquois and Their Neighbors in Indian North America, 1600–1800*, ed. Daniel K. Richter and James H. Merrell (Syracuse N.Y.: Syracuse University Press, 1987), 61–73.

Sarah might also have pondered the defection of another prominent praying Indian, John Sassamon, who had left Natick for Mount Hope at roughly the same time as her flight from Packemit. For an account of Sassamon that emphasizes his inability to belong fully in English or Indian society see Jill Lepore, "Dead Men Tell No Tales: John Sassamon and the Fatal Consequences of Literacy," *American Quarterly* 46: 4 (December 1994): 479–512. See also James P. Ronda and Jeanne Ronda, "The Death of John Sassamon: An Exploration in Writing New England Indian History," *American Indian Quarterly* 1 (fall 1974), 91–102.

86. Gookin, "Examination." On the suicide see Daniel T. V. Huntoon, *History of the Town of Canton, Norfolk County, Massachusetts* (Cambridge: J. Wilson, 1893), 23–4. For an analysis of how suicide was perceived in this period see Michael MacDonald and Terence R. Murphy, *Sleepless Souls: Suicide in Early Modern England* (Oxford: Clarendon Press, 1990).

87. On the importance of reciprocity in Algonquian cultures see Neal Salisbury, *Manitou and Providence: Indians, Europeans, and the Making of New England, 1500–1643* (New York: Oxford University Press, 1982), 10–1.

88. Pulsifer, *Acts of the Commissioners*, X:366. On Gookin's parallel efforts to

rescue the relatives of praying Indians from slavery, a fate he believed they did not deserve, see, for example, Massachusetts Archives Collection at Columbia Point (SC1, 45x), 30:221.

89. Massachusetts Archives Collection at Columbia Point (SC1, 45x), 30: 221a; Gookin, "Doings and Sufferings," 513–5.

90. Gookin, "Doings and Sufferings," 481.

91. Gookin, *Historical Collections*, 82.

92. Gookin, "Doings and Sufferings," 447–9; Hubbard, *Narrative*, I: 98–9, admitted that all would have been lost "had it not been for one well acquainted with those Woods, who led them in a By-path, by which Means they got thither [to Brookfield] a little before the Indians." But he does not mention that this skilled frontiersman was a praying Indian.

93. For examples of statements attesting to the worth of praying Indian troops see Gookin, "Doings and Sufferings," 524–5; and Massachusetts Archives Collection at Columbia Point (SC1, 45x) 30: 221, 228.

94. Gookin, *Historical Collections*, 84; "Doings and Sufferings," 476–7.

95. Gookin, "Doings and Sufferings," 527–9.

96. Ibid., 442.

97. Hubbard, *Narrative*, II:276.

98. In the 1680s and 1690s, British authors began to discuss military "strategy," as opposed to "pure valor," in more positive terms. Marcus d'Assigny presented to English readers in 1686 his translation of a book compiled by the Roman consul Sextus Julius Frontinus, containing "the most remarkable Stratagems of the Persians, Greeks, Romans, and Cathaginians." Well aware that the open and unhalting encouragement of "strategy" represented a departure from traditional English military thought, d'Assigny included in his dedication an extended explanation of the need for change: "No nation under the Sun have taken a greater Delight in War than ours, and none have been more successful in former Ages, and purchased more Honour in the field than the English. But this is remarkable in History, that their victories were gotten more by their plain Valour, than by their Policies. The Strength of other Nations consists in Subtilties and Ambushes; there are few that dare face an assaulting enemy in the open field and oppose their naked breasts to the showers of the the murthering shot. Behind a Hedge, or Ditch, or a Breastwork, and when they have the Advangages of Number and the ground, they may venture a Battel. But the English have been taken notice of for their Undaunted Courage in the midst of the greatest Difficulties, and have often snatcht the Victory out of the hands of thier insulting enemy. But if the English courage alone, without the Assistance of Art, hath been so victorious, what Wonders would it not be able to perform, if it were seconded by Policy and Craft?" Samuel d'Assigny, *A Collection of the Brave Exploits and Subtil Strategems of Several Famous Generals Since the Roman Empire with a Discourse Concerning Engines of War* (London, 1686), in "Dedication." Military writer William Freke, writing in the same vein seven years later, told officers they should not hesitate to employ spies, to ambush the enemy, to "plunder under mine enemies colours," or to make "false alarms," since " 'tis Jesting, not Fighting, to proclaim every blow we intend." Victory was no "less honourable" with the use of "strategem"; even Christ employed an artful strategy "after he was risen from the dead, and set his face as if he were going where he was not"; *Select Essays Tending to the Universal Reformation of Learning: Concluded with the Art of War, or a Summary of the Martial Precepts Necessary for an Officer* (London, 1693), 271–2.

"Stratagem" was, of course, used in military engagements in all periods, regardless of how it was presented in the literature. For the rules of engagement in various situations see Barbara Donagan, "Codes and Conduct in the English Civil War," *Past and Present* 118 (February, 1988), 65–95.

99. Hubbard, *Narrative*, I:201–3. Gookin's account also describes the nature of the spies' mission and emphasizes their craftiness. Gookin, "Doings and Sufferings," 485–91.

100. Hubbard, *Narrative*, I:199–200, emphasized One-Eyed John's canny ability to prey on English insecurities. Calling out to his victims at Groton, Hubbard recounted, One-Eyed John deliberately mocked the old friendships that had obtained between English and Indians, scoffed at the possibility of a "friendly Peace," and called into question English religious superiority.

101. See, for example, Anne Kusener Nelson, "King Philip's War and the Hubbard–Mather Rivalry," *WMQ* 27:4 (October 1970): 615–29. For a recent challenge to the argument that Hubbard was more "modern" or "rational" than other Bay Colony ministers, particularly Cotton Mather, see Winship, *Seers of God*, 22–7.

102. For Mather's account of how he lobbied in October for the "provoking evils" law see "Brief History," 105–6.

103. Mather, "An Earnest Exhortation To the Inhabitants of New England (Boston, 1676)," in *So Dreadfull a Judgment*,180.

104. Hubbard, *Narrative*, II:53–4.

105. Ibid., II:80.

106. Ibid., II: 258.

107. William Harris to Sir Joseph Williamson, State Papers in Frederick Lewis Gay Transcripts, II, Massachusetts Historical Society. For the English rationale that subject peoples in rebellion should be treated more harshly than other wartime enemies, see Ronald Dale Kerr, " 'Why Should You Be So Furious?': The Violence of the Pequot War," *Journal of American History* 85 (1998): 876–909.

108. "Diary of Increase Mather," *Massachusetts Historical Society Proceedings*, ser. 2, vol. 13 (Boston, 1899–1900): 358–9. See also Michael G. Hall, *The Last American Puritan: The Life of Increase Mather* (Middletown, Conn.: Wesleyan University Press, 1988), 113–4.

109. Mather, "Diary," 366.

110. See Michael G. Hall, ed., "The Autobiography of Increase Mather," American Antiquarian Society, *Proceedings* 71 (1961): 299, for Mather's grateful recognition of contributions made by Temple, Lake, and others. For an account of Temple's acceptance in Puritan society despite the rumors that circulated about how he lived in a dissolute manner and kept a mistress, see Arthur Buffinton, "Sir Thomas Temple in Boston: A Case of Benevolent Assimilation," Publications of the Colonial Society of Massachusetts, *Transactions* 27 (1932): 308–19.

111. Mather, "Diary," 359.

112. On Richards's opposition to the halfway covenant in North Church see Foster, *Long Argument*, 222–3. For his continuing opposition to covenant renewals and moves to liberalize rules concerning baptism see Cotton Mather to John Richards, 14 December 1692, in *Selected Letters of Cotton Mather*, ed. Kenneth Silverman (Baton Rouge: Louisiana State University Press, 1971), 46–50. Richards's ongoing interest in the Nova Scotia trade was evidenced by his marriage to a daughter of Captain Thomas Hawkins, who had participated in the 1640s on raids against French strongholds in French Acadia. Roberts, *Military Company*, I:143, 63.

113. On the extent of the Lake/Clark installation, destroyed by the Abenakis in 1676, see John G. Reid, *Acadia, Maine and New Scotland* (Toronto: University of Toronto Press, 1981), 130–1; and Hubbard, *Narrative*, II:72.

114. Massachusetts Archives Collection at Columbia Point (SC1, 45x) 30:221.

115. Saltonstall, "Present State," 35.

116. Gookin, "Doings and Sufferings," 503.

117. On Tyng see Martin, *Profits in the Wilderness*, 21–2; and Gookin, "Doings and Sufferings," 533. On investments in Dunstable see Elias Nason, *A History of the Town of Dunstable, Massachusetts, from its Earliest Settlement* (Boston, 1877), 7–16; and Wilkes Allen, *The History of Chelmsford, From its Origin in 1653, to the year 1820* (Haverhill, Mass., 1820).

118. Edmund Morgan, "A Boston Heiress and Her Husbands: A True Story," *Publications of the Colonial Society of Massachusetts* 34 (1937–42): 499–513; and Gookin, "Doings and Sufferings," 504.

119. On Lathrop see Charles M. Bodge, *Soldiers in King Philips War being a Critical Account of that War with a Concise History of the Indian Wars of New England from 1620–1677* (1906; reprint, Baltimore: Genealogical, 1967), 127–41.

120. Saltonstall, "Present State," 29–30.

121. Ibid., 29.

122. Gookin, "Doings and Sufferings," 501–2.

123. MBR, V:71; Gookin, "Doings and Sufferings," 496.

124. MBR, V:94–5. Mosely demanded also that "neither he nor any of his company may be ordered to keep garrison, but maybe alwayes at liberty to seeke out and molest the enemy"; that the colony avoid placing him "under the comand of any comander in chiefe that is or may be sent out, unless, upon a suddaine exigent . . . but not to be obliged to continue with them longer then that emergency may require"; and that "his commission may be as large as may consist with the safety of the country, and not to be bound up in his marches or executions to particular places, but to leave it to their best discretions for destroying the enemy." Interestingly, Mosely requested the use of "trusty" Indian adjuncts at this time.

125. Hubbard, *Narrative*, I:113–4.

126. Ibid., 115–9.

127. Saltonstall, "Present State," 39.

128. On the horrified reaction to the discovery of Joshua Tefft, a "renegade" Englishman who had married a Wampanoag woman and was thought to have aided the enemy militarily, see Colin G. Calloway, "Rhode Island Renegade: The Enigma of Joshua Tefft," *Rhode Island History* 43: 4 (November 1984): 137–45; and Hubbard, *Narrative*, I:162.

129. Hubbard marveled at the Indians' adroitness at what we would now call guerilla warfare, but in many cases his language betrayed his reservations about the adoption of such tactics. See, for example, Hubbard, *Narrative*, I: 175–6, for a chilling description of the ease with which an ally could blend in with the enemy.

130. Letter from Daniel Denision, 14 December 1676, in *Documentary History of the State of Maine*, ed. James Phinney Baxter, vols. 4–6, 9–16, *The Baxter Manuscripts* (Portland, Me., 1889–1916), VI:145–6; Noble, *Records of the Court of Assistants*, I:102. See also William S. Southgate, "History of Scarborough, from 1633 to 1783," *Maine Historical Society Collections* 1st ser., vol. 3 (Portland, Me., 1853), 135, 235; Hubbard, *Narrative*, II:171–5, 189, 191, 217; and Sybil Noyes, Charles Libby, and Walter Davis, *Genealogical Dictionary of Maine and New Hampshire*

(1928–39; reprint, Baltimore: Genealogical, 1988), 255–6. For Gendall's longstanding difficulties with Massachusetts authorities, and his prison break, see Augustus Corliss, ed., *Old Times of North Yarmouth, Maine* (1877–84; rep. Somersworth: New Hampshire Publishing Company, 1977), 511–37.

131. Drake, ed., *History of the Indian Wars in New England*, II:126–7, n. 155.

132. Ibid., 127. For testimony from residents who believed that Scottow had done his best to protect them, and to procure provisions and troops from a reluctant government in Massachusetts see Bodge, *Soldiers*, 325–41.

133. Hamilton A. Hill, "Joshua Scottow and John Alden," *Old South Church Memorial Addresses*, Boston Historical Pamphlets Connected with the Old South Church and Society, 1821–1884, comp. James F. Hunnewell (Boston: Old South Church, 1884), 6–9.

134. On the Hibbens case see Carol F. Karlsen, *The Devil in the Shape of a Woman: Witchcraft in Colonial New England* (New York: Norton, 1987).

135. Southgate, "History of Scarborough," 155.

136. Thomas Gardner to Governor Leverett, 22 September 1675, in Baxter, *Baxter Manuscripts*, VI:91–3. On Gardiner's support for the royal commissioners in Maine—which may have added to suspicions concerning his loyalty—see William D. Williamson, *The History of the State of Maine*, 2 vols. (Hallowell: Glazier, Masters, 1832), I: 421.

137. Att a Council at Boston, 16 October 1675, in Baxter, *Baxter Manuscripts*, VI:96–7.

138. Petition to the Honorable Court of Assistants, 5 September 1676, Massachusetts Archives Collection at Columbia Point (SC1, 45x), 30: 216.

139. Mather, "Diary," 359. On Chelmsford see Gookin, "Doings and Sufferings," 482–3.

140. Mather, "Earnest Exhortation," 187–88.

141. Kathryn Zabelle Derounian, "Puritan Orthodoxy and the 'Survivor Syndrome' in Mary Rowlandson's Indian Captivity Narrative," *Early American Literature* 22 (1987): 82–93, argues that the act of producing a narrative was a healing process for Rowlandson and effected her psychic deliverance from the trials of war. Christian Indians, of course, could achieve such deliverance only vicariously, through Gookin's work; whether they were aware of his manuscript, however, is unknown.

142. Gookin, "Doings and Sufferings," 454.

143. Mather, "Earnest Exhortation," 190.

144. Ibid., 188–9.

145. Mather, "Diary," 358; and "Earnest Exhortation," 189. On the efforts of clerics to make sure afflicted communicants blamed their sufferings on their own sinfulness see Richard Godbeer, *The Devil's Dominion: Magic and Religion in Early New England* (New York: Cambridge University Press, 1992), 85–121.

146. Gildrie, *The Profane, The Civil, and The Godly*, 203, puts missionary work into the context of the late-seventeenth- and early-eighteenth-century "proliferation of voluntary pious and reform associations," arguing that "the religious societies and the societies for the Reformation of Manners were a bridge between the Puritan impulses, both Anglican and Dissenter, of the late seventeenth century." It is important to recognize, however, that missionary endeavor often reflected not a genuine interest in Indian conversion but rather the need to adapt to the new imperial order while still appearing to be following the mandates of the founding generation. Hall, *Last American Puritan*, 310–13, emphasizes, for example, that the Indian work

helped Mather to cultivate influential persons in London, such as Major Robert Thompson; while in Massachusetts however, the Mathers had little or no direct contact with Indians.

147. Mather, *Brief History*, 100; Drake, *Book of the Indians*, bk. 3, pp. 102–3; and Hubbard, *Narrative*, II:135, 177.

148. Hubbard, *Narrative*, II: 177–8, 201–3.

149. Ibid., II: 270.

150. Increase Mather, *An Historical Discourse Concerning the Prevalency of Prayer* (Boston, 1677), 6; and Mather, "Exhortation," 189–90.

151. Harry S. Stout, *The New England Soul: Preaching and Religious Culture in Colonial New England* (New York: Oxford University Press, 1986), 127–47, has noted the prevalent use of the word "delight" in late-seventeenth-century cosmopolitan circles. Stout also provides a deft analysis of how ministers enabled colonists to retain their Puritan identity without the benefit of the Puritan state.

152. Amanda Porterfield, *Female Piety in Puritan New England* (New York: Oxford University Press, 1992), 116–56, sets this emphasis on domesticity in the context of the growing numbers of female church members. Interestingly, it was a group of women who carried out one of the most violent acts of King Philip's War, literally tearing apart some captured Indians in 1677. See James Axtell, "The Vengeful Women of Marblehead: Robert Roule's Deposition of 1677," *WMQ* 31: 4 (October 1974): 647–652.

153. On Bacon's Rebellion see Morgan, *American Slavery, American Freedom*. Virginia governor William Berkeley's speculations about the interconnectedness of the two events are discussed in Wilcomb E. Washburn, "Governor Berkeley and King Philip's War," *NEQ* 30:3 (September 1957): 363–77. For the eighteenth-century movement toward exclusivity see Gregory Evans Dowd, *A Spirited Resistance: The North American Indian Struggle for Unity, 1745–1815* (Baltimore: Johns Hopkins University Press, 1992).

154. For the connection between witchcraft and Indian war see John McWilliams, "Indian John and the Northern Tawnies," *NEQ* 69: 4 (December 1996), 580–604; and James E. Kences, "Some Unexplored Relationships of Essex County Witchcraft to the Indian Wars of 1675 and 1689," *Essex Institute Historical Collections* 120: 3 (July 1984), 179–212. According to Robert St. George, " 'Heated' Speech and Literacy in Seventeenth-Century New England," in *Seventeenth-Century New England*, ed. David D. Hall et al. (Boston: Colonial Society of Massachusetts, 1984), 275–317, the epithet "dog," which was also hurled at Gookin, could be used to describe persons who "had no hope for redemption" or who "might be working with Satan" (quoted at 294).

CHAPTER 5

1. Paul Boyer and Stephen Nissenbaum, eds., *The Salem Witchcraft Papers: Verbatim Transcripts of the Legal Documents of the Salem Witchcraft Outbreak of 1692*, 3 vols. (New York: De Capo Press, 1977), I:52.

2. See Richard Godbeer, *The Devil's Dominion: Magic and Religion in Early New England* (1992; reprint, New York: Cambridge University Press, 1994), 179–222, for a discussion of how colonists saw Andros, Indians, and witches as similar agents of assault against the godly colony.

3. On Phillips's founding membership in Third Church and his marriage to the widow Elizabeth Phillips Averill see Joseph W. Porter, "Captain John Alden,

Jr. of Boston and Maine," *Maine Historical Magazine* 7 (1891–92): 209–15; and Hamilton A. Hill, *History of the Old South Church (Third Church) Boston, 1669–1884*, 2 vols. (Boston: Houghton, Mifflin, 1890), I:118.

4. My interpretation of this colorful figure in this chapter is much indebted to Richard R. Johnson, *John Nelson, Merchant Adventurer: A Life between Empires* (New York: Oxford University Press, 1991).

5. For genealogical information concerning William Phillips and Bridget Hutchinson Phillips see Charles H. Pope, *The Pioneers of Maine and New Hampshire, 1623 to 1660* (1908; reprint, Baltimore: Genealogical, 1989), 160–63; Sybil Noyes, Charles Libby, and Walter Davis, *Genealogical Dictionary of Maine and New Hampshire* (1928–39; reprint, Baltimore: Genealogical, 1988), 548–9; and Joseph Lemuel Chester, *Notes Upon the Ancestry of William Hutchinson and Anne Marbury, From Researches Recently Made in England* (Boston, 1866), 17.

6. James Phinney Baxter, ed., *Documentary History of the State of Maine*, vols. 4–6, 9–16, *The Baxter Manuscripts* (Portland, M., 1889–1916), VI:344–5; and Bridget Phillips to Edward Rishworth, 29 July 1684, *Maine Historical Society Collections*, vol. 4 (Portland, M., 1856): 409.

7. Johnson, *Nelson*, 30–69. On Madockawando see Samuel Drake, *The Book of the Indians: Biography and History of the Indians of North America* (1841; reprint, New York: AMS Press, 1976), bk. 3, pp. 102–9.

8. On Parris's role see Paul Boyer and Stephen Nissenbaum, *Salem Possessed: Social Origins of Witchcraft* (Cambridge: Harvard University Press, 1974); and Larry D. Gragg, *A Quest for Security: The Life of Samuel Parris, 1653–1720* (New York: Greenwood Press, 1990). For a direct transcription of the ideas Parris was transmitting to his congregation in the years surrounding the witchcraft epidemic see James F. Cooper, Jr., and Kenneth P. Minkema, eds., *The Sermon Notebook of Samuel Parris* (Charlottesville, Va.: University Press of Virginia, 1993).

9. The connection between witchcraft and Indian war has been drawn in John McWilliams, "Indian John and the Northern Tawnies," *NEQ* 69: 4 (December 1996): 580–604; and James E. Kences, "Some Unexplored Relationships of Essex County Witchcraft to the Indian Wars of 1675 and 1689," *Essex Institute Historical Collections* 120: 3 (July 1984): 179–212.

10. Cotton Mather, "Decennium Luctuosum: An History of Remarkable Occurrences in the Long War, which New-England hath had with the Indian Salvages, from the year 1688, to the year 1698, faithfully Composed and Improved," in *Narratives of the Indian Wars, 1675–1699*, ed. Charles H. Lincoln (1913; reprint, New York: Barnes and Noble, 1959), 242.

11. Ibid., 243–7.

12. On this point see Kences, "Some Unexplored Relationships."

13. John Nelson, Letter to Benjamin Colman, 20 May 1699, Benjamin Colman Papers, Massachusetts Historical Society.

14. John Nelson, State of his Case and Affairs, n.d., Nova Scotia Papers in Frederick Lewis Gay Transcripts, I, Massachusetts Historical Society; Johnson, *Nelson*, 16–29, 46; and M. Halsey Thomas, ed., *The Diary of Samuel Sewall, 1674–1729*, 2 vols. (New York, 1973), I:145. According to Hamilton A. Hill, "Joshua Scottow and John Alden," in *Old South Church Memorial Addresses*, Boston Historical Pamphlets Connected with the Old South Church and Society, 1821–1884, comp. James F. Hunnewell (Boston: Old South Church, 1884), 15–16, Alden regularly captained vessels in which Sewall's father-in-law John Hull held shares; Sewall probably hoped to benefit from this connetion when seeking Nelson's aid.

15. Oliver Ayer Roberts, *History of the Military Company of the Massachusetts Now Called the Ancient and Honourable Artillery Company of Massachusetts, 1637–1888*, 4 vols. (A. Mudge, 1895–1909), I: 262; Francis Foxcroft to Francis Nicholson, 26 October 1691, State Papers in Frederick Lewis Gay Transcripts, III, Massachusetts Historical Society; and Samuel Ravenscroft to Francis Nicholson, 5 November 1691, ibid.

16. Johnson, *Nelson*, 31–48. On the Abenaki-French alliance and the missionary efforts of French Jesuits see Kenneth M. Morrison, *The Embattled Northeast: The Elusive Ideal of Alliance in Abenaki–Euramerican Relations* (Berkeley: University of California Press, 1984), 72–101.

17. John Nelson, Letter to Charles Talbot, 1695, Massachusetts Historical Society: Johnson, *Nelson*, 50–55.

18. Mather, "Decennium Luctuosum," 194.

19. Johnson, *Nelson*, 59–66. One Andros supporter, seeking to establish that anti-Andros merchants were equally guilty of frontier profiteering, included a denunciation of Foster and Waterhouse in a pro-Andros tract, asserting that one month prior to the rebellion these men had "loaded a Brigantine with Provision and Ammunition at Boston, and entered her for Bermudoes, but sent her to the eastward amongst the French and Indians then in actual War with us, and furnished and supplied them therewith, when the Governor and the Forces were out against them and had reduced them to the greatest want and necessity both for Provision and Ammunition; and soon after the Revolution that Vessel returned from those Parts with her Loading of Bever and Peltry, which was publickly known and talked, but no notice taken thereof, the grievous effects of which the country well knows, and are very sensible thereof." See [Joseph Dudley], *New England's Faction Discovered*, in *The Andros Tracts*, ed. W. H. Whitmore, 3 vols. (New York: Burt Franklin, 1868–74), II:216–17. On Waterhouse and Foster see also Roberts, *History of the Military Company*, I:254, 259.

20. Quoted in Johnson, *Nelson*, 61–2.

21. Ibid., 64–5.

22. Samuel Ravenscroft to Francis Nicolson, 5 November 1691, State Papers in Frederick Lewis Gay Transcripts, III, Massachusetts Historical Society; Kences, "Some Unexplored Relationships," 190; and Porter, "Alden of Boston and Maine."

23. Johnson, *Nelson*, 66–69; and Francis Foxcroft to Francis Nicolson, 26 October 1691, State Papers Colonial in Frederick Lewis Gay Transcripts, III, Massachusetts Historical Society.

24. Letter from Edward Tyng, 18 August 1688, *Baxter Manuscripts*, VI: 419–20; and Petition of the Inhabitants of Falmouth, 24 May 1689, 481–83. On Tyng's land acquisitions and officeholding in Maine see John Frederick Martin, *Profits in the Wilderness: Entrepreneurship and the Founding of New England Towns in the Seventeenth Century* (Chapel Hill: University of North Carolina Press, 1991), 20–22.

25. John Nelson's Statement of his Case and Affairs, n.d., Nova Scotia Papers in Frederick Lewis Gay Transcripts, I, Massachusetts Historical Society; and Johnson, *Nelson*, 66–85. On the complications that attended exchanges of captives see, for example, John Demos, *The Unredeemed Captive: A Family Story from Early America* (New York: Knopf, 1994); and Ian K. Steele, *Betrayals: Fort William Henry and the Massacre* (New York: Oxford University Press, 1990).

26. Johnson, *Nelson*, 70–85.

27. Boyer and Nissenbaum, *Salem Witchcraft Papers*, I:173.

28. On the distinctions between popular and elite conceptions of witchcraft

see Richard Weisman, *Witchcraft, Magic and Religion in Seventeenth-Century Massachusetts* (Amherst: University of Massachusetts Press, 1984); and Godbeer, *Devil's Dominion.*

29. For treatments that emphasize the importance of the Burroughs case as a turning point in the trials see Bernard Rosenthal, *Salem Story: Reading the Witch Trials of 1692* (New York: Cambridge University Press, 1993), 129–50; and Richard Gildrie, *The Profane, the Civil and the Godly: The Reformation of Manners in Orthodox New England, 1679–1749* (University Park: Pennsylavania State University Press, 1994), 172–80.

30. Deborah Willis, *Malevolent Nurture: Witch-Hunting and Maternal Power in Early Modern England* (Ithaca, N.Y.: Cornell University Press, 1995), has chronicled the tendency of "learned" witch hunters in Scotland and England to insist that the demonic family, a twisted parody of the Christian family complete with maternal witches and childlike imps, must be led by a male patriarchal figure—either the devil or an elite man. On the widespread fear during witchcraft panics of chaos and inversion see Stuart Clark, "Inversion, Misrule, and the Meaning of Witchcraft," *Past and Present* 87 (1980): 98–127.

31. Richard Slotkin, *Regeneration through Violence: The Mythology of the American Frontier, 1600–1860* (1973; reprint, New York: Harper Collins, 1996),141–2, shows how tales of Burroughs's seemingly preternatural strength, which linked him to the frontier, were used against him.

32. Boyer and Nissenbaum, *Salem Witchcraft Papers,* I:168–9. On the "sacramental renaissance" in late-seventeenth-century New England see E. Brooks Holifield, *The Covenant Sealed: The Development of Puritan Sacramental Theology in Old and New England, 1570–1720* (New Haven: Yale University Press, 1974), 197–224.

33. Mather, "Decennium Luctuosum," 278.

34. Roberts, *History of the Military Company,* I: 142; *MBR,* III: 372, 421; Herbert Ricard, ed., *Journal of John Bowne, 1650–1694* (New Orleans, 1975); Jack Minard Sanford, *President John Sanford of Boston, Massachusetts, and Portsmouth, Rhode Island* (Rutland, Vt., 1966); and Petition of William Phillips, 15 May 1661, *Baxter Manuscripts,* VI: 14–16.

35. On Phillips's frontier land activities see Martin, *Profits in the Wilderness,* 67, 106–7.

36. Phillips's Petition, *Baxter Manuscripts,* VI:14–6. On the attitude toward monopolies in Massachusetts and the conditions under which monopolies would be reluctantly granted see Stephen Innes, *Creating the Commonwealth: The Economic Culture of Puritan New England* (New York: Norton, 1995), 229–236.

37. Phillips's Petition, *Baxter Manuscripts,* VI:14–6.

38. On Quaker meetings in Maine see Jonathan Chu, *Neighbors, Friends or Madmen: The Puritan Adjustment to Quakerism in Seventeenth-Century Massachusetts Bay* (Westport, Conn.: Greenwood, 1985).

39. For an account of jurisdictional changes in Maine during this period see Charles E. Clark, *The Eastern Frontier: The Settlement of Northern New England, 1610–1763* (New York: Knopf, 1970), 63–4.

40. *Baxter Manuscripts,* VI:26–8, 20–1, 29–31.

41. On the destruction of the Phillips garrison and mills see William Hubbard, *A Narrative of the Troubles with the Indians in New England,* ed. Samuel G. Drake, *The History of the Indian Wars in New England,* 2 vols. in 1 (New York: Kraus Reprint, 1969), II: 109–110.

42. Mather, "Decennium Luctuosum," 277–8.

43. Elisha Sanford, Esborn Sanford, Eliphal Stratton, Elisha Hutchinson, Peleg Sanford, and Zechariah Gillam were all among the proprietors of the projected town of Sanford, which was to be built on an eight-square-mile tract of land deeded to them and others by William Phillips. See Edwin Emery, *The History of Sanford, Maine, 1661–1900* (Fall River, Mass.: n.p., 1901).

44. Anne Gillam and Eliphal Stratton were arrested together in 1673 for attending the same Quaker meeting (Moses Paine, Report on a Quaker meeting in Boston, 16 March 1673/74, Miscellaneous Bound Manuscripts, Massachusetts Historical Society). For evidence of the connection between the two families see Benjamin Gillam, letter to Hugh Gunnison, 23 March 1653/54, Photostats, Massachusetts Historical Society.

45. On Gunnison see Noyes, Libby, and Davis, *Genealogical Dictionary*, 292; and Pope, *Pioneers of Maine and New Hampshire*, 86–7.

46. See E. E. Rich, *The History of the Hudson's Bay Company, 1670–1680*, 2 vols. (London: Hudson's Bay Record Society, 1959), I:61–137. Interestingly, Robert Boyle, whom I have discussed as a sponsor of Gookin's and Eliot's work with the Indians, was also a central figure in the Hudson Bay Company. For references to Sanford and Gillam see also E. E. Rich, *Minutes of the Hudson's Bay Company, 1671–1674* (Toronto: Champlain Society, 1942); and E. E. Rich, *Minutes of the Hudson's Bay Company, 1679–1684*, 2 vols. (Toronto: Champlain Society, 1945–46). On Charles Bayly's release from the Tower in exchange for service to the Hudson Bay Company, as well as his proselytizing exploits in Rome and France and his residence in Maryland see Rich, *History*, 65; and [John Perrot], *A Narative of Some of the Sufferings of J. P. in the City of Rome* (London, 1661).

47. Boyer and Nissenbaum, *Salem Witchcraft Papers*, I:66.

48. Cotton Mather, "Decennium Luctuosum," 292.

49. Ibid., 278, 279, 287, 282–9. On Maule's role in the blasphemy trial of one of his neighbors see Carla Gardina Pestana, "The Social World of Salem: William King's 1681 Blasphemy Trial," *American Quarterly* 41: 2 (June 1989): 308–27. The voluminous writings of Thomas Maule are reprinted in James E. Maule, *Better That 100 Witches Should Live* (Villanova, Pa.: Jembook, 1995).

50. Rosenthal, *Salem Story*, 129–50, points out that the Mathers' rage against Burroughs was compounded by the inability to punish him as a dissenter. For a similar argument concerning the use of witchcraft accusations to discipline people who became too accepting of Quakers see Christine Leigh Heyrman, "Specters of Subversion, Societies of Friends: Dissent and the Devil in Provincial Essex County, Massachusetts," in *Saints and Revolutionaries: Essays on Early American History*, ed. David D. Hall, John M. Murrin, and Thad W. Tate (New York: Norton, 1984), 38–74.

51. David S. Lovejoy, *The Glorious Revolution in America* (1972; reprint, Middletown, Conn.: Wesleyan University Press, 1987), 179–95; Viola F. Barnes, *The Dominion of New England: A Study in British Colonial Policy* (New Haven: Yale University Press, 1923); Michael G. Hall, *Edward Randolph and the American Colonies, 1676–1703* (Chapel Hill: University of North Carolina Press, 1960); and Richard R. Johnson, *Adjustment to Empire: The New England Colonies, 1675–1715* (New Brunswick, N.J.: Rutgers University Press 1981). On the establishment of an Anglican enclave in Massachusetts see John Frederick Woolverton, *Colonial Anglicanism in North America* (Detroit: Wayne State University Press, 1984), 112–4.

52. For an excellent treatment of how the Bay Colony's defense of Whiggish

principles placed its leaders on common ground with "enlightened" postrevolutionary English intellectuals while at the same time allowing them to continue their century-long "reformation of manners," see Gildrie, *Profane, Civil and Godly*, 185–209.

53. Nathaniel Byfield, "The Revolution in New England Justified," in Whitmore, *Andros Tracts*, I:118.

54. Ibid., 105. See also "An Account of the Late Revolution in New England," in Whitmore, *Andros Tracts*, II: 194–5, for the argument that the "*Rose Frigat* now in our Harbour was intended to carry off our Late Governour for France, and to take any of our English Vessels that might be coming in unto us; and we apprehended our selves in the mean time very ill provided, if an Attacque from any of the French Fleet of the West Indies were perfidiously made upon us."

55. Roberts, *History of the Military Company*, I:253.

56. For an analysis of how anti-Catholic sentiments in New England continued to manifest themselves into the eighteenth century see Francis Cogliano, *No King, No Popery: Anti-Catholicism in Revolutionary New England* (Westport, Conn.: Greenwood Press, 1995).

57. For an in-depth assessment of Increase Mather's role in this process see Michael G. Hall, *The Last American Puritan: The Life of Increase Mather, 1639–1723* (Middletown, Conn.: Wesleyan University Press, 1988), 212–54.

58. [Joseph Dudley], *New England's Faction Discovered*, in Whitmore, *Andros Tracts*, II: 210–2, 215.

59. Ibid., 218–9.

60. Ibid., 214, 207–8.

61. Ibid., 208–9, 217.

62. See Daniel K. Richter, *The Ordeal of the Longhouse: The Peoples of the Iroquois League in the Era of European Colonization* (Chapel Hill: University of North Carolina Press, 1992), 135–41, 160.

63. "Petition of the Inhabitants of Maine," in Whitmore, *Andros Tracts*, I: 176–78.

64. "Revolution Justified," in Whitmore, *Andros Tracts*, I: 101–2.

65. Lovejoy, *Glorious Revolution in America*, 132–8, 103–6, 215–9, 261–70, 312, chronicles these rumors of plots involving indigenous peoples in numerous colonial settings.

66. Gordon S. Wood, *The Radicalism of the American Revolution* (1991; reprint, New York: Vintage Books, 1993), 369.

67. For the impact of these values in other contexts see Daniel H. Usner, *Indians, Settlers and Slaves in a Frontier Exchange Economy: The Lower Mississippi Valley Before 1783* (Chapel Hill: University of North Carolina Press, 1992); Richter, *Ordeal of the Longhouse*; James Merrell, *The Indians' New World: Catawbas and their Neighbors from European Contact through the Era of Removal* (Chapel Hill: University of North Carolina Press, 1989); Richard White, *The Middle Ground: Indians, Empires and Republics in the Great Lakes Region, 1650–181 5* (New York: Cambridge University Press, 1991); and Eric Hinderaker, *Elusive Empires: Constructing Colonialism in the Ohio Valley, 1673–1800* (New York: Cambridge University Press, 1997).

68. Gildrie, *Profane, Civil and Godly*, 1–15, emphasizes New England's "culture of discipline."

69. See William Cronon, George Miles, and Jay Gitlin, "Becoming West:

Toward a New Meaning for Western History," in *Under an Open Sky: Rethinking America's Western Past*, ed. William Cronon, George Miles and Jay Gitlin (New York: Norton, 1992), especially 6.

70. Paul E. Johnson and Sean Wilentz, *The Kingdom of Matthias* (New York: Oxford University Press, 1994), explains how, as late as the nineteenth century, rural men, who felt diminished by the expanding market economy, vented hostility toward women who had begun to move into new roles conferred upon them in part by the various types of "perfectionist" evangelical religions to which mercantile families subscribed. For these men, "democratic" aspirations were firmly tied to patriarchalism and independent land ownership. See also Stephanie McCurry, *Masters of Small Worlds: Yeoman Households, Gender Relations and the Political Culture of the South Carolina Low Country* (New York: Oxford University Press, 1995).

71. See Stephen Nissenbaum, "New England as Region and Nation," in *All over the Map: Rethinking American Regions*, ed. Edward L. Ayers et al. (Baltimore: Johns Hopkins University Press, 1996), 38–61; and Peter S. Onuf, "Federalism, Republicanism and the Origins of American Sectionalism," in the same volume, 11–37.

Index